FIRST PRINCIPLES OF
SPEECH TRAINING

This book is made in full compliance with
Government Directive L 120 limiting the
bulk of paper.

FIRST PRINCIPLES OF SPEECH TRAINING

BY

ELIZABETH AVERY, Ph.D.
PROFESSOR OF SPOKEN ENGLISH
SMITH COLLEGE

JANE DORSEY, A.M.
INSTRUCTOR IN SPEECH IN TEACHERS COLLEGE
COLUMBIA UNIVERSITY

AND

VERA A. SICKELS, B.S.
ASSOCIATE PROFESSOR OF SPOKEN ENGLISH
SMITH COLLEGE

D. APPLETON-CENTURY COMPANY
INCORPORATED
NEW YORK   LONDON

PREFACE

THE purpose of this book is to present the scientific principles of speech training as a basis for their practical application to the improvement of everyday speech. It is the outcome of many years of teaching and experimentation, chiefly at Smith College. For a detailed explanation of the authors' aims and point of view the reader is referred to the "Foreword to the Teacher" which follows at page xxiii.

The authors wish here to express their warm gratitude to President William Allan Neilson of Smith College for making possible many of the studies and experiments out of which the book has grown; to their associates in the Department of Spoken English, and especially to Professor Cary Franklin Jacob, for generous encouragement and coöperation; to various other members of the faculty of Smith College, and especially to Professor Mabelle B. Blake, Personnel Director, Professor Arthur T. Jones of the Department of Physics, Professor Myra M. Sampson of the Department of Zoölogy, Professor David C. Rogers of the Department of Psychology, and Professor Leah C. Thomas of the Department of Hygiene and Physical Education, for invaluable suggestions and criticisms relating to their special fields; to Mr. Alfred Dwight Sheffield of *The Inquiry* for assistance in the development of methods of group discussion; and to Professor Azubah J. Latham, of Teachers College, Columbia University, for generous sharing of her rich experience in speech education.

Special acknowledgment is due also to those teachers to whom the authors are indebted for their phonetic back-

ground, particularly Professors Daniel Jones, A. Lloyd
James, and Walter Ripman of London University, William
Grant of the Aberdeen Training Center, M. Pernault of the
Sorbonne, Professor G. Oscar Russell of the Ohio State Uni-
versity, and Professors Osmond T. Robert and Marthe
Sturm of Smith College; and to the writers on various
phases of speech training who have been their forerunners in
the movement to put the subject on a sounder basis.

For permission to reprint much of the illustrative and
practice material included in Part II the authors owe thanks
to many firms and individuals.

The selections listed below are used by permission of, and
special arrangement with, the following authorized publishers, authors, and individual holders of copyrights. The
authors acknowledge with thanks the courtesy shown in the
granting of these permissions.

Dodd, Mead & Company and Curtis Hidden Page, for the selections from *The Man Who Married a Dumb Wife* by Anatole France.

Doubleday, Doran & Company and the authors, for selections
from *Mr. and Mrs. Haddock Abroad* by Donald Ogden Stewart (copyright, 1924, by George H. Doran Company), and *Trivia* by Logan
Pearsall Smith (copyright, 1917, by Doubleday, Page & Company).

Four Seas Company, for the poem "At the British Museum"
from *Images Old and New* by Richard Aldington (copyright, 1918).

Henry Holt & Company, for the poems "Mending Wall" from
Selected Poems by Robert Frost, "The Listeners" from *Collected Poems*
by Walter de la Mare, two poems from *The Shropshire Lad* by A. E.
Housman, and a selection from *The Knowledge of English* by George
Philip Krapp.

Alfred Knopf, Inc., for selections from *The Dove's Nest* and *The
Garden Party* by Katherine Mansfield, the poems "Dirge," "Adven-
ture," "November Night," and "Triad" from *Verse* by Adelaide
Crapsey.

Harold Monro, for the poem "The Pedler" from *The Farmer's
Bride* by Charlotte Mew.

Sir Henry Newbolt, for his poem "Against Oblivion" from *Poems
New and Old* (published by John Murray) and the poem "Egypt's
Might is Tumbled Down" from *Poems* by Mary E. Coleridge (pub-
lished by Elkin, Mathews & Marrott).

Viking Press, Inc., for the poem "On the Road to Tch-Lii" from

Chinese Lyrics by Judith Gautier, translated by James Whitall (copyright, 1918, by B. W. Huebsch).

The authors are deeply grateful to the following publishers, authors, magazines, and individual holders of copyright, who graciously gave them the use of the poems and prose selections listed below.

D. Appleton & Company, for the selection from *Ariel* by André Maurois, the selection from *Primitive Hearths in the Pyrenees* by Ruth Otis Sawtell and Ida Treat, and the poems of Babette Deutsch and A. G. Prys-Jones.

Bobbs-Merrill Company, for the selection from *The Private Life of Helen of Troy* by John Erskine.

Cornell Alumni News, Teachers College Budget, and the *Journal of Education*, for selections from the pamphlet, "What the Colleges Are Doing," published by Ginn & Company.

John Day Company, for a paragraph from *Shadows Waiting* by Eleanor Carroll Chilton.

John Drinkwater, for his poem "Birthright" from *Poems, 1908–1919*, published by Houghton Mifflin Company.

The Forum, for a selection from "The School of Wisdom" by Count Hermann Keyserling.

Jun Fugita, for four of his tankas.

Harcourt, Brace & Company, for two selections from *The Common Reader* by Virginia Woolf.

Houghton Mifflin Company, for short passages and poems of Longfellow, Whittier and Emerson, and a paragraph from "The American Mind and American Idealism" by Bliss Perry.

Cary F. Jacob, for his poems "The Riveter" and "Autumn Days."

Daniel Jones, for selections from *Le Maître Phonétique*.

Little, Brown & Company, for an extract from Appendix II, "American Speech," in *A Glance toward Shakespeare* by John Jay Chapman, a selection from *Jalna* by Mazo de la Roche, and two passages from the essay *Voices* by Lucy Scarborough Conant.

The Living Age, for the selection from "Djaddesdé" by Melek Hanum, reprinted from *Pester Lloyd*.

Macmillan Company, for short selections from Browning, Tennyson, Matthew Arnold, Christina Rossetti, Thomas Hardy, Vachel Lindsay, and *The Voice and Spiritual Education* by Hiram Corson.

Marshall Jones Company and the author, for an extract from *The Liberal College* by Alexander Meiklejohn.

A. A. Milne, for "The Arrival of Blackman's Warbler," reprinted from *Punch*.

Edna St. Vincent Millay, for the poems "Tavern" from *Renascence* and "The Spring and the Fall" from *The Harp Weaver and other Poems* published by Harper & Brothers.

John Murray, for the poem "Spring Goeth All in White" and a stanza from "London Snow" by Robert Bridges.

William Allan Neilson, for an extract from one of his reports.

W. W. Norton & Company and the author, for a selection from *Influencing Human Behavior* by H. A. Overstreet.

Rose Mills Powers and her publishers, the Angel Alley Press, for two poems from *Psyche's Lamp*.

Charles Scribner's Sons, for the poem "Heredity," by Theta Kenyon, published in *Scribner's*, and the selections from Stevenson and *Art Epochs and their Leaders* by Oscar Hagen.

A. D. Sheffield, for several pages from "A Coöperative Technique for Conflict."

May Sinclair, for a selection from *The Dark Night*, published by the Macmillan Company.

W. R. Sorley, for the poem, "The Song of the Ungirt Runners," by Charles Hamilton Sorley.

Frederick A. Stokes Company, for the poems "A Wave of the Sea" and "White Waves on Water," from *Poems* by Joseph Mary Plunkett.

Teachers College Record and the author, for selections from an article entitled "Health Exercises for Everyday Use" by Dr. Jesse F. Williams.

Elinor Wylie, for the poem "Velvet Shoes" from *Nets to Catch the Wind*, published by Alfred A. Knopf, Inc.

Yale Alumni Quarterly and Mrs. Woodrow Wilson, for four pages from President Wilson's speech, "The Training of the Intellect."

E. A.
J. D.
V. A. S.

CONTENTS

PART I

THEORY OF VOICE AND SPEECH

PART II

MATERIAL FOR PRACTICE

ILLUSTRATIONS

FOREWORD TO THE TEACHER

GENERAL AIM OF THIS BOOK

ONE of the most striking features of educational development in the past ten years has been the rapidly growing interest in the improvement of American speech. It is encouraging to note that the general tendency in methods of speech training is away from the elocutionary and the purely imitative toward a scientific approach based on careful analysis of fundamental principles and their practical application. This scientific method of teaching voice and speech is being developed through experimentation and research, both in the classroom and in laboratories of phonetics, physics, physiology, and psychology. Such study has contributed to a better understanding of the structure and function of the speech mechanism, of the exact nature of the human voice and of speech sounds, of the importance of careful ear training, and of the need for social adjustment as a preparation for good speech, and for good speech as an aid in social adjustment. Especially has the more accurate and economical study of speech sounds which is the objective in phonetics done much to obtain for the subject of speech better academic standing and greater respect and interest among mature students.

Yet, in spite of improved methods, there is a more or less general feeling that the results are not commensurate with the effort expended. To us it seems that this relative lack of success may be attributed to five causes: first, failure to recognize that social adjustment has come to be regarded as the primary purpose of education, and that speech training should be one of the most effective elements in the educative process; second, failure on the part of the teacher to insist upon the importance of the best possible physical and mental basis for speech; third, failure to teach voice production and articulation as inseparable parts of the same speech process; fourth, failure to realize the basic importance of ear training; and fifth, failure to convince the student that speech is an integral and vital part of the whole life process, and that he should therefore take upon himself the responsibility of incorporating in his daily speech the skill which he has acquired in the classroom.

The failure to relate the study of speech to the modern idea of personal education for social adjustment has tended to narrow the scope of the subject and to devitalize it.

The failure to realize the importance in speech training of a high standard of physical and mental health has led to a method of teaching which is ineffectual and artificial.

In regard to the failure to coördinate voice and speech training, it is noteworthy that in many voice courses little attention is paid to articulation, the emphasis being placed on quality of tone, and that, on the other hand, in courses in articulation (phonetics) students are frequently allowed to produce sounds without giving due attention to voice production. Obviously, both methods are wasteful, since most speech sounds are merely modifications of voice, and since good speech consists of correct modifications of a properly produced tone.

The failure sufficiently to emphasize ear training is due to lack of realization by both teacher and student that to make any certain and rapid progress the student must be able to hear accurately his own speech and that of others. He must have this ability in order to determine what is desirable in voice and speech, which of these desirable qualities he lacks, and how he can best attain them.

Finally, the failure to form and fix right habits of speech

is due to the fact that the student has not established and maintained a proper attitude of mind, and that adequate provision for the right kind of practice has not been afforded him.

It is the aim of this book to meet these criticisms of speech work by providing both the elements of theory and the materials for practice needed to develop good habits of expression. This presupposes a broader aim, namely, to help the student to gain better adjustment, and to enable the socially adjusted individual to express himself more adequately and consequently to meet situations more successfully.

To clarify their thought on the subject teachers may well ask themselves two questions: (1) What kind of speech am I trying to help my students acquire? (2) What methods will enable them to acquire it most easily and most permanently?

In attempting to answer these questions open-minded teachers begin at once to realize that language has a scientific, as well as a practical and an æsthetic, side, and that if the scientific aspect is neglected, the others will suffer accordingly. There follows the realization that in solving their problems in regard to material and method they have much to learn from the sciences of physics, psychology, physiology, and linguistics, as well as from the arts of music, literature, and drama.

From physics, teachers of speech have already learned something, and are beginning to learn more, about the nature of sound in general and of speech sounds in particular, so that we can at least formulate fairly accurately the problems of pitch, force, quality, and duration as they relate to the human voice.

From physiology we have not only derived a conception of our bodies as capable of being brought into a finer sort of harmony, but also have learned to think of speech as a

secondary function—an afterthought of nature, as it were—
which is compelled to make the best of a mechanism primarily
intended for the life functions of breathing, eating, and
drinking. Our whole study of posture, of breathing for
speech, of voice production and articulation, is conditioned
by this realization of the difficulties inherent in our having
to use in talking a set of organs originally developed for
purposes other than speech and still used primarily for those
purposes. The problem is to attain the most pleasing and
effective speech with the least interference with normal life
habits and, consequently, with the least interruption of the
bodily rhythm.

In grappling with the problems of speech training,
teachers have received much help from the newer schools of
psychology and pedagogy. From modern case work they
have gained valuable information concerning social maladjustment both as a cause and as a result of ineffective speech.
The close coöperation of the speech department with the
personnel, psychology, and education departments in many
colleges is a sign of the rapid spread of recognition of the
nature of speech defects. The optimistic trend of the newer
psychology, emphasizing, as it does, the possibility of trans-
forming human nature by the substitution of good habits
for bad through better motivation, is especially helpful to
students of speech. Nowadays good speech is known to be
not necessarily a gift of fate, but a matter of faithful and
persistent effort in the establishment of right habits of living,
thinking, and speaking.

The study of all branches of linguistics, and especially of
phonetics, by furnishing a basic knowledge of speech sounds
and of the laws governing sound change, aids teachers in
assisting their students to formulate their ideas as to the
kind of speech they desire and to find sure and economical
ways of acquiring it.

A knowledge and appreciation of literature, by increasing

the sense of the value and dignity of life and of man's age-long struggle to realize its possibilities, builds more solidly the cultural foundation on which to base public and private speaking as well as reading and dramatic interpretation.

Much may be learned from teachers of singing, although their methods are still largely empirical. From actors and dramatic critics also may come practical help. But most aid can be gained from constant, accurate attention to the speech about one and from comparison of this with one's own pronunciation. By forming the habit of critical analysis and comparison one acquires what has been called the most valuable of all habits, the habit of criticising habits, and thus provides for constant improvement in speech throughout life, as well as better methods of teaching others.

PSYCHOLOGICAL PRINCIPLES INVOLVED

The method of using the material furnished for study and practice is essentially that applicable in any other course which includes both theory and practice. The pedagogical principles are those in general use by progressive teachers. A brief review of the most important of these may be helpful.

The educative process is one of determining the best attainable objectives or aims and of establishing a system of habits which will make possible the realization of these aims. Such a habit system is created by strengthening or weakening the connections between stimuli and responses, that is, by building desirable reaction patterns and breaking undesirable ones.

With adults the building of speech habits is largely a matter of reëducation. Voice and speech develop at an early age, and in many individuals bad habits of speaking are formed at this time. Poor models for imitation, careless instruction, untrained ears, physical defects, any or all of these may have contributed to the forming of the bad habits,

Whatever the cause, a double task must be undertaken if speech improvement is to follow: not only must desirable habits be firmly established, but undesirable ones must be eliminated. Only as the former replace the latter can progress be made.

There are several general rules of habit formation which should be known and applied. These are: (1) Have a clear idea of the whole behavior pattern of which the particular habit is a part. (2) Begin at once to exercise the desired reaction after thoroughly understanding its nature and particular application. (3) Having once started on the new habit path, never go back to the old; the new path is hard to make in any circumstances, and it is especially difficult to maintain if the old is kept open. (4) Practice the new habit every day until it is so firmly fixed that it becomes the inevitable response to the given stimulus. The effect of satisfaction or dissatisfaction accompanying practice has a very marked influence on the results accomplished; other things being equal, those habits will be most readily and securely formed which have pleasurable results.

These rules have an important bearing on the methods used in teaching speech. The acquisition of proficiency in any art requires a certain amount of drill. There is a tendency in speech training, even more than in other fields of education, to make the drill the end rather than a means towards an end. When this tendency is yielded to, the course is likely to become so dull and uninteresting that students gain little from it. To avoid waste, students must have a clear conception of good speech in general and of the particular excellence that each drill is intended to develop. When students are clear as to their far aim and the definite steps towards reaching it, they are more willing to practice and more intelligent in applying their newly acquired skills.

Improvement, however, often comes slowly, and the student sometimes feels that he is engaged in a hopeless task.

Hence the teacher not only should avoid destructive criticism, but should encourage every evidence of well-directed effort. Assurance on the part of the student that he is making some progress, or at least is working in the right direction, will serve as an incentive to still greater effort.

The final stage of the learning process is particularly applicable to speech—that is, the transfer of training. Since one of the purposes of a course in spoken English is to aid students in developing a pleasing and effective speaking voice, they are given as much practice as possible in the oral reading of passages of poetry and prose, in public speaking and group discussion, and in story-telling and dramatics. A student who has developed good habits of speech for special occasions, however, sometimes discards them on leaving the classroom. Consequently, he may have two forms of speech, the new habits not being carried over into daily life. If he thinks of his classroom voice as his "spoken English" voice and of his everyday voice as his "natural" one and sees little or no connection between the two, the instruction has been for him a failure. Everything possible should be done to prevent such failure. Students should be convinced that every good habit of speech can and should be carried over into their daily life, and that it is of no value unless it is thus carried over as a step toward the realization of their aim for better oral expression of thought. Much can be accomplished toward this end by turning the class period into a socialized recitation for group discussion. This will throw greater responsibility on the individual student and will give him constant opportunity to use his speaking voice in class in much the same way that he should use it whenever he has occasion to speak. But the teacher must realize that there will never be a complete and permanent carry-over until the student has convinced himself that the type of speech that he is trying to acquire is the one that will best satisfy his everyday needs.

PLAN OF THE BOOK

In their own teaching the authors find that in the long run they obtain best results by building on a somewhat solid foundation of scientific facts insofar as these have been determined. Teachers who feel that this method is unnecessary or wasteful, however, will find here sufficient material to permit a purely æsthetic or a purely practical approach. In recognition of the various approaches which teachers may wish to adopt, the book has been divided into two parts, the first part containing the theory of voice and speech, and the second, the material for practice.

The plan of Part I, as will be seen, is to begin with a discussion of speech in its relation to the general education of the student. The purpose of this is to give him a conception of speech as a total process—his chief means of social adaptation and of social control; having gained this general concept, he can start on the analytical study of the subject without danger of thinking of any particular speech skill as an end in itself. This introduction is followed by a study of voice and its articulation into speech. Then follow brief surveys of the elementary principles of group discussion, debate, public speaking, and oral reading.

Part II provides various types of material for the application of the principles taught in Part I. This material comprises exercises for posture, breathing, voice production, and articulation; material for study of the technique of reading and speaking; suggestive questions; topics for group discussion, debating, and public speaking; and bibliographies.

The bibliographies are arranged according to topics in the hope that they will be of service in providing teachers and students with material for more comprehensive study of the theories on which the present approach to speech training is based as well as in suggesting subject matter for more advanced work in group discussion and in public speaking.

The inclusion of much phonetic material has been made at the request of a number of teachers who have felt the lack of an adequate body of phonetic transcription of various types of American speech.

Voice and speech exercises are arranged according to the ability which each seems particularly suited to develop, but most of them would serve equally well in the acquisition of any or all of the desirable qualities of speech.

The selections for reading are arranged according to the four aspects under which the oral interpretation of literature is studied. They have been chosen with care in the hope that they may serve a number of different purposes. Many of those in the first division illustrate important points of theory and are intended to supplement the discussion of those points in the first part of the book. Some may be used as material for discussion or individual talks. Many selections (especially those for phonetic transcription) illustrate various types of humor; these, it is hoped, will cheer the student on his way to improvement. Some of the selections are very simple and can be easily and effectively used by beginners; others are difficult and should be reserved for students who have fairly mature minds.

The book is designed for a year's course of two or three hours or for a five-hour semester course. The purpose being development of power rather than acquisition of facts, over-conscientious teachers should be on their guard against feeling that they must use all the material provided.

The text is the outgrowth of several years of experimentation by the members of the Department of Spoken English in Smith College. In theory and aim it represents a substantial agreement of opinion among them. The illustrative material, however, reflects certain differences in the methods employed by the several instructors; the result is the inclusion of a large and varied body of selections for practice. The intelligent teacher will select the material that he finds best suited to his students and to his particular method of teaching.

A word of explanation should perhaps be given here concerning the inclusion of what may seem to some a preponderance of poetry and more purely literary prose. The reason for this abundance is twofold, (1) the knowledge that such material, if intelligently and sympathetically presented, serves as a special incentive towards acquiring a clear articulation and a flexible voice, and (2) the belief that the attempt to understand and interpret good literature from various ages and countries helps to create that sense le the continuity of human life and human aspiration which be the basis of true culture. It is hoped that the use of ts of material may help to make speech education a more via part of the general educative process and that students may be induced thereby to give it "hard study but willing."

THE QUESTION OF A SPEECH STANDARD

As to the standard of speech to be taught, the rule of this book is to suggest what the authors consider desirable for achieving clearness of articulation, pleasant voice quality, and a reasonable conformity to good usage, rather than to insist upon particular pronunciations.

If the purpose of education is to develop autonomous-minded rather than servile-minded individuals, training in speech is truly educational only in the degree to which it enables students to make wise choices after careful and intelligent study of the available facts. Further, in the present state of American thought and culture any attempt arbitrarily to impose a speech standard would be both futile and ridiculous. A standard of American speech, if there is ever to be one, must develop in consequence of a desire of the people for better speech, and better speech can come only as the expression of a better kind of thinking.

SUGGESTIONS FOR USE OF THE BOOK

From the fact that there is no universally accepted speech standard in America it follows that teachers of the subject, in order to secure the confidence and coöperation of their students, must avoid any appearance of dogmatism. On the other hand, to allow students to pass through a course in spoken English without making improvement in their speech is obviously going too far in the opposite direction. To avoid these extremes and at the same time to afford students most opportunity for practice in actual speaking, it has been found wise whenever possible to substitute group discussion for the lecture and recitation methods of instruction.

At their first meeting the class may well discuss their reasons for electing a speech course (if the course is required, they may discuss what they can reasonably hope to gain from it). If well conducted, this discussion, together with the reading of the first chapter of the text, should furnish adequate motivation for the work.

It is recommended that the chapter on group discussion be next assigned for reading or study, and that throughout the course an adequate technique for group discussion be gradually built up. At first, and particularly when the subject of discussion is fundamental to an understanding of the work, it will be well for the instructor to act as chairman. When a student is to preside, it is important for the teacher carefully to outline with him the objectives of the meeting and the pitfalls to be avoided.

Next the class may discuss the question of posture, working out further general standards of posture and the application of these standards to their special needs in public and private speaking, in reading, and in acting. The teacher should then give definite exercises for acquiring and maintaining good posture. Thenceforth the class should be held responsible for the posture of each student who takes part in the recitation.

Similarly, motivation for voice work is established through a discussion of what the students consider a desirable and reasonable voice standard. To save time it is wise to teach such fact material as the preliminary work in physiology and physics by means of lectures, demonstrations, recitations, and quizzes.[1] As to methods of voice training, such excellent results are obtained from widely different methods that it would be unwise to insist on the use of any particular one. On one point, however, most good teachers agree—that ear training is essential to sure and rapid progress. Whatever method of ear training the teacher prefers should be begun early and persisted in until all the class can accurately hear their own voices as well as one another's. One or two warnings must be given in regard to voice training. If the method used is that of singing, teacher and student should remember that the object is a speaking rather than a singing voice and should be careful to carry over the improved technique into speech. If the intoning method is largely relied on, care should be taken to avoid acquiring a monotonous quality or a tendency to overprolongation of vowels, which gives a sentimental and affected impression. If poetry is used as material for voice practice, reading in a meaningless singsong should never be allowed.

The study of speech, as of voice, should be motivated by a group discussion. The subject of this should be the standard of speech on which the class can agree and towards which they shall work. This standard once established, the class should be responsible for its maintenance. They should also discuss the value of phonetics as a basis for speech study.

---

[1] In teaching voice production the autophonoscope is very valuable since it gives a clear understanding of the action of the vocal cords and of the effect on tone of ridgidity in the muscles of the tongue, throat, and soft palate, and especially of the larynx.

Teachers should not expect students to undertake the task of analyzing their speech scientifically until they have convinced themselves that the result will be worth the effort. The actual phonetic analysis, if it is adequately motivated and skillfully presented in connection with training, will not prove a burden. The accurate formation of each sound should be taught first and practiced as a voice exercise until the vocal organs gain the habit of forming the sound quickly and surely. It should then be practiced in words, in sentences, and finally in everyday speech. Special care should be given to the practice of vowels without drawling, nasality, or glottal shock.

Since it is not possible to produce a tone without modeling it into some speech sound, *every voice exercise must be a speech exercise*; and since it is not possible to articulate any sounds (except voiceless consonants, and they are noises) without producing a tone, *each speech exercise must also be a voice exercise*. Except nonsense syllables, all speech sounds convey thought: hence *the problem of expression also must be constantly taken into consideration*.

The material on synthesis of sounds is not at all formidable provided the general laws have been explained one at a time as they have come up in phonetic transcription. As to the amount of time that should be spent on the writing and reading of phonetics, each teacher will decide for himself. The authors have found that this practice is one of the quickest and surest ways of teaching a class to think in terms of sounds instead of letters and thus to find out how they actually speak. If it is given in small assignments at first and clearly presented, it may be made to seem a new kind of game. The use of phonetic transcriptions is one of the easiest means of gaining the ability to make fine distinctions in sounds and to avoid extremes of pedantry and carelessness.

Each teacher will have his own methods of presenting the technique of discussion, debate, public speaking, and reading.

It is hoped that the material here given will be of service. In a fundamental course the emphasis should be on attaining, not a high degree of technical skill in any particular speech art, but a general expertness in the use of the most important tool for social adjustment.

For several reasons it has been necessary to reduce to a minimum certain important divisions of the subject, namely, the psychological and sociological approach, story-telling, and dramatics. By teachers who wish to supply such material for themselves, this practice book may be used as the sole text. By others, it may be supplemented by texts which deal with these subjects in greater detail.

The authors frankly recognize that speech as a college study is still in the experimental stage, both in subject matter and in method of approach. They have made, therefore, every effort to avoid the impression of dogmatism in their statements. They would welcome any constructive criticism by teachers, students, and others interested in the advancement of the cause of good speech.

E. A.
J. D.
V. A. S.

PART I

THEORY OF VOICE AND SPEECH

FIRST PRINCIPLES OF
SPEECH TRAINING

CHAPTER I

A TALK WITH THE STUDENT

STUDENTS enter an elementary course in speech hoping to improve the quality of their voices and their articulation. They are likely to look upon this anticipated change as a simple process and to trust that in some miraculous way the skill acquired in the classroom will pass over into their daily speech without any more effort on their part than the practice of a few exercises. Such faith might be justified if speech were merely a mechanical process. It is, however, much more than this. Although it becomes from early childhood an automatic response to our desire for communication, speech is so closely connected with the process of living that each response is an expression of the entire personality as well as of the mood of the moment.

This can be illustrated in so simple a matter as saying " Good morning." These words might seem to be merely the response of my speech mechanism to the greeting of an acquaintance, but consider how many factors complicate the matter. The stimulus is not merely some words of greeting. It includes the speaker's tone, facial expression, and general bearing, the occasion of meeting, perhaps the presence of other persons who affect us pleasantly or unpleasantly, the memory of our past encounters, and my feeling as to whether my acquaintance is greeting me wholeheartedly or only trying to dismiss me without too apparent brusqueness. So, too, my response is not simply the action of speech organs. My whole body is involved, its posture, gesture, facial expression; and these are the result of a complicated set of nervous, muscular, and glandular reactions—the response of my whole personality to the total situation. If my acquaintance's original tone is agreeable, my reaction will naturally tend to be one of pleasure. This will mean, if my voice is responsive to my mood, that my reply will have an added warmth, which, in turn, will tend to increase the feeling of mutual friendliness. If, however, the tone in which he addresses me is cold or querulous or harsh or flippant, the disagreeable effect of his greeting will color my reply and thus lessen the probability of clear and satisfactory relations between us.

Good Speech as a Factor in Social Adjustment

But the effect of speech on our relations with others goes deeper than this. In a society where the interest is in getting things done rather than in seeing that they are beautifully done, the manner of speaking loses some of its importance; in such an environment the effect of poor speech is less consciously felt by speaker and hearer, though even here its influence is greater than most of us realize. But in any community where even a part of the members have attained to some degree of beauty and effectiveness in speech, the matter becomes much more serious. Consciously or unconsciously all of us compare ourselves with our fellows, and our sense of inner well-being and power largely depends on the success with which we sustain that test. If we find ourselves in a group whose speech and manner are notably finer than ours, we have an obscure feeling of discomfort which undermines our power of free, natural, and forceful expression.

Conditions of this latter type are frequent causes of maladjustment in college. A student coming from a community where he has been accepted, and has accepted himself, quite simply and naturally as representative of the community's best standards, suddenly finds that he fails to make as good an impression as he desires. If he traces one of the causes of this failure to his way of speaking, the discovery cannot fail to increase his diffidence in the face of the many adjustments to be made in his new environment.

This common situation is met in various ways. One student frankly recognizes the inadequacy of his speech habits and promptly sets about acquiring new ones. Such a person stands an excellent chance both of overcoming his handicap and of developing a sane and judicious attitude toward college problems in general. Another student recognizes his deficiencies but through self-distrust or obstinacy or laziness or misplaced loyalty refuses to change his old habits. The result of this attitude is an increase in the ineffectiveness of his speech, sometimes to the extent of causing a stutter or some other evidence of his feeling of inferiority; and this in turn may lead to that more or less complete withdrawal from the normal occupations and associations of college life through which many students who need college most receive least benefit from it. A third student, refusing to acknowledge in any way the inadequacy of his habits of speaking, develops a self-assertive manner which becomes a further barrier between himself and his associates and a further obstacle to receiving and giving all that his abilities would permit.

It is in this view of speech as a factor in social adjustment, not as an end but as a means of contributing to a more abundant life for others as well as for oneself, that the newer conception of speech training has its greatest significance. The habit of thinking of speech work as a training for a more useful, a fuller, and a happier life helps to avert the danger of its leading to the affectation and self-admiration which sometimes was the unhappy result of the older elocutionary methods.

The Basis in Right Mental Habits

To this brief demonstration of the rôle of good speech in improving our relations with our fellow-beings, there is a very important corollary, that is, the desirability of developing the whole personality while evolving a better means of communication. With all its power for promoting social adjustment, improved speech alone cannot prevail against the handicap of personality defects. To improve the expression without improving that which is expressed is to apply an artificial adornment which must strike all discriminating hearers as insincere. Hence, a complementary aim in speech work should be the concurrent evolution of the whole personality, to the end that the improved speech may remain a true manifestation of the individual.

Granted the importance of this complement to speech improvement, the student who wishes to accomplish the twofold purpose may well ask, first, what tests of personality he can apply to himself, and second, what practical steps he can take toward making the best possible adjustment of his mental and physical make-up as a foundation for his efforts to achieve not only improved speech, but also the developed personality his improved speech is to express.

If the student has good physical habits and sane, constructive mental attitudes, including a zest for life, a wide range of interests and activities, genuine interest in his fellow-beings, and, above all, a definite and not too selfish aim, he may consider that he has a well-rounded personality. If, on the other hand, he has poor habits of living and thinking, if he habitually indulges in worry or depression or boredom or self-pity, if he lacks the desire or ability to make his life of value to himself and to others, he should feel that he falls short of adequate adjustment for happiness and success.

Colleges nowadays are realizing that a part of their service to students should be aid in solving personality and adjustment problems, most of which yield readily to intelligent and sympathetic guidance in the building of new attitudes and habits. Through deans, personnel departments, and psychological clinics, more and more colleges are providing help for students in adjustment to college life and to life in general. Every student must recognize, however, that the problem of adjustment is, in the last analysis, a problem for himself alone, and that the more frankly he faces it, the better will be his chance of solving it.

It is futile to discuss whether it would be wiser to work first for physical fitness and then for an improved mental state, or to start with an attempt to get the right mental attitude and from that work toward a more satisfactory physical condition. As a matter of obvious fact, the two objectives are so interdependent that the only sensible course is to work for both together and thus get the benefit of circular response.

The first requirement for all activity, mental or physical, æsthetic or practical, is freedom from undue tension. Strain always means waste of energy; it often involves complete inhibition of the desired action. It prevents the proper functioning of the nerves, muscles, organs, and glands; and their inadequate action, in turn, produces greater strain. Outwardly this strain is indicated by excitability, irritability, timidity, and general lack of confidence and control. In speech it may be evidenced by an unpleasantly high or an annoyingly low pitch, a flat or metallic or thin or hard quality of voice, an unrhythmical flow of tone, and too slow or too rapid articulation.

This does not mean that freedom from strain implies *complete* relaxation of nerves and muscles. That would be collapse. The desirable state is that degree of tension which insures free and vigorous functioning of the whole organism. Such balance is manifested in the qualities of courage, cheerfulness, vitality, confidence, and control. In speech it is

shown by a clear, full, resonant voice, well modulated, rhythmical, and melodious, and by clear-cut articulation.

How is this balance to be achieved? The problem is
somewhat different for each student, but the general procedure is the same for all. It consists in looking at the conditions of life as sanely as possible, in order, first, to find the
causes of strain, and second, to discover which of these
causes can be eliminated by intelligent effort and how the
others can be so subdued as to interfere as little as possible
with happiness and success. This appraisal must be made
with common sense and the realization that, within reasonable limits, one can become what one wishes to become.
If sometimes in the past such a facing of reality has led to
despondency and morbid introspection, more than likely
the resulting state was due to lack of confidence in the possibilities of reëducation of personality through determined
effort to establish right habits of thinking and living.

In substituting useful for wasteful habits it is well to
begin by replacing the habit of worry by the habit of courage.
The worry habit has less to commend it than almost any
other, not only because it destroys happiness and weakens
one's power of meeting situations successfully, but because it
has so harmful an effect on general health. In trying to con-
quer the nameless fears which are so often the causes of worry,
there is no greater help than looking the terrors squarely
in the face and reducing them to their elements. An inquiring and courageous temper of mind often puts ungrounded
fears to flight. Another strong ally is a sensible philosophy
of life. Perhaps the strongest is the habit of doing something
constructive toward bettering the situation that has caused
the worry. By this means an attitude of mind is developed
which, instead of being negative and destructive, is positive
and creative.

The relation of all this to speech seems almost too obvious
to need comment. Yet an astonishingly large number of

persons fail to see the connection between a weak, ineffective personality and a weak, ineffective manner of speaking. Fortunately educators are beginning to realize this connection and are insisting more and more on the importance, for speech training, of mental vigor, alertness, and balance.

The Basis in Right Physical Habits

The building of good mental habits, however, is only half the battle for personal hygiene. The other half, that of establishing good physical habits, is equally important. Indeed, physical health is almost essential to the maintenance of right mental states.

Among the most important aids to health are proper habits of eating. A balanced ration, particularly for persons of sedentary habit, demands less meat, starch, and sugar, and more milk, fruit, nuts, and vegetables, than are generally eaten. Very much more water should be drunk than is customary: perfect health requires the equivalent of at least eight glasses a day. But even a proper diet will not insure sufficient nourishment if meals are eaten too rapidly, or in the midst of noise and confusion, or in a state of worry, depression, or extreme fatigue.

Closely related to habits of eating are those of elimination. No less important than the choice of foods is the elimination of waste products through the lungs, skin, kidneys, and intestines. Proper diet, exercise, and rest and a healthy mental condition help to insure adequate elimination. If attention to correct living conditions is not sufficient to prevent the poisoning of the system by waste matter, a physician should be consulted before bad habits become fixed.

It is easy to see the relation between habits regarding food and elimination and the qualities of speech. A vibrant voice could hardly be expected from an ill-nourished and poison-ridden body, even if this physical state did not induce a low mental tone which is inevitably reflected in the speech.

Another set of habits which have considerable effect on both personality and power of expression are those of personal cleanliness—daily bathing; proper care of the hair, nails, and teeth; and neat and suitable dress. The effect of these habits, though pronounced, is chiefly indirect. They produce a feeling of self-respect and well-being which gives ease and confidence in bearing and speech.

More direct in their effect on expression are habits of exercise, rest, and recreation. Concerning exercise, Dr. Jesse F. Williams has this to say:[1] "Health, strength, and vigor in any person is health, strength, and vigor of the body, especially the nerve-centers of the spinal cord, and it should be clear and compelling that this strength comes largely from the use of the muscles of the body, especially the trunk muscles in youth."

In physical training, as in other branches of education, modern theories insist on subordination of the parts to the whole, or, rather, the coördination of the parts to attain the satisfactory working of the whole organism. This means that the ideal is not a system of exercises which develop muscles separately and without regard to their function, but one which evolves a more perfectly organized body by strengthening muscles in relation to one another and thus bringing about a better functioning of the body as a whole. Still more desirable than special exercises are games and such activities as swimming, boxing, fencing, dancing, and walking; these increase the sense of rhythm and stimulate the mind as well as the body, besides introducing the element of pleasure, doubly important as making exercise a true recreation. Especially beneficial is exercise in the open air.

Exercise is of particular value in speech training, not only in helping to establish the proper health basis, but specifically in developing the muscles of the chest and the abdomen and thus facilitating control of the breath, which is

---

[1] *Personal Hygiene Applied* (W. B. Saunders Company).

the basis of speech. The increasing sense of rhythm and the confidence and freedom from muscular strain which result from proper forms of exercise also help in vitalizing speech.

Relaxation and rest are important as well for speech as for general health. As the body needs activity for its proper functioning, so it needs relaxation for the accumulation of fresh stores of energy and for the maintenance of that equivalence between wearing down and building up which is necessary to the life rhythm. Moreover, this balance of exercise and rest is one of the chief means of creating in the tissues the resistance which serves as a barrier against disease. Neglect of this bodily need is, next to improper food and inadequate elimination, the chief cause of colds and of throat infections which play such havoc with the voice. In addition to the relaxation which comes in sleep, the ability to relax at will for a few minutes is of great value for ordinary conditions of life, since it makes possible long periods of sustained effort without great fatigue.

In speech training the ability to relax is indispensable. Zimbalist has said that every art is based on relaxation. Certainly of none is this truer than of speech. Strain in any part of the body lessens the freedom and beauty of tone.

Perhaps the most important law of hygiene for speech as well as for general health is that of good posture. Good posture must not be thought of as fixed and rigid, but as mobile and adaptable to changing conditions; it is *dynamic —the best adjustment of the body to the needs of the moment.* Walking, running, sitting, standing, playing various games, doing different kinds of work—all require different bodily adjustments. Emotional states, such as joy, sorrow, fear, rage, have their characteristic bodily attitudes. The fundamental principle of posture, however, is this: No matter what specific demands are made on the body, *correct posture means that state of balance which permits the muscles and organs to work together with a minimum expenditure of energy.*

The standing posture which permits the freest and most perfect functioning of the body as a whole and of the speech organs in particular is thus described by Dr. Joel F. Goldthwait: [2]

When the body is used rightly or fully erect, the feet, knees, hips, spine, shoulders, head, and all portions which represent the frame of the body, are used in balance, with the greatest range of movement possible without strain. In this position, the chest is held high and well expanded, the diaphragm is raised, and the breathing and heart action are performed more easily. The abdominal wall is firm and flat, and the shape of the abdominal cavity represents an inverted pear, large and rounded above, small below. The ribs have only a moderate downward inclination. The sub-diaphragmatic space is ample to accommodate the viscera. In this position, also, there is no undue pressure upon, or interference with, the pelvic viscera or with the large ganglia at the back of the abdomen and in the pelvis. On the other hand, if the body is drooped or relaxed, so that the shoulders drag forward and downward, the whole body suffers, the weight is thrown imperfectly upon the feet, so that the arch must be strained; the knees are slightly sprung, which shows by the crepitating joints; the pelvis is changed in its inclination, with strain to the sacro-iliac joints and lower back. In this position the chest is necessarily lowered, the lungs are much less fully expanded than normal, the diaphragm is depressed, the abdominal wall is relaxed, so that with the lessening support of the abdominal wall, together with the lowering of the diaphragm, the abdominal organs are necessarily forced downward and forward. Good posture requires an understanding of these conditions, and especially of the following facts: that the stomach and liver cannot work rightly if the ribs are contracted and narrowed so that there is practically no sub-diaphragmatic space; that the pelvic organs cannot work rightly and must be congested if the loose abdominal organs are crowded into the lower abdomen and pelvis, so that the nutrition must suffer; and that the physiology in general must be abnormal if the anatomic conditions under which the physiological function is expected to be performed are so markedly abnormal.

---

[2] Joel F. Goldthwait and Leah C. Thomas, *Body Mechanics and Health* (Houghton Mifflin Company).

To acquire such good physical habits as are here described may seem a forbidding task. Indeed, it is not an easy one. But if the effort is persisted in until the right habits become fixed, the gain in health and self-confidence is almost beyond belief. The lithe yet vigorous grace of the Winged Victory of Samothrace can be achieved by any normal young person who is willing to make the necessary effort.

Good Speech the Expression of a Developed Personality

The condition of physical and mental adjustment described in this chapter is often referred to as *poise*. It is, obviously, a necessary condition for effective speaking. Want of poise is manifested in rigidity of the muscles of the face and of the whole body, in a strained expression of the eyes, in mannerisms of various sorts, in lack of fullness and freedom of voice, and in absence of rhythm and force in speech. Usually, too, such tension hinders clear thinking. On the hearer the effect is one of greater or less discomfort, so that he finds it hard to give full value to the thoughts expressed.

Here we touch upon a point not always sufficiently considered in speech training, namely, the importance of good physical and mental equipment in relation not only to our way of speaking, but also to the thoughts we express. *Viewed as a means of social control, speech is of value only if its content is sound and constructive, or at least not definitely unsound and destructive.* Unintelligible speech might conceivably be regarded as an advantage in a person who habitually darkened counsel by words without wisdom. A definite part, then, of the "preparatory reactions" for speaking should be the development of that soundness of mind and body which will make utterance not only easy to hear, but also worth hearing.

CHAPTER II

THE PHYSICAL AND PHYSIOLOGICAL BASES OF SPEECH

SOUND is generally thought of as the sensation perceived through the ear. In terms of physics it is a form of wave motion, set up by a vibrating body (a violin string, the dome of a bell, the vocal cords) and transmitted through a medium, usually air. The production of air waves requires some motive force (the bow of the violin, the clapper of the bell, the breath expelled from the lungs) to start the vibrator. Very often some resounding (*re-sounding*) body (the violin box with the air contained in it, or that in the vocal passages) is required to reinforce the waves formed by the vibrator and make them effectively audible as sound.

Practically all musical instruments have these three elements—the *motor*, the *vibrator* or *generator*, and the *resonator*. The human musical instrument has still another—the *articulator* (the tongue, teeth, lips, etc.) by which the voice is shaped into the patterns of articulate speech, that is, converted into vowel and consonant sounds which, combined into words, are used to convey our thoughts audibly to others.

Since the purpose of our study is to understand the exact nature and use of speech, it is well for us to begin with a consideration of its physical and physiological bases.

THE PHYSICAL PROPERTIES OF SOUND

Sound has four properties or elements, *pitch, volume* (or *intensity*), *quality*, and *duration*. These physical properties of sound call for brief discussion as they relate to the human voice.

1. Pitch

The *pitch* of a sound, that is, its height or depth (also called its acuteness or gravity), is chiefly determined by the *rate* of vibration. Shortening a violin string or increasing its tension causes it to vibrate more rapidly when plucked and thus to emit a higher tone. The rate, or frequency, of vibration of the vocal cords depends on three factors, their tension, length, and thickness. An increase of tension of the cords causes an increase in the rate of their vibration, as does also a decrease in length or in thickness. Although there are only two vocal cords, they are capable of so many delicate adjustments in these respects that the human voice has a wide range of pitch.

2. Volume, or Intensity

The second property of a sound is *volume*, or *intensity*, that is, its loudness or softness. This depends chiefly on the *amplitude* of vibration [1] and on the degree of reinforcement by the co-vibration of another sonorous body. In other words, the sensation of loudness is primarily dependent on the amount of energy with which the sound is generated and on the extent of its reinforcement by resonance.

The result of the working together of these two factors can be seen in a familiar experiment with a violin string. If the string be stretched between fixed points and then lightly plucked, it will make slight oscillations back and forth and will set into motion correspondingly small waves of air, thus producing a scarcely audible sound. If the string be plucked more vigorously, it will swing through a much wider distance, set in motion larger waves of air, and

---

[1] The distance that the particular particles in vibration swing back and forth.

give a stronger sound. If now, however, the string be attached to a violin box and then plucked with the same force, the vibratory motion of the string will be conveyed to the body of the violin so that the box and the air within it oscillate with a corresponding vibratory movement, and the original waves, and consequently the effect they produce upon the ear, are greatly intensified.

There are various other factors that affect the loudness of sound. Among these are the distance of the hearer from the source of the sound and the amount of interference. A still more important factor is the apparent effect on volume of a change of pitch, a higher tone usually sounding louder than a lower one of the same amplitude.

3. Quality

The third property of a sound is *quality*, that characteristic which independently of pitch or loudness distinguishes one tone from another—the tone of a violin from that of some other musical instrument, the voice of one human being from that of another, or the voice of the same person under the influence of different mental or emotional states. Quality depends upon the *kind*, or *form*, of vibratory motion, that is, on the form of the wave corresponding to the tone emitted. If the vibration be represented by a curve, quality is determined by the peculiarities indicated by the shape of the curve. The modifications of the wave in form are due to the fact that the sounding body vibrates, not only as a whole, in the simplest way, but at the same time in parts, so that the different components of the sound have different frequencies.

The tone emitted when the generator vibrates in a certain simple way is called its *fundamental*, and the wave is represented by a simple curve; the tones produced when it vibrates in segments are called its *upper partials*, or *overtones*, or *harmonics*. The presence of these overtones gives a more complex form to the wave. To illustrate: If a stretched violin string be so tuned that when vibrating as a whole in a certain simple way it gives out a certain tone, it will emit a tone an octave higher when it is vibrating in halves. This harmonic ratio continues as the string is further subdivided. Since, however, the string vibrates as a whole as well as in sections, the latter vibrations must adapt themselves to the fundamental vibration, and they consequently appear as alternate elevations and depressions along the line of the vibrating string. The waves produced by this complex motion of the string are themselves correspondingly complex and give rise to a composite tone.

Most tones are complex, for only a few generators (tuning forks, some organ pipes, and flutes) are able to give tones that are approximately simple. If the overtones have frequencies (rates of vibration) that are exact multiples of that of the fundamental, they are called *harmonic partials*. If the overtones have frequencies whose relation to the fundamental cannot be expressed by whole numbers, they are called *inharmonic partials*. The upper partials of strings are nearly harmonic; those of bells and vibrating rods are inharmonic.

Experiments have shown the effect on quality of the addition or elimination of the upper partials in any complex tone. The fundamental when sounded alone gives a dull, uninteresting tone; as D. C. Miller says in his *Science of Musical Sounds*, "a pure tone is a poor tone." If upper partials are added in their harmonic order, the tone gains in richness and clearness, and as these are taken away, the tone becomes less brilliant. If upper partials are added that are not in harmonic ratio, the effect is generally less pleasing.

Helmholtz demonstrated the important law that the quality of an individual tone is determined by the number and relative frequency of the upper partials and their relative intensity. The selection and intensification of the particular, partials that determine the characteristic quality of any given sound depend on what happens to the tone after it is generated. How these partials are selected and reinforced will be considered when we come to discuss the subject of resonance.

4. Duration

The fourth property of sound, *duration*, may be defined as the period of time that it lasts. As long as the vocal cords are kept in vibration, the tone continues. In speech there are various "breathed consonants," such as the *s* in *see*, which may be continued without vibration of the vocal cords, but these are noises rather than tones.

Duration of speech tone may be thought of in two connections: first, as to the length of time it continues for each individual sound; and second, as to the length of time it continues for each group of sounds joined together to express a thought. We shall enter into a fuller discussion of the time element in speech when we come to the subject of rhythm in Chapter VII.

Resonance

In the discussion of volume and quality we have seen that these properties of sound are dependent not merely upon the action of the vibrator, but also upon its ability to transfer its vibratory motion to another sonorous body which reinforces the tone and gives it a distinct quality of its own. Such a sonorous body is called a *resonator*, and the power of reinforcement is called *resonance*.

In regard to volume, we saw that it is possible for a resonator materially to increase the loudness of a sound generated by a violin string. The vibrations of the string alone set into vibration so small a quantity of air that the sound is scarcely audible. When, however, the string is attached to the body of a violin, the vibratory motion is transmitted to the walls of the box and to the air within it; the box then becomes a co-vibrator, setting into motion a much larger quantity of air and thus intensifying the sound. Similar reinforcement of the sound of a tuning fork can be obtained by holding the vibrating fork at the mouth of a metal urn of appropriate size and shape; such a resonator can be made to ring with the tone faintly communicated to its enclosed air.

It should be understood that the resonator works more effectively the more nearly it is in tune with the vibrator, that is, the more nearly its rate of vibration corresponds harmonically to the rate of the generator. If the two are only slightly out of tune, there will still be resonance, though to a lesser degree; but if they are quite out of tune, there will be little, if any, reinforcement. The question whether or not an air resonator is in tune with the vibrator depends on its size and the size of its opening or openings: the larger the cavity, the slower the rate of vibration of the resonator; the larger the opening, the more rapid its rate of vibration. This means that high tones are reinforced by small resonators with large openings, and low tones by large resonators with small openings.

In regard to quality of tone, resonators exercise selective as well as intensifying power, choosing, by reason of the factors just mentioned, certain upper partials of the generated tone for reinforcement and ignoring the others. Two violin strings attached to different bodies may give the same fundamental tone, but the upper partials that are given very faintly on the one may be relatively loud on the other, and those which are intensified on the first may be rather faint on the second. In such a case the two tones differ appreciably in quality.

One way of classifying resonators is according to whether they are fixed in size, like the violin box, or whether they are capable of change in size, like those of most wind instruments.

The resonating cavities of the human voice belong to the latter class, being capable of a great variety of change both in capacity and in openings.

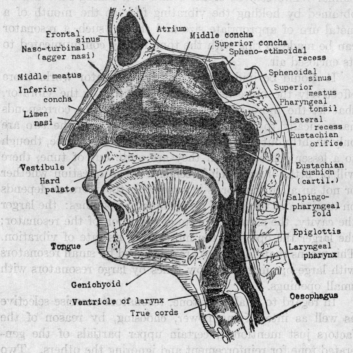

Frontal sinus
Naso-turbinal (agger nasi)
Middle meatus
Inferior concha
Limen nasi
Vestibule
Hard palate
Tongue
Geniohyoid
Ventricle of larynx
True cords

Atrium
Middle concha
Superior concha
Spheno-ethmoidal recess
Sphenoidal sinus
Superior meatus
Pharyngeal tonsil
Lateral recess
Eustachian orifice
Eustachian cushion (cartil.)
Salpingo-pharyngeal fold
Epiglottis
Laryngeal pharynx
Oesophagus

FIG. 1. SAGITTAL SECTION THROUGH THE NASAL FOSSA, MOUTH, PHARYNX, ŒSOPHAGUS, AND LARYNX

(From Buchanan, *A Manual of Anatomy*.)

Resonating Cavities of the Speech Mechanism

The cavities that seem to be the chief agents of resonance in the speech mechanism are those of the chest or thorax, the larynx, and the head. Of the nature and extent of the reinforcement furnished by the thoracic and laryngeal cavities so little is understood [2] that we shall limit our discussion to the supra-laryngeal system.

This system consists mainly of the passages of the throat, the mouth, and the nose (Figure 1). Each of these resonators may undergo many alterations both in capacity and in the size of its openings, so that the whole system is capable of very great possibilities for reinforcing tone. All three passages may act together as one complex resonator, or either the mouth or the nose may separately unite with the throat, the other being shut off by the action of the soft palate.

Like the rest of the speech mechanism, these cavities are only secondarily concerned with the production of voice, their primary functions having to do with the maintenance of life—breathing and the mastication and swallowing of food. In quiet breathing the cavities of the nose and pharynx form one passage, while in eating the mouth and pharynx act together. In breathing for speech all three adjustments may be used.

THE PHYSIOLOGICAL BASIS OF SPEECH

Study of the physiological basis of speech is usually limited to a consideration of those organs which are directly responsible for the production of speech. Such a narrowing of the subject, however, leaves out of account the fact that the action of these organs is dependent upon the assistance of many organs and muscles not usually regarded as part of the speech mechanism, and also upon the general condition and posture of the body as a whole.

Furthermore, these principal organs are often referred to as if they were formed and developed expressly for the purpose of producing speech. It is easily seen that this is not

---

[2] Though there is considerable evidence to support the theory that the tone is reinforced by sympathetic vibration of the walls of the chest.

true. They were originally used only for the life-sustaining functions of breathing and eating and drinking. These are still their primary functions, speech being a secondary one, a later development in the history both of the race and of the individual.

Breathing

Since breathing is a primary function of the speech mechanism and since the outgoing breath is the basis of speech, we shall begin our examination of the speech process with a description of breathing. It is necessary at the outset to make a distinction between quiet life breathing and breathing for speech, for although the inspiratory process is practically the same in the two, expiration is materially different, as to both manner and duration.

Under normal conditions these two processes of inspiration and expiration which constitute the cycle of breathing are automatically regulated by the needs of the blood. In the respiratory act air is taken through the nose and throat into the lungs, where it gives up a part of its oxygen to the blood and receives in exchange the exhaled waste product, carbon dioxide.

The Breathing Apparatus

The Lungs.—The lungs (Figure 2), the seat of the most important part of the respiratory act, are two spongy, cone-shaped structures which nearly fill the cavity of the chest, the base of each resting on the diaphragm and the rounded apex reaching about an inch above the first rib. The lungs are separated from each other by a median chamber, with thin-walled partitions, which contains the œsophagus, the trachea or windpipe, the heart, and certain large blood vessels.

Within the lungs the bronchial tubes branching from the trachea divide and subdivide into smaller tubes, and these in turn ramify into numerous fine branches which lead ulti-

mately into little pouches called *air sacs*. These air sacs
have very thin walls in which are embedded a network of
tiny blood vessels or capillaries, and it is here that the work of
the lungs, the interchange of gases, occurs. The air that
is taken into the expanded air sacs during inspiration loses
oyxgen and acquires carbon dioxide, and it is then expelled
from the sacs during expiration. The bronchial tubes and

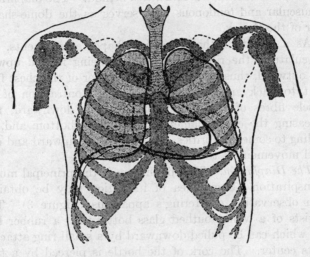

FIG. 2. DIAGRAM OF THE BREATHING APPARATUS, SHOWING THE
THORAX CONTAINING THE TRACHEA, BRONCHI, LUNGS, AND HEART,
AND ITS FLOOR, THE DIAPHRAGM

air sacs with their accompanying nerves and blood vessels,
held together by elastic connective tissue, constitute the
substance of the lungs.

The lungs, being passive though elastic organs, have often
been compared to rubber bags which can expand and contract only when acted upon by forces from without.

The Thorax.—The chest or thorax (Figure 2) is the upper
part of the trunk of the body. It has a framework consisting

of bones, cartilages, muscles, and tendons which encloses the upper of the two great ventral cavities. In this cavity are located the trachea, the lungs, the œsophagus, the heart, and the large arteries and veins. The framework consists of the ribs—twelve on each side, joined by muscular and connective tissue; the sternum or breast bone, to which the ribs are attached in front; and the thoracic vertebrae of the spinal column, to which they are attached behind. The diaphragm, a muscular and tendonous wall, serves as the dome-shaped floor of the thorax.

As a result of their peculiar shape, attachments, and musculature, the ribs are capable of being moved upward and outward, thus increasing the diameter of the chest from front to back and from side to side. Contraction of the muscle fibres of the diaphragm draws it downward, thus increasing the chest diameter from top to bottom and, according to some authorities, assisting in the upward and outward movement of the ribs.

The Diaphragm.—The diaphragm is the principal muscle of inspiration. Some idea of its action may be obtained from observation of Hering's apparatus (Figure 3). This consists of a wide-mouthed glass bottle with a rubber bottom which can be pulled downward by a small ring attached to its center. The cork of the bottle is pierced by a tube which branches at the lower end. Attached to each of the two branches of the tube is a rubber bag. The bottle represents the thorax with its elastic floor, the diaphragm. The part of the tube outside the bottle represents the upper air passages; the part within, the trachea and the bronchial tubes; the rubber bags, the lungs.

If we draw down the rubber floor of the bottle, the pressure within will be diminished; to compensate for this, air will be drawn through the tube into the rubber bags, causing them to expand. If now we release the floor and allow it to return to its position of rest, the pressure within the bottle will be increased, expelling the air in the bags through the tube. It should be remembered, however, that this apparatus only crudely represents the actual condition of the thorax since (1) the ribs, not being rigid like the walls of the bottle, can move; (2) the lungs, unlike the rubber bags, are in constant contact with the wall of the cavity; (3) the diaphragm, instead of being pulled down by an external force,

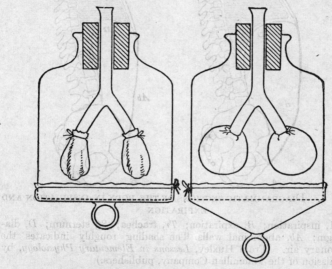

FIG. 3. HERING'S APPARATUS

descends as a result of the contraction of its own muscular fibres; and (4) instead of being drawn from a horizontal to a concave position, the diaphragm moves from a convex to a less convex position.

In respiration the contraction of its muscular fibres causes the central tendon of the diaphragm to descend, thus increasing the diameter of the thoracic cavity from top to bottom and partially displacing the visceral organs immediately below it. This displacement causes a slight protrusion of the upper abdominal wall.

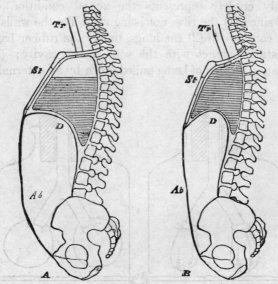

FIG. 4. DIAGRAMMATIC SECTIONS OF THE BODY IN INSPIRATION AND EXPIRATION

A, inspiration; *B*, expiration; *Tr*, trachea; *St*, sternum; *D*, diaphragm; *Ab*, abdominal walls. The shading roughly indicates the stationary air. (From Huxley, *Lessons in Elementary Physiology*, by permission of the Macmillan Company, publishers.)

The Mechanics of Respiration

In the human body the act of breathing seems to be carried on in the following manner: An excess of carbon dioxide in the blood passing through the brain stimulates certain nerve cells. These have long processes which conduct the nerve stimulus to the respiratory muscles, causing them to contract. At the same time that the diaphragm descends, certain other muscles are also stimulated to action. Chief among these are the *intercostals*, the *scaleni*, and the *levatores costarum*.

The *intercostal muscles* (the muscles between the ribs) are, in the opinion of some physiologists, the most important agents in raising the ribs. The external intercostals (that is, the outer layer of rib muscles) raise the ribs (with the exception of the first and, possibly, the second) and at the same time turn outward the lower borders of the ribs, thus increasing the capacity of the chest from front to back, and from side to side. It is commonly held that the internal intercostals have the reverse action and are thus chiefly expiratory in function.

In the meantime the first rib and to a certain extent the second have been raised and fixed by the action of the *scaleni*, three sets of strong muscles which rise from the vertebrae of the neck and are inserted in the upper borders of these two ribs.

The *levatores costarum*, twelve pairs of muscles which arise from the middle (seventh cervical to eleventh thoracic) vertebrae of the spinal column, each attached to the upper border of the rib immediately below the vertebra from which it originates, also assist in raising the ribs.

As the chest cavity increases in three dimensions, the air pressure is lowered in the lungs, the walls of which are in close contact with those of the thorax. Air rushes in until the pressure in the lungs equals that of the atmosphere.

When the act of inspiration is thus completed, the diaphragm and other respiratory muscles relax; the lungs, by their natural elasticity, contract, expelling the air until the pressure within the lungs again equals that of the atmosphere. The respiratory cycle is then completed. It will be seen that in ordinary breathing expiration is chiefly passive, but it is thought to be assisted by the contraction of some of the fibres of the internal intercostal muscles and also by the muscles of the abdominal wall, which compress the abdominal viscera, thus pushing the diaphragm upward and drawing the lower ribs downward.

Breathing for Speech

If in addition to the stimulus to ventilate the lungs, there is also a stimulus for speech, the response of the respiratory mechanism is somewhat different. Since it is desirable that

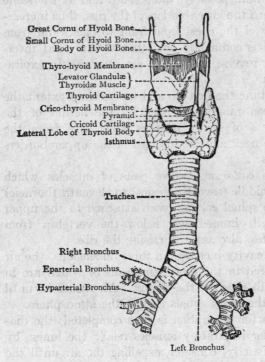

Great Cornu of Hyoid Bone

Small Cornu of Hyoid Bone
Body of Hyoid Bone

Thyro-hyoid Membrane
Levator Glandulæ
Thyroidæ Muscle
Thyroid Cartilage
Crico-thyroid Membrane
Pyramid
Cricoid Cartilage
Lateral Lobe of Thyroid Body
Isthmus

Trachea

Right Bronchus
Eparterial Bronchus
Hyparterial Bronchus

Left Bronchus

FIG. 5. ANTERIOR VIEW OF THE LARYNX, TRACHEA, AND BRONCHI
(From Buchanan, *A Manual of Anatomy.*)

the flow of speech, once it is started, shall be interrupted as little as possible by the intake of breath, inspiration must be rapid and inconspicuous. And since the outgoing air is the basis of speech, it must be adequately controlled, and expiration, therefore, becomes an active process.

There are various theories as to the best means of gaining this control. Excellent results have been accomplished by directly opposite methods. It seems to us that it is best achieved by maintaining in a considerable measure the front-to-back and side-to-side expansion of the chest walls

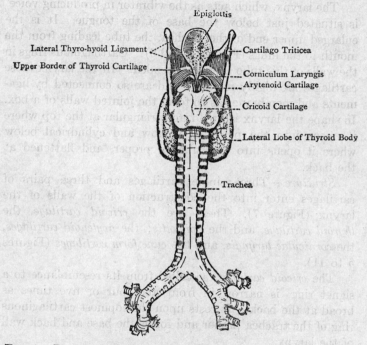

FIG. 6. POSTERIOR VIEW OF THE LARYNX, TRACHEA, AND BRONCHI
(From Buchanan, *A Manual of Anatomy*.)

and regulating the return of the diaphragm by pressure from below. This pressure is obtained by contraction of the muscles of the abdominal wall, which forces the organs below the diaphragm inward and upward. By this means a stream of air, with sufficient pressure to act as the motive power of tone, is sent from the lungs through the trachea to the larynx, where tone is generated.

The Speech Mechanism

The Larynx

The larynx, which acts as the vibrator in producing voice, is situated just below the base of the tongue. It is the enlarged upper end of the trachea, the tube leading from the mouth to the lungs (Figures 5 and 6). Cartilaginous rings in the walls of this tube keep it distended. In the larynx these cartilages are highly modified and are so connected by ligaments and membranes as to form the jointed walls of a box. In shape the larynx is broad and triangular at the top where it opens into the pharynx, narrow and cylindrical below where it opens into the trachea proper, and flattened at the back.

Structure.—Three single cartilages and three pairs of cartilages enter into the construction of the walls of the larynx (Figure 7). These are the *cricoid cartilage*, the *thyroid cartilage*, and the *epiglottis*; the *arytenoid cartilages*, the *corniculae laryngis*, and the *cuneiform cartilages* (Figures 5 to 11).

The *cricoid cartilage*, so-called from its resemblance to a signet ring, is narrow in front and four or five times as broad at the back. It rests upon the topmost cartilaginous ring of the trachea proper and forms the base and back wall of the larynx.

The *thyroid* (or shield-shaped) *cartilage*, the largest of these cartilages, rests on the cricoid and forms the front of the larynx. It consists of two plates which meet at an acute angle in front and are wide apart at the back. The front angle is popularly called the "Adam's apple."

The *arytenoid cartilages* are a pair of very irregular four-sided pyramids which rest on the top of the cricoid at the back (Figure 9).

The *corniculae laryngis* and the *cuneiform cartilages* are two pairs of very small cartilages on top and at the sides of the arytenoids (Figure 10).   Little is understood about their function.

The *epiglottis* (Figures 7 and 10), a fibrous, cartilaginous, leaf-shaped organ attached both to the back of the tongue and to the thyroid cartilage, is situated just above the upper open-

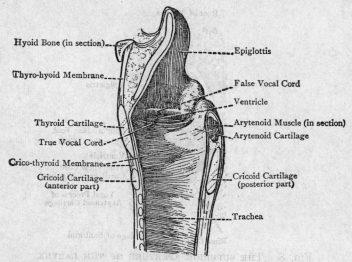

Hyoid Bone (in section)

Epiglottis

Thyro-hyoid Membrane

False Vocal Cord

Ventricle

Thyroid Cartilage

Arytenoid Muscle (in section)

Arytenoid Cartilage

True Vocal Cord

Crico-thyroid Membrane

Cricoid Cartilage (anterior part)

Cricoid Cartilage (posterior part)

Trachea

Fig. 7.   Sagittal section of the larynx and trachea
(From Buchanan, *A Manual of Anatomy.*)

ing of the larynx. The epiglottis is thought by some physiologists to have some connection with modification of tone quality, but its chief function is to help close the larynx during swallowing and thus prevent food on its way to the œsophagus from entering the trachea (Figure 1).

The Vocal Cords.—Extending into the cavity of the larynx on each side, near the upper opening, are two pairs of horizontal ridges consisting of elastic connective tissue covered with mucous membrane. The upper pair of these ridges are the *false vocal cords*, and the lower the *true vocal cords* (Figures 8 and 9).

The *false vocal cords* act in conjunction with the epiglottis in preventing food from entering the lungs. In the act of swallowing, their muscles contract powerfully, thus helping to close the larynx. In whispering they are somewhat

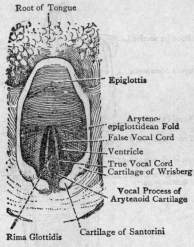

Root of Tongue

Epiglottis

Aryteno-
epiglottidean Fold
False Vocal Cord

Ventricle
True Vocal Cord
Cartilage of Wrisberg

Vocal Process of
Arytenoid Cartilage

Rima Glottidis   Cartilage of Santorini

FIG. 8.   THE SUPERIOR APERTURE OF THE LARYNX
(From Buchanan, *A Manual of Anatomy*.)

closely approximated. In coughing and in the glottal shock they are brought close together and then drawn quickly apart. In the speech of many persons they are more or less approximated.

The *true vocal cords* are the principal agents in the production of voice. They are attached in front to the inner angle of the thyroid cartilage and behind to the arytenoids.

When in the position of rest for quiet breathing, the free edges of the vocal cords enclose a triangular opening, with the apex in front and the base at the back. This space between the vocal cords is called the *rima glottidis*, or *glottis* (Figures 8, 9, and 12).

When tone is desired, the vocal cords are approximated, and air is sent through the narrowed slit of the glottis with sufficient force to set the delicate free edges of the elastic vocal cords into vibration, thus producing voice (Figure 9).

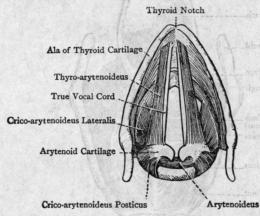

FIG. 9. SUPERIOR VIEW OF THE LARYNX, SHOWING THE MUSCLES, TRUE VOCAL CORDS AND RIMA GLOTTIDIS

(From Buchanan, *A Manual of Anatomy.*)

Muscular Control.—For the benefit of those who wish to make a more detailed study of the adjustments of the vocal cords, the following description of the action of the muscles of the larynx is given.

These muscles may be divided into two classes, those within the organ itself (*intrinsic*) and those which act upon it from without (*extrinsic*).

The *intrinsic muscles* (Figures 10 and 11) have two main functions, (1) to open and close the glottis and (2) to regulate the degree of tension (and the length) of the vocal cords.

The muscles that open the glottis are the *posterior crico-arytenoids*; these are attached to the arytenoid cartilages and to the back of the cricoid cartilage. By rotating the arytenoid cartilages outward they separate the vocal cords (Figure 10).

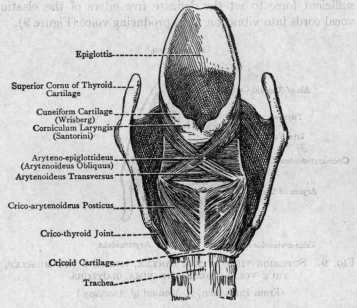

Epiglottis

Superior Cornu of Thyroid Cartilage

Cuneiform Cartilage (Wrisberg)
Corniculum Laryngis (Santorini)

Aryteno-epiglottideus (Arytenoideus Obliquus)
Arytenoideus Transversus

Crico-arytenoideus Posticus

Crico-thyroid Joint

Cricoid Cartilage

Trachea

FIG. 10. POSTERIOR VIEW OF THE INTRINSIC MUSCLES OF THE LARYNX

(From Buchanan *A Manual of Anatomy.*)

The closing of the glottis is effected by the *arytenoid* and the lateral *crico-arytenoid* muscles (Figure 11). The lateral crico-arytenoids extend from the side of the cricoid cartilage to the lower edge of the arytenoid cartilage, in front of the posterior crico-arytenoid muscles. By rotating the arytenoid cartilages inward they cause the vocal cords to be approximated. The arytenoid muscles themselves extend from the back and outer surface of one arytenoid cartilage to the corresponding surface of the other. These bring the arytenoid cartilages together and thus partially or completely close the glottis, especially at the back.

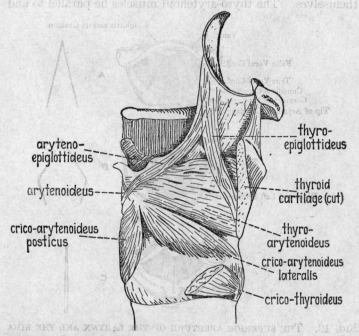

aryteno-
epiglottideus

arytenoideus

crico-arytenoideus
posticus

thyro-
epiglottideus

thyroid
cartilage (cut)

thyro-
arytenoideus

crico-arytenoideus
lateralis

crico-thyroideus

FIG. 11. LATERAL VIEW OF THE INTRINSIC MUSCLES OF THE
LARYNX

(From Buchanan. *A Manual of Anatomy.*)

The most important muscle used in lengthening and tensing the vocal cords is the *crico-thyroid* (Figure 11). It is triangular in form, arises from the front and side of the cricoid cartilage, and is attached to the lower border of the medial surface of the thyroid cartilage. This muscle draws the cricoid cartilage up in front, which action depresses the pack of the cricoid cartilage on which the arytenoid cartilages rest and thus produces tension in the vocal cords.

The vocal cords are relaxed and shortened by the *thyro-arytenoid* muscles and by the muscles in the vocal cords themselves. The thyro-arytenoid muscles lie parallel to and

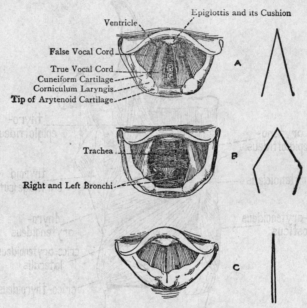

Ventricle

Epiglottis and its Cushion

False Vocal Cord

True Vocal Cord
Cuneiform Cartilage
Corniculum Laryngis
Tip of Arytenoid Cartilage

R.G.

A

Trachea

B

Right and Left Bronchi

C

FIG. 12. THE SUPERIOR APERTURE OF THE LARYNX AND THE RIMA GLOTTIDIS AS SEEN BY THE AID OF THE LARYNGOSCOPE UNDER DIFFERENT CONDITIONS

A, ordinary quiet inspiration; *B*, very deep inspiration; *C*, vocalization, especially in singing high notes; *R.G.*, rima glottidis. (From Buchanan, *A Manual of Anatomy.*)

continuous with the true vocal cords. They are attached in front to the lower front surface of the arytenoid cartilages, and their action is to bring the arytenoid cartilages nearer to the thyroid cartilage (Figure 11).

The larynx as a whole is acted upon by *extrinsic muscles*

connected with the sternum, the hyoid bone, the tongue, and the pharynx, by means of which it may be raised and lowered and tilted forward and backward. Some of these movements are necessary in swallowing and in various types of breathing; others seem to have a direct bearing upon resonance.

The Pharynx

The pharynx (Figure 1) is a vertical passage lying behind the mouth and extending from the base of the skull above to the larynx and œsophagus below. It is cone-shaped, wide above and narrow below. The back and side walls consist of muscular and fibrous tissue; in front the pharynx opens into three spaces which lie one immediately above the other, the larynx, the mouth, and the nasal cavity (Figure 1). In the production of voice the pharynx serves the double purpose of providing a free passage for the current of air and acting as a resonator to reinforce the tone generated in the larynx.

The pharynx is capable of modification in all of its dimensions. It can be shortened from above by lifting the soft palate against its back wall, thus cutting off the upper pharynx. It can be shortened from below by the contraction of the fibres that run lengthwise through its walls from the base of the skull to the larynx and by the raising of the larynx. The horizontal dimension can be modified by the contraction and relaxation of the circular fibres which make up the greater part of its muscular wall and by the moving forward or backward of the tongue and larynx (Figures 13 and 14).

Below, the pharynx has two openings which are capable of variation in size but which are not normally open at the same time. In eating, the pharynx is continuous with the œsophagus, the larynx being closed by the epiglottis and the false vocal cords, as has been described. In breathing, the opening into the œsophagus becomes a narrow slit, and the pharynx opens into the larynx (Figure 1).

The front opening from the pharynx into the mouth may be wholly or partially closed by the action of the tongue, the

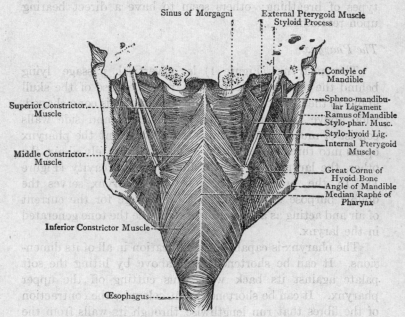

Sinus of Morgagni   External Pterygoid Muscle
Styloid Process

Condyle of Mandible

Spheno-mandibu-lar Ligament
Ramus of Mandible
Stylo-phar. Musc.
Stylo-hyoid Lig.
Internal Pterygoid Muscle

Superior Constrictor Muscle

Middle Constrictor Muscle

Great Cornu of Hyoid Bone
Angle of Mandible
Median Raphé of Pharynx

Inferior Constrictor Muscle

Œsophagus

FIG. 13. THE POSTERIOR WALL OF THE PHARYNX
(From Buchanan, *A Manual of Anatomy*.)

pillars of the fauces, and the soft palate. Above, the opening into the nasal passages may be partially or entirely closed by the elevation of the soft palate.

The Mouth

Like the pharynx, the mouth (Figure 15) is a resonator which is capable of many changes, both in capacity and in size of openings. It is nearly oval in shape and consists of two

cavities, the back cavity (the mouth proper) and a front
cavity having for its outer wall the lips and cheeks, and for
its inner, the teeth and gums.   The lips, which are of considerable use in eating, are of very particular importance

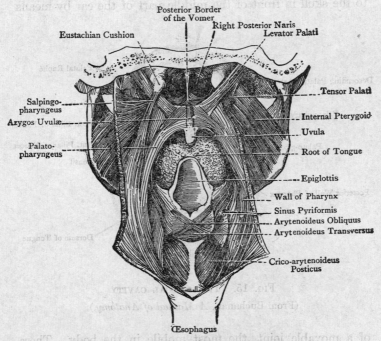

FIG. 14.   THE PHARYNX OPENED FROM BEHIND
(From Buchanan, *A Manual of Anatomy*.)

in the production of voice.   Through their system of muscles
they are capable of changing the size of the mouth aperture,
and by projection the size of the cavity itself, thus increasing
the adaptability of the mouth as a resonator.

The structural base of the mouth is the lower jaw or
mandible.   It is the largest and strongest bone of the face.

Its front part is shaped somewhat like a horseshoe and contains the lower teeth; at each extremity it bends sharply upward at an angle which is little short of a right angle. Each of these perpendicular extremities of the jaw is attached to the skull in front of the middle part of the ear by means

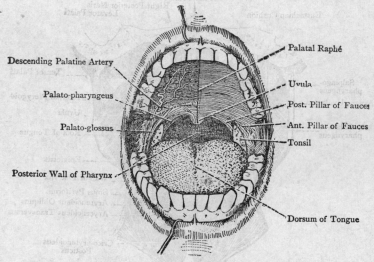

Descending Palatine Artery

Palato-pharyngeus

Palato-glossus

Posterior Wall of Pharynx

Palatal Raphé

Uvula

Post. Pillar of Fauces

Ant. Pillar of Fauces

Tonsil

Dorsum of Tongue

FIG. 15. THE BUCCAL CAVITY
(From Buchanan, *A Manual of Anatomy.*)

of a movable joint, the most mobile in the body. These joints, together with the strong muscles with which the jaw is furnished, make possible the powerful movements necessary for the mastication of food. The movements of the lower jaw also influence the character of the mouth resonator both as to capacity and to size of openings (Figure 1).

The mouth cavity proper is bounded in front by the teeth and gums, above by the hard and soft palates (the *roof of the mouth*), and below by the floor of the mouth, the greater part of which is taken up by the tongue. At the back it

opens into the pharynx through a narrow aperture between
two pairs of muscular folds (the *pillars of the fauces*) which
connect the soft palate with the tongue (Figure 15).

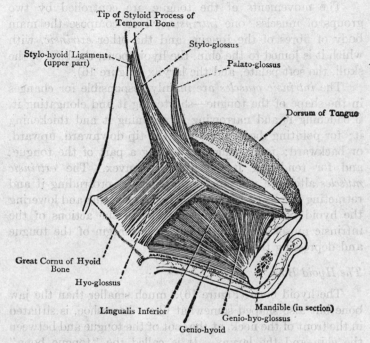

FIG. 16. THE EXTRINSIC MUSCLES OF THE TONGUE
(From Buchanan, *A Manual of Anatomy*.)

The Tongue

The tongue is an organ of the utmost importance in swallowing, in breathing, in controlling the shape of the resonator,
and in the articulation of sounds. It consists of a complicated system of muscle fibres, so constructed as to permit
the most minute and delicate adjustments. Below, it is
attached to the hyoid bone (to which the larynx also is

fastened), to the bone of the lower jaw, and to the inner wall of the chin. Above, as has been said, it is connected by the pillars of the fauces with the soft palate (Figure 15).

The movements of the tongue are controlled by two groups of muscles, one *intrinsic*, which compose the main body of fibres of the tongue, and the other *extrinsic*, with which it is joined to the chin, the hyoid bone, the base of the skull, the soft palate, and the larynx (Figure 16).

The *intrinsic muscles* are mainly responsible for changes in the shape of the tongue—shortening it and elongating it, broadening it and narrowing it, thinning it and thickening it; for pointing the tip, turning the tip downward, upward, or backward; for raising or lowering a part of the tongue; and for rendering it concave or convex. The *extrinsic muscles* alter the position of the tongue—protruding it and retracting it, raising it and lowering it, elevating and lowering the hyoid bone; and assist in some of the actions of the intrinsic muscles, such as raising the margin of the tongue and depressing the middle of it.

The Hyoid Bone

The hyoid bone (Figure 16), much smaller than the jaw bone but also shaped somewhat like a horseshoe, is situated in the front of the neck, at the root of the tongue and between the chin and the larynx. It is called the "tongue bone" because it supports the tongue and serves as an attachment for its muscles. The hyoid bone is the only bone in the body that is not articulated with some other bone. It is, however, suspended by a strong ligament from each side of the base of the skull behind the ear and is connected by other ligaments and muscles with the soft palate, the pharynx, the larynx, the shoulder blade, and the sternum, as well as with the tongue. It can be felt above the angle of the thyroid cartilage (Figure 5). By means of its muscular connections the hyoid bone can move freely upward and downward, forward and backward, from side to side and diagonally, taking with it some or all of the organs with which it is connected. It can also serve as a fixed point from which its muscles may act upon the movable cartilages and organs about it. For example, if the hyoid bone is in a fixed position, the contraction of the muscle by which it is connected with the larynx raises the larynx; but this muscle extends downward below the larynx to the sternum, so that when the muscle acts from the sternum as a fixed point, it will lower the larynx and with it the hyoid bone.

The Palates

The roof of the mouth consists of two parts, the *hard palate* in front and the *soft palate* at the back (Figure 1). The hard palate is a bony structure covered with mucous membrane; it extends in front and at the sides to the upper gum or teeth ridge. Continuous with the hard palate is the soft palate or *velum*, a movable fold of muscle fibres with a pendulous tip called the *uvula*.

By the contraction of its own muscles, the soft palate is raised against the back wall of the pharynx. By the contraction of other muscular fibres which arise in the soft palate and pass through the posterior pillars of the fauces, the pharynx, and the larynx, the soft palate is depressed, and the pharynx and larynx are elevated (Figure 14). By the contraction of muscles starting in the soft palate and passing through the front pillars of the fauces to the tongue, the sides of the soft palate are drawn forward, the sides of the tongue upward and backward, and the front pillars of the fauces are drawn together.

The Nose

The nasal cavity (Figure 1) is a long, narrow passage between the bones of the face, extending from the upper part of the pharynx to the edges of the nostrils. It lies immediately above the mouth, the roof of the mouth serving as its floor. It is divided into two parts by a vertical partition, the *septum*, the outer part of which consists of cartilage, the inner part of bone. The outer region with the cartilaginous septum comprises the *nostrils*; the inner part is divided by the bony septum into two passages called the *nares*. The entire nasal cavity is lined with mucous membrane.

The nose is furnished with small, weak muscles, those above serving to dilate the nostrils, those below, to depress and contract them. In forced breathing the former assist in enlarging the air passage. The nostrils are the only part of the nasal cavity that can change its size.

Sinuses.—Small openings from the nasal cavities lead into accessory air chambers called *sinuses*, situated in hollow bones of the face (Figure 1). These are thought by some physiologists to serve with the other cavities of the head in reinforcing tone. Since the nasal cavities and the sinuses are fixed in form and not subject to change, their effect in tone production is determined by their size, shape, and freedom from obstruction.

Action of the Muscles of the Resonators

The action of the muscles of the resonators has been more carefully studied and is better understood in relation to their primary physiological functions of breathing and eating than in relation to their secondary function of reinforcing tone. A brief examination of their action in breathing and eating, however, may help to make clear their probable action in resonation and to show how the muscular habit systems developed from these functions. Some of these habits seem to help in the resonation of tone, others to hinder.

At the beginning of the act of inspiration the nostrils dilate to facilitate the intake of air. This air passes through the nares into the pharynx, the soft palate being relaxed to provide a free passage and the pharynx being widely open.

The air then passes through the opened glottis of the larynx into the trachea and so into the lungs. In expiration the process is reversed.

In eating, the lower jaw drops to open the mouth to receive food. When the food has been taken into the mouth, the jaw is raised to close the mouth and to bring the lower teeth into contact with the upper for the purpose of mastication. In the first stage of swallowing, the tongue rises toward the hard palate to push the food backward in the mouth. The root of the tongue is at the same time retracted and the larynx is raised and carried forward. This elevation of the larynx closes that passage by bringing it toward the epiglottis, and it also opens the œsophagus to receive the food. As the food passes from the tongue to the pharynx, the pillars of the fauces are constricted and the soft palate is raised, thereby cutting off the entrances to the mouth and nose. In the meantime the constrictor muscles of the pharynx contract from above downward to force the food into the œsophagus.

An understanding of the function of these resonating cavities in the production of speech is made more difficult by the fact that they serve not only to reinforce the tone, but also to convert the tone into articulate sounds which we designate as vowels and consonants.

The Ear

A study of the speech mechanism would not be complete without some consideration of the part played by the ear, since it is the ear that tunes the instrument. The ear (Figure 17) consists of three portions, called the outer, the middle, and the inner ear. The *outer*, the ear commonly so-called, consists of an expanded shell-like portion which serves to collect the sound waves, and a passage which conveys the waves to the ear drum. The ear drum is a membranous wall between the outer and the middle ears.

The middle ear is a small chamber in the temporal bone. It contains a chain of three tiny bones, reaching from its outer to its inner wall, which transmit the sound vibrations from the ear drum to the inner ear. It communicates with the air in the pharynx by means of a connecting tube, the *Eustachian canal.*

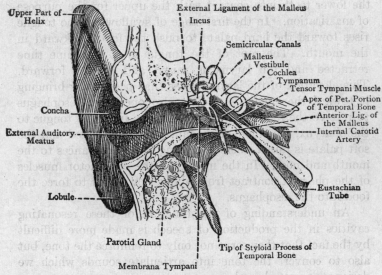

FIG. 17. SECTION THROUGH THE EAR

(From Buchanan, *A Manual of Anatomy.*)

The inner ear is made up of a series of passages stretching still farther into the temporal bone. Within these passages lies a corresponding membranous labyrinth in the walls of which are distributed the endings of the auditory nerve fibres. These nerve endings are sensitive to minute vibrations. Both the bony and the membranous labyrinths are filled with fluid.

Sound vibrations, then, are gathered in the outer ear and conveyed to the ear drum, in which they set up vibrations.

These vibrations are in turn transmitted by the bones of the middle ear to the fluid in which lie the endings of the auditory nerve in the inner ear. This nerve carries the stimuli to the brain, where they are interpreted in terms of sound. The brain has the power to discriminate between different tones and to translate these tones into symbols of thought.

There are great differences in the sensitiveness of individuals to vibrations and also in their power to translate them accurately in terms of sound. These differences are not so great, however, as was formerly thought: the number of persons who are really tone deaf is much smaller than has generally been supposed. Sensitiveness to sound is largely the result of training the ear to distinguish differences in pitch, volume, and quality. By some persons this is acquired with practically no conscious attention; by others it is acquired only with continued and rightly directed effort.

Sensitiveness to sound is so important an aid in enabling the student to recognize good speech and to make it his own that any adequate course in speech will give due attention to ear training. The need for ear training becomes all the more apparent when it is taken into account that people generally have no accurate idea of how their voices and speech sound to others. This is partly because they are so familiar with the sound of their own voices that they do not listen to them objectively, and partly because the close connection between the ear and the mechanism that produces the sound makes it extremely difficult to hear one's own voice as it sounds to others.

* * *

Our survey of the anatomical structure and primary functions of the speech mechanism has prepared us for the more detailed study of its secondary function—the production of voice and speech. This is the subject of the following chapter.

CHAPTER III

VOICE TRAINING

BEAUTY and power in voice production depend, as we intimated in our preliminary chapter, upon the healthy action of the whole body. The student of speech should work not only for physical control of the mechanism of utterance, but for the most perfect adjustment of the body for all conditions of everyday living.

Since tone is greatly dependent on mental attitudes and emotional responses as well as on physical conditions, skill in its control can never be considered as an end in itself, but rather as a part of that unconscious rhythmical balance of the whole neuro-muscular organism. Good tone is impossible without this coördination; even a slight disturbance in this balance is reflected in the voice. And it is unfortunately true that habits of faulty tone production remain long after the initial causes have disappeared. We may not speak "as we are," but we do speak "as we were" at some stage in our mental or physical adjustment to environmental conditions.

Moreover, sensitiveness to the æsthetic possibilities of tone greatly influences the result. Most persons would not speak as they do if they really "heard" their own voices. In order to make satisfactory progress the student must train his ear to analyze and appreciate a high standard in voice and speech production.

To obtain the best results, then, voice training must take into consideration the physical, mental, and æsthetic needs of the individual student. It goes without saying that such training cannot fail to be of invaluable aid in the maintenance of a healthy mental and physical state.

VOICE PRODUCTION

We shall now consider voice production in three main divisions: (1) the support of tone, (2) the initiation of tone, and (3) the reinforcement of tone. It must be definitely understood, however, that these are not three isolated and independent adjustments, but parts of a practically simultaneous process. A fourth element, that of articulation, is so involved that, except for certain general principles, its discussion is left to later chapters.

Control of the Breath for Speech

General Considerations

In the chapter on the physiology of the speech mechanism, normal life breathing was described as an unconscious, automatic process. Breathing should be that for speech also. The special demands made on the respiratory system should be met, as similar demands are met in running, jumping, and swimming, by an instantaneous and complete response of muscular action to nerve stimulus.

In athletic exercises the breathing is merely more vigorous than in ordinary respiration; hence, the chief consideration is to maintain in these more energetic actions as perfect a rhythm as in the quiet breathing of normal life. In speech, however, the problem is more difficult. Here the main consideration is not the intake of sufficient air, but the control of the outgoing breath. It follows that in breathing for speech, the expiratory phase, instead of being chiefly passive (the result of the relaxation of the diaphragmatic and intercostal muscles, the weight of the ribs, and the automatic recoil of the elastic lung tissue), must be actively controlled in order to give the necessary firmness and duration to the outgoing breath stream.

How can this change in the respiratory cycle be accomplished without interference with the normal functioning of the body?

The chief difficulty is that the change must be made without interrupting the bodily rhythm. The problem is somewhat similar to that in dancing. Each individual has his normal rhythm of movement, but he can learn to adjust this to the special rhythm required for a particular dance. A person whose natural rhythm is slow can with practice learn a rapid dance, though it will be harder for him than for one whose normal rhythm is quicker, and he will go back to his slower tempo as soon as the dance is over. In breathing for speech, instead of a fairly even rate of inspiration and expiration, we have a rapid intake of air followed by a relatively slow emission. This emission, moreover, is not always of the same duration, since it is dependent on the length of the phrase, which may vary from one syllable to a dozen words or more. Yet to prevent speech from being jerky and difficult to follow, the rhythm of breathing must be maintained.

To accomplish this requires, first, such control of the muscles that each successive phase of contraction and relaxation is begun smoothly and completed freely and unhurriedly within the proper period of time; and second, such coördination of mind and body that the flow of outgoing breath is easily sustained to the end of the phrase.

Mental Preparation for Speech

In our present strenuous age the greatest hindrance to quiet, rhythmical control of breath is not physical but mental, not muscular weakness but lack of confidence. With most beginners in the study of speech this lack of confidence is twofold: fear of not being able to take in enough breath without gasping, and fear of not being able to control the emission of breath so that it will last until the end of the phrase. Hence, the first step in gaining breath control should be to get rid of fear.

Overcoming Fear in Regard to Inspiration.—To eliminate apprehension regarding the supply of inspired air it is helpful to remember the physical fact of atmospheric pressure. For inspiration it is necessary only to maintain a free passage to the lungs and to create a vacuum in the chest by expansion of its walls. Under these conditions enough air flows into the lungs in the pause after each phrase to last through to the end of the next phrase. This knowledge is of great help in overcoming the nervous haste and jerkiness in inspiration which are among the chief causes of unrhythmical breathing.

Overcoming Fear in Regard to Expiration.—Fear concerning expiration is largely due to the mistaken idea that sounds consist of "blasts" of air instead of air waves merely. When one considers the speed at which sound travels, it is obvious that air blasts of that velocity would be veritable hurricanes. The student should remember that only a small stream of air is necessary to initiate sound waves, and that his problem is only to maintain such control of the outgoing breath that it will exert a firm but gentle pressure on the vocal cords. If the breath is emitted without waste, there is no need to fear that it will be exhausted before the end of the phrase is reached, provided, of course, that the inspiration has been adequate.

Overcoming Fear through Interest in One's Subject and Hearers.—A third means of gaining confidence is through interest in one's subject and one's hearers. This objective attitude of mind releases the tension caused by egocentricity or self-consciousness and permits free, rhythmical movement of the respiratory muscles.

Physical Preparation for Speech

The proper "mind set," having been gained the student's next step is to attain the most advantageous physical conditions for the rhythmical control of an adequate stream of air. The proper "stance" is as helpful in speech as in tennis or golf.

The following physical conditions are necessary for the best results in voice production:

1. *Maintenance of an easily erect posture* by (*a*) securing a firm base, the feet being far enough apart to suggest confidence without aggressiveness and the muscles of the legs being held in a state of elastic tension; (*b*) making the lumbar curve normal by contracting the lower abdominal and the gluteal [1] muscles and maintaining this contraction in a state of tonicity; [2] (*c*) holding the lower ribs extended and the chest high, thus increasing the thoracic cavity in all dimensions; and (*d*) holding the crown of the head high and the shoulders low.

2. *Inspiration of an easy, deep breath.*

3. *Release of the breath in a steadily controlled stream.*

Of these requirements, the one most apt to be misunderstood is that concerning the contraction of the gluteal and the lower abdominal muscles. This combined action not only (1) straightens the lumbar curve and makes possible a firm control of the posterior half of the diaphragm,[3] but (2) prevents the lower abdominal wall from being pushed forward by the depression of the viscera in inspiration, and (3) holds the liver and stomach firmly against the lower wall of the diaphragm.

A point not always clearly grasped is that the muscles of the upper and the lower abdominal walls act independently of one another, so that although in good posture the lower muscles are maintained in a state of constant tension, the upper ones are free to expand in inhalation and to contract

---

[1] The gluteal muscles are the fleshy muscles at the back of the hips.

[2] Tonicity may be defined as the exact degree of tension necessary to allow the muscles to function properly.

[3] See the preceding chapter.

in exhalation. It will be seen that the action of the upper abdominal muscles is the reverse of that of the diaphragm, that is, they contract as the diaphragm expands and *vice versa*. If all of these sets of muscles act correctly, (1) the viscera will be held in their normal position by the constant contraction of the gluteal and lower abdominal muscles; (2) the walls of the upper abdomen will expand from side to side and from front to back in inspiration through the descent of the diaphragm; and (3) the pressure of the relaxing diaphragm in expiration will be made firmer by the upward pressure of the abdominal viscera, and made slower by the maintenance of the upward and outward extension of the ribs. If the ribs are allowed to collapse, the air rushes out too rapidly, producing a noisy tone at the beginning of the phrase and a feeble, unsupported tone at the end. Control of breath for speech means, therefore, that *the action of the slowly relaxing diaphragm must be assisted by the upward pressure of the abdominal viscera and held in check by the extended ribs.*

Results of Faulty Breath Control

Faulty breath control for speech manifests itself in several ways, some connected with inspiration and some with expiration.

1. If the muscles do not act freely and vigorously in inspiration, the lung capacity is not increased sufficiently to receive the requisite amount of air, and the chest walls are not held firmly enough to make possible the forced vibrations which give buoyancy and vitality to the tone. For this reason actors and public speakers undergo long training to increase lung capacity and to strengthen the respiratory muscles.

2. Many persons who have failed to get a clear understanding of what is meant by breath control have a tendency to allow the intercostal and diaphragmatic muscles to relax

as in quiet breathing, thus failing to secure the controlled power that is gained by the firm pressure from the abdominal muscles held in check by the extended ribs. This is a fault in the voice production of many public speakers who fail to maintain a steadily controlled pressure to the ends of phrases or sentences, with the result that their voices become partially inaudible and wholly monotonous.

3. Speakers who have not learned to take in just sufficient breath for their needs, or who have been taught that air must be taken in vigorously rather than allowed to flow in quietly and easily, are inclined to take in more air than is needed for ordinary speech and to do so audibly and conspicuously. Gasping may also be caused by uncertain control of breath due to self-consciousness or lack of general nervous stability. Poor posture is usually a contributing factor in this condition.

4. Persons who have not thoroughly mastered the technique of respiration are apt to breathe jerkily instead of smoothly and rhythmically.

Correction of Wrong Habits of Breathing

The physical and mental disturbances of breath support can usually be prevented by taking more time in preparation for the intake of breath. Complete eradication of faults in breathing, however, may demand a change in the general physical and mental habits of the individual.

Since the foundation of all good voice production lies in the control of the respiratory forces, too much emphasis cannot be laid on the need for establishing the following correct habits in breathing for speech:

1. The association of the idea of voice production with that of outward-moving air waves;

2. The easy inhalation of an adequate quantity of breath;

3. The proper functioning of the intercostal, diaphragmatic, and abdominal muscles as the chief controls of the respiratory process;

4. *The maintenance of a rhythmical balance between the inspiratory and expiratory phases of the breathing process.*

The Initiation of Tone

General Requirements

A well initiated tone is the result of involuntary muscular adjustment under the direction of the ear. It is chiefly a matter of the perfect synchronizing of the respiratory muscles with those of the larynx. This involves two requirements: first, such control of the breath as will produce an air stream that is adequate in volume, rhythmically controlled, and rightly timed; and second, such adjustment of the vocal mechanism as will enable the vocal cords to respond freely to the direction of the ear.

Proper adjustment of the voice mechanism implies a sensation of freedom in the whole vocal instrument. This freedom is conditioned by the unimpeded action of the intrinsic muscles of the larynx, and the subsequent freedom from interference by the extrinsic muscles which connect the larynx with the root of the tongue, the soft palate, and the sternum. The chief value of a study of the anatomy and physiology of the vocal mechanism is to acquaint the student with the enormous complexity of the vocal process and thus to help him to guard against the almost unlimited possibilities for interference inherent in this complexity.

To repeat, a good tone is produced only when there is no hindrance to the free action of the vocal cords. Because of the two sets of muscles involved and the complicated character of the laryngeal adjustments for phonation, many kinds of damping are caused by the effort of the will to control the initiation of tone. The object of any vocal exercise, therefore, should be (1) to produce rhythmical vibrations and (2) to make the hindrance to resonation as slight as possible. This implies the necessity of breaking down old associations of the extrinsic muscles with phonation and of developing the required state of tonicity in all the muscles of the voice mechanism.

Results of Poorly Initiated Tone

The following are the chief faults due to poor initiation of tone, with their specific causes:

1. *Breathiness.*—(*a*) If the vocal cords are not brought together smartly enough to set all the outgoing air into vibration, the result is a breathy tone.

(*b*) If too violent a pressure of air is directed against the cords, breathiness will result. Many students waste so much breath in the first part of a phrase that the remainder is inadequately supported and thus becomes nearly, if not quite, inaudible.

2. *Harshness.*—(*a*) It has been shown by the autophonoscope that in the production of noisy or otherwise unpleasant tones the muscular fibres of the false vocal cords contract,[4] thus closing over the true vocal cords and preventing their free action. According to some authorities, it is this restriction that causes the harsh, jerky attack called the *glottal shock*, or *glottal stop;* according to others, the glottal stop is the result of rigidity in the action of the true vocal cords which causes them to remain too tightly closed, so that the air, instead of passing through smoothly, is completely checked and escapes with an explosive sound. Probably both conditions contribute to the result.

(*b*) The muscles of the throat, especially those attached to the lower jaw, to the root of the tongue, and to the soft palate, sometimes carry over into speech the vigorous contractions with which they facilitate the swallowing process. This overenergetic action, by hampering the free, rhythmical swing of the vocal cords, is one of the commonest contributing causes of badly initiated tone.

---

[4] As they do in swallowing; see Chapter II.

(c) Harshness results also from too great pressure of the breath stream, which causes heavy, unrhythmical vibrations and thus produces noisy tones.

3. *Weakness.*—Lack of general muscular tonicity causes too weak pressure of the breath stream and inadequate response of the vocal cords. The resulting tone gives an impression of bodily weakness and permanent or temporary mental inertness.

Correction of Faulty Initiation of Tone

The student should have for his aim an easy, rhythmical initiation of tone, remembering that a forced, jerky attack always means a noisy tone.

He should keep in mind also that although the tone is initiated at the larynx, it should always be associated with the outward movement of the air waves. Since, as has repeatedly been said, the control of the intrinsic muscles of the larynx rests entirely with the ear, the student must consider the development of sensitiveness to the sound of his own voice the primary essential to the correct initiation of tone.

Resonance

General Requirements for Reinforcement of Tone

We have already learned that no matter how well supported and smoothly initiated a vocal tone may be, it has little beauty or carrying power unless it is properly reinforced. Such reinforcement requires (1) that the resonating chambers shall be free from obstruction and capable of instantly adjusting their capacity and the size of their openings to meet the needs of the constantly changing tones;[5] (2) that the muscles

---

[5] Since beauty of tone greatly depends on the adequate reinforcement of the fundamental and the lower overtones and since the pharynx is by its size especially adapted to produce this resonation, it is particularly important that this part of the resonator be kept as open and free from strain as possible.

which control the tongue, lips, jaw, and soft palate shall be so flexible that they can make the articulatory movements with the least possible interference with the sonority of the tone; and (3) that the breath stream shall be not only well supported, but directed forward, through the mouth for oral sounds and through the nose for nasal sounds.

This does not mean that in speech one should be consciously thinking of breath support or of initiation of tone. It means that a definite tone standard should be established in the student's mind and attention given to the various steps in reaching that standard until they have become automatic.

Results of Poor Resonation

The chief faults due to poor reinforcement of tone, with their specific causes, are:

1. *Inadequate Resonance Due to Weak Initiation of Tone.*—If the breath support is weak, the tone is thin and colorless. Such tone is often the result of physical weakness or mental depression.

2. *Lack of Reinforcement through Forced Vibration of the Chest Walls.*—It seems to be established by the experiments of Simon and Keller [6] that if the chest walls are taut and the breath pressure is adequate to cause firm vibrations of the vocal cords, the air waves thus generated will be reinforced by the sympathetic vibrations of the chest walls. If the upper chest is not held high, if the lower chest is not fully expanded, and if the breath is not well controlled by the combined action of diaphragmatic, intercostal, and abdominal muscles, this reinforcement is not sufficient to produce appreciable effect on the tone.

3. *Inadequate Resonation of Upper Partials Due to Failure to Direct the Tone Forward.*—If through failure to direct the tone forward the resonation of the upper partials or over-

---

[6] See the article by these writers in the *Quarterly Journal of Speech Education*, November, 1927.

tones is neglected, the tone, though it may have sufficient pharyngeal resonance, will be hollow and lacking in brilliance. Many persons in attempting to correct a loud, harsh, shrill, or nasal tone acquire this kind of voice.

4. *Reinforcement of Discordant Partials.*—(a) If the breath pressure is violent or irregular, the resulting air waves will be unrhythmical and, when reinforced, will produce a harsh and noisy tone.

(b) If the free swing of the vocal cords is hindered by undue tension of the vocal muscles, the resulting tone will have a weak fundamental and relatively strong overtones. When these are reinforced, the tone lacks depth and beauty.

(c) If the resonator is not properly adjusted to reinforce the fundamental and the lower overtones, the tone, even though properly initiated, will be shrill and unpleasant.

(d) If, with the muscles of the false vocal cords and the walls of the resonating cavities in a rigid condition, the air is sent through the nasal passages, a particularly unpleasant nasal twang results.

The reinforcement of discordant partials may be caused by carrying over into speech the muscular habits of eating. It will be remembered that in eating (1) the muscles of the lips and tongue tip are relatively inactive and the lower jaw acts very vigorously; (2) the muscles of the back of the tongue and of the side and back walls of the pharynx act energetically in forcing the food into the œsophagus; (3) those of the soft palate become rigid in order to hold it firmly pressed against the pharyngeal wall and so prevent food from entering the nasal passages; and (4) those of the false vocal cords contract strongly in order to help the epiglottis in preventing food from entering the larynx. It will readily be seen that powerful contraction of the false cords tends to bring them down over the true vocal cords, preventing their free upward and downward swing and thus hindering tone initiation. Rigidity of the soft palate makes impossible the rapid adjustments necessary in going from nasal to oral tones. A strong backward movement of the tongue blocks the pharyngeal resonator. Undue tension of the muscles of the tongue, palate, throat, and jaw is communicated to the larynx, with which these muscles are directly connected, and prevents the free, rhythmic swing of the vocal cords. On the other hand, the relative lack of exercise of the lips and tongue tip prevents the articulatory movements from being swift and light and sure and thus hinders oral resonace.

Correction of Faults Due to Poor Resonation

To correct the faults of resonation and gain proper reinforcement of desirable partials is no easy task. In fact, no other phase of speech training requires more intelligent and persistent effort.

A rhythmically initiated tone, a breath stream steadily controlled and directed well forward, and a chest well expanded and slightly raised are prime essentials. But most necessary and most difficult of attainment is the power to reverse in speech the muscular habits of eating. How is it possible to change habits as deeply rooted as these? Chiefly by establishing, with the aid of the ear, the imagination, and the kinæsthetic or motor sense, an entirely different reaction pattern. It will be found helpful to think of the throat and the back of the mouth as being a resonator only, and of articulation as occurring chiefly in the front of the mouth. In order to make the resonator as useful as possible, it must be kept open and its walls free from all strain. Singing teachers have many devices to help in achieving this condition. Some speak constantly of the "open throat." Others ask their students to think of the sensation of yawning. Some are more explicit and recommend a " low " yawn, with the idea of relaxing and lowering the back of the tongue; others recommend a "high" yawn in the effort to counteract the nasality due to rigidity or overrelaxation of the soft palate.[7] Some try to gain this desired condition through promoting greater bodily and mental relaxation and repose. In the last analysis, however, this is a problem which each student will have to solve for himself.

For gaining greater precision and firmness in the use of the lips and tongue tip, it will help to have a clear idea of how each vowel and each consonant should be made and to gain the power of making each sound with precision and lightness and of passing easily and smoothly from one sound to the next. It will help also to remember that for every vowel the tongue tip should rest close to the lower front teeth and that all but four of the consonants are made with the tongue tip touching the teeth or the upper gum. Shakespeare's recommendation to speak "trippingly on the tongue" should be literally followed. Lastly, the firm rounding of the lips in forming the back vowels and the consonants *w* and *wh* helps to give harmonious reinforcement to the tone.

In order, therefore, to ensure the carrying over into daily speech of these improved habits of tone reinforcement, it is important to fix once and for all these general principles:

1. The pharynx and the back of the mouth should be thought of as the chief resonator and should be kept as open and free from obstruction as possible.

2. Their muscles must be free from rigidity so that they will not communicate tension to the muscles of the vocal cords.

3. The front of the mouth should be thought of as the chief articulator, but the lips and the tongue tip should be trained to make the speech sounds with such accuracy and yet with such delicacy that this cavity becomes as perfect a resonator as possible for the upper partials which characterize the vowels and sonorous consonants.

---

[7] This latter condition is perhaps due to the fact that in quiet breathing the soft palate is very low in order to allow the breath to pass freely in and out of the nose.

4. The soft palate should be free from rigidity or sluggishness, thus insuring desirable nasal resonance and preventing undesirable nasalization.

THE ELEMENTS OF TONE

Having discussed the physiological aspects of voice production, we shall now make a brief study of the physical properties of vocal tone—pitch, volume or intensity, quality, and duration—building on what we learned in the preceding chapter concerning these properties of sound in general.

Pitch

Pitch has been explained as the property of sound that depends on the frequency at which the air waves strike the ear drum. In discussing pitch in relation to the human voice we shall consider (1) *key*, or the average pitch from which the tone rises and falls, and (2) *intonation*, or the melody patterns which the voice makes in moving up or down from one pitch to another.

Key

Every voice has its natural pitch, determined by the length and the thickness of the vocal cords. Speaking in this key, therefore, ensures the best tones of which the voice is capable and also the greatest comfort to the instrument. Hence it is important for the student, with the aid of a piano or a teacher, to find his natural pitch and to key his voice to this. Every voice, however, has a considerable range up and down from this median tone, and if the natural pitch is used as the basis, it is easy to change the key according to the demands of the thought or emotion to be expressed and to make the natural intonation curves without getting out of one's vocal range.

Since pitch is chiefly determined by the tension of the

vocal cords, it is not surprising that one of the most common
defects of American voices is that of being keyed too high.
The results of this fault are more or less conscious discomfort
in the voice mechanism of the speaker and strain on the
nervous system of the listener.   The cause lies sometimes in
the high tension of American life and sometimes in lack of
consideration for the hearer—sometimes in both.   The remedy is to be found in the cultivation of greater sensitiveness
to pitch, in greater regard for the comfort of others, and in
freer relaxation and better bodily and mental control.
Most of all, perhaps, it lies in freedom from an urge to be
the most conspicuous and dominant person in the group to
which one belongs.   When combined with a harsh and guttural quality, extremes of pitch are sometimes the result of
self-sufficiency or of overcompensation for a feeling of inferiority.

The first step in correction is for the student to become
better adjusted socially.   Next, his ear should be trained
to hear his own pitch and to form a concept of the key to be
desired.   Then should follow practice of voice exercises, pref-
erably with the piano, and the reading of light, cheerful
lyrics [8] or the acting of youthful and gay rôles in amateur
theatricals.

Intonation, or Inflection

A study of changes in pitch brings us to recognition of
what is called *speech melody*.   In song the melody is very
evident, since it consists of definitely marked changes made
by *leaps* of the voice from one musical note to another.   In
speech the melody is not so apparent, since it is caused by
glides [9] of the voice from one level of pitch to another.

---

[8] Children's verses such as those of A. A. Milne are particularly good
for this purpose.

[9] Some authorities prefer to call the syllabic glides *inflections* and
the phrasal patterns *intonation curves*.

Such a glide is called an *inflection,* or *intonation curve.* Although these glides of the voice have more or less definite patterns according to the thoughts and the emotions they express, they vary with the individual and do not represent fixed musical intervals. Nevertheless, speech tunes are no less important than those of song; possibly they are more important, since not only the musical quality of speech but also its subtler meanings depend on them. Although very little experimental study has been given to the intonations of American speech (which differ considerably from those of English speech), it may be helpful to consider a few of the fundamental facts concerning them.

An inflection may occur in a single syllable or extend throughout a whole phrase. Inflections may be *rising, falling, compound* (that is, rising-falling or falling-rising), and *level.* In a general way a *falling inflection* indicates finality, decision, deep conviction, assertiveness. It is the inflection used at the end of an assertion or of a command. *Rising inflection* indicates incompleteness, uncertainty, doubt, inquiry, deference, humility, weakness of mind or character. It is the normal inflection for the ends of phrases that express unfinished thought and for certain types of questions. A *compound,* or *circumflex, inflection* generally occurs when there is a conflict in the mind of the speaker or between the words and their meaning. It is used to express vacillation, irony, insinuation, and real or feigned surprise. A *level intonation,* or progression of the voice on one pitch, may mean suspension of thought, deliberation, or great elevation or deep impressiveness of thought. For practical purposes in oral reading perhaps the most important point with regard to the use of intonation is what may be called falling-rising or *suspensive inflection.* This occurs at the end of a phrase which does not complete a thought. It consists of a downward movement of the voice ending in a slight upward turn.

The following sentences may serve to illustrate these intonation changes. The dots representing the intonation patterns and the lines the average pitch of the voice:

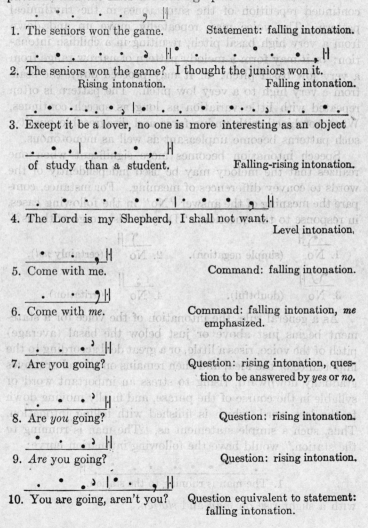

1. The seniors won the game. Statement: falling intonation.

2. The seniors won the game? I thought the juniors won it.
       Rising intonation. Falling intonation.

3. Except it be a lover, no one is more interesting as an object

   of study than a student. Falling-rising intonation.

4. The Lord is my Shepherd, I shall not want.
           Level intonation.

5. Come with me. Command: falling intonation.

6. Come with *me*. Command: falling intonation, *me* emphasized.

7. Are you going? Question: rising intonation, question to be answered by *yes* or *no*.

8. Are *you* going? Question: rising intonation.

9. *Are* you going? Question: rising intonation.

10. You are going, aren't you? Question equivalent to statement: falling intonation.

Monotony of intonation distracts the attention of the hearer from the thought to the melody. A striking example of monotony of tune is the "sing-song" voice, caused by the continued repetition of the same tones in the rhythmical pattern. The voice may repeatedly move up and down from a very high basal pitch, resulting in a childish intonation; or it may form a melody pattern of narrow range from a very low basal pitch; or it may proceed down the scale from a very high to a very low pitch. The pattern is often repeated with little variation as long as speech continues. When combined with undue force and disagreeable quality, such patterns become unpleasant as well as monotonous.

Speech intonation becomes more significant when one realizes that the melody may be used independently of the words to convey differences of meaning. For instance, compare the meaning of the answer "No" in the following cases, in response to the question, "Do you wish to go with us?"

1. No (simple negation).   2. No (certainly *not*).

3. No (doubtful).   4. No (irritation).

As a general rule, the intonation of the voice for a statement begins just above or just below the basal (average) pitch of the voice, rises a little, or a great deal according to the importance of the idea, and then remains on a level or moves gradually downward, rising to stress an important word or syllable in the course of the phrase, and finally moving down to the last word, which is finished with falling intonation. Thus, such a simple statement as, "The man is running to the station," would have the following intonation curve:

1. The man is running to the station.

with a slight rise on *man* and *station*.

Had some particular man been pointed out, the melody would have been slightly changed, thus:

2. *That* man is running to the station.

that being spoken in a pitch quite a little above the basal pitch, the voice then moving downward.

If the fact of his *running* had been the important matter, there would have been a rising intonation on that word, and the melody pattern would have been:

3. That man is running to the station.

The following illustrate patterns in longer passages:

Tiger, Tiger, burning bright,

In the forests of the night,

What immortal hand or eye

Could shape thy fearful symmetry?

WILLIAM BLAKE

Heard the phoebe note of the chickadee today for the first time; I had at first heard their 'day, 'day, 'day ungratefully. "Oh! You but carry my thoughts back to winter!" But anon I found that they, too, had become spring birds. They had changed their note.

THOREAU

Volume, Intensity, or Force

The property of volume of tone, which the ear interprets as loudness or softness, depends upon two factors—the intensity of the air waves and their reinforcement by the resonance chambers and by the forced vibrations of the bony walls of the chest [10] (perhaps also of the head).[11] Of these two factors, that of resonation concerns us most. A voice that depends for its carrying power on vigorous initiation will reach the ear as loud, noisy, and difficult to listen to because of its lack of rhythm. One that depends on delicate precision of initiation and reinforcement by properly tuned resonators, forward articulation, and mental projection will reach the ear as a smooth, full tone, agreeable to listen to and easy to understand. Overenergetic initiation of tone is, like too high pitch, a common characteristic of American voices, especially of women. Its causes are similar to those of high pitch. Its cure is also similar—cultivation of the sensitiveness of the ear, regard for the feelings of others, knowledge of the fundamental principles of voice production, and constant practice of these principles until right habits have become second nature. To repeat, *proper resonance, or full use of the reinforcement possibilities of tone, is more important than energetic initiation in achieving volume.*

Quality

Tone quality, even more than volume, depends on resonance, though here also right initiation of tone is essential, since only rhythmical air waves can be agreeably reinforced. If the muscular walls of the resonator are so flexible that

---

[10] See note, page 58.

[11] Subjectively, a third element enters into the matter—that of pitch, since a high-keyed voice sounds louder than a low one. The use of the expression, "a low voice," to mean either a voice in a low key or a soft voice, is evidence of this. A good way, then, to avoid the effect of a loud voice is to lower the pitch.

they respond promptly and accurately to the demands of the ear, both as to the characteristic quality of the various speech sounds and as to emotional color, a properly initiated and adequately supported tone will receive such reinforcement as will give it beauty and harmony. If, however, there is constriction or rigidity in the resonating passages, the tone will be reinforced by inharmonic overtones, in which case the voice will be flat, strident, metallic, harsh, rough, or nasal. Or the tone may be reinforced by so few overtones that it will be dull, muffled, guttural, or somber in quality.

To a greater degree even than pitch and volume, the quality of a tone depends on general mental and physical states. If the throat is congested or infected by a cold or other cause, the tone will be husky or hoarse. Chronic hoarseness is often the result of misuse of the voice when the condition of the throat is impaired. Constriction or stoppage of the nasal resonator resulting from adenoids, catarrh, colds, rigidity following an operation, or bad habits of breathing [12] causes a lack of nasal resonance which is often wrongly called nasality.[13] The various types of real nasality may result from one or more of a number of physical and mental causes—tightness of throat, tongue, and velar muscles, overrelaxation of the velum, self-pity, and bad habits due to imitation of poor models. A metallic or strident voice is usually the result of a highstrung, irritable temperament or mood. The voice of a physically weak, despondent person

---

[12] The pinched nostrils of many persons living in northern New York and New England suggests generations of avoidance of the "frosty pepper" which so abundantly seasons the winters in those latitudes.

[13] True nasal resonance on vowels and all consonants except *n*, *m*, and *ng* requires that the throat be open and the soft palate lowered ever so slightly so that the air in the nasal cavities may be set in vibration, but that the air stream be directed through the mouth, not emitted through the nose.

will usually be dull and monotonous, and frequently nasal
as well because the air is allowed to take its more natural
course through the nostrils instead of being directed through
the mouth.

Actors depend for characterization quite as much on tone
quality as on gesture and facial expression; for power and
charm, even more. No one who has heard such a voice as
that of Duse, Sarah Bernhardt, Salvini, Ellen Terry, Julia
Marlowe, or Edith Wynne Matthison will ever forget it.
One of the reasons why a play loses so much of its beauty
and effectiveness when converted into a motion picture is
that the characterization, lacking the voice, becomes thin
and inadequate.

So revelatory of character and mood is the quality of the
voice that it often expresses the thoughts and emotions of a
speaker more truly than do his words. Frequently, indeed, it
contradicts the words, and in such cases no one but the most
stupid would fail to believe the voice rather than the words.
Insincere persons seldom deceive anyone but themselves.

In working for improvement in voice quality, then, the
student must start with a definite idea as to what kind of quality he desires and then make sure he has the physical and mental characteristics of which that quality is the natural expression. Otherwise his speech, though it may have some pleasing
elements, will lack the one ultimately satisfying characteristic
—that of sincerity. Sensible persons generally prefer a voice
with little charm except the ring of sincerity to a melodious
voice which sounds mincing and affected. But the student
who has developed a sound and sensible mind in a sound and
flexible body has all the more reason for developing the voice
qualities that shall adequately express this fully balanced
personality. In acquiring these, the skills described in the
discussion of resonance and those to be described in the
following chapters on speech, sounds and oral reading are
necessary.

Duration

The time element in speech comprehends (1) the general rate of speed in reading and speaking; (2) adjustment of the speaker's normal tempo to the demands of a particular thought or mood or of a particular audience; (3) the relative length of individual speech sounds; (4) pause, whether for emphasis or for replenishing the breath and indicating the ends of phrases; and (5) speech rhythm, whether the free rhythm of prose and unmetrical poetry or the patterned rhythm of metrical verse.

Rate is of great practical importance since it involves timing one's speech so that the key word of each phrase meets the crest of the wave of the hearer's attention. One of the commonest causes of ineffective speaking is failure thus to synchronize the phrasing with the attention waves of the audience. To do this calls for the kind of rhythm that means freedom from nervous tension. But it also demands considerable practice. Benjamin Franklin tells of a famous preacher who had such mastery of this art that, especially after he had given a sermon two or three times, he could time his points so perfectly that not one of them failed to reach and move his audience. Of all the speakers in America during the last generation, William Jennings Bryan probably had this power in the highest degree, and this ability combined with a somewhat musical voice gave the effect of impressiveness to his often mediocre thought.

The physiological, physical, and psychological aspects of the time element have already been touched upon and will be more fully discussed, together with the practical and æsthetic aspects, in the chapters on speech sounds and oral reading.

* * *

In conclusion, it must be reiterated that a pleasant and effective speaking voice is one of the most important factors in achieving success and happiness and is richly worth the effort its development requires. It must also be emphasized again that attention to any one phase of voice education without reference to the total effect desired is not only futile, but likely to produce an artificial and affected tone quality which will be a liability rather than an asset. Voice training should aim at giving the student such knowledge as will enable him to develop a voice expressive of the best of which his personality is capable at a given time. To accomplish its full purpose it must do more than this—it must help him to the further development of his personality. To be successful, voice training and integration of personality must be reciprocal: each must serve in turn as cause and as effect.

CHAPTER IV

REPRESENTATION AND CLASSIFICATION OF SPEECH SOUNDS

VOICE and speech are sometimes spoken of as if they could be considered independently of each other. A little reflection will show this to be a fallacy. As the air waves which originate in the larynx proceed through the vocal passages, they are not only reinforced, but shaped into speech sounds. When the mouth is sufficiently open to allow the air waves to pass out freely, the sound is some sort of vowel (though not necessarily an English vowel).[1] When the waves are impeded somewhere in their outward passage, the sound is some sort of consonant. No voice teacher tells a student to practice voice in the abstract. "Abstract voice," to paraphrase Burke, "like other abstractions, does not exist." The student of singing or speaking practices voice by practicing certain vowels or resonant consonants or even words or connected passages. Thus it will be seen that voice is the raw material of speech,[2] and that speech sounds are not well made unless they are properly initiated and properly reinforced, as well as properly articulated.

If you say the sentence, "Come unto these yellow sands," you will realize that it consists of a series of air waves

---

[1] If the voiced air passes out with the vocal organs in their natural position of rest, the vowel produced is the annoying sound (sometimes written *er* or *ah*) that is made by speakers who fail to relax the vocal cords while they are thinking of a word. It is sometimes called the *natural*, or *neutral*, *vowel*.

[2] Though it is true that a few speech sounds like *p* and *s* are merely noises produced by the unvoiced breath.

FIG. 18. KYMOGRAPH RECORD OF THE SENTENCE, "COME UNTO THESE YELLOW SANDS"

which are made by one impulse of the breath and are modified or hindered in their outward course through the vocal passage. By means of the kymograph the nature of these air waves can be shown. Opposite is a graphic representation of the air waves that constitute this spoken sentence. It will be seen that they form an unbroken series except for the slight interruption made by the breathed consonants *c* (phonetically [k]), *t*, and *s*.

The fact that speech consists of connected series of air waves instead of separate letters or even words is of vital importance not only for the study of speech proper, but also for a right understanding of voice production and of the use of speech to convey thought.[3]

The Phonetic Method of Speech Study

The study of the individual speech sounds and of the changes that they undergo in connected speech is called *phonetics*. For this reason phonetics is sometimes defined as "the science of speech sounds."

This scientific method of studying speech is comparatively new, but its advantages are readily seen. First, speech improvement, if it is to be genuine, must be the result of intelligent choice; phonetics gives students the power to hear their own sounds accurately, to compare them with those of other speakers, and to decide what changes they wish to make in their own ways of speaking. Secondly, phonetics trains the auditory, visual, and kinæsthetic senses instead of relying, as the old method did, on the untrained ear alone; with this equipment it is easier to recognize unsatisfactory speech habits and quickly and surely to substitute

---

[3] It is believed by most modern students of linguistics that in the evolution of language phrase-consciousness developed first, then word-consciousness, and much later letter-consciousness. See W. B. Pillsbury and C. L. Meader, *The Psychology of Language* (D. Appleton and Company), and G. A. de Laguna, *Speech* (Yale University Press).

good ones than under the old method. Thirdly, this scientific method of training the organs of speech and hearing helps to achieve a good voice quality in place of a nasal, flat, drawled, or guttural tone. Finally, by teaching the laws that govern the combining of sounds into connected speech, phonetics helps students to avoid extremes of pedantry and of slovenliness; to improve their speech without seeming affected; and to acquire principles that will tend to make speech improvement a continuing process through life.

One of the greatest sources of difficulty under the old method was the bewildering inconsistency of our spelling. Its illogical character becomes apparent when we consider that in English a letter may have as many different sounds as *a* [4] in *at, ate, ask, car, care, intricate,* while one sound may be spelled in many ways, as the vowel sound in the words *me, see, cease, yield, seize,* and *clique;* and that one letter may represent two sounds, as the *x* in *six,*[5] while one sound may be represented by two letters, as the *ng* in *sing;* not to mention the fact that a large percentage of our words have letters that represent no sound at all, like the *k* in *knee,* the *b* in *comb,* the *l* in *calm,* the *e* in *ate,* and the second *t* in *pretty.*

In contrast with this, the phonetic system has only a single symbol for each speech sound,[6] so that once these symbols are mastered, there is no difficulty in representing sounds accurately and unequivocally.

The symbols used in this book are those of the International Phonetics Association. Granted reasonable intelli-

---

[4] When a letter is *italicized* in this book it means the letter name; when not italicized but enclosed in brackets it means the phonetic symbol: for example, *i* means the first letter in the word *it,* [i] means the sound of the vowel in *me.*

[5] Equivalent to *kš*.

[6] One of the first steps in phonetic training is to learn to think in terms not of letters but of sounds. The first sound in *cat,* for example, must not be spoken of as the letter *c* (*see*), but as its actual sound, phonetically written [k].

gence and application, they can be mastered in a few hours.[7]
The symbol for a sound is usually the letter that represents
it in ordinary spelling. This is true of all the consonants for
which a letter is available for representing the sound: they
are *p, b, t, d, k, g, m, n, s, z, r, l, w, h, f, v*. Where there is a
sound for which we have no single letter, as *th, sh, ng*, a symbol
has been borrowed from some foreign language that has a
single letter to represent it, as [θ] and [ð] for the two sounds
of *th* and [ʃ] for *sh*; or a new symbol has been invented, as
[ŋ] for *ng*. The letters *c, q, y*, and *x* are not used in the
English phonetic system since their various sounds are
represented by other symbols. The hard sound of *c* is
represented by [k], its soft sound by [s]; *q* is replaced by
[k]; the three sounds of *x* (in *exercise, exert,* and *Xenophon*)
are represented by [ks], [gz], and [z]; and the consonant
sound of *y* by [j].[8] The sound indicated in our spelling
by the letter *j* is represented in the phonetic alphabet by
the symbol [dʒ].

When we come to vowels, the system of symbols may
at first appear somewhat formidable and confusing,[9] but it
ceases to seem so once we realize that the symbols represent
the values of these vowels in the modern languages of Con-
tinental Europe. The committee who devised the International System of Phonetics was composed almost entirely
of scholars from the Continent, so that these symbols
represent the sounds that they associated with the letters.
The matter becomes easy if we remember that these symbols have approximately the values that the corresponding
vowels have in French, German, Italian, Spanish, and also
in Latin. Our reason for adopting the International System

---

[7] This does not mean, of course, that everyone could learn in so short
a time to make accurately the sounds represented by the symbols.

[8] *j* is the letter that represents this sound in Teutonic languages,
as in the German word *ja*.

[9] Since [i] is used for long *e* as in *me*, [ɑ] for *ah*, [u] for *oo* as in *boot*,
and so on.

is that it is the simplest system and also the one used by most of the leading teachers of modern languages, so that it is of great value to students of foreign languages as a basis of comparison.

Moreover, in English also the vowels originally had the sounds indicated by the International symbols, the *a* in *name* having been pronounced *ah*, the *i* in *ride, ee,* and so on, so that English spelling originally represented the actual pronunciation of the words. But in the last five centuries nearly all the vowel sounds have undergone changes, several consonants meanwhile having been altered and many consonant groups simplified. Spelling, however, during this period has changed very little, and so it is several hundred years behind the pronunciation. It can readily be seen how unsafe a guide to pronunciation is our antiquated spelling, and how untenable is the position of anyone who claims to pronounce words as they are spelled. Yet in this age of many books we are all so eye-minded that we need considerable training in hearing what we actually say and in writing it down in phonetic symbols in order to learn to think in terms of sounds rather than of letters and thus to hear our speech as it really is.

That learning to read and write in phonetic script is not a very arduous task may be proved by discovering how easy it is to read the following sentence if we know that [ð] represents the sound of *th* in *thine*, that [ŋ] represents *ng*, that [ɑ] stands for *ah*, [ɔ] for the vowel sound in *all*, [ɒ] for that in *not*, [u] for that in *boot*, and [ə] for the *a* in *above*:

ɪts nɒt tru ðət mɛn ɑr ɔlwɪz strɒŋɡər ət twɛntɪ ðən ət fɪftɪ.

At this point it may be well to reiterate that in the method here recommended, phonetics is to be considered, not as an end in itself, but as the most practical and economical approach to the study of speech. It is practical since it teaches us to hear with accuracy and discrimination our own speech and that of others and trains the vocal organs to pronounce correctly and easily the form of language that we select as best suited to our needs and desires. It is economical since by teaching us the definite laws of sound

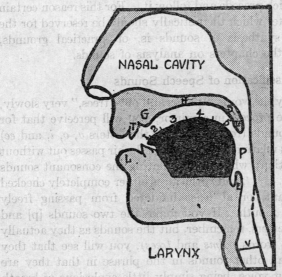

Fig. 19. Diagram of the elements of the articulatory organs used in describing the formation of speech sounds

L, lips; T, teeth; G, gum, or teeth ridge; H, hard palate; S, soft palate; U, uvula; P, pharynx; E, epiglottis; V, vocal cords; 1, tip of tongue; 2, blade of tongue; 3, front of tongue; 4, middle of tongue; 5, back of tongue.

production and sound change it enables us to acquire the desired excellence of voice and speech in the shortest possible time and without affectation.

The complete study of phonetics implies, as has been said, (1) an analysis, that is, a study of the formation of each speech sound taken individually without reference to neighboring sounds; and (2) a synthesis, that is, a consideration of the changes that these sounds undergo in connected speech. The two following chapters deal primarily with the analysis of sounds, but the nature of speech is such that the essential character of any one sound cannot be fully understood without some knowledge of the way it is influenced by those which precede and follow it. For this reason certain subject matter which theoretically should be reserved for the section on synthesis of sounds is, on practical grounds, included in the chapters on analysis of sounds.

General Classification of Speech Sounds

If you say the words, "palms and olive trees," very slowly, watching the process in a mirror, you will perceive that for the vowel sounds (represented by the letters *a*, *o*, *i*, and *ee*) the mouth is relatively open so that the air passes out without any obstruction; while in articulating the consonant sounds (*p*, *m*, *s*, *n*, *d*, *l*, *v*, *t*, and *r*) the air is either completely checked for an instant, or at least hindered from passing freely through the mouth. If you make the two sounds [p] and [t] (not the letters, remember, but the sounds as they actually occur in the words *palms* and *trees*), you will see that they differ from all other sounds in the phrase in that they are made without voice, being simply little explosions of breath that has not been set into vibration at the vocal cords. If now you isolate the sounds [m] and [n], you will discover that they differ from all the other sounds in the phrase by the fact that in forming them the air is emitted through the nose instead of through the mouth. From these three differences in the way the outgoing breath is conditioned by the vocal organs, we have the threefold classification of speech sounds as (1) *vowel* and *consonant*, (2) *voiced* and *voiceless*, and (3) *oral* and *nasal*.

1. *Vowels and Consonants*

A *vowel* is a speech sound in which the voiced breath is emitted with relatively little obstruction, its special character [10] being the result of the size of the mouth and throat cavities and the size of their openings.

A *consonant* is a speech sound in which the outgoing air, whether voiced or not, is checked or impeded somewhere in the vocal passage.

In certain cases the distinction between vowel and consonant sounds is very slight. For instance, if we bring the back of the tongue near the soft palate, purse the lips as for whistling, and voice the outgoing air, we form the vowel *u* as in *rule*. If, however, we bring the tongue slightly nearer the soft palate and purse the lips a little more closely, we have the consonant *w* as in *wool*. In this case it is practically impossible to determine the exact point at which the vowel leaves off and the consonant begins. For this reason some phoneticians make a third class and give the name *semi-vowels* or *glide consonants* to the sound of *w* in *was* and of *y* in *yes*. Others go further and consider *v, l, r, m, n,* and *ng* as semi-vowels since they contain so slight an element of noise when properly made.

2. *Voiced and Voiceless, or Breathed, Sounds*

Voiced sounds are those in which the outgoing air has been set into vibration by the vocal cords so that a murmur is produced.

Voiceless, or *breathed, sounds* are those in which the air passes through the glottis without being voiced but meets with interference in its outward passage so that it makes a slight noise. All vowels and most consonants are voiced. The exceptions are *p, t, k, wh, f, th* as in *thin, s, sh,* and *h,* which are noises made by checking or hindering the unvoiced air as it is sent through the vocal passage.

---

[10] That is, its individual resonance, due to the reinforcement (in the vocal passage) of certain partials of the tone that was initiated at the vocal cords.

3. Oral and Nasal Sounds

Oral sounds are those formed by emission of air through the mouth. In our language all vowels and all but three consonants are (at least theoretically) oral sounds.

Nasal sounds are those in which the air is emitted through the nose. The only recognized nasals in the English language are the three consonants *m*, *n*, and *ng*, though other consonants and some vowels are *nasalized* in the speech of many persons, that is, they are pronounced with a considerable part of the air stream passing through the nose.

The classification into vowels and consonants is not only the most familiar but the most practical for the analysis of speech sounds. We shall therefore use it as a basis for the study of the individual sounds, beginning with the consonants.[11]

The Phonetic Alphabet

For convenience in learning the phonetic symbols they are listed on page 83 in alphabetical order.[12] Both script and type forms of the symbols are given, followed by keywords in ordinary and in phonetic spelling.

The sound values of the phonetic symbols are those described in the succeeding chapters. In order to use the symbols accurately the student must be sure that he associates with each the sound described. Until the student's ear has become a reliable guide, he should be constantly checked as to accuracy in use of the symbols.

---

[11] Although for purposes of voice training many teachers prefer to begin with the vowels, it has seemed wiser to analyze the consonants first, since they are more clearly defined and therefore easier to analyze than vowels. For voice practice, the teacher may perfectly well begin with individual vowel sounds, being careful, of course, that they are well formed.

[12] The symbols used are those found in the "narrow" form of the International Phonetic Association alphabet. The "broad" form of this alphabet is that used in *An English Pronouncing Dictionary* by Daniel Jones.

Fig. 20. THE PHONETIC ALPHABET

Symbols		Key Words		Symbols		Key Words	
a	[ɑ]	father	[fɑðə]	ŋ	[ŋ]	sing	[sɪŋ]
aʋ	[aʊ]	vow	[vaʊ]	o	[o]	obey	[obeɪ]
a	[a]	ask	[ask]	oʋ	[oʊ]	low	[loʊ]
aɪ	[aɪ]	by	[baɪ]	ɛə	[oə]	bore	[boə]
æ	[æ]	hat	[hæt]	ɔ	[ɔ]	hall	[hɔl]
b	[b]	ball	[bɔl]	ɒ	[ɒ]	long	[lɒŋ]
d	[d]	dog	[dɒg]	ɔɪ	[ɔɪ]	boy	[bɔɪ]
e	[e]	débris	[debri]	ɒə	[ɒə]	bore	[bɒə]
eɪ	[eɪ]	say	[seɪ]	p	[p]	pan	[pæn]
ɛ	[ɛ]	met	[mɛt]	r	[r]	red	[rɛd]
ɛə	[ɛə]	there	[ðɛə]	s	[s]	so	[soʊ]
ɜ	[ə]	bird	[bəd]	ʃ	[ʃ]	shoe	[ʃu]
ə	[ə]	above	[əbʌv]	t	[t]	tell	[tɛl]
f	[f]	fan	[fæn]	θ	[θ]	thin	[θɪn]
g	[g]	go	[goʊ]	ð	[ð]	then	[ðɛn]
h	[h]	hot	[hɒt]	u	[u]	pool	[pul]
i	[i]	eat	[it]	ʊ	[ʊ]	book	[bʊk]
ɪ	[ɪ]	it	[ɪt]	ʊə	[ʊə]	poor	[pʊə]
ɪə	[ɪə]	here	[hɪə]	ʌ	[ʌ]	nut	[nʌt]
j	[j]	yes	[jɛs]	ʋ	[v]	vine	[vaɪn]
k	[k]	call	[kɔl]	hʋ	[ʊ]	what	[hʊt]
l	[l]	lamb	[læm]	ʊr	[w]	way	[weɪ]
m	[m]	mat	[mæt]	z	[z]	zone	[zoʊn]
n	[n]	not	[nɒt]	ʒ	[ʒ]	azure	[æʒə]

CHAPTER V

ANALYSIS OF SPEECH SOUNDS: CONSONANTS

Definition

A *consonant* is a speech sound caused by the stoppage or hindrance of the voiced or voiceless breath.[1]

Classification

Since consonants are the result of breath subjected to various modifying conditions in its emission, it is natural that they should be classified according to the nature of these conditions. Consonants may accordingly be classified as to (i) whether or not the air has been set into vibration at the vocal cords; (ii) the manner in which the air is impeded; and (iii) the place at which it is impeded.

I. *As to Production with Voiced or Voiceless Breath*

We have already seen that certain consonants, like *d*, *v*, and *l*, are made with air that has been set into vibration at the vocal cords, while others, like *p*, *t*, and *f*, are made without this vibration or vocal murmur. These two types of sounds are called *voiced* and *voiceless* (or *breath* or *breathed*) consonants.

---

[1] According to the English phonetician, Henry Sweet, "a consonant is the result of audible friction, squeezing, or stopping of the breath in some part of the mouth (occasionally the throat). The main distinction between vowels and consonants is that while in the former the mouth configuration merely modifies the vocalized breath, which is therefore an essential element of the vowels, in consonants the *narrowing or the stopping of the oral passage is the foundation of the sound, and the state of the glottis is something secondary.*"

84

II. *As to the Manner of Articulation*

A. *Stops or Plosives.*[2]—If the breath is checked in its outward passage and then suddenly released through the mouth with a slight explosion, the sound thus produced is called a *stop* or *plosive*. The English plosives are *p, b, t, d, k,* and *g*.

B. *Continuants*[3] (*Nasals, Laterals, Fricatives*).—If the air, instead of being stopped, is merely impeded in its passage through the mouth or diverted and sent through the nose, the sound is called a *continuant*. The chief continuants in the English language are *nasals*—*m, n,* and *ng* (phonetically [ŋ])—made by stopping the air in the mouth and emitting it through the nostrils; one *lateral*—*l*—formed by pressing the tip of the tongue against the upper teeth ridge and emitting the air at the sides of the tongue; and *fricatives*[4]—*f, v, h, s,* for example—which are murmurs, breathings, or hisses caused by the narrowing of the vocal passage at some point.

---

[2] Neither of these terms is entirely satisfactory since each calls attention to only one part of the process of the formation of the sound. *Stop* is a useful term in bringing out one very striking characteristic of these consonants—the momentary checking of the smooth flow of breath. *Plosive*, on the other hand, is valuable in calling attention to the element of noise which they introduce into speech.

[3] The term *continuant* is not used by all phoneticians. It serves a useful purpose, however, in calling attention to the fact that these consonants should be pronounced with a smooth flow of breath, thus helping the student to remember that "every speech exercise should be a voice exercise."

[4] Some students, notably Dr. Floyd S. Muckey, author of *The Natural Method of Voice Production,* maintain that none of these sounds is due to friction, but rather to an "air blade" produced by the focusing of streams of breath which have been caused by interference in expiration. Experiments seem to afford a certain amount of evidence of the truth of this theory, but since it is still under dispute and since we are here concerned with the practical application of phonetics to voice and speech training, we may for the present content ourselves with the attempt to articulate these sounds as clearly as possible.

III. *As to the Place of Articulation*

1. *Lip, or Labial, or Bi-Labial, Consonants.*—If the breath is stopped or impeded at the lips, the sound is called a *lip,* or *labial,* or *bi-labial, consonant.* The English labials are *p, b, m, wh* [ʜʋ], and *w.*

2. *Lip-Teeth, or Labio-Dental, Consonants.*—If the breath is hindered by the lower lip being brought against the upper teeth, the sound is a *lip-teeth,* or *labio-dental, consonant.* The language has only two labio-dentals, *f* and *v.*

3. *Tongue-Teeth, or Dental, Consonants.*—If the breath emission is impeded by the tongue tip being placed against the upper teeth, the sound is a *tongue-teeth,* or *dental, consonant.* English has two dentals (both spelled *th*): one is the voiceless sound in *thin,* [θ], the other is the voiced sound in *thine,* [ð].

4. *Teeth-Ridge, or Post-Dental, Consonants.*—If the tip of the tongue articulates against the upper teeth ridge, the sound is called a *teeth-ridge,* or *post-dental, consonant.* The English post-dentals are *t, d, n, s, z, l, r, sh* [ʃ], and the sound of *z* in *azure,* [ʒ].

5. *Palatal Consonants.*—If the front of the tongue articulates against the hard palate, the sound is a *palatal consonant.* Our only palatal is in the sound of *y* in *yes,* [j].

6. *Soft-Palate, or Velar, Consonants.*—If the back of the tongue articulates against the soft palate, or velum, the consonant formed is called a *soft-palate,* or *velar, consonant.* The English velars are *k, g,* and *ng* [ŋ].

7. *Glottal Consonants.*—If the glottis is so narrowed that the air in passing through causes friction [5] but not sufficient vibration to produce voice, the sound is called a *glottal consonant.* *h* is the only authorized glottal consonant in English, but there is another, the glottal plosive, which plays an insistent, though unrecognized, part in the speech of many persons.

---

[5] Or an "air blade."

Study of Individual Consonants

Thus we have a three-fold classification of consonants—as to voice, place of formation, and manner of formation. For instance, *b* is a voiced bi-labial plosive; *f* is a breathed labio-dental fricative; *n* is a voiced post-dental nasal, etc. According to this classification we may now proceed to study the individual consonant sounds.

A. STOPS OR PLOSIVES

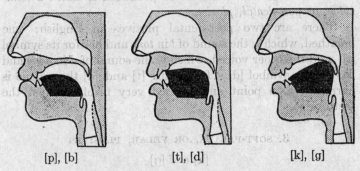

| [p], [b] | [t], [d] | [k], [g] |

FIG. 21. THE PLOSIVES

Stops or *plosives* are consonants formed by stopping the outgoing breath and then releasing it with a slight explosion.

1. LIP, OR LABIAL, OR BI-LABIAL, PLOSIVES

[p] *and* [b]

If the outgoing breath is checked for an instant by the closing of the lips and the elevation of the soft palate, so that no air can escape through the mouth or nose, and the compressed air is then released by a quick separation of the lips, the sound produced is a *lip*, or *labial*, or *bi-labial*, *plosive*.

There are two bi-labial plosives in English: one breathed, which is the sound of *p* in *poor* and has for its symbol [p];

and one voiced, which is the sound of the *b* in *boor* and has for its symbol [b].

2. TEETH-RIDGE, OR POST-DENTAL, PLOSIVES

[t] *and* [d]

If the outgoing air is checked by pressing the tip of the tongue firmly against the upper teeth ridge and by raising the soft palate, and then is quickly released by the withdrawal of the tongue, the sound produced is called a *teeth-ridge*, or *post-dental*, *plosive*.

There are two post-dental plosives in English: one breathed, which is the sound of *t* in *tone* and has for its symbol [t]; and the other voiced, which is the sound of *d* in *done* and has for its symbol [d]. In making [t] and [d] the tongue is narrowed to a point and pressed very firmly against the teeth ridge.

3. SOFT-PALATE, OR VELAR, PLOSIVES

[k] *and* [g]

If the outgoing air is checked by the pressure of the back of the tongue against the raised soft palate, and the compressed air is then quickly released with a slight explosion by the withdrawal of the tongue from the palate, the sound is called a *soft-palate*, or *velar*, *plosive*.

There are two velar plosives in English: one breathed, the sound of *k* in *king*, which has for its symbol [k]; and the other voiced, the sound of *g* in *go*, which has for its symbol [g].

4. GLOTTAL PLOSIVE

[?]

In addition to the recognized plosives in English speech there is another sound which is often substituted for them. It is called the *glottal plosive*, which is made as the result of

CONSONANTS 89

checking the air in the larynx and then releasing it with an explosion like a slight cough.[6] Its phonetic symbol is [ʔ].

This is an accepted speech sound in certain languages, but not in English. It is frequently heard in careless speech, however, in place of other sounds, as, for instance, the *t* in "What was I saying?" [hʊɒʔ wəz aɪ seɪɪŋ]. The sound is further described on page 56.

Plosives in Connected Speech

When a plosive is doubled, as in the word *bookcase*, there are not really two stops (as there would be if each word were pronounced separately) but one, made with a prolongation of the pause between the closure and the release. In this word, for instance, the first [k] is represented by the pressure of the tongue against the soft palate; the closure is held for a relatively long time; then comes the release, which represents the second [k]. Compare [bʊkkeɪs] (*bookcase*) with [bukeɪ] (*bouquet*). In careless speech one or other of the doubled consonants is apt to be omitted; in pedantic speech both are apt to be fully enunciated with an explosion for each.

A similar modification takes place when two different plosives come together, whether they occur in the same word, as *apt* [æpt], *act* [ækt], *sagged* [sægd]; or in two consecutive words, as *hot drink* [hɒt drɪŋk], *big cats* [bɪg kæts], *sad case* [sæd keɪs].

When a plosive is followed by a lateral, as the [tl] in *shuttle*, the plosive is not released in the usual way: it is held for an instant and the air emitted at the sides of the tongue. In *shuttle* we have the pressure for the [t] and the lateral release for the [l]. In this case, since the tip of the tongue is in the same place for both sounds, it naturally does not shift for the [l]. In making these double articulations the greatest

---

[6] The autophonoscope shows that in making the glottal plosive the false vocal cords generally close over the true cords; the compressed air then bursts through with a trigger-like action.

care should be taken to prevent a vowel-like sound between the plosive and the lateral, and to prevent any turning back of the tip of the tongue for [l]. This matter of the "inversion" of [l] is treated on page 95.

When a plosive is followed by a nasal, the stop is made in the usual way, held an instant while the soft palate is lowered, and the air is then emitted through the nasal passages. Examples of this are found in the words *mutton* [mʌtn], *sudden* [sʌdn], *shaken* [ʃeɪkn], *happen* [hæpn]. Here also care must be taken to prevent the insertion of a vowel between the plosive and the nasal [7] and the inversion of the tongue in forming the post-dental consonants.

When a plosive is followed by a fricative, the closure is made, the breath is held back a moment at that point, and is then released through the narrow passage of the following fricative, as in the words *hats* [hæts], *cads* [kædz], *hatch* [hætʃ], *judge* [dʒʌdʒ]. These combinations are called *affricates* and are by some phoneticians regarded as single sounds.

In all these plosive combinations it is very important, as we cannot too often repeat, to make a firm closure. Failure to do so is one of the most common causes of slovenly articulation. Especially is this true in the case of [t] and [d], which in American speech are often *flapped* consonants rather than true plosives. Such carelessness is not only unpleasant but also tends to make the meaning unclear, causing confusion between such words as *hurtle* [hɜ(r)tl] and *hurdle* [hɜ(r)dl], which become indistinguishable unless the narrowed tongue tip is firmly pressed against the teeth ridge for the [t] and the vocal cords are made to stop vibrating for an instant.[8]

---

[7] The fact that there is a vowel between the plosive and the nasal in the spelling is misleading; pronouncing this vowel is one of the causes of the American drawl.

[8] The firm action of the tongue in forming the voiced plosive helps also in overcoming a tendency toward nasalization.

Faults in the Articulation of Plosives

In order to form plosives properly, three things are necessary: (1) a firm closure of the articulating organs; (2) a steady control of the air through the lungs; (3) a quick release.

1. A frequent result of lax closure of the articulating organs is that breathed plosives are almost indistinguishable from their voiced cognates, the slackness in articulation being accompanied by slackness regarding the approximation of the vocal cords, so that *waiting* [weɪtɪŋ] sounds like *wading* [weɪdɪŋ] and *bitter* [bɪtə(r)] like *bidder* [bɪdə(r)]. To the ears of a foreigner this flapped [t] in our American speech often gives the impression of some strange form of [r], the word *tomato* [təmɑto] being heard as tomorrow [təmɒro], for example.

2. The result of lack of control of the air stream is particularly noticeable in breathed plosives, which have little carrying power unless the pressure of air is continuous and forceful. Especially is this true when they occur medially or finally, as in *hating* [heɪtɪŋ] and *that* [ðæt], and still more so at the end of a phrase, as in "I will go if I must" [aɪ wɪl goʊ ɪf aɪ mʌs(t)], where the plosive often becomes entirely inaudible. Lack of firm direction of the air through the mouth also results in nasality.

3. The result of too slow release is that breathed plosives seem to be followed by a slight fricative, so that *what* sounds like [hʊts] and *it* like [its].

4. *Inversion of Post-Dental Plosives.*—In forming [t] and [d] the tip of the tongue is often turned back to the hard palate instead of being pressed against the teeth ridge. This "inversion" gives a labored quality to the articulation. Furthermore, the turning back of the tongue requires more effort than does the more natural articulation at the teeth ridge. This extra effort almost always causes strain at the

back of the tongue and interferes with the proper resonation of the adjacent vowels. On the grounds of pleasant and effective voice production, therefore, this articulation is not to be recommended.

5. *Substitution of the Glottal Plosive for an Oral Plosive.*—This is an unfortunate habit, (since it gives a harsh, guttural quality to the voice), and one which seems to be increasing. It is a compensatory articulation—the result of that general sluggishness of lips and tongue which have led to our being called lip-lazy and tongue-lazy Americans.[9]

B. CONTINUANTS

I. NASAL CONSONANTS

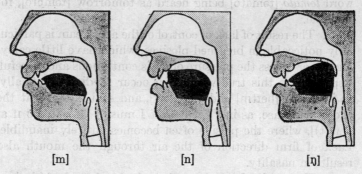

[m]   [n]   [ŋ]

FIG. 22. THE NASAL CONSONANTS

Nasal consonants are made by closing the mouth passage, lowering the soft palate, and allowing the air to pass out through the nose.

---

[9] It would be interesting to know how large a percentage of Americans say the [t] in *good night* with the tongue tip quietly resting behind the lower teeth and with the stop made at the vocal cords—a custom "more honored in the breach than the observance."

1. BI-LABIAL NASAL

[m]

If with the lips pressed together as for [b] the soft palate is lowered and the voiced breath is allowed to pass out through the nasal passages, the sound is that of *m* in *me*. It is called the *bi-labial nasal consonant* and is represented by the phonetic symbol [m].

2. POST-DENTAL NASAL

[n]

Sending the air through the nose in the same way while the tongue and vocal cords are in the position for [d] causes the sound of *n* in *no*. It is called the *post-dental nasal consonant* and is phonetically written [n].

3. VELAR NASAL

[ŋ]

Similarly, if the back of the tongue is pressed against the lowered soft palate so that the voiced air passes out through the nose, the sound is that of *ng* in *sing*.

It is called the *velar nasal consonant*, and its phonetic symbol is [ŋ].

Nasals in Connected Speech

When [m] is followed by [f], as in the word *comfort*, it is usually made in the position of the lips for [f]. Compare the [m] in *comfort* with the [m] in *come*.

When [n] is followed by [k], as in *Lincoln* and *twinkle*, it is drawn to the position of that consonant and is pronounced [ŋ]. The same change sometimes occurs in rapid speech when the [k] precedes the [n], as in *bacon* [beikŋ].

On the other hand, careless speakers often substitute [n] for [ŋ] in words ending in *ing*, as in [pleɪɪn] for [pleɪɪŋ].

In very careless speech the [m] and [ŋ] in *something* are both replaced by an [n], and the word is pronounced [sʌnθɪn].

There are no breathed nasals among the recognized speech sounds in English, but in certain combinations, as in *warmth*, nasals are often wholly or partly unvoiced.

The letters *ng* in certain words, as *song, singer, singing*, are pronounced [ŋ]; in certain other words, as *finger* and *English*, they are pronounced [ŋg]: [sɒŋ], [sɪŋə(r)], [sɪŋɪŋ], but [fɪŋgə(r)], [ɪŋglɪʃ]. This is a frequent cause of difficulty: the words that should be pronounced with [ŋ] alone are often pronounced [ŋg], as [sɪŋgɪŋ] for [sɪŋɪŋ]; and, on the other hand, those which should be pronounced [ŋg] are pronounced with the [ŋ] alone, as [fɪŋə(r)] for [fɪŋgə(r)].

Lists for practice in making these distinctions will be found in the "Articulation Exercises" in Part II.

II. The Lateral Consonant

A *lateral consonant* is a sound made by the emission of the air at the sides of the tongue.

1. THE POST-DENTAL LATERAL

[l]

English has only one lateral consonant sound, that of *l*. In forming it the tip of the tongue is pressed against the teeth ridge and the air allowed to pass out of the mouth over the sides of the tongue, the soft palate being raised to prevent the escape of air through the nose. It is the voiced *post-dental lateral* and is phonetically written [l].

In English this consonant has two principal forms, called the *clear* [l] and the *dark* [l]. The clear variety occurs initially or after an initial consonant, as in *look* and *glance*. The

dark variety is used finally or before a final consonant, as in
full and *told*. [10]   In both varieties of [l] the tip of the tongue
should be pressed against the teeth ridge; it is only the back
of the tongue that changes position.   In the clear [l] the
back of the tongue curves downward; in the dark [l] it is
raised toward the soft palate, which gives the consonant a
somewhat [u]-like character.   Most foreigners use the clear
[l] in all positions.   Some Americans use the dark [l] where
the clear one is preferred.   This is undesirable as it changes
the character of the adjacent vowels.

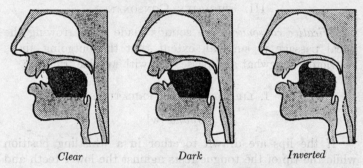

Clear   *Dark*   *Inverted*

FIG. 23.   THE THREE FORMS OF THE LATERAL CONSONANT [l]

A third variety of the lateral is the *inverted*, or *retroflex*,
[l].   This is formed with the tip of the tongue turned back
toward the soft palate.   The inversion gives a dull, unreso-
nant quality, not merely to the [l], but also to the vowels that
precede and follow it.   In dialect stories this pronunciation
is indicated by such spelling as "wal" or "wul" for *well*.

---

[10] It is difficult to go from a vowel to [l] without some intermediate
sound, that is, [l] tends to develop a strong off-glide in the preceding
vowel, so that [pul] (*pool*) is often heard as [puəl], and [toʊl] (*toll*) as
[touəl].   This drawling tendency is sometimes carried so far that a
vowel is developed where none exists, so that [kætl] (cattle) becomes
[kætəl] and [pædl] (*paddle*), [pædəl].   The student should practice the [l]
word lists until this drawling habit is overcome.

Persons who invert the [l] are likely also to nasalize it, not only lowering the soft palate, but contracting the muscles of the throat, in which case the sound, instead of being one of the most musical in our language, becomes one of the ugliest.

There is no recognized form of the breathed [l] in English. But the consonant is usually unvoiced, in part at least, after a breathed consonant, as in *clear* and *please*; and, too often, at the end of words, as in *tell*.

III. Fricative Consonants

Fricative consonants are sounds made by narrowing the vocal passage to such an extent that the outgoing air is restricted somewhat and passes out with audible friction.[11]

1. lip, or labial, fricatives

[ʜ] *and* [w]

If the lips are drawn together in a whistling position while the tip of the tongue rests against the lower teeth and the back of the tongue is raised toward the soft palate, so that the air in passing out causes friction, the sound is called a *lip,* or *labial, fricative.*

There are two lip fricatives in English: one breathed, the first sound in *when,* which has for its phonetic symbol [ʜ]; the other voiced, the initial sound in *wear,* which has for its symbol [w].

The sound of [w] is probably more often a semi-vowel or glide consonant than a fricative; that is, the articulating organs are not approximated closely enough to cause audible friction, but they move quickly from their original position to that of the following vowel, producing a vowel-like sound, often called a *glide consonant* or *glide vowel.*

---

[11] See note 3 of this chapter.

In some parts of the United States and England the breathed form of this consonant [ʜ] has been almost entirely supplanted by its voiced cognate [w]. The result is that in such speech *where* and *wear* are both pronounced [weə(r),) *white* and *wight* are both pronounced [waɪt]. This variation does not suggest vulgarity or even carelessness of speech, but it is not to be recommended for imitation since it tends to produce many homophones,[12] which are a disadvantage in

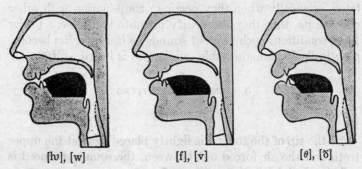

[ʜ], [w]   [f], [v]   [θ], [ð]

FIG. 24. THE LABIAL, LABIO-DENTAL, AND DENTAL FRICATIVES

any language. Occasionally this use of [w] for [ʜ] quite changes the meaning of the sentence, as in Masefield's "Sea Fever," where the phrase, "the wind's like a whetted knife," becomes, "the wind's like a wetted knife."

2. LABIO-DENTAL FRICATIVES

[f] *and* [v]

If the lower lip is raised to the upper teeth and the breath sent audibly between the lip and the edges of the teeth or through the openings between the teeth, the sound is a *labio-dental fricative*.

---

[12] *Homophones* are words that are different in spelling and meaning but alike in pronunciation.

There are two labio-dental fricatives: one breathed, the initial sound in *few*, which has for its phonetic symbol [f]; the other voiced, the initial consonant in *view*, which has for its symbol [v].

The voiced sound of the labio-dental fricative is often replaced by the breathed cognate [f] when a breathed consonant follows it, as in the expression *have to* [hæv tu], heard as [hæf tə].[13] Both [f] and [v] are often so weakly articulated, especially when they occur in combination with other consonants, that they are nearly or quite inaudible. Under these conditions such pairs of sounds as *lives* and *lies* become practically indistinguishable, while *fifth* is heard as [fɪθ].

3. DENTAL FRICATIVES

[θ] *and* [ð]

If the tip of the tongue is lightly placed against the upper teeth and the air forced out between, the sound produced is called a *dental fricative*.

The breathed form is the sound represented by the letters *th* in *thin*, and its symbol is [θ]; the voiced form is represented by the letters *th* in *then*, and its symbol is [ð].

[θ] and [ð] are the only pure dentals in the English language, and even they are often pronounced as intra-dentals, the tongue being allowed to protrude between the teeth instead of being placed against the upper teeth. On the grounds of appearance this method of forming the sounds is not to be recommended. Observe the effect in your mirror.

The voiced form of the dental fricative most often disappears in words that contain several consonants in combination; for example, *hundredths* may be heard as [hʌndrɪdz] and *clothes* as [kloʊz]. See the discussion of the omission of sounds in Chapter VII.

---

[13] See also the section on "Assimilation" in Chapter VII.

4. POST-DENTAL FRICATIVES

There are five consonants in this class: [r], [s], [z], [ʃ], and [ʒ].

[r]

If, without being grooved, the tip of the tongue is raised so near the teeth ridge that the voiced breath in passing though causes audible friction (or an " air blade "), the sound is that of *r* in *rose*. It is called the voiced *tip post-dental fricative*, its symbol being [r]. This consonant has no breathed equivalent, but when it follows a breathed consonant, as in pray [preɪ] or *pretty* [prɪtɪ], the [r] is usually unvoiced, in part at least.

This sound is often produced practically without noise and is then almost completely vowel-like in character. It is sometimes called a glide consonant or semi-vowel, its quality being due to the swift movement of the tongue from its original position to that of the following vowel.

On the other hand, it is sometimes rolled or trilled, especially when it occurs medially or initially or after an initial consonant. This trilled form, because of its great carrying power, is sometimes used by actors and telephone operators. In ordinary speech its use is apt to be regarded as slightly elocutionary. The practice of trilling the [r] is, however, one of the best exercises for gaining control of the tip of the tongue.

In many parts of the country an inverted or retroflex [rᵢ is used. This sound is made by turning the tongue backward toward the hard palate (as in the inverted [t], [d], [l], etc.). Like other inversions, the inverted [r] changes the quality of the adjacent vowels: the spelling "Amurrucan" is an attempt to represent this inversion of the vowels. There is another form of [r] which sounds very much like the inverted variety. It is made by raising the back of the

tongue toward the soft palate while keeping the tip behind
the lower teeth. This method of formation also gives an
altered quality to the adjacent vowels. Both of these varieties of [r] are likely to be accompanied by undue tension at
the back of the tongue, which gives a rather hard and
unpleasant quality to the tone. For this reason they are not
recommended by voice teachers.

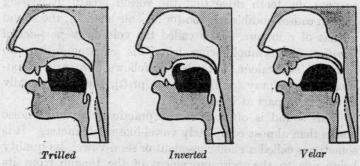

Trilled   *Inverted*   *Velar*

FIG. 25. THE THREE FORMS OF THE FRICATIVE [r]

In some parts of the United States, especially in the East
and South, [r] is not sounded when it occurs at the end of a
syllable or before a final consonant, as in *war* [wɔ] and *ward*
[wɔd]. Final [r] is usually sounded, however, when the following word begins with a vowel. Even a speaker who does
not ordinarily pronounce the [r] in *war* would sound it in
the expression "War is cruel" [wɔr ɪz kruəl].

Sometimes an unrounded [w] is substituted for [r], *rose*
[roʊz] being pronounced nearly like [woʊz]. In this pronunciation the tip of the tongue is held behind the lower
teeth instead of being raised toward the upper teeth ridge.
Small children are apt to make this substitution after they
have learned to make the [w] and before they can make the
more difficult [r]. Its use gives an infantile character to the
speech and should be corrected as early as possible.

[s] *and* [z]

If the grooved tip of the tongue is pressed lightly against the teeth ridge and the breath is sent in a narrow stream through this groove and between the teeth, the sound produced is called the *tip post-dental fricative.*

There are two such fricatives: the one breathed, which is the consonant in *so* and has for its symbol [s]; the other voiced, which is the initial sound in *zone* and has for its symbol [z]. These sounds can also be made with the tip of the tongue low in the mouth.

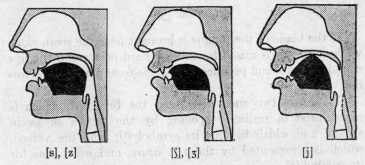

[s], [z]   [ʃ], [ʒ]   [j]

FIG. 26. THE POST-DENTAL AND PALATAL FRICATIVES

In English spelling the breathed form is represented not only by *s*, but also by *ss* as in *miss* [mɪs] and by *c* as in *mice* [maɪs]; it is also the second of the two sounds represented by *x* in such words as *axe* [æks]. The voiced form is represented not only by *z*, but by *s* as in *has* and by *zz* as in *puzzle;* it is also the second of the sounds represented by *x* in such words as *exist* [ɪgzɪst].

Of all the sounds in our language, [s] and [z] are perhaps the least agreeable even at their best, and they are the most frequently and most unpleasantly mispronounced. In addition to the commonly recognized intra-dental lisp, there are more than a dozen other forms of lisped [s] and [z]. Besides these, there is the disagreeable hissing sound produced by imperfect control of the breath stream or by throat strain or by undue prolongation of the sound, and the almost inaudible sound produced by too weak pressure of the air.

To make these sounds lightly yet clearly requires for most speakers a considerable training, but there is perhaps no other phase of speech improvement that so amply rewards faithful and intelligent practice.

[ʃ] *and* [ʒ]

If the blade of the tongue is brought near the teeth ridge while the front is raised toward the hard palate and the lips rounded, the sound produced is a *blade-front post-dental fricative.*

There are two such fricatives: the breathed, which is represented in ordinary spelling by the letters *sh* as in *should,* and which has for its symbol [ʃ]; and the voiced, which is represented by the *z* in *azure,* and which has for its symbol [ʒ].

The sound [ʃ] occurs also in *ci* in *precious, ce* in *ocean, ti* in *election, si* in *pension, ss* in *tissue, s* in *sugar,* and *c* in *specie.* The sound [ʒ] is represented by *g* in *rouge, s* in *pleasure,* and *si* in *explosion,* as well as by the letter *z.*

Like [s] and [z], these sounds are frequently lisped; often also they are articulated with too little firmness and precision of the tongue and lip muscles, the result being very slovenly and noisy speech. Many persons through overassimilation [14] use [ʃ] and [ʒ] more frequently than is necessary, the result being an unpleasantly sibilant speech.

---

[14] In such expressions as *did you, don't you, that year.* See the section on "Assimilation" in Chapter VII.

5. THE PALATAL FRICATIVE

[j]

If the front of the tongue is raised nearly to the hard palate, the voiced breath in passing through the narrow opening produces a sound called the voiced *palatal fricative*. It is the sound of *y* in *yes*, and its phonetic symbol is [j]; it is the consonantal form of the high front vowel [i].

Like [w], this sound is perhaps more often a semi-vowel or glide consonant than a fricative.

When the letter *u* is used initially, or after certain consonants (as [b], [p], [m], and [k]), it is preceded by [j], as in *use* [juz], *pew* [pju], *beauty* [bjutɪ], *mute* [mjut], and *cue* [kju].

6. THE GLOTTAL FRICATIVE

[h]

If the vocal cords are sufficiently approximated to cause friction but not voice, the sound produced is called the *glottal fricative.* It is the sound of *h* in *house*, and its symbol is [h].

This consonant is sometimes called a "voiceless vowel." In forming it the tongue is in the position of the vowel that follows, so that in the word *he* the [h] may be said to be a breathed [i], and in the word *ha* it may be called a breathed [ɑ]. It occurs in English only at the beginning of a syllable, though it is retained in the spelling of such words as *ah* and *shah*.

Consonant Chart

In the horizontal rows of the summary chart on page 104 will be found the consonant sounds articulated in the same manner, and in the vertical rows will be found the sounds articulated by the same organs. The order of arrangement is that suggested by the diagrams, the lips being at the left.

Fig. 27. CONSONANT CHART

Manner of Articulation	Place of Articulation															
	Lips		Lip–Teeth		Tip of Tongue–Teeth		Tip of Tongue–Teeth Ridge		Blade of Tongue–Teeth Ridge		Middle or Front of Tongue–Hard Palate		Back of Tongue–Soft Palate		Glottis	
	b	*v*	*b*	*v*	*b*	*v*	*b*	*v*	*b*	*v*	*b*	*v*	*b*	*v*	*b*	*v*
Plosive.	[p]	[b]					[t]	[d]					[k]	[g]		?
Nasal.		[m]						[n]						[ŋ]		
Lateral.								[l]								
Fricative.	[hʊ]	[w]	[f]	[v]	[θ]	[ð]	[s]	[z] [r]	[ʃ]	[ʒ]		[j]			[h]	

Note.—*b* and *v* are abbreviations for "breathed" and "voiced."

Key Words

[p] *pin, cap, taper*
[b] *bin, cab, tabor*
[t] *tin, bit, bitter*
[d] *din, bid, bidder*
[k] *kit, lick, asked*
[g] *go, flag, bugle*

[m] *me, maim, summer*
[n] *no, noon, dinner*
[ŋ] *sing, singer*
[l] *loo, all, stifling*
[hʊ] *why*
[w] *we, away*

[f] *fee, if, muffin*
[v] *vie, live, loved*
[θ] *thin, oath, Ethel*
[ð] *thine, with, other*
[r] *row, far, sorry*
[s] *see, miss, fussy*

[z] *zoo, haze, dazzle*
[ʃ] *she, hush, session*
[ʒ] *rouge, azure*
[j] *ye, human*
[h] *ha, inherit*

CHAPTER VI

ANALYSIS OF SPEECH SOUNDS: VOWELS

Definition

A *vowel*, as we defined it in Chapter IV, is a speech sound in which the voiced breath is emitted with relatively little obstruction, its special character being the result of the size of the mouth and throat cavities and the size of their openings.[1]

Make the sound of *ee* in *see*, of *oo* in *moon*, and of *a* in *calm*. Watching the process in a mirror, you will observe that the positions of the jaw, lips, and tongue change for each of these vowels. There is the possibility of an infinite number of variations in tongue and lip positions, and consequently of an infinite number of vowels. Of the possible vowel sounds the English language recognizes only about twenty-five, including diphthongs; but as each of these vowels has several different forms according to the consonants that precede and follow it, there are in reality many more. Besides, the vowel positions are so much less exact than those of the consonants that there is a considerable variation in the form of the same vowel in the speech of different persons, and even of the same person at different times.

---

[1] A more scientific definition is:

A *vowel* is the effect produced upon the ear by sound waves (1) set in motion as air in passing from the lungs comes into contact with the vocal cords, (2) modified in their component parts (the overtones) by the size of the vocal cavities and by the size of their openings, and (3) allowed to pass out unobstructed.

Nor are vowel changes limited to the mouth cavity. By the aid of the autophonoscope, the laryngo-periskop, and X-ray photographs it has been proved that for every vowel other changes occur—in the size and shape of the pharyngeal cavity and in the adjustment of the vocal cords, and that these changes are probably of even greater importance than those relating to the mouth cavity. It can easily be demonstrated, for instance, that a perfectly good [ɑ] can be made with the tongue in any one of a number of positions, there being in each case compensatory adjustments in the walls of the pharynx.[2] In normal conditions a certain adjustment of jaw, lips, and tongue automatically brings with it the suitable adjustment of larnyx and pharynx. For this reason it has been thought wise to follow here the traditional classification and analysis of vowels according to mouth positions.

The student must bear in mind, however, that this basis of classification is merely one of convenience, and since in the last analysis the matter is one of acoustics, the final criterion is the ear. Hence the most important part of the study of vowels is training the ear to recognize the different sounds and, incidentally, to associate them with their proper symbols.

Classification

1. *According to Position of the Tongue*

For convenience in studying its articulation with other organs, as we have seen in Figure 19, the tongue may be divided into five parts—back, middle, front, blade, and tip. In the formation of vowels *the blade and tip should rest behind*

---

[2] Much new light has been thrown on this subject by the investigations of Professor G. Oscar Russell, whose books, *The Vowel* (Ohio State University Press) and *Speech and Voice* (Macmillan Co.), will be of interest to the advanced student.

the lower front teeth. The remainder of the tongue moves up and down. In this vertical movement of the tongue the front approaches the fore part of the hard palate, the back approaches the soft palate, and the middle rises toward a point somewhere between these two positions.

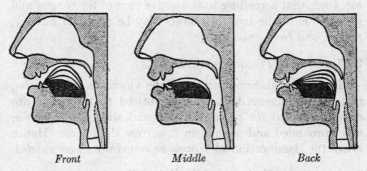

Front   Middle   Back

FIG. 28. APPROXIMATE TONGUE POSITIONS IN FORMING VOWELS

If we start with the active part of the tongue in the high front position and let it slowly descend until it reaches the lowest possible position (the vocal cords vibrating meanwhile), we hear a variety of vowel sounds, including the vowels in *see, it, at,* and *path.* All of these, since they are made in the fore part of the mouth and with the front of the tongue, are called *front vowels.*

Close observation will show that in sounding the *ee* in *see* the part of the tongue that phoneticians call the front is raised nearly to the hard palate; while in making the sound of *oo* in *moon* the back of the tongue is raised, and for *a* in *calm* the whole tongue is low in the mouth with a slight elevation toward the back. If the back of the tongue starts from the position of the vowel in *moon* and descends without interrupting the vibration of the vocal cords, a series of sounds called *back vowels* will be produced, those in English being the vowels in *moon, good, hope, saw, song,* and

calm. In the same way a group of vowels are made with
the middle of the tongue slightly raised in the middle of the
mouth and descending. These are called the *middle,* or *neutral, vowels,* and there are three of them in our speech,
namely, the vowel in *bird* and the two vowels in *butter.* We
see, then, that according to the active part of the tongue and
its position in the mouth, vowels may be classified as *back,
middle,* and *front vowels.*

2. *According to Position of the Lips*

If the lip positions for the three vowels in *moon, calm,*
and *see* are observed, it will be noticed that the lips are
closely rounded for *oo,* unrounded and widely open for *a,*
and unrounded and opened in a narrow slit for *ee.* Hence
arises the classification of vowels as *rounded* and *unrounded.*

3. *According to Emission of the Voiced Breath*

Vowels are also classified according to whether the air is
emitted through the mouth only, or whether the breath
stream divides, part being allowed to pass through the nose.
When the air passes out through the mouth, the vowel so
formed is called an *oral* sound. If, however, some of the air
is allowed to escape through the nose as well as through the
mouth, the sound is called a *nasal vowel.* The French language has four such nasal vowels, as in the expression
"*Un bon vin blanc*" [œ̃ bɔ̃ vɛ̃ blã].[3] In English all vowels
properly produced are oral, there being no recognized nasal
vowels.[4]

4. *According to Tension of the Vocal Organs*

In forming certain vowels the muscles of the vocal organs
are tense, in forming others they are slack. For instance,

---

[3] ~ is the symbol of nasalization.
[4] For a more detailed discussion of nasalization see the section on
"Assimilation" in Chapter VII.

the vowel in *eat* is formed with tense muscles; in forming that in *it* they are relatively lax. We have, then, the further classification of vowels as *tense* and *lax*. This tension causes a decided difference in the shape not only of the mouth, but of the pharynx. It also causes a difference in the texture of the walls of the vocal passages. Until more is known about the effect of these changes on vowel quality, however, this classification is of minor value.

5. *According to Length*

Furthermore, vowels differ in their duration, there being three recognized degrees of length—*long, half-long,* and *short*. English vowels, however, unlike those of the Latin and many other languages, have no fixed quantity. For instance, the first vowel in *rheumatism* is usually long, but in the word *rheumatic*, the same vowel may be either half-long or short. On the other hand, many so-called short vowels are often lengthened, *mat* being pronounced by certain speakers as if it were *maat*. In phonetic transcription [ː] after a vowel means that it is long, while [ˑ] means that it is half-long.

6. *According to Stability of the Vocal Organs; Diphthongization*

Further, as a result of the difficulty of controlling the vocal organs so that the desired vowel position can be promptly taken, and of holding it unchanged once it has been taken, the vowels, especially if long, tend to become unstable. In some instances this instability is scarcely evident and the vowel character is distinct; in such case the sound is called a *simple vowel*. In others the tongue and lips move nearly or quite into the position for another vowel, so that a reasonably keen ear detects two different sounds which blend into one another instead of being separated by a slight break or slackening of the breath pressure. Such sounds are called *diphthongs*. In the word *cawing* (phonetically written [kɔɪŋ]⁵ there is a definite pause between the two vowel sounds, and they are consequently regarded as two separate, *simple* vowels; while in the word *coin* (phonetically [kɒɪn]) the tongue and lips move from the [ɒ] to the [ɪ] position without pause or diminution of the air stream, thus producing a *compound vowel*, or *diphthong*. Hence the following definition: If a sound is characterized by two distinct vowel qualities which are caused by a change in the position of the tongue or lips but are made with no diminution of the air pressure, it is called a *diphthong*. Examples of such sounds are found in the words *now*, *my*, and *coin*. Diphthongs are further discussed later in this chapter.

Thus we see from these various bases of classification that vowel sounds are affected by a great number of factors, any or all of which can influence the quality of the sound either slightly or materially.

The Phoneme Theory

We come to the study of vowels with a problem to solve. Our study would be simplified if it were possible to assert that there is one definite and fixed position of the vocal organs for each vowel. A very little experimentation will prove, however, that this is not so. Two persons trying to make the same sound (as, for instance, the vowel in *it*) might make sounds which would be recognized as this vowel, but examination would prove that the sounds were not exactly the same and that the difference was due to slight differences in the position, shape, or tension of their vocal organs. A third person, perhaps a Frenchman, in attempting to make the sound might make it with so marked a change in the

---

⁵ Here the student is again warned against the confusion caused by our English spelling. The letters *aw* represent one position of the vocal organs and therefore one sound—the vowel which is written *a* in the word *call*, *o* in *lord*, *au* in *applaud*, *oa* in *broad*, *aw* in *caw*, but which phonetically is always [ɔ].

position or tension of the vocal organs that it would strike the ear as an entirely different sound, that of the vowel in *eat*. In the same way the word *full* may be pronounced with slight variations and still be recognizable as *full*, but with greater variations it becomes a different word, such as *fool*.

It is apparent that *for each vowel there are certain space limits in all directions—up and down, front and back, and diagonally, and so long as the vowel is produced within those limits, it is recognized as the sound intended; but as soon as those limits are passed, it strikes the ear as a different vowel.*[6] In other words, within certain limits a sound may be produced with decided differences in the position and tension of the vocal organs and yet be clearly recognized as the sound intended; but outside these limits changes in position and tension produce sounds which are entirely different in the impression they make on the ear. This gives us, not one exact mould for each vowel sound, but several, with approximately the same characteristics and quality.

Instead, then, of speaking of each vowel as if it represented one absolutely fixed position of the vocal organs, it is more helpful to think of it as a group of very closely related sounds, each of which represents a slightly different position. A group of vowel sounds so nearly alike that they impress the ordinary ear as the same sound may be called a *phoneme*, or *vowel family*.[7] This may be illustrated by reverting to our example of the vowel in *it*. So long as any or all of the vari-

---

[6] These changes, it will be remembered, involve not only to the mouth, but the pharynx as well. Furthermore, the quality of the vowel is affected by (1) the position of the larynx; (2) the length, tension, and approximation of the vocal cards; (3) the extent to which they are covered by the false vocal cords and the cushion of the epiglottis; and (4) the amount of muscular tension in the walls of the vocal passages. See G. Oscar Russell, *The Vowel*.

[7] The term *phoneme* is also applied to a group of consonants that are so nearly alike that they seem to be the same sound. In English, voiceless [l] is in the [l] phoneme. In Welsh, however, it is a separate phoneme and is written *ll*, as in *Llewelyn*.

ants give the sound that we are in the habit of calling short *i*, they are in the phoneme represented by the phonetic symbol [ɪ]; but as soon as the speaker in pronouncing *it* suggests the vowel in *eat* (phonetically [i]), the sound can no longer be considered as belonging in this phoneme.

Study of Individual Vowels

Proceeding from this phoneme theory, we shall make a detailed study of the English vowel system, which consists of fifteen vowels, or vowel phonemes, not including the diphthongs. The diphthongs will be discussed later.

In the correct formation of all English vowels, the tip of the tongue rests behind the lower teeth, the vocal cords are in vibration, and the air is sent through the mouth. It will be remembered that vowels have been classified as *front, back,* and *middle,* according to the place in the mouth where they are formed and the part of the tongue used. This classification will be used as the basis for our study of the individual vowels.

To encourage careful observation of the sounds as they are formed, some of them are described with definite directions for observing the action of the vocal organs (in so far as this is possible) with the aid of a mirror. These directions are not repeated in the descriptions of all the vowels, but students are strongly recommended to make continued and diligent use of their mirrors in every phase of their phonetics study. By this means much can be accomplished in the direction of improvement of speech long before the ears are trained to make distinctions accurately. With the aid of descriptions, diagrams, and models, students can, by using their mirrors, "see" what they are saying; can, if necessary, change the action of their articulatory organs; and can observe whether or not changes in individual sounds are carried over into connected speech. The ultimate goal, however, is to train the ear to distinguish and to demand accurately articulated speech.

A. Simple Vowels

I. Front Vowels

[i]

With your mirror in hand for observation, make the sound of the vowel in *see*.

You will notice that the front of the tongue, somewhat tensed, is raised nearly to the hard palate, the tip resting behind the lower front teeth; the lips, also slightly tense, are opened in a narrow slit, the vocal cords are vibrating, and the air is emitted through the mouth.

This is the highest front vowel.

Phonetic Symbol: [i] **Diacritical Marks:** [8] (ē), (ĭ), often called "long e"

Spellings: *e* as in *me*, *i* as in *machine*, *ee* as in *seen*, *ie* as in *yield*, *ei* as in *receive*, and *ea* as in *cease*.

In accented syllables [i] is usually long or half-long, for example, *mean* [miːn]; in unaccented, it is often short, for example, *meander* [m[i]ændə(r)].

In unaccented syllables and in unstressed monosyllables [i] often passes into the vowel sound in *it* or the first sound in *above*. For example, *be* as an accented word is pronounced [bi]; in an unstressed position, as in *become*, it is pronounced [bɪ] or [bə].[9]

Because of lack of precision in taking the tongue and lip positions, the vowel is often started with a moving tongue, so that [i], like most other long vowels, is apt to start with an on-glide; and because of the difficulty of holding the position once it has been taken, it sometimes ends with an off-glide. Thus, in the sentence "Give it to me," the word *me* is heard as [mɪi] or [miɪ] or even [mɪiɪ].

---

[8] An effort has been made to choose from the infinite variety of diacritical marks those most commonly used.

[9] See the next two vowels.

[i] has the highest natural pitch of all the vowels. For this reason it is used by singing teachers to produce a bright, clear tone. Singing or intoning this vowel helps to give consciousness of the facial resonators.

By reason of its being a tense vowel, there is a natural tendency to pronounce [i] with undue tension of the throat muscles. To avoid this it will be helpful to keep a firm breath support and to maintain the sensation of a free throat.

[ɪ]

The next vowel phoneme is the first sound in *it*. It is made by allowing the front of the tongue to relax into a position slightly lower and farther back than for [i], at the same time slightly relaxing the lips; the tip of the tongue is behind the lower teeth, the vocal cords are in vibration, and the air is emitted through the mouth.

Phonetic Symbol: [ɪ]   **Diacritical Mark:** (ĭ), " short i "

Spellings: *i* as in *it*, *y* as in *myth*, *u* as in *busy*, *e* as in *behind*, *ai* as in *fountain*, *ie* as in *daisies*, *a* as in *plumage*.

[ɪ] is a short vowel, but Americans have a tendency to lengthen and diphthongize it. Thus *it* becomes [ɪit] or [ɪət]. This is a form of the American drawl and is to be avoided for good speech.

The sound is sometimes made with the tongue too low and too far back in the mouth. This is especially true of speakers who invert their [t]'s, [d]'s, [l']s, [r]'s, and [s]'s, notably in the suffixes *-ed, -est, -es, -less, -ness*. In the speech of such persons *added* [ædɪd] becomes [ædəd]; *tallest* [tɔlɪst] becomes [tɔləst]; and *goodness* [gʊdnɪs] becomes [gʊdnəs].

By certain speakers a spelling pronunciation is used in the suffixes mentioned above; goodness [gʊdnɪs], for example, is pronounced [gʊdnɛs]. Such a pronunciation strikes most ears as pedantic.

[e]

Pronounce the word *they*. As you say the vowel in this word, does your tongue remain in one position or move from its initial position to another very near the first? Use the mirror to verify your conclusion.

If your tongue remains in one position, you form this sound as a pure vowel; but if, instead of maintaining the initial position, your tongue moves into the area of the phoneme [ɪ], the vowel is a diphthong. The initial position of this sound is a little lower, more forward, and more tense than [ɪ].

By some phoneticians this sound is considered only as a pure vowel, and such words as *day*, *play*, *say*, *make*, and *pale* are considered as belonging to the phoneme of the initial position, which is [e]. Tests given to some of our students have revealed a difference in the pronunciations of the words *play* and *take* by the same person, there being a more noticeable off-glide in *play* than in *take*. However, we have found few instances of this sound being made as a simple vowel, and for this reason it will be described as a diphthong,[10] although there is no objection to its being made as a simple vowel; indeed many voice teachers prefer this pronunciation.

[ɛ]

Pronounce the vowel in *get*. You will observe that the front of the tongue is considerably lower and slightly farther back than for [e] and that the lips are more open; the tip of the tongue is behind the lower teeth, the vocal cords are vibrating, and the air passes out through the mouth.

Phonetic Symbol: [ɛ]   **Diacritical Mark:** (ĕ), " short e "

Spellings: *e* as in *red*, *ea* as in *deaf*, *ay* as in *says*, *eo* as in *leopard*, *ai* as in *said*, *u* as in *bury*, *a* as in *Thames*.

---

[10] See the description of the diphthong [eɪ] later in this chapter.

This vowel is sometimes pronounced as if it belonged to the phoneme [e], the word *measure* [mɛʒə(r)] being heard as [meʒə(r)] or even [meɪʒə(r)]. On the other hand, the front of the tongue is sometimes dropped down and back until it enters the area of the phoneme of the vowel in *at*, so that a word like *yes* [jɛs] is heard as [jæs] (written "yaas" in dialect stories).

The vowel [ɛ] is normally short, but it is often drawled and even diphthongized. Then [mɛt] (*met*) becomes [mɛɛt] or [mɛət]. A lowered form of this vowel is used in the diphthong in the word *fair*, as we shall see later, but it should not be confused with the pure vowel sound of [ɛ].

The vowel [ɛ] is often begun with a glottal plosive, a sound resembling a slight cough,[11] which in American speech is usually accompanied by throat strain and so gives a flat and unpleasant quality to the sound. The word *effort* [ɛfə(r)t], if glottalized, would be pronounced [ʔɛfə(r)t].

[ɛ] is frequently nasalized when it is in the vicinity of nasal consonants, [mɛn] (*men*), for instance, being pronounced [mɛ̃n], because the air stream continues to pass through the nose instead of being sent through the mouth for the vowel. This nasalization, especially if accompanied by undue tension of the throat and back of the tongue, is undesirable, since it produces a kind of twang.

[æ]

Pronounce the vowel in *at*. You will observe that there is still a slight elevation of the front of the tongue, though less than for [ɛ], and the front is further retracted; while the tip remains behind the lower teeth, the vocal cords are vibrating, and the air passes out through the mouth.

Phonetic Symbol: [æ] . **Diacritical Mark:** (ă), " short a "

Spellings: The spelling form of this sound is always *a*.

---

[11] Described in the preceding chapter.

This sound is often made with undue tension in the throat, especially in the false vocal cords, which gives rise to a glottal plosive with its initiation: [ækt] (*act*) thus becomes [ˀækt]. Because of this tension many singing teachers require students to use the vowel sound in *calm* for such words as [mæn], [ænd], [hænd], and thus change them to [mɑn], [ɑnd], [hɑnd].

[æ] is the most frequently nasalized of all our vowel sounds. This nasalization, with the tension described above, makes it one of the least pleasant of our vowels. For this reason many speakers substitute for [æ] the first sound of the diphthong in *my* (phonetically written [a]) and say [man] and [hand] and [and]. Instead of following this practice it is recommended that students learn to make [æ] correctly, with throat free and soft palate raised.

[æ] is used interchangeably with [a] and [ɑ] in such words as *grass, ask, path,* etc. This will be discussed more fully under the next vowel heading.

[a]

Pronounce the vowel sound in *ask*. Note carefully whether your tongue takes the position for [æ] described above, making the vowel in this word sound like the vowel in *at*, or whether it drops a little farther down and back. If the latter, you are in the next front-vowel phoneme, which is [a], a sound slightly lower and farther back than [æ].

Phonetic Symbol: [a]   **Diacritical Mark:** (à), "intermediate a"

Spellings: Except ın the diphthong [aɪ] ("long i") the spelling form of this sound is always *a*. (As a simple vowel the sound is correctly used only when the vowel is followed by *ss, sk, st, sp, th, f, lf, ft, gh, nce, nt,* and by *nd* in words of Latin origin.)

In New England and some other sections this sound is often substituted for [ɑ] in such words as *art, department,*

Harvard, garden, etc. This practice has no authority, and it is not recommended.

In the speech of many persons the sound does not occur except in the diphthong [aɪ], as in *my*.

The problem of using this sound is one of the most troublesome that confronts a student of speech. As we have stated above, three different vowels are acceptable for the sound [a]. There are many arguments in favor of each. [æ] is used by a large number of speakers in this country. Others consider this form undesirable from the point of view of voice quality, since, as has been said, it is a difficult sound to make perfectly. On the stage and in certain localities [ɑ] is the preferred pronunciation. Yet many good speakers in all parts of the country prefer [a], because it is the only form of the vowel that the American dictionaries permit in such words as *ask, half,* and *past,* and it is the mean between the two extremes [æ] and [ɑ]. In view of these facts it seems wiser to make no recommendation, leaving it to the individual to choose the pronunciation that seems to him preferable.

II. BACK VOWELS

[u]

The highest back vowel is the vowel sound in *moon.* You will observe that it is made with the back of the tongue raised nearly to the soft palate and with closely rounded lips. Both the lips and the back of the tongue are tense. The tip of the tongue is behind the lower teeth, the vocal cords are in vibration, and the air is emitted through the mouth.

Phonetic Symbol: [u]   **Diacritical Marks:** (u̩), (o͞o), (o̩)

Spellings: *u* as in *rule, oo* as in *pool, o* as in *do, ou* as in *soup, ue* as in *blue, eu* as in *Reuben, ew* as in *flew, oe* as in *shoe.*

[u] is usually long in quantity, but it is sometimes made half-long or even short: for example, in *rue* [u] is generally long, in *rudimentary* it is half-long, while in *prudential* it is short.

[u] is frequently made with insufficient lip-rounding.

It is often slackened and lowered till it enters the next phoneme, so that [sun] (*soon*) becomes [sʊn] and [spun] (*spoon*) becomes [spʊn].

In some parts of the country, especially in the South, the back of the tongue is brought too far forward, giving to the vowel somewhat the character of the vowel in the French word *tu* [ty].

[u] is often diphthongized as a result of failure to bring the back of the tongue quickly and definitely to the right position and hold it there. In this faulty formation the tongue is placed too low at the start and is then pushed up to the correct position, or it passes from the correct position to a lower one. This produces a typical example of the so-called American drawl. Thus [du] (*do*) may become [dru], [dʊu], [duʊ], or [duə]. This drawled articulation occurs especially before *l*, [skul] (*school*) becoming [skuəl], and [pul] (*pool*) becoming [puəl].

The primary essential for this vowel is one that can be demonstrated only by the use of apparatus—a very large pharyngeal resonator with a small opening (the passage between the tongue and the palate). This gives the characteristically low, dull tone of the vowel, a tone which can be imitated by blowing over the top of a large bottle with a small neck. The soft surfaces, the closely approximated tongue and velum, serve to filter out the harsh upper partials, thus giving a particularly mellow quality to the tone. This fact, combined with the rounding and projection of the lips, which help to give the consciousness of a forward tone, makes [u] one of the best vowels for voice practice. It is essential, however, that the student should have a clear tone image and correct placing of the vocal organs before starting the tone. This will eliminate the danger of an on-glide and will make certain the initiation of the tone with what singers call a " clean attack." For these reasons many teachers make practice on the vowel [u], alone and in syllables, the foundation of voice training.

[ʊ]

This phoneme, the vowel sound in *foot*, bears the same resemblance to [u] that [ɪ] bears to [i]. It is sometimes regarded as the relaxed form of [u], there being less tension of the vocal organs. This release of tension tends to make the tongue drop a little down and forward in a slightly grooved shape and to make the circle of the lips slightly larger.

Phonetic Symbol: [ʊ]   **Diacritical Marks:** (ŭ), (o̦), (o͞o)

Spellings: *u* as in *pull, oo* as in *good, o* as in *wolf, ou* as in *could.*

[ʊ] is classed as a short vowel, but it is lengthened in drawling speech, [pʊt] (*put*) becoming [pʊʊt] or [pʊət]. As in [u], the drawl occurs most often before *l*, [pʊl] (*pull*) being heard as [pʊəl].

Like [u], this sound is often unrounded, and in some parts of the country it is made with the tongue too low and too far forward; then *put* sounds somewhat like [pʌt],[12] *pulpit* like [pʌlpɪt], etc.

As noted above, there seems to be a growing tendency to substitute some form of the phoneme [ʊ] for [u] in such words as *soon, hoop, room, root, roof,* and *hoof,* though most dictionaries still give only the [u] pronunciation. As a means of practice for voice production we recommend the more tense form, since, as has been said, it is so valuable in keeping the tone forward.

---

[12] See page 127 for [ʌ].

[o]

This phoneme balances [e], that is, it is made at about the same height in the mouth and is generally (though not always) pronounced with an off-glide. In the speech of many persons it is chiefly heard as the first element of a diphthong—the sound of the vowel in *no*. As heard in the unaccented syllable of words such as *hotel*, it is a simple vowel. It is formed with the back of the tongue considerably lower than for [ʊ] and with the lips rounded in a larger circle; the tip of the tongue is behind the lower teeth, the vocal cords are in vibration, and the air is sent out through the mouth. [o] will be discussed more fully under the diphthong [oʊ].

[ɔ]

The sound of this phoneme is that of the vowel in *saw*. It is made with almost as much tension of the tongue and lips as for [u]. The back of the tongue is much lower than for [o], the lips are rounded in an ellipse and are more projected than for any other vowel; the tongue tip is behind the lower teeth, the vocal cords are in vibration, and the air is emitted through the mouth.

Phonetic Symbol: [ɔ]   **Diacritical Marks:** (ô), (a̧), (â)

Spellings: *o* as in *short*, *a* as in *fall*, *au* as in *sauce*, *ou* as in *thought*, *aw* as in *thaw*, *eo* as in *George*, *oa* as in *broad*.

This is a sound which in our American speech has wide variations, ranging from a tongue position of the phoneme [o] to that of [a] and from close lip-rounding to complete unrounding. Thus *water* is heard, on the one hand as very nearly [wotə(r)], and on the other as [watə(r)], with the more generally accepted pronunciation, [wɔtə(r)], between the two.

[ɔ] is often diphthongized, [wɔtə(r)] becoming [wɔətə(r)]. It is frequently inverted, *for* being heard as [fᶗ] or [fᶗᶒ] or [fɔr].[12]

The lip projection with which this sound is correctly formed makes it valuable in speech training for keeping the tone forward; its tension helps to keep the flow of tone steady. Hence, if perfectly made, it is excellent for voice practice.

[ɒ]

This phoneme, heard in the word *John* as it is pronounced in many parts of the country, is the lowest vowel made with lip-rounding. The tongue is nearly flat in the mouth, the back being very slightly raised, and the lips are somewhat rounded but without great tension; the tip of the tongue is behind the lower teeth, the soft palate is raised, and the vocal cords are in vibration.

Phonetic Symbol: [ɒ]   **Diacritical Marks:** (ŏ), (ạ)

Spellings: *o* as in *doll*, *a* as in *watch*, *au* as in *laurel*, *aw* as in *Lawrence*

Of all the vowels in our language, this has perhaps the widest range of variation in tongue position, lip-rounding, and duration.

[ɒ] is sometimes diphthongized, that is, followed by an off-glide. In the word *boy* the vowel is a legitimate diphthong, but when diphthongization occurs in pronouncing a word that should have a pure vowel, it is incorrect. This happens when [ɒd] (*odd*) is heard as [ɒəd], or [ɑəd], or even [aəd].

[ɒ] is not heard at all in the speech of some persons, being pronounced as some form of the phoneme [ɔ], in which case *dog* [dɒg] becomes [dɔg]; or as some form of the phoneme of the vowel in *calm*, [nɒt] (*not*) being heard as [nɑt].

The front vowel phoneme [a] also is often substituted

---

[12] A dot under a symbol means inversion.

for this sound, [ɒd] becoming [ad], [nɒt] becoming [nat], and [gɒd] becoming [gad].

The variations [a] and [ɔ] are felt as provincialisms in certain localities and for that reason are apt to call attention to themselves as unusual pronunciations. The variation [ɑ], on the other hand, is a very common one and does not offend the ears of careful speakers. From the point of view of tone production [ɒ] is to be recommended because it is made with lip-rounding, which, as we have noted, is helpful in developing projection of tone.

[ɑ]

This phoneme is the sound of the vowel in *calm*. The tongue is low in the mouth, with perhaps a slight elevation at the back; the lips are completely unrounded but are rather widely open; the tongue tip is behind the lower teeth, the vocal cords are vibrating, and the air is sent through the mouth.

Phonetic Symbol: [ɑ]   **Diacritical Mark:** (ä)

Spellings: *a* as in *far*, *au* as in *laundry*, *e* as in *sergeant*, *oi* as in *memoir*, *ea* as in *hearth*. It is the sound of *a* when followed by *h* or *r*.

[ɑ] has the following undesirable modifications:

1. It may be made too far forward in the mouth, being carried into the phoneme [a]; in that case [kɑm] (*calm*) would sound like [kam].

2. It may be made too far back and rounded, [kɑm] then sounding like [kɒm].

3. It may be made with the back of the tongue raised too high and with the lips rounded, [kɑm] being heard as [kɔm].

4. It may be nasalized so that [kɑm] sounds like [kãm] or [kãm].

5. It may be inverted, especially if it comes before a teeth ridge consonant. If this occurs, *art*, instead of being pronounced [ɑt] or [ɑ(r)t], is heard as [ɑ̣ṛṭ].

6. It is frequently drawled, an off-glide being heard which is made by raising the middle of the tongue slightly so that [kɑm] becomes [kɑəm].

This vowel is often made with unnecessary tension at the back of the tongue and in the throat, which prevents its being properly resonated. It should be made with the vocal organs as free from strain as possible.

[ɑ] is not an easy sound to make correctly because it is less clearly defined than many of the others as to both tongue and lip positions. However, with ear training and practice in directing the action of the vocal organs it is possible to make this vowel properly, when it becomes a very beautiful sound and adds greatly to the resonant effect of speech.

III. MIDDLE, NEUTRAL, OR MIXED VOWELS

[ɜ]

This is the vowel sound in *fur*. It is made with the middle of the tongue raised about half way to the hard palate; the lips are unrounded, the tip of the tongue is behind the lower teeth, and the breath is sent out through the mouth.

Phonetic Symbol: [ɜ]   **Diacritical Marks:** (û), (ẽ), (ĩ), (y̆)

Spellings: *e* as in *fern*, *i* as in *sir*, *u* as in *turn*, *o* as in *attorney*, *y* as in *myrtle*, *ou* as in *courteous*, *ea* as in *earnest*, *eu* as in *connoisseur*.

[ɜ] is frequently lip-rounded, especially in New York City. It is also diphthongized, the off-glide being heard as some form of the phoneme [ɪ]: thus [bɜ(r)d] (*bird*) becomes somewhat like [bɜɪd] and ʃtɜ(r)n] (*turn*) like [tɜɪn].[13]

It is often made too far forward, causing [sɜ(r)] (*sir*) to sound somewhat like [sɛ(r)].

---

[13] This is the pronunciation represented in dialect stories by "boid" and "toin."

It is also made with the tongue too high and too tense.

This is one of the vowels in which the strongest inversions are likely to occur. Care should be taken to hold the tip of the tongue behind the lower front teeth and to keep the whole tongue free from strain.

[ə]

In forming this vowel, the second vowel sound in *father*, the tongue is slightly lower than it is in the position that it naturally assumes when at rest, with the middle of the tongue lowered and retracted slightly from the position for [ɜ]. The tip of the tongue rests behind the lower teeth, and the whole tongue is relaxed; the soft palate is raised, and the vocal cords are in vibration.

Phonetic Symbol: [ə] **Diacritical Marks:** (à), (ĕ), (ẽ) (a), (e), (ŏ), (u), (a̱), (e̱), (i̱), (o̱), (a̱), (e̱), (u̱)

Spellings: *a* as in *about, final, sofa, monarch*; *e* as in *over, mystery*; *i* as in *affirmation*; *o* as in *arbor*; *u* as in *surprise*; *y* as in *martyr*; *io* as in *national*; *ou* as in *porous*; *oi* as in *porpoise*, etc.

This sound is called by phoneticians the *neutral*, or *natural*, or *indefinite, vowel*. It is made with the tongue at rest and is the sound to which all vowels in unaccented syllables tend to be leveled. The only ones to resist this tendency are the high front vowel and the high back vowel, which are more likely to be weakened by relaxation of the tongue so that [u] becomes [ʊ], as in [daɪnɪŋ rʊm] (*dining room*), and [i] becomes [ɪ], as in [bɪkʌm] (*become*).

Many persons who think in terms of letters rather than of sounds feel that the use of the neutral vowel is to be avoided and take great pains to say [prɔfɛsɔ(r)] (*professor*) for [prəfɛsə(r)] and [pɑ(r)tɪkjulɑ(r)lɪ] (*particularly*) for [pətikjʊlə(r)lɪ]. The effects of this overconscientiousness are discussed on pages 158–163.

Fig. 29. VOWEL DIAGRAM

The upper curve represents the roof of the mouth, the lower curve represents the low position of tongue. The symbols are placed on the diagram to indicate approximate tongue positions.

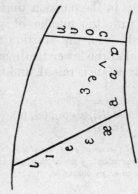

Key Words [15]

[i]	eat	(ē), (ī)		[ɜ]	fir	(û), (ē̃), (ĩ), (ȳ)		[u]	moon	(ụ̈), (o͞o), (ọ̈)
[I]	it	(ĭ)		[e]	above	(a), (ẹ̈), (ị̈), (ọ), (ụ̈), etc.		[ʊ]	book	(ṳ), (o͝o), (ọ̈)
[e]	débris	(ā)		[ʌ]	up	(ŭ), (ŏ),		[o]	hotel	(ō), (o)
[ɛ]	met	(ĕ)						[ɔ]	saw	(ô), (ạ), (â)
[æ]	at	(ă)						[ɒ]	not	(ŏ), (ạ̈)
[a]	ask	(à)						[ɑ]	calm	(ä)

[15] The phonetic symbol for the vowel precedes the key word and is enclosed in brackets; the diacritical marks following are enclosed in parentheses.

[ʌ]

This vowel, heard in the word *but*, has many variations, not only as to the elevation, but also as to the part of the tongue used in its formation. In America it is generally made with the middle of the tongue and is therefore classed as a neutral or mixed vowel. In the speech of many persons, however, it is formed with the back of the tongue and when so made should be classified as a low back unrounded vowel.

As a mixed vowel [ʌ] is made with the middle of the tongue slightly lower than for [ə] but considerably retracted, being somewhat near the area of the [ɑ] phoneme. The tip of the tongue rests behind the lower teeth, the soft palate is raised, and the vocal cords are in vibration.

Phonetic Symbol: [ʌ]   **Diacritical Marks:** (ŭ), (ò)

Spellings: *u* as in *much*, *o* as in *come*, *ou* as in *trouble*, *oo* as in *flood*, *oe* as in *does*.

In words like *current*, *worry*, etc., the vowel [ɜ] is often substituted for [ʌ]. So frequently, indeed, does this pronunciation occur in American speech that it will doubtless find its place in our dictionaries, and it can even now be regarded as an accepted pronunciation in many parts of the country.

B. DIPHTHONGS

In our study of the vowels so far, emphasis has been laid upon the necessity for promptly taking and firmly maintaining the position for each vowel, thus eliminating, as far as possible, the on-glide and off-glide caused by moving the tongue or lips, so that the quality of the vowel shall be pure and distinctive. There is, however, a group of vowels in the pronunciation of which the off-glide is so important a factor that it adds another element to the simple vowel and causes the two elements (the first fairly strong and the other relatively weak) to give the effect of a compound sound, though there is no increase or decrease in the air pressure. These compound sounds are called *diphthongs*.

If the formation of the word *I* (the so-called "long *i*") is carefully observed in a mirror, it will be seen that the tongue starts with the position of the vowel [a], but, instead of maintaining this, moves toward the position of the vowel [ɪ]. Thus it is seen that "long *i*," instead of being a simple vowel sound as is often thought, is a compound vowel or diphthong. Professor Daniel Jones calls a diphthong "two vowels so placed and so pronounced that there is no diminution of sonority between them (that is, that they do not form more than one syllable)." In the word *doing* [duɪŋ] we have the consecutive vowels [u] and [ɪ], but they do not form a diphthong because there is a slackening of the air pressure between them, so that they occur in different syllables. In the word *foil* [fɒɪl] on the other hand, the [ɒ] and [ɪ] are pronounced with sustained pressure of the air; they are, therefore, in the same syllable and form a diphthong.

Of the sounds *a*, *e*, *i*, *o*, and *u*, commonly called the five English vowels, only the second is a simple vowel. The first, third, and fourth are usually diphthongs, and the fifth is a vowel preceded by the consonant that is phonetically written [j].

As was observed in the formation of the word *I* (phonetically written [aɪ]), a diphthong consists of two elements. The more important of these represents the initial position of the vocal organs, and it is phonetically designated by the symbol of this position. The second element consists of a movement of the tongue toward a point just below the highest position in one of three vowel groups (front, neutral, or back) and is expressed by the symbol that corresponds to that point. It is understood, of course, that in the enunciation of both elements the positions of the tongue are accompanied by the corresponding positions of the lips and other vocal organs.

Diphthongs may for convenience be classified in groups according to their second element. They will now be briefly described under this classification.

I. Diphthongs Ending in [ɪ]

The first group has for its second element the vowel [ɪ].

[eɪ]

This diphthong is the compound sound heard in the word *bay*. The front of the tongue starts in the [e] position and makes an off-glide toward the position for [ɪ].

Phonetic Symbol: [eɪ]   **Diacritical Mark:** (ā)

Spellings: [eɪ] is represented in ordinary spelling by *a* as in *fame*, *e* as in *detour*, *ey* as in *prey*, *ea* as in *great*, *ei* as in *neighbor*, and *ai* as in *wait*.

By some phoneticians this sound is not considered a diphthong, but is listed as a pure vowel, [eɪt] (*ate*) being pronounced [et] and [pleɪ] (*play*) pronounced [ple]. We find differences in the extent to which this vowel is diphthongized in the speech of different persons, and even in that of the same person in different words, there being less of an off-glide on [keɪk] (*cake*) than on [pleɪ], but we have seldom heard it with complete elimination of the off-glide in accented syllables except in the speech of foreigners.

A lowered form of this diphthong is heard when the phoneme [ɛ] is substituted for [e], [pleɪ] becoming [plɛɪ].

Before *l* this diphthong often becomes a triphthong, [peɪl] (*pale*) being pronounced as [peɪəl]. When, as often occurs, the [ə] and the [l] are inverted or nasalized or both, the result is most unpleasant.

[aɪ]

This is the vowel heard in the word *buy*. It has for its
first element the phoneme [a] and for its second, [ɪ].

Phonetic Symbol: [aɪ]   **Diacritical Marks:** (ī), (ȳ)

Spellings: *i* as in *pine*, *ai* as in *aisle*, *ei* as in *height*, *y* as in *type*, *ie* as
in *pie*.

The first element in this vowel is often replaced by [ɑ]
or [ɒ] or even [ɔ]. Thus [maɪ] (*my*) may be heard as [mɑɪ],
[mɒɪ], or [mɔɪ]. The first of these does not call undue attention to itself, but the last two, because they are unusual
provincialisms, are apt to do so.

This vowel is very often nasalized, particularly if preceded or followed by a nasal consonant: thus *my*, *mine*, *nine*,
etc., become pronounced [maĩ], [maĩn], [naĩn], etc.

There is a tendency to drawl this diphthong, and if that
is combined with nasality, as often happens the effect is very
unpleasant.

The off-glide of this vowel is sometimes partially or
entirely eliminated and [maɪ taɪm] (*my time*) becomes
[mɑ tɑəm].

The second element sometimes becomes an [i], [maɪ]
being heard as [mai].

[ɒɪ]

This is the vowel sound in the word *boy*. Its first element
is the phoneme [ɒ], and its second element is [ɪ].

Phonetic Symbol: [ɒɪ]   **Diacritical Marks:** (ði), (ðy), (oi)

Spellings: *oi* as in *oil*, *oy* as in *boy*.

The first element is often heard as [ɔ], [bɒɪ] (*boy*) becoming [bɔɪ]. Indeed, the International Phonetic Association
represents this diphthong by [ɔɪ].

The first element may be the neutral [ə], so that [bɒɪ]

becomes [bəɪ]. This is one of the forms heard in careless New York speech.

The second element is occasionally a sound in the phoneme [j], [bɒɪ] being heard as [bɒi] or [bɒj].

II. Diphthongs Ending in [ə]

The second group of diphthongs have the neutral vowel [ə] as the second element.

[ɪə]

. This diphthong, the vowel in *ear*, begins with the vowel [ɪ] and has for its off-glide the neutral [ə].

Phonetic Symbol: [ɪə]   **Diacritical Mark:** (ē) [16]

Spellings: *ea* as in *idea*, *ee* as in *sheer*, *ie* as in *tier*, *e* as in *here*.

The tense form [i] is often substituted for the more lax [ɪ], so that [ɪə(r)] (*ear*) becomes [iə(r)].

The front of the tongue is sometimes too low when the first element is sounded, so that it is heard as [e] or [ɛ], [ɪə(r)] being heard as [eə(r)].

The second element [ə] is frequently inverted, [ɪə(r)] becoming [ɪə̣] or [ɪə̣r].

[ɛə]

This is the diphthong heard in the word *bear*, having a lowered form of the vowel [ɛ] as its first element and [ə] as the off-glide.

Phonetic Symbol: [ɛə]   **Diacritical Mark:** (â)

Spellings: *a* as in *fare*, *ai* as in *air*, *ea* as in *pear*, *ei* as in *heir*, *e* as in *there*.

---

[16] The diacritical mark for this sound completely misrepresents it. For instance, the word *fear* is pronounced in Webster's Dictionary fēr, without an off-glide from the ē to the *r*, which is practically impossible.

In making the first element of this diphthong the front of the tongue is sometimes lowered to the area of the [æ] phoneme; [bɛə(r)] (*bear*) is then heard as [bæ̯əə(r)].

This diphthong, like the one preceding, is often inverted, [bɛə(r)] becoming [bɛ̣ə̣] or [bɛ̣ə̣r].

[ɒə] *or* [oə]

The diphthong, heard in the word *bore*, has for its second element the neutral vowel [ə], but the first element may be either [ɒ] or [o]. Thus *bore* may be pronounced [bɒə(r)] or [boə(r)].

Phonetic Symbols: [ɒə], [oə]   **Diacritical Mark:** (ō)

Spellings: *oa* as in *oar*, *o* as in *more*, *oo* as in *floor*, *ou* as in *pour*.

This diphthong is frequently inverted, [bɒə(r)] or [boə(r)] being heard as [bɒə̣r] or [boə̣r].

The second element [ə] is sometimes made with the middle of the tongue lowered to the position for the phoneme [ʌ], [bɒə] (*bore*) being heard as [bɒʌ].

[ʊə]

The diphthong in *boor* is made up of the two elements [ʊ] and [ə].

Phonetic Symbol: [ʊə]   **Diacritical Mark:** (ōō)

Spellings: *oo* as in *boor*, *u* as in *lure*, *ou* as in *tour*.

The first element [ʊ], is often made with too great a degree of tension of the back of the tongue and the lips, resulting in a substitution of [u] for [ʊ]; [bʊə(r)] (*boor*) is then heard as [buə(r)].

Like the other diphthongs ending in the neutral vowel, [ʊə] is frequently inverted, [bʊə(r)] becoming [bʊ̣ə̣] or [bʊ̣ə̣r].

[ʊə] may be replaced by [oə] or [ʋə], [pʊə] (*poor*) becoming [poə(r)] or [pʋə(r)]. The pronunciation [pʋə(r)] is used by many careful speakers so that it is recognized in England and in some parts of America as an acceptable variant, but the form [poə(r)] is generally felt as provincial.

III. Diphthongs Ending in [ʊ]

The third group of diphthongs have [ʊ] as their second element.

[aʊ]

This is the diphthong heard in the word *bough*. The first element is [a] and the second [ʊ].

Phonetic Symbol: [aʊ]   **Diacritical Marks:** (ou), (ow)

Spellings: *ou* as in *bough*, *ow* as in *now*, *au* as in *sauerkraut*.

The first element in this diphthong, [a], is frequently replaced by [a] or [æ] or even [ɛ], in which case [baʊ] (*bough*) is heard as [baʊ], [bæʊ], or [bɛʊ]. These substitutions are often accompanied by nasalization of the diphthong, especially if it is preceded or followed by a nasal consonant, as in *noun*. The International Phonetic Association represents this diphthong by [aʊ].

The second element is sometimes heard as the tense [u] instead of the more lax [ʊ], [baʊ] becoming [bau].

These two modifications in the elements may be combined, [baʊ] being heard as [bæu].

The second element may be absent entirely, the vowel in the word being then a pure one. Thus, [baʊ] may be heard as [ba]; or if there is a slight off-glide, it may be some form of the phoneme [ə], [baə].

Except perhaps [aɪ], no other diphthong is so often pronounced with poor tone quality. Most students require long practice on this sound to realize its possibilities for beauty.

[oʊ]

This diphthong, the vowel sound in the word *beau*, has for its first element [o] and its second [ʊ].

Phonetic Symbol: [oʊ]   **Diacritical Mark:** (ō)

> **Spellings:** *o* as in *go*, *ow* as in *blow*, *ou* as in *soul*, *oa* as in *goat*, *eau* as in *beau*.

Although [o] in accented syllables is rarely pronounced without some diphthonization by English-speaking people, the simple vowel is sometimes substituted by foreigners for the diphthong, [boʊ] (*beau*) being heard as [bo]. This is generally described as a "tense" pronunciation of the diphthong.

The first element [o] may be replaced by [ɒ], [ɑ], [ə], or [ʌ], giving to [boʊ] the pronunciations [bɒʊ], [bɑʊ], [bəʊ], or [bʌə].

The second element [ʊ] may be replaced by the more tense [u], [boʊ] then being heard as [bou].

Fɪɢ. 30. DIPHTHONG DIAGRAM

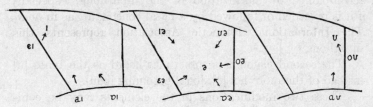

The arrows indicate the direction in which the tongue glides from the position of the first element to that of the second.

Key Words

[eɪ]	*bay* (ā)	[ɪə]	*beer* (ē)	[aʊ]	*bough* (ou), (ow)
[aɪ]	*buy* (ī), (ȳ)	[ɛə]	*bear* (å)	[oʊ]	*beau* (ō)
[ɒɪ]	*boy* (ŏi),(ŏy),(oi)	[oə] [ɒə] } *bore* { (ō) (ō)			
		[ʊə]	*boor* (ōō)		

Diphthongs in Connected Speech

Good vowels are absolutely necessary to good speech, and there should be constant practice in making each vowel accurately and in prolonging it indefinitely without change in the position of the vocal organs. Not until the ability to do this has been acquired should the student practice diphthongs. In making these compound vowels it is important to gain perfect control of the lips as well as of the tongue. For instance, in the diphthong [ɒɪ] it is essential to unround the lips for the second element. Failure to do so gives a strong foreign accent to words containing this diphthong. A good exercise is to practice saying [ɒɪ], [ɒɪ], very rapidly before a mirror, being careful to unround the lips for each [ɪ], while at the same time training the ear to distinguish the difference in sound. There is no better training for beauty and precision of speech than such practice in the rapid articulation of diphthongs.

When considered in relation to voice production, diphthongs present an even greater problem than simple vowels in the establishment of good qualities of tone; for although each element may be correctly made when pronounced alone, the combination of front and back, lip-rounded and unrounded, tense and lax vowels presents new difficulties of enunciation which can be overcome only with practice and ear-training.

The effects produced by nasalization and inversion are most undesirable and must be eliminated if the tone quality is to be clear and smooth.

Delicacy, precision, and purity of tone in the enunciation of diphthongs may be regarded as one of the final tests of excellence in speech.

Diphthongs in Connected Speech

CHAPTER VII

SYNTHESIS OF SOUNDS IN CONNECTED SPEECH

IN order to speak well we must be able to make every individual sound in our language with perfect ease and accuracy. But this is only the first step toward good speech, for when sounds are combined in speech, they are modified not only by neighboring sounds, but by such influences as stress, rhythm, and analogy with other combinations of sounds.

To learn all the laws that govern the connecting of sounds in a language is so difficult that practically no one ever really masters a foreign tongue. In our own language we have been learning these laws, for the most part unconsciously, since our early childhood, and one would think that we ought to be able to read and speak English perfectly. But several causes have combined to prevent most of us from even approximating to perfect English speech.

One of these causes has already been mentioned—the bewildering inconsistency of our spelling. If we depended chiefly on our ears as guides in speech, this condition might not be so disastrous, but in modern education sight is trained at the expense of hearing, so that we rely on visual rather than auditory images.

To make a bad matter worse, most of us are brought up with the idea that we must, so far as possible, make our pronunciation conform to the spelling of words—as Oxford newsboys take great pains to pronounce *Magdalen College* as it is spelled instead of using the standard pronunciation [mɔːdlɪn]. Reverence for the printed page is so strong in most teachers of reading, unless they have been phonetically

136

trained, that they encourage this tendency toward slavish following of the letters, especially in reading aloud. The result is a habit of reading, and to a lesser extent of speaking, which is pedantic and entirely foreign to the genius of our language.

The other extreme, which is perhaps even more common in our speech, is the habit of pronouncing words in the easiest way, with little regard for the sounds that compose them. The result of this is to make speech slovenly and difficult to understand.

And lastly, so large a part of our population is foreign-born that the pronunciation of our language is more or less affected by the speech habits of other nationalities. In some of the public schools of New York City various foreign influences have combined to produce a form of English which is different from that spoken anywhere else in the world. And even in less extreme instances students of our language find tendencies which seem to be the result of foreign speech habits.

ASSIMILATION

Definition

In view of all these adverse influences it is of particular importance to study the laws that govern the synthesis of sounds in English. The most general law is probably that of *economy of effort*,[1] that is, the greatest ease consistent with clearness of articulation. The largest number of cases of the working of this law are grouped under the general heading of *assimilation*, which means the influence of one sound upon another, or, as Professor Daniel Jones expresses it, *the law by which one sound becomes a different sound under the influence of a third.*

---

[1] Many students of linguistics deny the importance of this factor, but every teacher knows how natural is the tendency of the vocal muscles to accomplish their end with the least possible expenditure of effort.

So many movements of the vocal organs are required to make the sounds of a single sentence that talking would become a painfully tedious process if we made every sound with scrupulous accuracy and completeness. As a matter of fact, no speaker, even the most precise, does make each sound ,in this theoretically perfect way. The articulation of sounds is eased by assimilation in several ways. The laws of assimilation may therefore be studied from several points of view.

A. Assimilations Classified as to Direction of Influence

1. *Due to the Influence of One Sound on the Following Sound (Progressive Assimilation)*

In the first place, in going from one sound to the next it is often difficult to make instantly all the changes necessary for an accurate articulation of the second sound. Accordingly this second sound, or sometimes only the first part of it, is formed before these changes have been entirely made, and it thus acquires some of the character of the first sound, or is, as we say, *assimilated* to it. For example, the word *want* was originally pronounced [wɑnt] as it is spelled. But because it is difficult to unround the lips instantly from the close position required for [w], the [ɑ] has come to be pronounced with lip-rounding, which makes it a form of [ɒ]. Hence the accepted pronunciation is [wɒnt].

Another instance of a sound being influenced by a previous sound is found in the word *looked*. When the *e* was dropped, bringing the voiced [d] next to the breathed [k], it was so much easier to make the final sound with the vocal cords still in the relaxed position than to draw them tautly together that the [d] was unvoiced. The word, therefore, though it retains its old spelling, is pronounced [lʊkt].

Also [k], though ordinarily formed with the back of the tongue on the soft palate, is made with the front on the hard palate when the [k] follows a front vowel. Compare, for example, the [k] in [liːk] (*leak*) with that in [lʊk] (*look*). Such bringing of a sound from the soft palate to the hard palate is called *palatalization*.

2. Due to the Influence of One Sound on the Preceding Sound (Regressive Assimilation)

Secondly, while pronouncing one sound we are sometimes getting ready for the next, so that the first sound is made with the vocal organs partly in the position required for the second. For instance, the velar [k] may be palatalized by a succeeding as well as by a preceding front vowel. Compare the palatal [k] in [ki] with the velar [k] in [ku]; or, still better, compare [kɪk] (*kick*) with [kʊk] (*cook*). In [kɪk] the [ɪ] influences both [k]'s, so that the whole word is made with the tongue in the front of the mouth. This word, therefore, illustrates both progressive and regressive assimilation and shows that several movements of the tongue may be eliminated in one syllable.

The sound [ʃ] is usually rounded, but when it is followed by an unrounded vowel, it is often partially unrounded: compare the [ʃ] in [ʃi] (*she*) with that in [ʃu] (*shoe*). On the other hand, [l], though normally unrounded, is often rounded in anticipation of a lip-rounded vowel: compare [lɪk] (*lick*) with [lulu] (*Lulu*).

3. Due to the Mutual Influence of Two Sounds (Reciprocal Assimilation)

Thirdly, two consecutive sounds may be modified as a result of their influence upon one another. In the word *vision*, formerly pronounced [vɪzjən], the [z], normally made with the tongue tip, tends to bring forward the [j], normally made with the front of the tongue; at the same time [j] tends to draw the [z] backward. The result is that the two sounds merge in the sound [ʒ], which is made with the blade of the tongue, that is, the point midway between the tip and the front. In the word *action*, formerly pronounced [æktjən], the [t] has been drawn backward under the influence of the [j]; the [j] has been unvoiced under the influence of the [t]; and the two have finally coalesced to form the intermediate unvoiced sibilant [ʃ].

B. Assimilations Classified as to Position of the Vocal Cords

In the expressions [ðə kæt ɪz kruəl] (*the cat is cruel*) and [ðə kæt həz kʌm] (*the cat has come*) the consonant in *is* and *has* is voiced. If, however, the verb is contracted to [z] (written '*s*), it is much easier to make this consonant with the vocal cords relaxed as they already are for [t] than to draw them closely enough together to produce voice. The [z] is therefore unvoiced.

On the other hand, when the word *serve* is compounded with a prefix that ends in a voiced sound, like *de-* or *ob-*, the vocal cords, being tense for the voiced sound, remain tense in making the [s], which is accordingly voiced as in *preserve*, *observe*, and similar words.

At this point it is well to note an English speech habit which, though not properly an assimilation, is frequently classified as one by phoneticians. When voiced consonants occur initially, the vocal cords are seldom brought smartly enough together to make these sounds voiced from the beginning; and when voiced consonants occur finally, the vocal cords are not held tensely until the end; so that initial voiced consonants begin as breathed sounds, and final voiced consonants end as breathed sounds. Thus *zone* is approximately [szoʊn], and dogs, [dɒgzs]. The failure of foreigners to observe this law of partial unvoicing gives rise to one of the most characteristic peculiarities of a foreign accent. Clergymen and public speakers, in an attempt to enunciate very clearly, sometimes voice their final consonants to the bitter end, producing an unpleasantly labored impression.

On the other hand, many persons unvoice final voiced consonants almost or quite completely, making them indistinct and sometimes changing the meaning of a word.

C. Assimilations Classified as to Place of Articulation

1. *In Forming Consonants*

Originally the [n] in *sink* was a genuine [n], but as a result of the influence of the [k] the post-dental nasal [n] was drawn back to the velar position, and in this way the word gained its modern pronunciation [sɪŋk]. The word *Lincoln* is another example of this form of assimilation, that is, the substitution of the velar nasal [ŋ] for the post-dental nasal [n]; some persons, however, in an attempt to follow the spelling, use the post-dental nasal. *Angry* is another example of the velarization of [n] under the influence of [g], being pronounced [æŋgrɪ]. Words having the prefix *in-* followed by a velar sometimes have the velarized nasal, especially in rapid speech; an example of this is the word *incompatible*, sometimes pronounced [ɪŋkəmpætəbl].

The opposite assimilation, that is, from [ŋ] to [n], occurs in the words *length* and *strength* as pronounced by many Americans and most Scotch people. H. C. Wyld, in his *History of Modern Colloquial English*, says that [lɛŋgθ] is so frequently [lɛnθ] in Scotland that the word has become the Scottish shibboleth. This pronunciation, however, is not considered good either in America or in Scotland.

The word *virtue* [vɜ(r)tju] is frequently assimilated to [vɜ(r)tʃu], since the post-dental [ʃ] is more easily made after [t] than the palatal [j]. This assimilation is generally accepted as justifiable in rapid colloquial speech. Many persons prefer the unassimilated form in reading poetry or formal prose and in public speaking. The assimilation of [ɛdjukeɪʃən] (*education*) to [ɛdʒəkeɪʃən] is considered by many as rather slovenly even in rapid speech.

In the compound *horseshoe* the [ʃ] in [ʃuː] assimilates the *s* in [hɔ(r)s] to [ʃ], and the word is pronounced with one prolonged [ʃ]. The same assimilation frequently occurs in such expressions as *Miss Shaw* [mɪʃʃɔː], *has she* [hæʒʃi] or [hæʃʃiː], etc. Often in very rapid speech these expressions are still further simplified to [mɪʃɔː], [hæʃi], or [hæʒi]. These last two assimilations are not recommended.

An expression like "I shall miss you," if spoken very quickly, illustrates the way in which two sounds mutually influence each other (reciprocal assimilation). The *s* in [mɪs] is attracted to the [ʃ] position under the influence of the palatal [j]; this [j], meanwhile, is drawn forward to the [ʃ] position and unvoiced under the influence of the [s]; so that we have the pronunciation [mɪʃʃu]. Similarly, *Miss Young* becomes [mɪʃʃʌŋ].

English speakers are inclined to avoid this type of assimilation, even to the point of pronouncing *issue* [ɪsju]. In American speech such assimilations have excellent, though unconscious, authority. At a recent Phi Beta Kappa dinner one of our most distinguished scholars spoke of his Alma Mater as [oʊldʒeɪl]. Here the palatal [j] was assimilated to the post-dental [ʒ] under the influence of the preceding [d]. In spite of such authority, however, these assimilations suggest careless articulation and are not recommended.

Such assimilations as [oʊpm] for [oʊpn] (*open*), [beɪkŋ] for [beɪkn] (*bacon*), [aɪ kŋ goʊ] for [aɪ kən goʊ] (*I can go*), are sometimes heard but are not accepted pronunciations.

In a word like *clean* [kliːn], the post-dental [l] draws the velar [k] forward and is in turn drawn backward by this [k] until they meet at a point half way between their normal points of articulation. Careless speakers sometimes assimilate these sounds differently. They substitute the post-dental plosive for the velar plosive, so that the word becomes [tliːn]. This change, however, is so slight that only trained ears would perceive it.

2. *In Forming Vowels*

In discussing assimilation many phoneticians confine themselves to changes in consonants. Vowels, however, are influenced by the adjacent sounds even more than consonants, though these changes are so subtle that they are less easily perceived. For instance, there is a different form of the vowel in each of the words *bet* [bɛt], *bed* [bɛd], and *bell* [bɛl]; but the difference is too slight for the untrained ear to observe, and the same phonetic symbol is used for all three, that is, they are regarded as being in the same phoneme group.

In the words just mentioned it is the succeeding consonant that causes the change. When the vowel [ɑ] is preceded by a lip-rounded consonant [w] or [ʍ], it is difficult to unround the lips instantly, as has already been explained, and the unrounded [ɑ] is rounded to [ɔ] or [ɒ], as in *water* [wɔtə], *want* [wɒnt], *was* [wɒz], *what* [ʍɒt], *quality* [kwɒlɪtɪ], *Washington* [wɒʃɪŋtən], etc. In certain parts of the country lip-rounding does not occur in all these cases: for instance, one often hears the word *Washington* pronounced [wɑʃɪŋtən]. In regard to this type of assimilation E. H. Sturtevant, in his *Linguistic Change* (page 75), says that in Shakespeare's time the use in England was also vacillating and that *wanting* rhymed with *granting*. "In the nineteenth century," he continues, "the modern pronunciation of such words was the common one, but many people kept the old sound in certain words such as *wart, warp, waddle, wad, wallop*. For the last hundred years or so the standard English pronunciation has constantly employed the sound-group [wɔ] or [wɒ], for the earlier [wɑ]; whereas the change was irregular in the eighteenth century it was regular in the nineteenth. In American English the irregularity still persists. Some of us say [ɑ] in the words [wɑdl], [wɑd], [wɑləp]; many of us in [wɑʃ] (*wash*); and most of us in [wɑtə] (*water*). Probably

American English will eventually work its way to uniformity as the English of the mother country has already done.'' There is, however, another influence which may prevent this—our tendency to unround the [w]. This is a part of a very widespread drift in our American speech which is practically doing away with lip-rounding. If this continues, all [ə]'s and [ɒ]'s will tend to become [ɑ]'s. At present, however, the pronunciations [wɑʃ] and [wɑtə] for *wash* and *water* strike many Americans as provincial.

It has already been said that pronouncing the postdentals [t], [d], [n], [l], [r], with the tongue turned back to the hard palate greatly changes the adjacent vowels. Examples of this vowel change are seen in the pronunciations of such words as *American, very, lyric, spirit, telephone, lady,* when these words are pronounced with inversions of the consonant. It is easy to perceive this assimilation of the vowels to the inverted position of the consonants in reading the following sentence with the tip of the tongue turned back to the hard palate in forming all post-dentals:

bɪhoʊld ðə lɪlɪz əv ðə fiːld haʊ ðeɪ groʊ | ðeɪ tɒɪl nɒt niˑðər du ðeɪ spɪn | jet aɪ seɪ ʌntʊ ju ðət sɒləmən ɪn ɒl hɪz glɔrɪ wəz nɒt əreɪd laɪk wʌn əv ðiz |·|

Similarly, the use of an initial dark [l] changes the following vowel. In general, any faulty formation of the consonants has a marked effect upon the character of the contiguous vowels.

D. Assimilations Classified as to Manner of Articulation or Emission of Breath

1. *Changes Affecting Plosive Combinations*

(a) *Two Consecutive Plosives.*—When a plosive is doubled, as in the word *bookcase*, there are not really two steps, but one, made with a prolongation of the pause between the closure and the release. In this word *bookcase*, for instance, the first [k] is represented by the pressure of the back of the tongue against the hard palate; the closure is held for a relatively long time; then comes the release, which represents the second [k]. Compare [bʊkkeɪs] with [bʊkeɪ] (*bouquet*).

A similar modification occurs with two different plosives, whether they occur in the same words as [æpt] (*apt*), [askt] (*asked*), [sægd] (*sagged*), [rʊbd] (*robbed*), or in two consecutive words as [hʊt drɪŋk] (*hot drink*), [bɪg kæts] (*big cats*), [sæd keɪs] (*sad case*).

This form of assimilation may be briefly defined thus: when two plosives follow one another, only one explosion takes place, the first consonant being represented by the closure, and the second by the release. This assimilation is according to the phonetic principle that "when two consecutive sounds have certain articulatory movements in common, these movements are generally executed only once."

(*b*) *A Plosive Followed by a Lateral.*—When a plosive is followed by a lateral, the plosive is not released in the usual way: it is held for an instant, and the air is then emitted at the sides of the tongue. An instance of this is heard in the word [ʃʌtl] (*shuttle*); here we have the pressure for the [t] and the lateral release for the [l]. In this case, since the tip of the tongue is in the same place for both, it naturally does not change for the [l]. In [fɪkl] (*fickle*), however, the closure is made with the back of the tongue against the soft palate and without the vibration of the vocal cords; the tip is then pressed against the teeth ridge, the vocal cords are brought into vibration, and the voiced breath is released at the sides of the tongue. In the word [eɪbl] (*able*) the air is checked at the lips and then released at the sides of the tongue and at the lips simultaneously. In all these cases it is difficult for untrained muscles to make this articulation quickly and smoothly, and for that reason the words in question are often pronounced with a glide before the [l], so that they become [ʃʌtəl], [fɪkəl], [eɪbəl]. This is a form of drawl and should be avoided. Care should be taken also to prevent inversion of the tongue for the [l].

(c) *A Plosive Followed by a Nasal.*—When a plosive is followed by a nasal, the stop is made in the usual way and held an instant while the soft palate is lowered; the air is then emitted through the nasal passages. Examples of this are heard in the words [mʌtn] (*mutton*), [sʌdn] (*sudden*), [ʃeɪkn] (*shaken*), [hæpn] (*happen*). Here also care must be taken to prevent the insertion of a vowel between the plosive and the nasal, and the inversion of the tongue in forming the post-dental consonants.

(d) *A Plosive Followed by a Fricative.*—When a plosive is followed by a fricative, the closure is made, the breath is held back for a moment at that point, and is then released through the narrow passage of the following fricative, as in the words [hæts] (*hats*), [hætʃ] (*hatch*), [bʌdz] (*buds*), [bʌdʒ] (*budge*), and [dʒʌdʒ] (*judge*). The sounds in these combinations are so closely welded together that by some phoneticians they are considered to be single sounds and are called *affricates*.

2. *Nasalization*

One of the most common types of assimilation in American English is nasalization. Its effects are most noticeable in vowels, though consonants also are often nasalized. This assimilation is caused by the influence of [m], [n], or [ŋ] on the sound that precedes or follows it. In the assimilation [meɪ̃d] (*made*), for instance, the soft palate, which has been lowered for [m], is not raised quickly enough to prevent the nasalization of the [eɪ]. In the pronunciation [tæ̃n] (*tan*) the soft palate is lowered too soon and part of the air stream allowed to pass through the nose, so that the [æ] is nasalized.

This assimilation occurs in a slight degree with even good speakers in America; but when allowed to excess, especially if it is accompanied by muscular strain, it becomes extremely unpleasant. The student is recommended to make a special effort to avoid it. To do so, exercises for gaining control of the soft palate are important, sluggishness and rigidity of the velum being equally common causes of this form of nasality. It is also important to cultivate the habit of directing the air through the mouth. It is most important and most difficult of all to train the ear to recognize nasalization. Until nasalized sounds are recognized as such, the habit will never be completely overcome.

Recognition of Assimilations in Good Speech

According to whether or not assimilations have become recognized elements in speech, they may be classified as *established* and *accidental*. An assimilation that has been generally accepted by good speakers, like the change of [soʊldjə(r)] (*soldier*) to [soʊldʒə(r)], is an established assimilation. The voicing of [t] between two voiced sounds, as in [ʃʌd ʌp] for [ʃʌt ʌp] (*shut up*), is an instance of the accidental type. Other accidental assimilations are [oʊpm] for [oʊpn] (*open*); [beɪkŋ] for [beɪkn] (*bacon*); [gʊbbaɪ] for [gʊdbaɪ] (*goodby*); and [wʊdʒə] for [wʊd ju] (*would you*).

Since there is no absolute authority in English pronunciation, it is often a question of some difficulty to decide what assimilations are established. This can be settled only by cultivation of one's sense of hearing and by acquiring the habit of observing the pronunciation of persons whose speech one considers good enough to serve as a standard.

It is often difficult to know how far we are justified in using assimilations that are frequently employed though not absolutely established. It is well to remember that many of these relaxed forms are reasonably acceptable in rapid and familiar speech and yet are quite out of place in formal speaking or in the reading of poetry or elevated prose. One of the most common types of assimilation—that from [dj],

and [tj] to [dʒ] and [tʃ], as in the expressions *did you* ([dɪd ju],
[dɪd ʒə]), *didn't you* ([dɪdnt ju], [dɪdntʃə]), *that year* ([ðæt
jɪə(r)], [ðætʃɪə(r)]), etc.—is to be avoided for reasons of
euphony, since it tends greatly to increase the already
excessive number of sibilants in our language. Too much
assimilation makes speech slovenly and difficult to understand; the speech of drunken persons and of the mentally
deficient are examples of assimilation carried to an extreme.
Too little assimilation, on the other hand, makes speech
pedantic and ineffective. It is for each person to fit himself by ear training and observation to find the golden
mean which makes speech clear-cut and beautiful yet easy
and natural.

OMISSION AND INSERTION OF SOUNDS

Omission of Sounds

There are certain sound combinations which for one or
or another reason present special difficulties to the speaker.
This matter of difficulty, however, must be regarded, not as
absolute and universal, but as more or less relative and individual. Certain sounds and combinations of sounds may be
easy for one race or one generation and difficult for another;
or easy for most speakers and hard for particular individuals;
or easy for persons to whom they are familiar and difficult
for persons to whom they are strange.

1. *Simplification of Consonant Groups*

The English language has an unusually large number of
consonant groups which not only foreigners but most native
speakers find difficult, at least in rapid speech. As a result,
the whole history of the language has been a gradual simplification of these groups—sometimes, as has already been explained, by assimilation, very often by the omission of one or
more sounds. The earlier forms of the words *best* and *last*

were [bɛtst] and [lɑtst], but they were soon reduced to [bɛst] and [last]. (In careless speech they are still further simplified to [bes] and [las] or [læs] or [lɑs]).

In certain periods of our history there has been great laxity, and in others extreme care, in pronunciation. For several centuries following the Norman Conquest little attention was given to the pronunciation of the English language. During this time an enormous number of simplifications occurred. On the other hand, the last part of the eighteenth century and nearly all of the nineteenth were characterized in England, and to a lesser degree in America, by an anxious effort for accuracy in speech. The tendency, as H. C. Wyld says, was "toward the regular and solemn and away from the cursory and colloquial."

During this period the fetish of pronouncing according to the spelling developed. As a result, many of the relaxed forms of an earlier happy-go-lucky period were replaced by pronunciations which conformed more nearly to the spelling. Many of the simplified pronunciations, however, have survived: as [krɪsməs] for *Christmas*, but [krɪstjən] or [krɪstʃən] for *Christian*; [heɪsn] for *hasten*; [rʌsl] for *rustle*; [raɪt] for *wright* and *write*; [θɔt] for *thought*; [hu] for *who*; [ni] for *knee*; [noʊm] for *gnome*; [læm] for *lamb*; [kɑm] for *calm*; and (though not universally) [fɑm] for *farm*.

All of these changes with the exception of the last are universal in the usage of good speakers at the present time. Many other simplifications are often heard, some of which are more or less generally accepted: examples are [sədʒɛst] for *suggest* [sʌgdʒɛst] ([sədʒɛst] is now the more usual pronunciation); [eɪts] for *eighths* [eɪtθs]; [dʒʌs] for *just* [dʒʌst]; [dɪrɛklɪ] for *directly* [dɪrɛktlɪ]; [nɛks] for *next* [nɛkst]; [kɛp] for *kept* [kɛpt]; [ask] or [ast] for *asked* [ɑskt].

This word *asked* is typical. The combination of a particularly difficult post-dental like [s] with the velar plosive [k] and the post-dental plosive [t] requires so many movements that only a well-trained tongue can make them all in rapid speech without a definite effort. The articulation is accordingly eased in the speech of many persons by elimination of either the [k] or the [t]. It is an interesting point in this connection that although many persons are not seriously offended by the omission of the [k] in very rapid speech, most good speakers are grievously tormented by the dropping of the [t]. Many persons are equally annoyed by the omission of the [t] in *kept*; the dropping of the [t] in *just* and *next*, however, is more apt to pass unnoticed, though it may make the judicious grieve.

The wholesale dropping of final consonants suggests that the English language may be tending toward a condition similar to that of the French in the elimination of final consonants.

In regard to these simplifications of pronunciation, it is for each person to decide how far he wishes to go along the easiest way. But it should be remembered that as it is the consonants that give definition to speech, too great laxity in regard to them makes for unclear articulation. An element of courtesy, too, enters into the matter—that is, an obligation to take pains ourselves in order to save trouble for our hearers. In speaking to a large audience, in acting any but vulgar rôles, and in reading poetry or literary prose it is well to give most consonant groups their full value.

2. *Omission of* [r]

The question of the omission of the [r] when final or followed by another consonant is one of great difficulty, especially since discussions concerning the matter are apt to be colored by emotional reactions. For an amusingly detached and historically accurate account of the [r], the student is referred to Professor Charles Grandgent's essay "The Dog's Letter," in his *Old and New*.

Briefly, the history seems to be this: In the parent stock

of European languages the [r] was evidently a very vigorous sound, made perhaps by a strong trilling of the inverted tip of the tongue. Gradually the tongue tip assumed its more natural place of articulation, that is, against the teeth ridge; and still more gradually the violence of the trill was abated, though in Italian it is still vigorous. In French and German the sound was softened by being made with the uvula; in both these languages at the present time final [r] is very weak. In English the trill became less and less vigorous until it was finally reduced to one tap (or more recently to a fricative glide consonant) when initial or between vowels, and was eliminated entirely when final or before a consonant. In the local dialects of certain parts of England and in the accepted speech of a large part of the United States, a form of the inverted [r] is still retained in all positions.

As a matter of fact, however, few Americans do pronounce a consonantal [r] when it is final or before a consonant. To illustrate this the word *are* will serve. If it were to be pronounced as spelled (omitting, of course, the final *e*, which has long been silent), the [ɑ] would be formed with the tongue flat in the mouth, the tip being behind the lower front teeth. The tip of the tongue would then be raised to the teeth ridge (or to the hard palate) to form the [r]. But in the speech of most Americans who say they "pronounce their final *r*'s," something quite different happens. The tongue, instead of taking the [ɑ] position and then going directly to the [r] position, forms the [ɑ] with the tip turned back toward the hard palate; the tip is then drawn a little farther back to form the [r].

Still other speakers who maintain that they "pronounce their *r*'s" make the [ɑ] with the back of the tongue raised; for the [r], the back is raised still farther. The acoustic effect of this sound is very similar to that of the [r] made with the tongue turned back. To anyone unaccustomed to these pronunciations the effect is not that of a vowel followed by a consonant, but of a peculiar form of diphthong-ized [ɑ].

The positions of the tongue required for producing these inverted sounds change the shape of the oral cavity in such a way as to interfere with the full resonant quality associated with the vowel [ɑ] and to substitute for this a comparatively dull and unmusical tone. Besides, the articulation is usually accompanied by considerable tension at the back of the tongue, which has an unpleasant effect on the tone of the voice. For these reasons this inverted vowel is not generally popular outside of the area where it prevails. But it is the accepted pronunciation in that large part of the United States between the Hudson and the Rockies and north of the Ohio River and as such must be considered in any study of American sounds.

Insertion of Sounds

1. To Ease the Pronunciation of Difficult Consonant Groups

Certain groups of sounds are simplified by the addition of a sound: for instance, [æŋʃəs] (anxious) becomes [æŋkʃəs] and [sɛns] (sense) becomes [sɛnts]. In [æŋʃəs] five changes are necessary in going from [ŋ] to [ʃ];ᐟ for [ŋ] is made with the vocal cords tense, the soft palate lowered, lips neutral, back of tongue pressed against the soft palate, and tip resting behind the lower front teeth; whereas [ʃ] is made with vocal cords relaxed, soft palate raised, lips rounded, back of tongue lowered, and tip raised against the teeth ridge. To make instantly so great a number of changes as this is practically impossible except for a well-trained speech mechanism, and it is easier to make them a few at a time. For this reason many speakers raise the soft palate and relax the vocal cords before lowering the tongue. When the tongue is taken away in preparation for the [ʃ], there is a breathed explosion [k], and the word becomes [æŋkʃəs].

Such easings, though frowned upon by purists, are so common that they may almost be considered the accepted form in this country, especially in rapid speech. There are many other interpolations, however, with regard to which this is not true. Very few educated persons approve of such forms as [æθəlɛtɪk], [ʌmbərɛlə], [hʊaɪəl], [spuəl], [θɪmbəl], [rɪðəm], and [kæzəm] for *athletic, umbrella, while, spool, thimble, rhythm,* and *chasm,* though the last five are frequently used even by fairly good speakers. The pronunciation of [sɛvən] *(seven)* for [sɛvn] is also common. [smɜ(r)nə] *(Smyrna)* is sometimes pronounced [səmɜ(r)nə]. Professor Ortel in his *Lectures on the Study of Languages* speaks of having often heard Dwight Street in New Haven pronounced [dəwaɪt].

2. *To Avoid the Coming Together of Two Vowels*

Analogous to the insertion of a vowel between two consonants is the use of a consonant between two vowels. The coming together of two vowels (called a *hiatus*—for example, *clawing* [klɔɪŋ]) is difficult for most speakers, and the English race from Anglo-Saxon days has been especially impatient of it. In Old English, hiatus within a word was regularly avoided by contraction or by elision of an unaccented vowel. Moden English shows the same tendency to avoid hiatus, whether within a word or between words, and uses a variety of means for this purpose. The most common of these is the insertion of a consonant.

(a) *Insertion of* [r].—The most familiar example of an intrusive consonant is perhaps the use of an [r] in such expressions as [ðɪ aɪdɪər ɒv ɪt] *(the idea of it)* when the first of the two consecutive vowels is the neutral [ə]. This use of the [r] is the easier to account for since sounding a final [r] before a word beginning with a vowel is usual even among persons who do not regularly sound their final [r]'s. Many persons do not seriously object to the intrusive [r] after a neutral vowel, but nearly everyone dislikes such expressions as [aɪ sɔr ɪt] (*I saw it*). Since any form of the intrusive [r] is offensive to many persons, it is better wholly to avoid its use.

(*b*) *Insertion of the Semi-Vowel* [j] *or* [w].—When a front vowel or one of the diphthongs that end in [ɪ]—[eɪ], [aɪ], [ɒɪ]—is followed by another vowel, the hiatus is often avoided by the use of the semi-vowel [j]. Examples are [flaɪjɪŋ], [haɪjə(r)], [hijə(r)], [krijeɪtə(r)], [θriɪjɪn wʌn], for *flying, higher, here, creator, three in one.*

After a back vowel or one of the diphthongs that end in [ʊ]—[aʊ], [oʊ]—the hiatus is often avoided by raising the tongue to the position of the semi-vowel [w], as in the pronunciations [floʊwɪŋ], [flaʊwə(r)], [duwɪŋ], [haʊ waɪ ðeɪ], for *flowing, flower, doing, how are they.*

(*c*) *Insertion of a Glottal Plosive.*—The use of these semi-vowels, though slightly less noticeable than the use of [r], is not considered good articulation. Many persons in attempting to avoid one of these intrusive consonants use a glottal plosive, as in [ðɪ ʔaɪdɪə], [krɪʔeɪt], [aɪ sɔ ʔə mæn], for *the idea, create, I saw a man.* This is especially undesirable, for although to untrained ears the glottal plosive does not suggest an interpolated consonant, its use gives a tense and unpleasant quality to the voice.

(*d*) *Other Methods.*—Certain other methods of easing the pronunciation of two consecutive vowels will for convenience be mentioned here.

When the first of two vowels is an unstressed [ɪ], as in the suffixes *-ious, -eous, -ial, -ion,* this vowel is often replaced by the semi-vowel [j], as in [tidjəs] for [tidɪəs] (*tedious*); [raɪtjəs], or by assimilation [raɪtʃəs], for [raɪtɪəs] (*righteous*); [bestjəl] or [bestʃəl] for [bestɪəl] (*bestial*); [bətæljən] for [bətæ1ɪən] (*battalion*). These forms are now considered correct, and the earlier forms are regarded as pedantic.

Still another method of avoiding hiatus is by changing the order of sounds so that a following consonant is brought between the vowels, as in the pronunciation [ɛrɪənɔt] for [ɛərənɔt] (*aeronaut*). This pronunication, though frequently heard, is not recognized as standard.

The difficulty of pronouncing two contiguous vowels is often met in the easiest way of all—by eliminating one of them. In some cases, as [haɪdʒin] for [haɪdʒiin] (*hygiene*), the simplification has been generally accepted. In other instances it is frowned on, as in [dʒɪŋgrəfɪ] for [dʒɪŋgrəfɪ] (*geography*), [poʊm] for [poʊɪm] (*poem*), and [poʊtrɪ], for [poʊɪtrɪ] (*poetry*).

All students of speech should be able to pronounce combinations of vowels, as well as of consonants, clearly and smoothly. Abundant exercises for practice on vowel and consonant groups are given in Part II.

ISOLATIVE CHANGES

There are certain changes of sounds in connected speech that do not seem to be the result of assimilation or indeed of economy of time and effort. They are accounted for by some authorities as being the result of a general drift in the language, the causes of which are not at present perfectly understood.

1. *Changes in Position of the Tongue*

An example of such a change is the raising or lowering or the advancing or retracting of vowels. Such changes have apparently been going on in our language from the start. At the beginning of the Modern English period the vowel in such words as *hate* and *came* was still pronounced as in *calm*, but it was gradually raised to the [e] position. At the same time the vowel in such words as *see* and *tree* (which had been [e]) was raised to the [i] position. At present, in America at least, the opposite change is taking place in certain vowels. The [e] in the diphthong [eɪ] as in *day, pale,* and *same* is often lowered even into the [ɛ] phoneme. Such changes, because they seem not to be the result of the influence of neighboring sounds, are called *isolative*.

2. *Changes in Regard to Nasalization*

Another type of isolative change is the tendency to nasalize vowels even when they are not in proximity with a nasal consonant. Such pronunciations as [aʊ̃t] or [æʊ̃t] or even [ɛʊ̃t] for [aʊt] (*out*) may be considered isolative and due to rigidity in the muscles of the tongue, throat, and soft palate. Some forms of nasality seem to be due to a sluggishly relaxed soft palate.

3. *Changes Due to a Tendency to Substitute a Glottal Plosive for True Plosive Sounds*

A tendency which is growing both in England and in America is the use of the glottal plosive in place of one of the other plosives, especially [t]. Only persons whose attention has been called to the matter will realize the extent of this substitution in such expressions as [ɔ raɪʔ] (or even [ɔʔ raɪʔ]), [gʊdnaɪʔ], [hʊɒʔ wɒz ɪʔ], [ðæʔ wʌn], for *all right, good night, what was it,* and *that one.* Its use seems to be particularly common before [w], [n], and [m] and at the end of a word. This substitution seems to be the result of a general drift in American speech toward an increasing lack of vigor in the use of the tongue and lips. The glottal plosive in these cases is compensatory articulation—that is, the air, instead of being checked at the lips or the back or tip of the tongue, is checked at the vocal cords. This habit makes for excessively unclear articulation and backward tone production.

4. *Tendency toward Instability of Vocal Organs in Forming Long Vowels*

A general characteristic of our language from earliest times has been the instability of long vowels. There has been a tendency not only to raise or lower, to retract or advance them, but also to diphthongize them. For instance, when the vowel [e] was raised to the [i] position, as has been described above, the original [i] in such words as *write* (Anglo-Saxon *writan*) underwent a diphthongizing process. The first element was begun lower and lower in the mouth until at the present time the diphthong starts in the [a] position. In some parts of the country this process has continued still further, and many persons pronounce the diphthong [ɑɪ]. Practically all long vowels in the language are more or less diphthongized in ordinary speech.

5. *Tendency to Substitute the Post-Dental for the Velar Nasal*

Another change often considered isolative is the use of the post-dental nasal [n] for the velar nasal [ŋ] in participles and verbal nouns—the so-called "dropping of *g*." This seems to have been an almost universal speech habit in early Modern English, but in the eighteenth century, under the influence of printing and the desire for better speech, it gradually came to be considered provincial. It is still very general in certain rural communities, particularly in New England and the South.

6. *Tendency to Omit the* [h]

The question is often asked why the dropping of *h*'s so common among all but the most cultivated in England is seldom heard in America. The answer is that this instability in regard to the [h] did not become prevalent in England until after the settlement of America, and this country had so stable an [h] that it was not disturbed by the uncertainty in England. Australia, which was colonized after the English [h] had become unsettled, has the same difficulty as England in the matter.

However, the [h] in the pronouns *he, his, her,* and the auxiliaries *had* and *have* is usually dropped in unstressed

positions in America as well as in England, as the following
section on weak forms will show. Failure to use the weakened forms of these words is a frequent cause of pedantry and
lack of rhythm in reading and speaking.

Emphasis

Since the purpose of combining sounds in speech is to
express thought, it is obvious that the words that express
the main ideas should be made to stand out. In the sentence, "Faithful are the wounds of a friend, but the kisses
of an enemy are deceitful," the words that carry the thought
are, of course, *faithful, wounds, friend, kisses, enemy,
deceitful*. The others are simply connecting words, none of
which, except *but*, is important. It goes without saying that
the thought-carrying words should be read with greater
emphasis—that is, with greater stress or force, with greater
slowness, with a change of pitch or of tone quality, or with a
pause before or after them.

Rhythm

Now if the sentence is read naturally, that is, with
emphasis on the important ideas, it is found to have a definite
rhythm. All normal speech has a more or less rhythmical
character. When the brain and the body are properly
coördinated in speech, this rhythmical accent and the
thought-accent correspond. The same is true in good reading—in good reading, that is, of well-written prose or poetry,
for unfortunately not all writing has this organic rhythm.

Weak Forms of Vowels

In order to keep the rhythm in speaking or reading, it is
necessary not only that the main points be given greater
prominence, but also that the unimportant ones be definitely

put into the background.   This is done partly by lightening the stress on the insignificant words and saying them quickly. As a result of this subordinating process the vowels in the unstressed words and syllables are reduced from their original value to *weak forms*, usually to the neutral vowel [ə], but sometimes to [ɪ] or [ʊ].

If, in reading the sentence quoted above, all the vowels were given their full value, the sentence would be:

feɪθfʊl ɑɪ ðiː wundz ɒv eɪ frɛnd bʌt ðiː kɪsez ɒv æn ɛnɛmɪ ɑɪ diːsiːtfʊl

So read, the sentence would lose both its emphasis and its rhythm, and such reading would soon exhaust both reader and listener.   If, however, the passage is read:

feɪθfəl ə ðə wundz əv ə frɛnd bət ðə kɪsɪz əv ən ɛnɛmɪ ə diːsiːtfəl

the natural stress of the voice coincides with proper sub-ordination of the thought, and the reading process is not only easier for the reader, but clearer and more pleasing for the listener.

Some of the most common weak vowel forms are listed below:

Pronouns:	Strong form	Weak forms
he	[hiː]	[i], [hɪ], [ɪ]
her	[hɜɪ(r)]	[hə(r)], [ə]
she	[ʃiː]	[ʃɪ]
his	[hɪz]	[ɪz]
some	[sʌm]	[səm]
that	[ðæt]	[ðət]
them	[ðɛm]	[ðəm], [əm]
their	[ðɛə(r)]	[ðɛ(r)], [ðə(r)]
they're	[ðeɪ ə(r)]	[ðɛə(r)], [ðə(r)]
your	{ [jʊə(r)] } { [jɒə(r)] }	[jʊ], [jə(r)]

PREPOSITIONS:	STRONG FORM	WEAK FORMS
at	[æt]	[ət]
by	[baɪ]	[bə], [bɪ]
for	[fɔ(ː)(r)], [fʊə(r)]	[fə(r)]
from	[frɒm]	[frəm]
of	[ɒv]	[əv]
to	[tuː]	[tʊ], [tə]
upon	[ʌpɒn]	[əpɒn], [əpen], [əpn]
into	[ɪntu]	[ɪntʊ], [ɪntə]

CONJUNCTIONS:		
and	[ænd]	[ənd], [ən], [nd], [n]
as	[æz]	[əz]
but	[bʌt]	[bət]
for	[fɔː(r)], [fʊə(r)]	[fə(r)]
nor	[nɔː(r)], [nʊə(r)]	[nə(r)]
or	[ɔː(r)], [ʊə(r)]	[ə(r)]
than	[ðæn]	[ðən]
that	[ðæt]	[ðət]

VERBS:		
am	[æm]	[əm], [m]
are	[ɑː(r)]	[ə(r)]
can	[kæn]	[kən], [kn]
could	[kʊd]	[kəd]
do	[duː]	[dʊ], [də], [d]
does	[dʌz]	[dəz]
had	[hæd]	[həd], [əd], [d]
has	[hæz]	[həz], [əz], [z], [s]
must	[mʌst]	[məst]
shall	[ʃæl]	[ʃəl], [ʃl]
should	[ʃʊd]	[ʃəd], [ʃd], [ʃt]
was	[wɒz]	[wəz]
were	[wɜː(r)]	[wə(r)]
will	[wɪl]	[l]
would	[wʊd]	[wəd], [d]

ARTICLES:		
a	[eɪ]	[ə]
an	[æn]	[ən]
the	[ðiː]	[ðɪ], [ðə]

ADVERB:		
there	[ðɛə(r)]	[ðə(r)]

It is of the greatest importance to use the weak forms of these words in speaking and reading except where for some special reason they are emphatic.   The idea of many teachers that clearness and effectiveness are achieved by giving full value to every word and every syllable is contrary to the principle of economy of attention: first, because if the attention is wasted on words that have little or no meaning, there is just so much less for the important words; and second, because attention goes in rhythmical waves, and if words are spoken without rhythm, it is much harder to attend to them.

This rule of using weakened vowels applies not only to words, but to syllables as well.   In the sentence already quoted the suffix of the word *deceitful* (which would, as the independent word *full*, be pronounced [fʊl]) is weakened to [fəl].   The prefix also, instead of being given its full value [di], is weakened to [dɪ], so that we have the form [dɪsitfəl]. The pronunciation [disitfʊl] not only sounds slow, heavy, and pedantic, but ruins the rhythm of the sentence.

From earliest times our language (as contrasted, for example, with the French) has been characterized by a very strong stress on the important syllables.   This is doubtless one of the chief reasons for the use of the weakened vowel so prevalent in English, since the vocal organs save themselves trouble after the vigorous effort of the stressed syllable.   In the sentence "Can he go?" we have three forms according to whether the *can* receives the main stress, or is next to the accented syllable, or is two removed from it (in which case it receives a slight accent): thus, ['kæn hi goʊ], [kn'hi goʊ], and [kən hi 'goʊ].[2]   Similarly we have ['kɒnvɪkt] (*con'vict*), [rekn] (*reckon*), and lastly [kən'vɪkt] (*convict'*) where the vowel of the prefix retains some value because of its etymological importance.

---

[2] Phoneticians usually place the stress mark (') before the accented syllable, as [rɪ'fɜ], [repju'teɪʃən], ['ædmɪrəbl], etc.

Syllable Stress, or Accent

The question of syllable stress or accent is one of the most difficult features of our language. In general, English stress is recessive, that is, it tends toward the beginning of the word. An instance of this recessive tendency is seen in the word *automobile*.[3] When it was first introduced into the language, it retained its accent on the last syllable, and the usual pronunciation was [ɔtomo'bil]. Very soon, however, the stress receded to the penult, and many dictionaries still give as the preferred pronunciation [ɔto'moʊbɪl]. Now it has receded still further and ['ɔtomobil] is the favorite pronunciation, at least in the groups in which we have tested it.

But the matter is unfortunately not so simple as this, for there are several influences in our language which prevent the uniform working of this tendency.

The first of these is the influence of the Old English or Anglo-Saxon system of root accent. To this day words of Anglo-Saxon stock are stressed on the root syllable: examples are *hand*some, *hand*ily, two-*hand*ed, and second*hand*.

The second is the influence of the French progressive system. A good many anglicized French words like *prestige*, *caprice*, *machine*, still retain their final accent. In regard to others there is uncertainty: *chauffeur*, *garage*, *valet*, are accented sometimes in the English and sometimes in the French fashion. Many words, like *crochet*, *croquet*, *sachet*, which with us are still accented on the last syllable, are accented on the first syllable in England.

The third influence is that of the mutable accent of Latin. English words of Latin origin preserve their tendency to shift the accent, so that we have groups like *mut*able, mu*t*ation, and muta*bil*ity; *con*stitute, con*sti*tuent, constit*u*tion, constitution*al*ity.

---

[3] The French accent is progressive—that is, it tends toward the end of the word.

The fourth influence is that of sentence rhythm, especially in words of level stress, as: *sixteen*, but, "It happened in *six*teen-*eight*" and "She is sweet six*teen*"; *red cross*, but "He contributed to the Red *Cross*" and "A *Red* Cross knight forever kneeled to a lady in his shield."

The fifth influence is the preservation of the distinction between two uses of the same word, as *A*ugust, au*gust*; *fre*quent, fre*quent*; *sub*ject, sub*ject*.

The sixth is the shifting of accent for contrast or special emphasis: as, im*prov*ident, but "I didn't say *prov*ident, I said *im*provident"; and *ab*solutely, but (sometimes) "I believe her abso*lute*ly."

And lastly, there is the difficulty, especially for an untrained tongue, of saying a number of unaccented syllables in succession. This develops a secondary accent, as *labora-tory*, *depart*ment*al*; or leads to the dropping out of a syllable or two, as ['læbrətrɪ]; or pulls the accent forward again, as is observable in the growing tendency to such pronunciations as con*dol*ence, la*ment*able, hos*pit*able, ex*quis*ite.

The student who wants to speak well should master these general principles of accent and train his ears to recognize the exceptional cases, so that he may be able to decide intelligently whether he prefers ['læbərə'torɪ] or ['læbrətərɪ] or ['læbrətrɪ] and whether he wishes to say ['ɛkskwɪsɪt] or [ək'skwɪsɪt].

The matter of word stress will be discussed more fully in later chapters,

CHAPTER VIII

FIRST PRINCIPLES OF GROUP DISCUSSION

Need for a Technique of Group Discussion

LIFE is increasingly a complicated affair of demands and obligations. It is no longer possible, as it was in colonial days, for human beings to live in comparative isolation and independence. But if individual liberty is in some respects curtailed by this modern scheme of living, it is in others greatly increased. To an extent never before dreamed, the average man, provided he has the necessary wisdom and skill, can control the conditions of his own life and help others to control theirs. The keynote of life today is not *independence* but *interdependence*.

One of the most important skills for this complicated modern life is the ability to help in formulating such group opinions and group plans as will ensure for each individual the greatest liberty consistent with the general good. One would naturally suppose that a group of persons who are discussing a question in which they are all interested would have only one object—to arrive at the truth. In reality such a condition is extremely rare. Most of us, even in matters where it is vitally important for us to reach the truth, are more eager to prove ourselves right and our fellows wrong than to build up a group opinion that would be nearer the truth than the guess of any individual member. Similarly, in discussing a plan the average person is more interested in carrying through his pet project than in helping to formulate a course of action that would represent the mature judgment of the group and thus have, since it reflected, in some measure at least, the thought and desires of all, the best possible chance of winning whole-hearted support.

Why is this true, even among intelligent persons? Partly because one of the most deeply ingrained traits of human nature is that of forming judgments hastily and then cling-ing to them tenaciously. Having once uttered an opinion, no matter how little it may represent our sober judgment, we feel that our honor is involved in proving it wise and just. Everett Dean Martin says in his *Psychology*: "Intelligent public discussion is almost impossible for the reason that people ordinarily are not using their language habits to solve their problems. They are striving to vin-dicate their principles, not to verify their hypotheses." In some of the mediæval lists of the Seven Deadly Sins a promi-nent place is given to self-justification.

A little honest self-examination will convince most of us that one of the hardest things we ever have to do is to say, even in a small matter, "You are right and I am wrong." No doubt one reason for this is that our opinions are in the main so insecurely founded and so jerry-built that we voice them with tremendous assurance to cover our self-distrust, and having thus boldly asserted them, we feel humiliated if we are obliged to retract or modify them. Chiefly, how-ever, our dogmatism and contentiousness are due to the fact that almost never in the history of the world has there been a system of education of which the main purpose was to give human beings the desire and the ability to think together for the common good.

Perhaps the sole instance in which the method was ever given a fair trial was in the ancient republic of Athens. Thucydides puts into the mouth of Pericles these notable words: "We differ from other states in regarding the man who holds aloof from public life, not as 'quiet,' but as use-less; we decide and debate, carefully and in person, all matters of policy, holding, not that words and deeds go ill together, but that acts are foreordained to failure when undertaken undiscussed. For we are noted for being at once the most adventurous in action and most reflective beforehand." [1]

It is strange that so signal an example of the value of public discussion should have been so little followed. In the Middle Ages, it is true, the schoolmen tried to arrive at truth by discussion, but they were more concerned with saving their lonely souls than with building up a better world order. Hence their discussions became more and more formal in character and increasingly barren of results. In recent years there has been a growing realization that the right kind of training in this subject is necessary if democracy is to function successfully,[2] and a number of educators have emphasized the importance of developing what is, after all, a specialized and difficult skill—that of taking effective part in group discussion.

Preparations for Gaining a Technique

How can this skill be developed? Before the actual training begins, it is important that the student gain the right point of view toward group discussion. To achieve this requires not only a clear understanding of its purpose, but also a realization of the most constructive attitudes toward the other members of the group and toward his own handicaps in discussion.

Understanding the Purpose of Group Discussion

As has already been said, the purpose of group discussion is to reach a consensus of opinion or to formulate a plan.

---

[1] Quoted by F. C. Young, "Commonwealth Conference."
[2] See the books of Graham Wallas, M. P. Follett, Everett Dean Martin, H. A. Overstreet, A. D. Sheffield, F. C. Young, and John Dewey, listed in the bibliography for this chapter in Section V of Part II.

In order to be a helpful member of a group one must realize that the purpose of discussion is, as Professor Sheffield points out, not to win an argument or even to effect a compromise, but to bring about a real consensus of opinion. In order that this consensus may represent the best of which the group is capable, each member should come prepared with a tentative opinion which is the result of his best thinking and should present that opinion as clearly and vigorously as possible in order to win from the group the acceptance of whatever it contains of value. He should constantly remember, however, that what is desired is not the acceptance of one person's theory, but the integration of the thought of the whole number, and that he must be ready to modify his opinion or even discard it altogether if it prove inadequate or ill-advised.

It has been said that in committees, which are perhaps the most usual sort of discussion group, two types of members are thoroughly unwelcome. The first is the person who says that he will be glad to serve and that he has exactly the plan the committee should adopt. The second is the person who says that he will be glad to serve though he has no knowledge of the subject and that he will approve whatever the others decide. A third undesirable might be added—the person who has given no thought to the matter but who speaks glibly, adding to the discussion "a vast deal of nothing."

Attitude toward Other Members of the Group

In order to take a useful part in discussion, each participant must think in terms, not of orator and audience, but of membership in a group discussing a topic in regard to which all are interested and informed.[3] This latter relationship has a number of implications. The tone to

---

[3] For this reason it is important that the group be small enough to permit everyone to participate in the discussion. Ten to twenty members make the most satisfactory number.

be desired is plain but forceful speech rather than per-fervid oratory. There is no idea that one person will be lifted above the crowd to instruct them or to dazzle them with his brilliance. Nor is there any question of opponents to be confuted. The member who differs from another is to be regarded as a co-worker who has a new and perhaps a valuable contribution to make to the discussion. To at-tempt to nullify this contribution by clever strategy instead of investigating it in a fair spirit would be contrary to the ethics and the common sense of discussion, since the purpose is not that one side shall win, but that the final decision shall represent the best thinking of the group. In order that this result may be achieved, each member should try to understand the points of view of the various factions represented and to find some principle by which these diver-gent opinions can be reconciled. To persons accustomed to the excitement of formal debate this may seem tame sport, but those who have once taken part in a genuinely fine dis-cussion find ample compensation in the pleasure of trailing down an elusive idea and in increased respect for the intelli-gence and fair-mindedness of their fellows.

Attitude toward Oneself

It follows from what has been said that one of the great differences between debate and discussion is that in debate one is chiefly concerned with understanding and exploiting the opponent's weaknesses, whereas in discussion one is mainly interested in understanding and as far as possible overcoming one's own.

In preparing, then, to take part as effectively as possible in discussion, it is well to begin by trying to find out what are the conditions that may interfere with one's success. These group themselves under two general heads—those outside oneself and those having to do with one's own nature.

Of the external conditions that may be obstacles to

success in discussion, the most common are lack of time for necessary research or thought; inability to obtain first-hand information; lack of adequate apparatus or other equipment for investigation; and, particularly in college communities, difficulty in finding a quiet place for hard thinking. Of the conditions within the individual that may hinder effectiveness in discussion, some of the most common are physical, such as poor eyesight, defective hearing, or impaired general health. Others are mental, such as stupidity, laziness, conceit, and indifference. There are also temperamental handicaps, the result of inheritance or early training: among these are political, religious, racial, and social prejudices, and extremes of conservatism and radicalism, of optimism and pessimism, of idealism and materialism. Lastly there are hindrances which result from inadequate training in the art of thought—habits of hasty generalization, carelessness in the use of terms, arguing from false analogy, and failure to get at the causes of things.

Methods of Dealing with Personal Handicaps

Even this partial list of difficulties to be surmounted is so formidable that the student may be inclined to be discouraged at the outset, but by facing the situation fairly he will find that with patience and determined effort many of these obstacles can be overcome and the others compensated for more or less satisfactorily.

External Difficulties.—Much can surely be done to offset external difficulties. Lack of time can be partly compensated for by concentration and ingenuity in the discovery of short cuts. If original documents are not to be had, copies, careful abstracts, or other reliable secondary sources are often available. Lacking adequate equipment, ingenious persons can often construct satisfactory substitutes. And a really studious person can find some quiet corner even on a college campus.

Physical Handicaps.—As to physical conditions, modern science makes almost anything possible. Glasses compensate for imperfect eyesight, mechanical devices help defective hearing, and increased knowledge concerning diet, exercise, rest, and preventive hygiene make reasonably good health possible for nearly everyone.

Mental Handicaps.—What seems to be laziness or stupidity is often merely indifference, due to lack of self-confidence or of understanding of the basic significance of the subject or its relation to the student's own problems. If he comes to see the question as vitally important to his own development, he may surprise even himself by his zeal and intelligence.

Temperamental Handicaps.—Prejudices are not easily overcome, as everyone knows who has ever striven for fair-mindedness. One reason is that we are unconsciously rather proud of them. They are often bound up with various kinds of loyalty. Often, too, they give us a sense of superiority. If, however, one really wishes to overcome these obstacles to constructive thought, he can make a beginning by carefully analyzing his particular prejudices and thereby discovering how insecurely grounded they are. "Why," he may ask himself, "do I dislike Baptists or Roman Catholics or Democrats or teachers or lawyers or socialists?" The answer will usually be that the prejudice is either an unanalyzed inheritance from parents or early associates or the result of a small number of unpleasant experiences with representatives of the group in question. Recognition of the illogical nature of prejudice, however, is not enough to uproot it. The task is an arduous one, and no one will accomplish it who does not care so much for truth that he is willing to make a determined effort to remove this obstacle to mental freedom.

With regard to such personality traits as extremes of conservatism and radicalism, optimism and pessimism, idealism and materialism, it is doubtful whether much can be accomplished except to recognize and allow for them as the scientist allows for "the margin of error" in an experiment or the archer allows for the wind in aiming his arrow.

Faults of Reasoning.—Faults of reasoning can be overcome by any intelligent person who is willing to undergo the proper discipline. Hasty generalization is the result of thoughtlessness, laziness, and the desire to shine in conversation without effort. We know two students of Z College who are frivolous, and we announce jauntily that Z College has a low standard of scholarship. When we begin really to care for the truth, we shall learn to investigate a sufficient number of typical cases before making the "inductive hazard." But with most of us the habit of hasty generalization is so ingrained that to overcome it completely will be a challenge to our best efforts.

Loose employment of terms also is due to laziness and lack of mental discipline. Really to understand the meaning of a word like *culture* or *education* or *communism* or *relativity* or *democracy* or *complex* or *personality* or *propaganda* requires much study and close thinking. Most persons use such a term without even being conscious of how little they understand it. Numberless disagreements and futile discussions are the result of misuse of words. Contestants often think they are arguing a definite point when in reality they are discussing two entirely different things. Or a person may use a word in a certain sense in one part of his argument and in quite a different sense in another part. There is no better mental training than the habit of making sure that one does not use words in vague and misleading ways. A piece of advice that cannot be too often repeated is, "Define your terms."

The habit of false analogy is closely connected with that of hasty generalization. It is well known that resemblances are more readily observed than differences. All of us, unless

we are constantly on our guard, find ourselves observing a
superficial likeness between two persons or objects or ideas
and assuming that because they are alike in this one respect,
they must be alike in general character. A student argues
that because a friend of approximately equal intelligence
can do the mathematics assignment in half an hour, he can do
the same—and his pride and class record suffer in consequence. A parent reasons that because a method of discipline works with one child, it will work with its brother
or sister—and open rebellion or hypocrisy or a broken spirit
results. The only way to correct the habit of false analogy
is to recognize that Nature never repeats herself. The
tendency to reduce individuals to categories is extremely
dangerous. It is safer to treat persons and things and ideas
as independent phenomena until they are found to be related
to others by some principle of fundamental resemblance.

But of all the obstacles to good reasoning, the deadliest
is carelessness in regard to the causal relation. We use the
word *because* many times a day, but we are usually satisfied
if we have found the most obvious and superficial reason for
the statement it purports to explain. As a matter of fact,
it is seldom that the cause of any phenomenon is simple and
immediately apparent. The ringing of an electric bell is
sometimes given as an example of the complexity of the
causal relationship. The obvious cause, the pressing of the
button, is merely the releasing cause. The wire is the conduct-
ing, and the dynamo the generating, cause. But even then the
chain is not complete. Before the button was pressed, there
was some stimulus, perhaps the contraction of certain muscles
or some glandular action, which affected a certain nerve,
which sent a message to the brain, which in turn sent a message over other nerves to the muscles of the arm and finger,
ordering them to push the button. Thus the chain of causation is seen to be as lengthy as that which led to the House
that Jack Built.   In the world of thought we often encounter

elaborate cause systems, the unraveling of which requires patient and careful investigation. Most of us are content with an explanation as easy and as inadequate as the pressing of a button.

It is a start in the right direction to recognize that for any phenomenon there is usually a chain of causation rather than a simple cause. The student who is unfamiliar with Mill's methods of testing cause and effect will do well to look them up.[4] The careful solution by Mill's methods of even one problem in causation will give him a sense of power which will encourage him to continue in this important exercise for developing his mentality.

The methods of reasoning and the fallacies connected with them are discussed at length in any good work on logic or argumentation.[5] The student who wishes to become a clear thinker and a forceful speaker will do well to learn the tests for each and to apply them to his own thinking and to that of others. Having thus sharpened his tools, he is ready to proceed intelligently to the preparation for a specific discussion, the first step of which is the formulation of a tentative opinion.

Forming a Tentative Opinion

To clear the way for constructive thinking on a given subject, unless one is very familiar with it, it is well to begin by making a careful appraisal of what one already knows and thinks about it. Here it is important to distinguish accurately between knowledge and opinion and between reasoned opinion and prejudice. After this inventory has been made, it will often be found that if anything

---

[4] In Mill's *Logic* or any of the textbooks logic or argumentation listed in the bibliography for this chapter in Section V of Part II.

[5] A particularly interesting treatment of the principles of reasoning is D. S. Robinson's *Illustrations of the Methods of Reasoning* which by examples shows the various methods in actual use.

of value is to be brought to the discussion, considerable further preparation is necessary. This preparation consists of several processes: (1) collecting material on which to base one's judgment; (2) testing and weighing this material; (3) giving it time to mature and take definite shape; (4) verifying the results of this process of "incubation"; and (5) organizing these results for effective presentation to the group.

Collecting the Material

The material on which we form our opinions and beliefs is called *evidence*. This may be obtained (*a*) from our own observation and (*b*) from reports of the observations of others.

Evidence from Personal Observation.—In collecting evidence, the student will need to overcome or compensate for such of the personal handicaps discussed above as he possesses. Prejudice and passion, quite as much as defective sight or hearing, will cause him to overlook whole groups of important facts. The inability of the average person accurately to observe and record facts is emphasized in practically all elementary books on psychology and logic. Amusing examples are given in Lippmann's *Public Opinion* and Wigmore's *Principles of Judicial Proof*.

Graham Wallas once said that most of us go about with our heads encased in boxes on the inside of which are painted pictures of human events and human characters as we conceive them, and that when we think we are seeing the world as it really is, we are merely looking at the pictures on our painted boxes. Walter Lippmann in *Public Opinion* expresses the same theory by his figure of "stereotypes." All of us, he says, have preconceived ideas of things, and we do not see them as they are because the "stereotype" comes between us and the actual object or character or event. If, for instance, we watch a dog fight and attempt to describe it afterward, we shall be very likely to alter the details unconsciously to make it more like our stereotype of a dog fight.

A group of students can easily test the reliability of their powers of observation and recall by looking briefly at a collection of miscellaneous objects and then seeing how many of them they can remember and how accurately they can describe them. A similar test can be made by attempting to describe an unusual and complicated object or an exciting scene in the theater or in real life. Comparison of the reports of several observers will show how great a number of significant facts the average person observes inaccurately or entirely overlooks.

Moreover, since it is well established that we notice chiefly the objects which in some way interest us and that we are interested only in objects of which we know something, it is obvious that our ability to collect a representative body of facts will depend greatly on the range of our interests and knowledge. Compare, for instance, the number and variety of natural phenomena observed by an Indian and by a city clerk during a walk through the woods.

Evidence from the Records of Other Observers.—In these days of the making of many books there is seldom difficulty in finding material on any subject under discussion. More often the problem is to make a wise selection from the bewildering wealth of testimony. Much time may be saved by cultivating the habit of finding out which writers on a given subject are most likely to have something of value to say. For this purpose the following tests may be applied:

1. Is the writer especially fitted by education or experience to write authoritatively on the subject in question?

2. Has he a reputation for intelligence, honesty, and reliability?

3. Is there any reason why he might be unfitted through prejudice or self-interest to be an impartial observer in this matter?

4. Has he been recently in touch with the subject so that his testimony is likely to be up to date?

After a little reading of an author one may add the further questions:

5. Are his statements consistent with one another?
6. Are they consistent with the known facts on the subject?
7. Are they consistent with probability and common sense?

Answers to the first series of questions can usually be deduced from such biographical reference books as *Who's Who* and *Who's Who in America* or from articles in magazines like *The World's Work* and *The Literary Digest*. Many periodicals have the convenient custom of giving such information concerning their contributors.

On present-day questions the recency of information is often a deciding factor in selection. For a discussion of the present economic situation in Russia, for example, it would be foolish, except for gaining the necessary historical background, to spend much time on articles written even a few years ago, no matter how learned and reliable their authors may have been.

General Suggestions.—Perhaps the most helpful plan in collecting material is to approach the quest, not with a ready-made opinion to be proved correct nor yet in a state of passive ignorance, but in an attitude of suspended judgment and with a series of questions, answers to which are to be sought as a basis for formulating a tentative opinion. Such a state of open-mindedness is of the greatest importance, no less than intelligent choice of questions.

Suppose, for instance, that the topic for discussion is: "Should this college adopt a system of student government?". The following questions might then be helpful:

1. Is the present system attended by such evils that a new one should be tried?
2. If so, would student government correct these evils?
3. Granted it would do so, would its adoption be followed by other equally undesirable results?

4. If so, is there some other plan that would correct the evils of the existing system without being attended by equally serious drawbacks?

Or a different set of questions might be investigated, as, for instance:

1. Has student government ever been tried in this college?
2. If so, what led to its being abandoned?
3. Do similar conditions exist today?
4. Does experience in colleges similar to this seem to indicate that it would be successful here?
5. What do educational authorities think about the desirability and the practicability of the system in colleges of this type?
6. Does the character of the student body lead one to believe that the plan would ensure the best results for the students themselves and for the standing of the college?

If the subject for discussion is the meaning of some term, as *education*, the search for material will be facilitated by such questions as:

1. What is the derivation and history of the word?
2. What is its logical definition, that is, *genus* and *differentia*?
3. What are its most common synonyms and how does it differ in meaning from each of these?
4. What are its antonyms?
5. What are the various types of education?
6. What are the means or processes by which it is attained?
7. What are the results of education?
8. What persons serve as examples of different types of education?

One warning about the gathering of material. Be sure that you have not overlooked any important aspect or point of view of the subject. One such omission will sometimes invalidate a carefully built up opinion. And remember that the aspects you are most likely to overlook are those toward which you are not naturally sympathetic. Here, as always, one must guard against the insidious effects of prejudice.

Recording Material.—The most satisfactory system of recording notes for such purposes as this is the use of cards. At the top of each card should be written the special topic; at the bottom, the author and title of the special reference and the page of the book or magazine in which it is found. If two or more cards are needed for one reference, they can be fastened together with a clip.

The convenience of this system is obvious. It is especially useful in that it permits the grouping of all material relating to one question and its rearrangement for refutation or any other special purpose.

Testing the Material

Having collected an adequate body of material, indeed during the whole process of gathering it, the student should test its value as evidence in forming his tentative opinion. A simple way to do this is to ask concerning each item the questions: (1) Is it true? (2) Is it pertinent? (3) Is it important?

Testing the Truth of Evidence.—In collecting material, whether the result of his own observation or of that of others, the student should be careful to include only what seems unquestionably true. Before finally accepting any statement he should ask himself whether it is consistent with the facts of the subject as he has so far established them, and with common sense and general probability. Here, perhaps more often than anywhere else in the whole process of preparation, the untrained student will be likely to go wrong. He must be constantly on his guard against the extremes of credulity and scepticism and must try in every way to develop the power of discriminating between truth and error. The greater his store of general information and experience, the more capable he will be of evaluating each separate piece of information. Even granted a fair amount of both, however, he will need to be constantly on his guard against the human failing which Virgil long ago noted—that of believing most readily what one wants to believe. The only safe course is to cultivate the detached and impartial attitude of a scientist or a judge, whose success depends largely on ability to evaluate and test the truth of evidence.

Testing the Pertinence of Evidence.—Having formed his opinion as to the trustworthiness of an alleged fact, the student should next consider whether or not it has definite bearing on the question to be decided. If he is trying to form an opinion regarding the economic situation of Russia, he will eliminate material that deals primarily with educational or religious conditions. If he keeps the basic questions in mind and does his weighing and testing as he goes along, he will not only save time in the collection of material, but have a more valuable body of evidence at the end of his search.

Testing the Importance of Evidence.—Lastly, of every piece of information the student will ask, "Is this important for the particular question under discussion?" A relatively small body of material that represents the actual and recent experience of a trained and impartial observer will have more weight with an intelligent seeker than a great deal of second-hand information and scattered testimony of doubtful witnesses. This is a point which inexperienced persons do not appreciate. They often act upon the assumption that if they have a great body of what they call "facts," their case is practically established. Nothing could be further from the truth. Indeed, the very fact that a person shows so little judgment in the selection of his material predisposes a discriminating critic to doubt his general intelligence and to give proportionately less weight to his really important evidence. A nail is much more securely driven by two or three strong blows than by a dozen taps with a tack hammer.

Reasoning about the Material

A sufficient body of trustworthy and important evidence having been collected, the next step is to derive from it answers to the questions with which the investigation started. For this purpose the cards containing the material relating to each question should be sorted out and divided into two sets according to whether the references support a negative or an affirmative answer. A process of reasoning must now decide whether the total body of evidence leads to a negative or an affirmative answer to each subordinate question and to the main point under discussion.

Here the student must be on his guard against drawing conclusions from insufficient or unrepresentative data. He may find at this stage that in order to counteract the natural and dangerous tendency toward hasty generalization, he will have to collect more evidence before forming even a tentative opinion. Take, for example, the investigation of student government described above. He may discover that in two of the five colleges he has investigated, faculty government does not seem to meet with serious opposition from the students and that it apparently maintains a satisfactory condition of affairs, whereas in the other three it seems to be accompanied by much dissatisfaction and considerable open rebellion on the part of the students. It will be evident that before any sound conclusion can be reached, more cases must be investigated.

Another pitfall to be guarded against is that involved in causation. To illustrate again from the investigation of student government. The student must make very sure that the evils attending the present system are not the result of general conditions or a legacy from some earlier régime. An effort must be made to find out whether the wholesale breaking of laws in the college in question is due to resentment against rules imposed by the administration, or to a general wave of revolt against discipline, or to the natural tendency toward license of persons who have recently come to feel themselves old enough for autonomy. Here the student must consult his evidence regarding colleges in which student government prevails to discover whether there, too, considerable delinquency in behavior is indicated.[6]

"Incubation" of an Opinion

Having subjected his evidence to this rigorous reasoning process, the student should give his mind a chance to do the kind of creative work that Graham Wallas calls "incubation." This is the result of free association in a mind which for some time has been concentrating powerfully on a body of material. It is the process by which the imagination hits upon the salient points in a mass of material and arranges them in some new and effective pattern. One reason why so many debates, discussions, and public speeches are dull and unconvincing is that the speaker has omitted this step in his preparation.

Unfortunately no very definite instruction can be offered for developing this most important skill, though helpful suggestions are given in Wallas' *The Art of Thought*, and in Dewey's *How We Think*. Writers on the subject and other creative thinkers agree that the spirit seldom moves unless a deal of very hard work has been done beforehand. In the technique of the process, however, they seem to differ materially. Some find that they are most successful in this kind of thinking when they are walking or riding or driving alone; others, when they are playing the piano; others, after they have gone to bed at night or when they first waken in the morning; still others, under the stimulation of talk with one or more intelligent persons; one writer does his most fertile thinking while he is playing solitaire. What-

---

[6] In a study of this kind the methods advocated by Mill will be found exceedingly helpful.

ever may be the best means of promoting this kind of mental activity, certain it is that no original contributions to thought occur without it.

Verification of Conclusions

Last of all, the tentative judgment thus formed should be subjected to thorough critical analysis. Are the answers to the individual questions the logical inferences from the evidence? Are they consistent with one another? Is the final result sound and constructive and uninfluenced by personal considerations or prejudices? If this kind of scrutiny can be successfully met, the student is ready to consider the way in which the opinion can be most effectively presented.

Presentation of a Tentative Opinion

It is very natural that after having given so much time and effort to formulating his tentative opinion, the student should feel a just pride and proprietorship in it and be ready to defend it against all comers. But this very natural complacency he must resist. Again he must emulate the scientist who, notwithstanding a long time spent in research on a promising theory, is quite ready to modify it or give it up altogether if he finds it does not explain all the facts of the case. The student should come to the discussion with a determination to present his contribution so clearly and effectively that it will be assured a fair hearing, but with perfect readiness also to recognize the element of truth in the opinions of others and to coöperate with them in building up a group opinion which shall include what is best in the opinions of all.

Organizing the Material

If he has prepared his contribution according to the method outlined above, his thoughts will have arranged themselves in a more or less logical order. It may be well, however, to make certain changes, looking toward an order that is psychologically as well as logically sound—that is, which considers the mental habits of the group concerned instead of being based entirely on theoretical ideas of the way in which perfectly logical minds would work. This will involve such decisions as the choice between the inductive and the deductive method of reasoning, the number and nature of the examples to be used, and the order in which correlative ideas are to be arranged. Suppose, for instance, a number of reasons for a certain conclusion are to be given. Maximum effectiveness will be ensured by offering first one with which the group is likely to agree unquestioningly. Having thus made a favorable opening, the clever speaker will next give points which are more difficult to grasp, less welcome, or less important. These will be accompanied by such evidence and explanatory matter as will make them seem more intelligible, convincing, and acceptable to the group. Finally should come the most important points, arranged in climactic order and usually followed by a short and striking summary.

Choosing the Style

It must not be inferred that in group discussion a speaker need have no concern for style, but rather that his style should be suited to the subject, the occasion, and his hearers. Since the subject and purpose of group discussion are usually serious, the style should be simple, straightforward, and free from flippancy. The hearers, however, being presumably as intelligent and well informed as the speaker, he should guard against a heavy and impressive or patronizing style. Moreover, the small size of the group makes the informal style of rather serious conversation the appropriate medium of expression.

As to choice of words, since the group is usually fairly

homogeneous, it is allowable to use a more specialized vocabulary than would be suitable in addressing an ordinary mixed audience. The speaker's greatest care in this respect should be to avoid words that, though harmless in his thought, would be likely to set off unfavorable reaction tendencies in some of his hearers. In certain groups, for example, the mere use of the word *conservative* would arouse antagonism; in others, the word *radical* would have equally disastrous results. The wise course, as Professor Sheffield suggests, is to "let sleeping dogs lie."

Short sentences or the somewhat loose sentences of ordinary conversation are preferable to elaborate periods. Figures of speech should be used sparingly and discriminatingly. Humor, if good-natured and spontaneous, is a great help in disarming antagonism and encouraging a constructive attitude of mind, but if used tactlessly it may produce exactly the opposite effect.

It is seldom that notes are excusable in group discussion. If used at all they should consist merely of quotations or statistics. It is taken for granted that the speaker should have given enough thought to the subject and should feel intensely enough concerning it to make notes unnecessary.

Presenting the Material

In manner of presentation the keynote again should be that of a group conversing about a subject in which the members are deeply interested. Whether the speaker sits or stands will depend on the size of the group and the formality of the occasion. In either case his posture should suggest ease and alertness.

He should begin by addressing the chair, but he should speak to the group. To fix his eyes on one person, or, worse yet, on some real or imaginary object, would be to lose touch with his hearers and to suggest discomfort rather than confidence and interest. By watching the group, moreover,

he can discover when his tempo is too fast or too slow, when
he is laboring a point or failing to make it clear, and when
he is antagonizing his audience or not reaching them at all.
Thus he can constantly adapt his methods to the needs of the
situation and obtain for his theory or plan a fair, if not a
sympathetic, hearing.

General Technique of Group Discussion

The technique of group discussion is little more than
a formalizing of the methods of good conversation, with the
difference that in conversation the primary object is pleasure,
whereas in discussion it is the crystallization of thought.
It may be worth while, by way of comparison, to consider
for a moment the nature of conversation.

The Nature of Conversation

In good conversation everyone is expected to contribute
something, if only an intelligent and stimulating interest.
A conversation may survive one or even two blanks, but
three kill it utterly.   Equally fatal to good talk is the person
who feels that the whole burden of entertaining the company
rests on him.   Even brilliant minds are not always free from
this vice.   Coleridge had it, and Oliver Wendell Holmes, and
George Meredith. A contemporary of Meredith relates that
at a dinner where the guests were talking animatedly in small
groups, he suddenly announced in exasperation, "If this
sort of thing continues, conversation will become impossible."   Another deadly enemy of good talk is the contentious person who holds forth aggressively on subjects concerning which some of the guests are sensitive or have intense
convictions.   Deadliest of all perhaps is the humorless
person who fancies himself a wit and tells long, pointless
stories from his personal experience or from some repository
of humor.   With one or more such persons about, conversation does indeed become impossible.

It is upon the host and hostess that the responsibility rests of saving a social gathering from the disaster which is threatened by the presence of any or all of these enemies of pleasant talk. In other ways also the success of an occasion when conversation is the chief form of entertainment depends on them. Good hosts and hostesses are always good listeners. They know how to draw out the diffident and gently but firmly to discourage the loquacious. They know how to bring up interesting and amusing subjects and to steer the talk away from those which are dangerous or tiresome. They know how to prevent dead spots, where the conversation seems to turn mournfully round and round one point. Over and above all this, they have as much delight in good talk as old Sarah Battles had in good whist, and through their zest for the game they succeed in bringing out the skill and team play and good feeling of the whole company. Thus there is released in each member a certain power and charm and gaiety of which perhaps he has been only dimly aware. The result is not only the immediate satisfaction that comes from the release of power, but added confidence in meeting other situations. The difference between persons who have always taken part in free, intelligent conversation and those who have not is apparent to the least observant.

This brings us to realization of the fact that the lay members, as well as the host and hostess, need special skills for this most fascinating of games. First, they require the kind of imaginative sympathy and insight that prevents them from boring others by stolid taciturnity or self-centered garrulity and from hurting or antagonizing them by tactlessness or contentiousness. Next, they need sufficient interest in things of the mind to make them eager to discuss any subject on which new and stimulating points of view are likely to be expressed. Still more they need that lively interest in life and in human beings which will make them skillful allies of the host and hostess in drawing out the various members of the group so that each shall contribute his share toward the pleasure of the occasion. And, lastly, they need the sportsman's knowledge and scrupulous observance of the rules of the game and the sportsman's keen zest for playing it rigorously.

Now let us see how all this applies to group discussion, beginning with the duties of the chairman.

The Duties of the Chairman of a Group

The function of the chairman is to see not merely that some conclusion is arrived at, but that it is the one which represents the best thinking of the group and that it is reached as expeditiously and as amicably as possible.

To further this purpose, the chairman should have made beforehand every effort to gain a broad view of the question, including the facts of the subject and the various opinions concerning those facts. He should have a general idea of the course the discussion should take,[7] but this should not be so rigid that he is tempted to follow a prearranged plan. Rather he should be sure that all the essential points receive fair exposition. The more the chairman seems to be letting the discussion take its course, the better. Yet he must keep it from straying into eddies and backwaters. He can do this by occasionally summarizing the progress already made and asking what point the group wish to discuss next. Sometimes it will be necessary to raise the question whether the discussion is not wandering too far from the main point to be decided. The skillful chairman will do this sort of thing in such a way as not to offend or antagonize the others. Like the skillful leader in conversation, he should know how to draw out the modest and to restrain the overzealous. If a tendency toward ill will or bad manners appear, he should

---

[7] This does not of course mean that he should have a fixed idea of the *conclusion* to be reached.

try to restore the right atmosphere by restating a tactless remark in such a way as to prevent its causing ill feeling. Or if there is indulgence in large, emotionally overcolored terms, he can ask the speaker to restate them more explicitly. His greatest influence in this respect will come through setting an example of fairness and courtesy. In fact, an intelligent and resourceful group chairman can usually establish and maintain favorable conditions for discussion.

In summary, the principal duties of a group chairman are:

1. To make the discussion progressive by insisting on the following conditions:

(*a*) That confusion as to the exact nature and purpose of the discussion is avoided by a clear statement of the question to be discussed.

(*b*) That at the outset the meaning of the terms used in the discussion is clearly understood and agreed on by all the members, and throughout the discussion that question-begging terms and vague expressions are restated unequivocally.

(*c*) That the basic facts are stated accurately and fully and that discussions of opinion are prevented whenever facts are available. (If possible, the chairman should see that adequate source material is at hand to make possible the immediate settlement of disputes concerning matters of fact.)

(*d*) That each side of the question, or each interest if it is a matter of policy, is fully and fairly stated. (This is especially important in the case of unpopular opinions, which a chairman should never allow to be ridiculed or refused fair presentation.)

(*e*) That each faction is urged to make a real effort to see the question from the opposite point of view and to give other groups credit for being as honest, intelligent, and right-minded as themselves. (Especially important is it to discourage any attempt on the part of one faction to discredit the motives of another.)

(*f*) That the issues involved are stated as far as possible in terms of common sense, practicability, and constructiveness rather than of right and wrong.

(*g*) That the discussion is kept as definite and practical as possible by use of the "case method"—that is, the examination of specific examples instead of idealistic theorizing and generalization.

(*h*) That every large issue is broken up into its elements and that these are examined separately and in their relation to the whole situation.

(*i*) That egotistic and long-winded speakers do not waste the time of the group and that persons with something constructive to contribute are not, by their own modesty or by the much-speaking of others, prevented from giving it.

(*j*) That time is saved by frequent brief summaries and statements of the exact point reached and the next point to be discussed. (It is helpful, whenever possible, to make clear that a substantial agreement has been reached regarding one phase of the subject and that the logical thing is to proceed from this common ground to a further point in regard to which the group can find some basis either of agreement or of reasonably satisfactory compromise.)

(*k*) That in the interest of saving time the discussion must not be allowed to reach a premature and unsatisfactory conclusion. (The chairman must constantly remember that in discussion meetings the main purpose is not to get business transacted but to bring about a true integration of thought. He must sometimes be courageous enough to acknowledge that the meeting has not brought about a consensus of opinion and to ask the members to suspend judgment until there has been more time for thought and research and possibly discussion in still smaller groups.)

(*l*) That the conclusion that is finally reached is stated clearly.

(*m*) That if any reasonable number disagree with the conclusion, they are invited to draw up a minority report or that an opportunity is given to reopen the discussion at some future time.

2. To maintain dignity and courtesy in the discussion through the following means:

(*a*) Preventing discourtesy and confusion by insisting that all speakers address the chair.

(*b*) Preventing irritation and hurt feelings by restating tactless remarks in a way to make them seem less offensive.

(*c*) Preventing feelings of injustice by maintaining what in the British Parliament is called "the austerity of the chair"—meticulous regard for the rights of each individual and faction. (To succeed in this respect, the chairman needs not only a strong sense of justice, but a thorough knowledge of the principles of parliamentary usage.)

(d) Preventing mob-mindedness by insisting on the translation into plain terms of emotional phraseology and thus counteracting any undue appeal to prejudice and class or party or personal feeling.

(e) Preventing loss of dignity by refusing to tolerate undignified or frivolous or scurrilous language.

The Duties of Group Members

No matter how experienced and effective the chairman may be, however, he alone cannot make the discussion a success. To achieve this result every member must coöperate. And it is not enough that each individual bring a tentative opinion carefully prepared from an adequate body of tested facts; he should bring also keen interest in the subject, respect for the chairman, and good will toward the other members. He should make his own contribution as effectively as possible and should try to discover whatever in the contributions of the others will help toward a final solution. He should not speak too often or too long or contentiously or off the point. He should have enough knowledge of parliamentary usage to enable him to obtain fair treatment, but he should not use this knowledge to take unfair advantage of those who are less informed or more scrupulous. In short, his whole desire should be to help in all ways toward the formulation of a representative and satisfactory opinion or plan.

The Use of Parliamentary Practice in Discussion

Parliamentary practice has been developed as the result of centuries of experimentation in discussion. Its chief requirements are: (1) that business shall be transacted by motions passed by the majority after free discussion open to the whole assembly; (2) that there shall be a definite order of business in general and of motions in particular; (3) that all business shall be conducted through the chair; and (4) that personalities and rude or undignified behavior shall be avoided.

The extent to which parliamentary practice need be followed depends on the occasion, the subject, and the size and nature of the group.

Informal Discussion.—In very informal discussion little more strictness of procedure is necessary than in ordinary conversation, though even here it is better to address the chair in order to keep the talk general and progressive. This is usually adequate restriction for a discussion whose purpose is to agree on the meaning of a term or to test the truth of an hypothesis or for meetings of small committees. Practice in committee meetings is of very great value both for college life and for life after graduation.

Formal Group Discussion.—In more formal discussion, especially when a policy or a plan is under consideration, it will usually be found helpful to have the question stated as a motion. In such case it may sometimes be well to have the discussion started by four rather formally prepared speeches, those of the mover and seconder of the resolution and of the first two speakers in opposition. Others may then speak more informally, the floor being given alternately to speakers on each side.

A type of somewhat formal discussion in which parliamentary practice is strictly observed is a form of the so-called "socialized recitation." Over such a recitation a chairman presides, and a secretary takes the minutes. Sometimes there is a parliamentarian who makes sure that no slips in procedure are allowed to pass unchallenged. The subject or subjects under consideration are proposed and discussed in the form of motions, and the whole recitation is carried on as if it were the meeting of a club or deliberative body. Often a lecture period may profitably be turned into a "committee of the whole" to discuss some disputed point or to decide on the best way of carrying on some phase of class work.

Parliamentary Debates.—Sometimes it will be found interesting, especially to classes that have studied history or government, to conduct a discussion as if it were a debate in Congress or some foreign parliament. Such an exercise is valuable, not merely for the encouragement it gives to the mastery of parliamentary practice, but in the effect of reality it lends both to the study of institutions and to the discussion itself.

Formal Debates.—From this point it is but a short step to formal debate, which many students find a particularly exciting means of developing intellectual keenness and subtlety as well as power of coöperation and ability to play a game hard without loss of courtesy and fairness. A convenient form of debate is that in which there are three speakers on a side. Since the burden of proof rests on the affirmative group, they are given the benefit of both the first and the last word. The first speaker on this side begins with an introduction which includes any necessary definition of terms, the history of the question (including the reasons for its timeliness), statement of the conceded and waived matter, and a summary of the special issues; in all this he should give the impression of perfect fairness in stating conditions. Next he explains the general line of argument his side intends to follow, and then usually begins to establish the affirmative answer to the question embodied in the first issue. Since in all debates of policy the affirmative is arguing in favor of a change, the first issue is very likely to be concerned with the need for change or, if this is assumed to be self-evident, with proof that the proposed change is desirable or practicable or constitutional.

The first speaker on the negative is then given the floor. If his opponent in the course of the introduction has made any misstatements or warped the facts in order to make them seem favorable to his side, the present speaker calls attention to these points in such a way as not merely to correct the unfairness but to weaken the influence of the affirmative. In the same way he calls attention to any slips in fact or inference in his opponent's argument, and then starts his own proof. Since the burden of proving that any change, or at least the proposed change, is desirable rests with the affirmative, the negative side, at least in the early stages of the debate, can usually afford to content itself with evidence that the proposed change is not desirable. In other words, their tactics are chiefly those of defensive warfare; they are in possession of the fort and need only see that it is not demolished or captured by the enemy.

The debate proceeds with alternating affirmative and negative speakers until all have had their turn. Then (usually after a short intermission) the rebuttal begins. Sometimes speeches in rebuttal are made by all the debaters, sometimes by the leaders of the two sides only. In either case the affirmative leader has the great advantage of the last speech. He has no right, however, to introduce any new evidence in this final speech, as that would be manifestly unfair.

The decision is made either by a committee of judges or by the vote of the whole audience. It may be rendered on the merits of the question or on the merits of the debate.

It must be frankly admitted that debates as sometimes conducted are dead and dull affairs. This is usually true when the disputants have either given little time to preparation or devoted too much of their time to fact-getting and too little to reasoning and "incubation." It is always the result when they depend on set speeches, whether memorized or openly read or delivered from voluminous notes. The effect is particularly painful when each member gives his little speech as an independent exhibit, without reference to the preceding speaker or to the general line of argument of the opposition. The more nearly a debate approaches a lively discussion between two groups of well-informed and witty persons, the more interesting it is to the audience.

On the ethical side also debates are sometimes open to

question. "The danger of debating is that if it is wrongly conducted it may encourage cheapness, trickery, and deceit —qualities which need no encouragement in the human race." [8] The answer to this is, of course, that in any game a contestant may cheat or show bad sportsmanship, but the desirable course is not that games should be given up, but that people should be taught to play them hard but fairly. If debates are so conducted that the participants and the audience gain not only new light on disputed questions, but a finer sense of team play and of courtesy to opponents, the time spent on them will have been justified. But in view of the difficulty of gaining an inquiring and impartial temper and a habit of constructive rather than destructive thought, it will usually be wiser for the student to practice debate only after considerable training in group discussion. In speech training discussion is especially to be recommended, since it serves the double purpose of extending the intellectual background and of developing the effectiveness in expression which is the final purpose of the work.

[8] Stone and Garrison, *Essentials of Argument*.

CHAPTER IX

FIRST PRINCIPLES OF PUBLIC SPEAKING

Overcoming Dread of Public Speaking

IN their book on *The Psychology of Language* Pillsbury and Meader say that it is natural to speak and unnatural to refrain from saying what we think and feel. To anyone who has studied the behavior of children this seems a logical deduction from the general law that expression is natural and the habit of repression unnatural and often painfully acquired. Why, then, do so many persons feel an intense fear and dislike of speaking in public?

It is probable that the dislike is chiefly due to the distaste felt by most persons for the old-fashioned florid oratory with which public speaking is commonly associated. The dread is partly due to the fear of failure which comes from lack of early training. Most schools fail to make practice in speaking before a group so much a part of the regular curriculum that it comes to be considered a natural phase of school work. Without such practice the student is likely to feel nervous and uncomfortable in appearing before an audience even of his schoolfellows.

By Thinking of It as a Form of Conversation

It will be well at the outset to examine these states of mind and see whether they cannot be overcome. The dislike for public speaking is diminished when it is thought of as merely an enlarged and slightly more formal type of conversation or discussion, in which the speaker, for greater convenience in making himself heard, stands a little out from

195

the group. As a matter of fact, this direct and unpretentious manner of speaking has practically superseded the more oratorical style except for rare and impressive occasions, though survivals of it in its less inspiring form are sometimes heard at political meetings and Fourth-of-July celebrations.

By Thinking of the Audience as Individuals

Fear of an audience and of one's own inadequacy can best be combatted together. And first, by analysis of the audience. The speaker's sense of its formidableness is greatly diminished if he learns to think of it, not as a hydra-headed monster or as "a beast without a head," but as a group of well-disposed and fairly intelligent individuals. Timidity is still further lessened if he becomes really interested in the individuals in the audience and their reaction to his ideas. It disappears entirely if he learns to feel that he is not talking *to* an audience, but *with* each member of it. Hence, if instead of wasting energy in painful anticipation of making the speech, the prospective speaker gives his entire attention to preparing something of real interest to say, he will find his confidence rapidly increasing. Furthermore, as soon as his fear of the audience turns to interest in them and in what he is going to say to them, their interest and confidence in him will increase. This in turn, by what psychologists call "circular response," will add still more to his self-assurance.

By Understanding the "Preparatory Reactions"

But perhaps the greatest help of all is to analyze the distressing physical and mental reactions which so often add to the dread of speaking in public. Everyone knows what these sensations are—the trembling of the limbs, the heavy thumping of the heart, the irregular breathing, the constriction of the throat, and the loss of power to think logically.

These sensations are so terrifying that they discourage many persons from attempting to speak in public. When analyzed they are seen to be merely the preparatory reactions for flight, which centuries of experience in the dangers of running away have transformed into preparations for fight. Let us examine them in detail. The bodily apparatus, which has been in comparative rest and is now called upon to perform a somewhat difficult task, starts to prepare for this. The breathing, which has been going on very gently, becomes deeper and more vigorous in order that there may be plenty of air to support the voice and to supply brain and muscles with the extra oxygen they will require. At the same time, the beating of the heart is accelerated, and the endocrine glands begin pouring into the blood stream a greater supply of adrenalin and the other secretions that help to put the body into good fighting trim. But this all happens so suddenly that the quiet rhythm of the body is disturbed, and with it the calmness of the nerves. If, however, instead of being terrified by this condition, the speaker recognizes it as nature's way of preparing him for greater exertion, and if by two or three quiet, deep breaths he swings this increased activity into a larger rhythm, he will find his fear giving place to confidence. If now he walks quietly and rhythmically to the platform and stands quiet for a moment, looking at his auditors and thinking of them as human beings, he will find, at least after a little practice, that his fear has changed to a sense of exhilaration. Yet this does not mean that he will ever reach a point where he can anticipate a public speech entirely without concern. It would not be well for him to do so. If he did, he would be like a football player who has become so confident of his powers that he ceases to have these preparatory reactions and suddenly discovers at a crucial point in the game that he lacks his usual physical and mental alertness.

By Beginning with Group Discussion

The very nature of public speaking implies a certain tension and feeling of challenge. An hour's talk to a thousand persons consumes a thousand hours of the time of the world. The responsibility for making an adequate return for such an expenditure would give pause to the most thoughtless. But the knowledge that nature's preparatory reactions are helpful if properly controlled, together with the support that comes from conscientious preparation and from frequent practice in talking to small groups, will turn public speaking from a terror to a pleasure. Especially will this be true if the practice has been preceded by group discussion, so that a feeling of contact with one's audience has been developed naturally through working with others to build up a group opinion

Choosing a Subject

Before undertaking to make a speech the prospective speaker may well ask himself why he should make it. In class the situation is unnatural—we are frankly practicing different types of talks in order to acquire necessary skills. Even here the student can get some effect of reality by imagining a definite situation which would call for the kind of speech he is to make or by choosing a subject of interest to the class. In real life it is the occasion that decides. One may have certain information which he feels would be of interest or value, or a plan that he believes should be adopted, or he may have been chosen to do honor to some person, or to celebrate some public occasion, or to amuse and entertain. In any of these cases he should decline unless he feels he has something of interest to say—not necessarily brilliant and startling or deep and impressive, but at least the result of some sort of creative thinking on his part. If it is impossible to escape making a speech for which the speaker feels himself inadequately prepared, he can at least make sure that it has one virtue—that of brevity.

In deciding what to talk about, the speaker will do well to choose, whenever possible, a subject about which he already knows something. As was said in the last chapter, the perfunctory utterance of material which has been hastily collected and has not undergone a process of "incubation" is apt to be little more impressive than the crackling of thorns under a pot.

Secondly, he should choose a subject in which he is genuinely interested. Unless he really cares about the subject, he can hardly hope to hold the attention of his audience. The beginner should not let this requirement worry him. Very often students fail to realize how many interests they have, or they hesitate to talk of these interests for fear of being ridiculed. To overcome such foolish and cramping inhibitions and to learn the pleasure that comes from regaining freedom and naturalness of expression are among the most valuable by-products of a class in public speaking. If through practice in discussion the fear of an audience has been overcome and group-consciousness substituted for self-consciousness, the power to talk about real interests will develop rapidly. In this way class speeches, instead of being the most artificial things in the world, will come to have a certain reality and directness.

Finally, the speaker's task is easiest if he selects a subject in which his audience is interested or which is nearly related to one of their interests. People will listen to a relatively dull talk on a subject about which they know something and wish to know more. It requires a skillful speaker to arouse the attention of his hearers to a subject regarding which they are ignorant and indifferent.

The Speaker's Problems

This matter of attention is the great problem of the public speaker. The questions he must ask himself are:

"How can I get the attention of my audience?" and "Having got it, how can I hold it and use it to accomplish the purpose of my speech?" If he knows anything about the nature of audiences, he will realize that in the beginning he can expect from his hearers only involuntary attention. Unless he begins by presenting ideas to which it is possible for his hearers to listen without effort of the will, he need not hope for the attention of more than a small number of them. Their interest once thoroughly aroused, however, they may be relied on to make a slight voluntary effort to follow a line of thought if it is vividly presented and interesting and not too difficult. But at best only a *slight* mental effort can be expected of them. In capacity for hard thinking, as in everything else, "the average man is far below the average."

Getting Attention in the Introduction.

How can the speaker lay hold on this reluctant and wavering attention and rivet it to his subject? The problem would be a formidable one were it not for certain favoring conditions. Often the audience is predisposed in his favor by his reputation as an interesting speaker or an authority on his subject, or by his relationship to some member of the community, or for some other less logical but equally effective reason. If he is unknown to the audience, the speaker is usually put in a favorable light by the person who introduces him. A member of a class in public speaking who has given one really good talk will readily have the interest of the others to see if on a second occasion he will do as well or better.

The Initial Challenge

By the mere act of walking to the platform the speaker focuses all eyes upon himself, since motion is one of the surest challenges to attention. If he pauses a moment and looks at his audience with friendly interest unmixed with fear, he not only ensures quiet for his opening words, but takes advantage of the fact that suspense is one of the surest means to his desired end. Another certain means is the use of so clear and pleasant a tone and so distinct an articulation that the audience listen involuntarily. The adoption of a moderate speech tempo and a rhythm so timed that the speaker's main idea hits the crest of the wave of his hearers' attention helps to make his problem easier. Still further help comes from using in the introductory passages questions and short, direct sentences which require only involuntary attention.

The Introduction

Speakers too often fail to realize that in their introductory remarks they should rely entirely on involuntary attention. Often the battle for attention is lost before the discussion is begun. A speaker who begins by boring or annoying his audience will have little chance of winning them to his point of view.

What exactly, then, should the introduction to a speech accomplish? Cicero says it should make the hearers *attentos, dociles, et benevolentes*—not merely attentive but willing to be informed and kindly disposed toward the speaker and his message. We have suggested the more obvious and superficial ways of challenging the attention of the auditors. How can the speaker by the thought expressed in the introduction still further arouse their interest and at the same time win their respect and sympathy?

Humor and Other Devices.—Many speakers find they can accomplish this most easily by means of humor. At its best and in the right place this is the ideal method. Laughter produces an agreeable relaxation of bodily tensions and thus contributes to a sense of physical well-being. Shared enjoyment of an amusing idea is one of the surest means of establishing community of feeling. The ability to see a joke gives a pleasant sense of mental superiority. All these agreeable feelings tend to make an audience kindly disposed toward the person who has aroused them.

It is only in ideal conditions, however, that these happy results follow. First of all, the humor itself must be genuine and unforced. If it grows out of the immediate situation—from something the chairman or a previous speaker has said, for instance—it seems spontaneous and delightful. If, on the other hand, it gives the impression of having been carefully prepared beforehand, the audience, unless they are in a complacent mood, may take coldly and even resentfully what appears too obvious a bid for their approval. Especially is this likely to happen if the witticism is felt not to be in perfect taste. The whole problem of good taste is extremely important for the public speaker. The relation of humor to taste is a subject well worth discussing, but it is too large a question to be settled here. One element, however, must be mentioned—that of appropriateness. Persons (usually humorless) who feel that a funny story is the approved way of beginning a speech often fail to see that by their ineptitude they are arousing in their hearers a feeling of contempt rather than of admiration and are thus creating an entirely wrong attitude toward their message. A speaker who begins a tearful plea for Near East Relief by a rollicking story will scarcely accomplish his purpose.

What means other than humor help to create the desired introductory impression? Study good speakers, or, better yet, make a case study of some excellent speaker whom you hear often, and you will find that there are a number of effective devices. One of these is direct challenge in the form of a question or a startling assertion; another, an arresting quotation or the clever adaptation of a well-known quotation. A third is an anecdote, still another, an epigram. Incidents and hypothetical cases are sometimes useful. The student who is really interested in gaining a technique of public speaking will try various devices until he learns the value of each for various types of material, occasion, and audience.

The Speaker's Triangle.—Phillips in his book on *Effective Speaking* has a useful suggestion. He says that the introduction to a speech should establish clear and satisfactory relations between the speaker and the audience, the speaker and the subject, and the audience and the subject. Sometimes not all sides of the triangle need be equally stressed. Suppose, for instance, a well-known and popular lecturer were speaking on a subject quite out of his ordinary line. He could very well assume that the connection between himself and his audience was adequately established, and he would accordingly stress his reasons for his unexpected choice of subject and, incidentally, his qualifications for treating it. A relatively unknown person suddenly called on to speak in place of an authority in a given field might well give first his qualifications for speaking on the subject, unless the chairman had been tactful enough to forestall him. He should state, convincingly but without boasting, the training and experience that have made him also more or less of an authority in the field. This kind of introduction requires infinite tact in order that the audience shall be *dociles et benevolentes*. To find the golden mean between an unattractive overconfidence and that "'umbleness" of which Uriah Heep is the classical example is a severe test of balance and integration of personality.

Indicating the Motivation of the Speech.—A thoroughly good introduction, then, should win the interest, the respect, and the good will of the audience and should give a general idea of the subject to be discussed. But it should do more than this. It should outline, or at least suggest, the course the discussion is to take and hint at the nature of the conclusion to be reached. In other words, it should give reality to the talk by suggesting the motivation. In a properly motivated speech the hearer is not likely to "lose the drift": the speaker knows so well where he is going that the hearer finds it easy and pleasant to go with him. This seems self-evident, but any observant person will have discovered that hardly a third of the speeches he is expected to listen to have a clearly defined purpose. It is not enough that the speaker have a general interest in his subject: the good speaker has a special interest in a particular phase of the subject and explains clearly in his introduction from what point of view he intends to discuss this phase. The introductory matter must be given briefly, however, for American audiences have this in common with those of ancient Greece, that they are quickly and easily interested and as quickly and easily bored.

Holding Attention in the Body of the Speech

The technique of preparing the material for a speech and of organizing it for presentation has already been discussed in the chapter on group discussion. To the present chapter, however, it has seemed best to leave a fuller discussion of the manner of presentation, since public speaking, much more than discussion, demands knowledge and skill for sustaining the interest of the audience. The members of a discussion group have a favorable mind set toward the speaker's subject; since they have helped select it and have given it considerable study, any clear presentation of a reasonably original opinion concerning it will hold their interest. But to hold the attention of an audience to a subject regarding which they may have little knowledge and less interest, a speaker must make use of all his psychological knowledge and technical skill.

Principles of Stimulus and Response

How can the speaker best equip himself for this supreme test of his effectiveness? Perhaps by reviewing what he knows of the laws of attention and seeing how they apply to this problem of securing the voluntary attention of an audience.[1]

Beginning with the Known.—He will remember that it is practically impossible to hold the interest of people in anything of which they have no knowledge. Hence he will start with a phase of the subject about which his hearers already know something. When he comes to points concerning which he cannot safely assume any knowledge on their part, he will explain these by analogy with something with which they are acquainted. On the other hand, since people are easily bored with what they know well, he will give a novel presentation of whatever is familiar yet necessary to the discussion.

Achieving Variety.—Another principle of attention is that it soon lapses if the stimulus is not frequently changed. The good speaker will be careful not to labor a point. If it is necessary to dwell for some time on a difficult and important matter, he will turn it about and look at it from various points of view so that variety is achieved. This is particularly important in the restatement and expansion of difficult ideas. An observant speaker will often see that his audience has not fully grasped a significant point. He realizes that unless he makes this clear, his auditors will not be able to follow his reasoning and will accordingly lose interest. To say the same thing over in the same way would be to bore and to insult them. The obvious course is to restate the point in some more striking fashion so that the imaginations of his hearers will come to their aid in grasping the thought. Sometimes the use of a more concrete term, a figure of speech, an analogy borrowed from their own experience, a specific instance, or a humorous story will not only clear up a difficult matter, but freshen the lagging interest of the

---

[1] This matter is clearly treated in Prof. J. A. Winans' excellent book on *Public Speaking*.

audience. For this reason, as the preceding chapter has already shown, it is of the utmost importance for the speaker to keep in close contact with his audience so that he may prevent their losing interest through failure to understand a pivotal point in the development of his theme.

Maintaining Clearness.—Of all the problems that confront a speaker, this matter of clearness is the most difficult. Students of public speaking do not sufficiently consider that a listener has not a reader's opportunity for pondering a difficult point or going over an argument a second time; that he loses interest if he fails to follow the thought easily, yet resents any implied insult to his intelligence. The first requirement for the speaker is to have done such hard thinking beforehand that every step in the development of his thought is perfectly clear in his own mind. The second is to have written the speech out, or, better yet, spoken it out, many times, experimenting with various ways of stating the ideas until he has discovered the clearest as well as the most novel and striking terms of expression. The third is to sense the habits of thought of the audience and to adapt to their thinking the kind of illustrative material they will find most interesting and enlightening. In this respect the study of great orators like Cicero and Burke is instructive: notice how often Burke borrows his figures from gambling and similar interests of his contemporaries in the House of Commons. An effective device is to make the audience participate in developing the thought through skillful use of questions and direct appeals of various kinds.

Gauging the Intensity of Stimulus.—An important matter to be remembered in this connection is the relation between interest and *intensity of stimulus*. No one can fail to pay attention to a loud explosion outside the window, or a sharp blow, or a blinding light flashed suddenly in his eyes. Speakers often make use of powerful stimuli to maintain attention. They shout at their hearers, use violent gestures, walk excitedly up and down the stage, tell boisterous jokes, and use slang and other highly colored expressions. All this certainly attracts attention. Sometimes, if coupled with sincerity, vigorous thinking, and attractive personality, it holds attention. With some audiences it even helps in achieving the desired effect. Ford Madox Ford once said he intended to have attention if he had to turn handsprings to get it. No one remembering hours of deadly boredom endured at the hands of public speakers will be inclined to be too critical of any method that gives interest to a speech. But a number of considerations have to be taken into account.

There is perhaps no aspect of modern life to which more thought is given than to advertising, and a study of advertising methods helpfully reveals what has been discovered about attention by those men whose livelihood depends on arousing and maintaining the *right kind of attention*. In the changed technique of advertising we have an important suggestion. Some years ago the most violent combinations of colors were used in street-car and subway advertising. It was finally discovered, however, that although such garish signs inevitably caught the eye, they made so unpleasant a visual impression that the association with the advertised article was the opposite of what was intended. Within a few years a striking change occurred in the color schemes of advertisements. Colors came to be chosen, not according to the intensity of the impression they would make, but to its pleasurableness.

In public speaking likewise there is danger of antagonizing many persons in an audience by a method that strikes them as being in bad taste. Because of the *relativity* of taste no one can set an absolute standard. Hamlet's dictum, "Let discretion be your tutor," is as good as any that has ever been devised. Sometimes a speaker is willing to antagonize a small element of his audience in order to make the desired impression on the majority, or to antagonize them all momentarily in order to win them more enthusiastically afterwards. But a word of caution on the use of these extreme measures. Striking or even violent means may produce the result intended provided the audience feel sure of the intense conviction of the speaker. But if they for a moment suspect that these are the deliberate devices of the actor, they are apt to resent them intensely and to give the speaker credit for being even less sincere than he is.

Nevertheless Hamlet's warning, "Be not too tame neither," is also needed in these days of repression and colorless speaking. Many persons are so afraid of being accused of emotionalism and sentimentality that they eliminate from their speaking all emotion and all sentiment. The result is an uninspired and arid manner which leaves the audience cold. The cure for this attitude of mind is a deeper interest in life, freer play of the imagination, and greater faith in the good sense and good will of the audience.

Appealing to Human Motives.—Still another element of our knowledge concerning the principles of stimulus and response is extremely helpful to the public speaker. Interests, we know, may be natural or acquired. The natural ones, which relate to our most primitive needs—for food, warmth, perpetuation of the race, and so on, are the strongest and most universal appeals. These, then, are the most powerful stimuli, not merely for getting and holding attention, but for using it to achieve our desired ends. A study of advertisements indicates how clearly this is realized by firms who want to influence others in the difficult matter of loosening purse strings. A tabulation of the kinds of motivation represented in a successful advertising medium like the *Saturday Evening Post* will show that all but a very small number of advertisements appeal to desire for personal safety, comfort, power, and attractiveness or for the safety and comfort of the family. In a speech to an ordinary audience, therefore, and especially in the early part of it, it is well to appeal to these universal motives.

But what of acquired, or socially conditioned, interests? Are they to be altogether neglected? Certainly it would be unwise to neglect them in speaking to a group of more than average mental and cultural development. Even with the ordinary audience one may risk an occasional appeal to such motives as love of beauty for its own sake, interest in the quest of truth, ideals of social and political betterment. Especially is it practicable if these appeals are somehow related to the instinctive behavior level and are presented with a certain imaginative and emotional warmth. Here again the audience, the subject, the occasion, and the speaker's sincerity and tact are all conditioning factors.

Developing an Effective Style

The speaker's style is also a powerful factor in maintaining interest and in stimulating the desired reaction. A varied sentence structure is extremely desirable—long, flowing periods alternating with loosely constructed conversational sentences, interrupted by sharp questions or terse statements, with an occasional finely balanced sentence to emphasize a contrast or comparison. This variety, however, must be the natural expression of a keen and well-trained mind. If the result sounds labored and artificial, the effect is worse than that produced by a dry, monotonous style which is at least natural and spontaneous. But if the speaker is thoroughly familiar with his subject matter and has done original thinking upon it and if all his forces are bent upon making it live for his hearers, there is little danger of his sentence structure being dull and nerveless.

Like his syntax, the speaker's vocabulary will reflect his thinking and prove a help or a hindrance in his task of holding and swaying his audience. If he really cares for words and has formed the habit of learning their accurate meanings, if he reads discriminatingly and spends some time each day in intelligent conversation, he will have a rich treasury at his command when the need arises, at least after he has had sufficient practice to be free from nervousness. Concrete and specific words, since they arouse definite images, make for clearness and vividness. Figures of speech, if natural and suited to the subject and the audience, give color and vigor to style. Discrimination in the use of words is a particularly valuable asset in maintaining interest over transitions Sharp, clear, striking phrases not only prevent the listeners from losing their way in the mazes of thought, but enable the speaker to make a fresh and forceful attack.

Changes in the speaker's position at the end of thought divisions help to make the organization clear and thus prevent his hearers from losing the drift. Useful too in driving home a point or in arousing lagging interest are gestures, provided they are spontaneous, suitable, and forceful. Variations in pitch, volume, tempo, and quality of voice give effectiveness to the thought, and relieve monotony and sense of strain. They also lend an effect of beauty to the whole, provided always that they are (or at least seem to be) the natural result of changes of thought and mood.

Fixing the Desired Impression in the Conclusion

We now come to the conclusion of the speech. How can the speaker use it as a means of driving home his main contentions and making them memorable?

Like the introduction, the conclusion should be brief but striking. If the introduction is important in being the means of starting the speech with the right kind of impression, the conclusion is still more important since it is the means of making on the audience the final and lasting impression.

It must be *conclusive* and not merely an end of speaking. It may take the form of (1) a brief summary of the points made; (2) a conclusion from the arguments or incidents given in the body of the speech; (3) an application of the points to some specific case; (4) an appeal to action; (5) an anecdote, historical reference, analogy, or quotation in prose or poetry which illustrates the main point; (6) a question that has grown out of the discussion; or (7) a brief and epigrammatic, or a long and periodic, restatement of the main contention.

Not only should the conclusion be the inevitable outcome of the discussion, it should also balance the introduction. The introduction says in effect, "This is where we are going"; the conclusion counters with, "You see, we have arrived." This is rather neatly illustrated by the story of the man who said that in reading Browning's "Sordello" he had understood two lines, the first and the last, and that they were both lies. Lies they may have been, but otherwise excellent as introduction and conclusion, for they are:

> Who will, shall hear Sordello's story told.

and

> Who would, has heard Sordello's story told.

Equally perfect are the opening and closing paragraphs of Strachey's essay on Lady Hester Stanhope in his *Eminent Victorians*.

Not everyone, of course, can achieve this balance with such consummate art, but everyone can at least avoid the trite and the banal. Study of the methods of good speakers of the past and of the present; cultivation of the faculties of observation, imagination, and humor; and the sense that public speaking is a delightful game to be played with greater and greater skill—all this will produce good craftsmen, if not great artists.

"Platform Manners"

A word concerning what are sometimes called "platform manners" may be helpful. As public speaking is merely an enlarged conversation, so the etiquette of public occasions is merely a slightly more formal sort of everyday etiquette. Suppose, for example, you are to introduce a speaker. In bringing him to his place on the platform it might be natural for you to go ahead, since he presumably does not know the way as well as you do. Having brought him to the front of the stage, you would probably think it courteous to indicate a chair so that he might be seated during your speech. In introducing him your duty would be to tell what the audience wants to know about him—his name, the topic on which he is to speak, and his qualifications for speaking on this theme. This you would tell as graciously as possible and in such a way as to arouse the listeners' interest and curiosity. Fulsome flattery is, of course, out of place here as elsewhere, but a warm recommendation of the speaker to the sympathy of the group helps to give him confidence and ease in addressing them. After having introduced him, you would sit down without crossing in front of him. At the end of his talk it would be your place to say some gracious word of appreciation. Then without passing in front of the speaker you would precede him, or walk beside him, to the door. In this and in similar circumstances the rule is to do what any considerate and tactful person would do—the thing that will make the situation as smooth and easy as possible for everyone concerned.

Instructions for particular occasions and for the various types of speeches are beyond the scope of this brief introduction; they will be found in any good book on public speaking. By far the best way of gaining ease and confidence, however, is to watch carefully the behavior of speakers who seem most successful in meeting situations, to compare different methods of meeting a given situation, and so to gain general theories and principles for guidance in similar circumstances. The most helpful guiding principle is the realization that on the platform, as in all other human relations, the requirement is not an inflexible rule of conduct for each situation, but a sense of what makes for the greatest freedom from general strain and the least discomfort to the individual.

CHAPTER X

FIRST PRINCIPLES OF ORAL READING

In the earlier chapters of this book, oral reading has been used chiefly as a means of developing skills in voice and speech production. In this chapter the emphasis is reversed: reading is here considered as one of the ends for which these skills are developed. It need hardly be repeated that good voice and good speech are important only as aids toward the adequate expression of thought. The preceding chapters have been chiefly concerned with providing means for developing the student's power of expressing his own thoughts. This chapter gives some of the principles that should guide his attempts to interpret the thoughts of others.

The treatment is divided according to the qualities necessary for literary interpretation: (1) clearness through understanding of the content; (2) unity through grasp of the rhythm; (3) interest through appreciation of the dramatic movement; and (4) color through realization of the mood.

THE INTELLECTUAL APPROACH: THROUGH ANALYSIS OF THOUGHT

It may seem an insult to the intelligence of the advanced student to suggest that before attempting to express the thought of another, he should fully understand that thought, as in expressing his own ideas he should be sure that he has clear ideas to express. Many otherwise intelligent persons, however, seem to think that reading is merely the mechanical pronunciation of series of words. Frequently they do not realize that they have failed to grasp the content themselves, to say nothing of mastering the more difficult problem of

214

communicating it to others. There is an Oriental proverb which says, "One candle lights a thousand." But obviously the candle must itself be alight.

Since ordinary prose is written primarily to appeal to the intelligence of the reader, the most natural approach to it is through the intellect. The following steps, therefore, are necessary in preparing a prose passage for oral reading, and in commencing the preparation of a difficult poem or play:

1. Reading the selection as a whole in order to grasp the author's thought and intention.

2. Separating it into its parts and analyzing the steps by which the author attains his conclusion.

3. Discovering the logical relations of these parts to one another and to the general intention of the author.

4. Finding the key words that must be given direct and definite emphasis in order that the thought and intention of the author shall be unmistakable, and identifying for subordination everything that is merely repetitious, obvious, purely decorative, or otherwise unimportant.

5. Reading the selection aloud until the various elements are built into such a structural whole that the reader becomes a re-creator of the thought at the time he is reading it, and the reading becomes the expression of active and present thinking.

Grasping the Thought as a Whole

The reader who fails to comprehend thoroughly the basic thought and general purpose of a selection is like an architect building a house room by room without a plan. The power of grasping thought from the printed page is so little developed in the average student that the only way for him to be sure of mastering this first requirement of oral interpretation is to train himself to summarize the thought of a passage in a clear, unified sentence. He will find it necessary to recapitulate the thought of many passages of various degrees of difficulty before he has gained this power of getting a bird's-eye view of the whole. If the selection is long, he, should read it paragraph by paragraph until he can reduce each to a single sentence.

Carefully read the following:

No one can understand America with his brains. It is too big, too puzzling. It tempts, and it deceives. But many an illiterate immigrant has felt the true America in his pulses before he ever crossed the Atlantic. The descendant of the Pilgrims still remains ignorant of our national life if he does not respond to its glorious zest, its throbbing energy, its forward urge, its uncomprehending belief in the future, its sense of the fresh and mighty world just beyond to-day's horizon. Whitman's 'Pioneers, O Pioneers' is one of the truest of American poems because it beats with the pulse of this onward movement, because it is full of this laughing and conquering fellowship and undefeated faith.

BLISS PERRY, "The American Mind"

You will discover that Bliss Perry is saying: "The American spirit cannot be comprehended by the intellect alone since it consists of such dynamic and intangible ele- ments as gaiety and fellowship and faith."

Grouping or Phrasing

In the passage quoted above, the words naturally group themselves not merely into paragraphs and sentences, but into shorter divisions called *breath groups*, or *phrases*. These thought units are not phrases in the grammatical sense, but groups of words spoken on one breath and so closely con- nected in meaning that for purposes of reading aloud each phrase may be considered as one word. Phrases always end with a special bend of the voice called an *inflection*, or *intonation curve*. For this reason they are sometimes called *intonation groups*.[1]

Grouping or phrasing is of the utmost importance in oral reading since it enables the reader (1) to replenish his breath supply, (2) to formulate the next group, (3) to allow his

[1] See page 64.

hearers time to grasp the meaning of the phrase just read, and (4) to maintain the rhythmical flow of the sentence.

The length of phrases cannot be absolutely or arbitrarily fixed. Punctuation does not always indicate correct phrasing. Punctuation marks are intended to show the syntax and to help the reader in grasping the thought. Having grasped it, he should divide it for reading into groups regardless of punctuation. The amount of thought to be included in a phrase depends on (1) the difficulty or unfamiliarity of the thought, (2) the size and character of the audience, and (3) the purpose of the reader. For example, a scientist reading a paper on relativity to a large mixed audience would use shorter phrases and pause longer between them than a person reading a story to a small group.

Re-read the quotation from "The American Mind" and see if you would divide the thought into the phrases indicated below. You will observe that some phrases are more closely connected in thought than others, and that the closer the connection between phrases, the shorter will be the pause. Certain symbols may be used to show these various gradations. When phrases are so closely related that there should be only a slight pause between them, this pause may be indicated by a single vertical line, thus, |. Phrases that are nearly complete in thought yet are felt to be parts of a larger unit are separated by two vertical lines, ||. Phrases that express entirely independent thoughts are separated by two vertical lines with a dot between them, |·|. Sometimes a phrase is broken by a slight pause for emphasis or clearness; such a pause may be indicated by a shorter vertical line, thus, ¹.

No one can understand America with his brains |·| It is too big || too puzzling |·| It tempts || and it deceives |·| But many an illiterate immigrant¹ has felt the true America in his pulses | before he ever crossed the Atlantic |·| The descendant of the Pilgrims¹ still remains ignorant of our national life | if he does not respond to its glorious zest | its throbbing energy | its forward urge | its uncomprehending belief in the future | its sense of the fresh and mighty world¹ just beyond to-day's horizon |·| Whitman's 'Pioneers, O Pioneers'¹ is one of the truest of American poems | because it beats with the pulse of this onward movement || because it is full of this laughing and conquering fellowship¹ and undefeated faith |·|

Subordination and Coördination of Phrases

After the habit of thinking in phrases has been established, the next step is to recognize that, while some phrases carry on the main current of the author's thought, others merely add qualifying or explanatory matter. The reader indicates this relationship between phrases by giving due prominence to the principal groups and subordinating the others. In the last sentence of the paragraph from "The American Mind" it is clear that the two clauses beginning with *because* are subordinate to the first clause, although they are coördinate with regard to one another. Sometimes the thought is so involved that there are several levels of importance. Often two elements of equal importance are separated by another of less or of greater value. In such cases subordination and coördination of phrases must be carefully considered, since the clearness of the passage depends upon the nicety with which these gradations are indicated by the voice.

Emphasis to Indicate the Progression of Thought

If you read again the passage concerning the spirit of America, you will find that the author's thought is carried on by means of the underlined words:

No one can understand America with his brains. It is too big, too puzzling. It tempts, and it deceives. But many an illiterate immigrant has felt the true America in his pulses before he ever crossed the Atlantic. The descendant of the Pilgrims still remains ignorant of our national life if he does not respond to its glorious zest, its throbbing energy, its forward urge, its uncomprehending belief in the future, its sense of the fresh and mighty world just beyond to-day's horizon. Whitman's 'Pioneers, O Pioneers' is one of the truest of American poems because it beats with the pulse of this onward movement, because it is full of this laughing and conquering fellowship and undefeated faith.

There is nothing in the whole technique of reading more important than this matter of giving to the basic, key words such unmistakable emphasis that the hearer's mind follows easily and inevitably the path which the writer has marked out. To give primary emphasis to an idea that has already been expressed or implied, or that is unimportant, may reduce a whole passage to nonsense. To avoid this misleading emphasis requires an intensity of concentration of which few minds are capable without much training.

This difficulty will be better understood through study of the underlined words in the passage above. It will be noted that the word *America* in the fourth sentence is not a new idea, but is essential to the structure of the sentence, being the object of the verb *has felt.* For this reason it naturally receives some measure of emphasis, as has been indicated by underscoring with a dotted line. If, however, it is spoken with the same strong, direct stroke of the voice that the word receives in the first place, the impression is either that a different America is being referred to or that the reader thinks his hearers too stupid to get the idea the first time it is mentioned. Similarly, in the last sentence the expressions "onward movement," "laughing and conquering fellowship," and "undefeated faith" are not new concepts, but restatements of ideas expressed in the preceding sentence. They are important elements in the sentence and must, therefore, have due emphasis, but this must not be the same kind of emphasis that is given to the expressions "glorious

zest," "throbbing energy," "forward urge," "uncomprehending belief in the future," and "fresh and mighty world
just beyond to-day's horizon." Similarly, the phrase
"American poems" expresses, not a new idea, but one which
may be considered obvious, to a college student at least.

The first principle of emphasis, then, is to distinguish
between *new* ideas and those which have been *mentioned*
or *implied before*.

Old ideas are often expressed by pronouns or synonyms,
in which case they are easily recognized as repetitions. But
the matter is much more difficult when the repetition of
thought is not so obvious or when it is implied rather than
expressed, as in such an expression as "In the springtime, as
the days grow full." Here the conception of lengthening
days is so much a part of the idea of spring that it should not
receive special emphasis. To emphasize it would imply that
the reader gives his audience credit for very little observation
of the ways of nature.

Emphasis for Intensification of Thought

The emphasis so far discussed has to do primarily with
making the thought clear and progressive. Often, however,
ideas are added for the purpose of intensifying the thought
or of revealing the author's personal feeling about it. In
Shakespeare's lines,

> From you have I been absent in the spring,
> When proud-pied April, drest in all his trim,
> Hath put a spirit of youth in everything,
> That heavy Saturn laughed and leaped with him.

it is apparent that the factual content is expressed in the
first line; the remainder of the passage, and, indeed, of the
whole sonnet, merely expresses the intensity of the poet's
feeling concerning that absence. Such intensification of
thought calls for emphasis of another kind.

The difference between these two types of emphasis—
that for intellectual clearness and that for emotional intensification—can perhaps be best understood by thinking of the
first as *objective* and the second as *subjective* in character.
Consider the use of the word *mad* in the following sentences:
"The mad king is a pathetic rather than a tragic figure,"
and "Thou'rt mad to say so." In the first, the word is
used simply to convey the information that the king is
insane and is used without particular coloring from the
mood of the speaker. In the second, the word is saturated
with the speaker's emotion.

The nicest discrimination is needed in this whole matter,
not only in distinguishing between what is primarily factual
and what is essentially emotional, but in making sure that
the emotional elements are given exactly the kind and the
degree of intensification that the author desired. Failure to
express the emotion intended makes dry, dull reading. For
this reason a reader who aims only at clearness often fails to
achieve even that, since he loses the attention of his hearers
and thus makes no impression on them. On the other hand,
emotion that is false or exaggerated or insincere on the part
of the reader leaves the intelligent hearer with a feeling of
profound disgust. This problem of emphasis for expressing
the mood of the author will be discussed more fully in a later
section of this chapter.

Means of Emphasis

When one has decided what words and phrases must be
emphasized in order that the meaning and mood of the
author may be made clear to the hearer, there remains the
problem of how this emphasis can best be achieved. There
are four chief means of emphasis, dependent on the four
properties of voice described in Chapter III: (1) *force*, or
volume; (2) *pitch*; (3) *duration*, or *time*; and (4) *quality*.
All of these elements, of course, are present whenever a voice

is speaking. It is by special uses of each that we achieve emphasis.

1. *Emphasis by Means of Volume or Force*

Variation of Volume.—Force is, in its broad sense, merely the vigor or vitality of the voice, a quality necessary to all good reading. This is true no matter how much the force is held in check, as strength of muscles is necessary to the pianist even when he is playing *pianissimo*.

Certain ideas are made emphatic by a deliberate lessening of the volume of the voice; for example, in the phrase, "But if you keep quite still," the emphasis is obtained by saying the last two words as softly as possible. To say them loudly would negative the whole meaning of the passage.

A special form of emphasis is achieved by gradually increasing the volume. Since an author usually puts his most important idea at the end of a phrase, sentence, paragraph, stanza, or scene, this power of gradual *crescendo* is one of the first requirements of an effective reader. This cumulative force is sometimes carried through a series of words, phrases, or even sentences, for the purpose of attaining a climax. The ability steadily to increase the volume of the voice in this way requires considerable training. It is essential to begin with moderate force and to increase it gradually and smoothly rather than explosively and stridently. To achieve this demands adequate technique in the control of the breath and ability to increase the volume of tone without undue tension of the vocal organs.

In Walter de la Mare's "The Listeners" there is increasing force in each challenge of the traveler; the third (which follows) is in itself an example of climax:

> For he suddenly smote on the door, even
> Louder, and lifted his head: —
> "Tell them I came, and no one answered,
> That I kept my word," he said.

Stress.—Stress, or increase of force on special words, is the most physical, the most primitive, the least subtle way of obtaining emphasis. It is the most natural method in the reading of ballads and other vigorous narratives, in strongly emotional scenes in the drama, in dogmatic statements and heated argument. No other form of emphasis is so natural or effective in reading "How They Brought the Good News from Ghent to Aix," "Boot, Saddle, to Horse and Away," the description of the fight in "Helen of Kirconnel," and such passages from Shakespeare as those beginning, "Ye blocks, ye stones, ye worse than senseless things," "Once more unto the breach, dear friends," and "Accoutred as I was, I plunged in." For subtler rhythms and subtler thought this use of mere physical energy is inadequate and inappropriate. In lyric poetry especially, where the musical element is so essential, sharp stress is to be avoided.

2. *Emphasis by Means of Pitch*

Under pitch we shall discuss *key*, or the basic pitch from which the voice travels up and down, and *inflection*, or the slides of the voice from one pitch to another.

Key.—Every passage is most effective when read in a particular key. A high key suggests the irresponsible gaiety of childhood. To read a sad or reflective passage thus would be to falsify its meaning. If our ears are trained, our voices flexible, and our imaginations alert, we shall not have to say to ourselves: "This is a passage of deep and solemn thought; I must read it in a low key." At first, however, it may be necessary consciously to tune the voice to the pitch that the mood of each selection requires, for reading a passage "out of key" destroys the emphasis completely.

A very important function of pitch in attaining emphasis is in facilitating fresh attack. Whenever we have finished a division of a subject or reached a climax, we should start the next thought on a different pitch. This not only indicates to the hearer the beginning of a new phase of the subject, but serves as a challenge to his attention.

Inflection.—It must not be supposed, however, that a passage should be read in a single key. In speaking, the voice continually goes from one pitch to another in order to express varying shades of relationship and degrees of emphasis; only sluggish-minded persons talk without these constant slides of the voice.[2] In reading, however, partly from failure to grasp the content and partly from self-consciousness in attempting to interpret another's thoughts and emotions, many persons either fail to make these constant changes or else repeat one or two intonation patterns endlessly. The result of the first fault is monotony so sedative that the hearer acquires little idea of the whole or of the especial significance of the principal points. The result of the second is a dreary sing-song which robs the selection of all meaning and beauty.

The correction of these faults is among the most important and difficult of all speech problems. First, the ear must be trained to such a point of sensitiveness to pitch that it detects at once this monotone and these meaningless inflections. Second, the various inflections of the voice must be practiced until great flexibility has been gained. And third, the mind must be trained to concentrate powerfully on the author's thought; if the reader ceases for an instant to concentrate on what he is reading and to be interested in it, he is in danger of falling into one or the other of these deadly sins.

Of all the modifications of the voice, inflection is the most intellectual. By its use, as we have already said, the phrasing is indicated. Each phrase ends with a bend of the voice which not only binds together as a unit the group of words it terminates, but shows whether the phrase is complete in itself or closely connected with what follows. If the phrase

[2] See page 63.

expresses a completed thought, it is ended with a downward stroke of the voice. If the thought is incomplete, the voice, though its general direction may be downward, ends with a slight upward curve.

Usually downward inflection indicates completion, decisiveness, self-assurance; sometimes it denotes bluntness and intolerance. An upward inflection indicates incompleteness, uncertainty, doubt, deference, courtesy, and sometimes weakness and mental cowardice. A waved (or circumflex) movement of the voice generally indicates insincerity or irony or some form of mental confusion. A strong downward stroke of the voice, whether on a whole phrase or on a single word or syllable, is a most important means of giving prominence to an idea. By its finality and decisiveness it makes the element thus emphasized stand out sharply from the rest of the sentence. This downward inflection for the sake of emphasis often occurs when the thought is incomplete and hence would normally take a rising inflection. The following sentence is an illustration of this apparently contradictory use of the downward intonation:

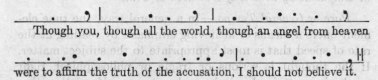

Though you, though all the world, though an angel from heaven were to affirm the truth of the accusation, I should not believe it.

It will be noticed that the words *you, world* and *heaven*, though they occur at the ends of phrases which express incomplete thought, take the downward inflection because they are all so emphatic.

It is chiefly by difference in inflection that the distinction is made between a new idea and one that has already been mentioned or implied. Read the following naturally and intelligently: "What Kezia liked more than anything was the lamp. It stood in the middle of the dining table, an exquisite little amber lamp with a white globe." You will notice that the voice behaves quite differently in saying the word *lamp* in the two sentences. In the first it comes down with a firm stroke as if to warn the hearer to give attention to this new and important idea. In the second sentence the voice takes a slightly upward turn, thus making the word less prominent and allowing the stronger emphasis to fall on the new idea, *amber*.

Since inflection is the chief means of emphasis used in conversation, it is of the greatest importance in dramatic presentation and in narration. Since it is the most logical and intellectual form of emphasis, it is employed where clearness and convincingness are particularly needed, as in exposition and argumentation. Since it appeals to the intellect rather than to the imagination and interferes with the subtler music of vowel pitch, its excessive use in reading poetry is to be discouraged. Most poets, in England especially, emphatically resent a too conversational reading of their poems.

3. *Emphasis by Means of Duration or Time*

Pace or General Tempo.—In a general way, the time element offers a means of achieving emphasis by reading at the rate of speed that is most appropriate to the subject matter. If the thought is serious or tragic or philosophical, right emphasis is attained only by a slow tempo. If, on the other hand, the subject matter is gay or exciting or trivial, the general tempo should, of course, be quick and staccato.

Emphasis on a particular element may be gained through the time element in three ways: (1) by pausing before or after it; (2) by giving it more time through prolongation of the vowels and sonorous consonants; (3) by intensifying the rhythm.

Pause.—A pause before a word or phrase (sometimes called the *anticipatory*, or *dramatic*, pause) emphasizes it by arousing interest through suspense. "Of nothing you will at last, after much lost labor, produce only nothing," is feeble unless there is considerable pause before the last word. The use of the anticipatory pause often makes a special demand on the intelligence and dramatic sense of the reader since the punctuation (as in this case) may fail to indicate the need for it.

A pause after an element (which may be called the *deliberative* pause) emphasizes it by allowing the hearer's mind to grasp the idea in its full significance. A passage which requires this sort of pause is the opening sentence of Lamb's "Poor Relations":

A Poor Relation is the most irrelevant thing in nature,—a piece of impertiment correspondency,—an odious approximation,— a haunting conscience,—a preposterous shadow, lengthening in the noontide of our prosperity,—an unwelcome remembrancer,— a perpetually recurring mortification,—a drain on your purse,— a more intolerable dun upon your pride,—a drawback upon suc- cess,—a rebuke to your rising,—a stain in your blood,—a blot on your scutcheon,—a rent in your garment,—a death's head at your banquet,—Agathocles' pot,—a Mordecai in your gate,—a Lazarus at your door,—a lion in your path,—a frog in your chamber,— a fly in your ointment,—a mote in your eye,—a triumph to your enemy,—an apology to your friends,—the one thing not needful,— the hail in harvest,—the ounce of sour in a pound of sweet.

Here the reader must stop after each accusation in order to allow himself and his hearer time to grasp each several enor- mity in all its hideous significance.

Sometimes an idea is of such importance that it should be both preceded and followed by a pause and thus stand out completely framed in silence. An instance of this sort occurs in the following lines from Lyly's "Cupid and Cam- paspe":

At last he set her both her eyes;
She won, and Cupid blind doth rise.

The whole point of the poem lies in the fact of Cupid's gambling away his eyes in a card game with Campaspe, and the word *blind* thus becomes so significant as to demand a pause both before and after it. Here again we see that we must rely, not on punctuation alone, but on our own realization of the author's intention.

Prolonging Vowels and Consonants.—Emphasis gained by prolonging a word through the lengthening of a vowel or voiced consonant is sometimes very effective, especially in lyric poetry where the poet has deliberately chosen beautiful vowel and consonantal resonances. This method always enhances the impressiveness in passages where the thought is somewhat grandiose, as:

> My name is Ozymandias, king of kings,

and

> . . . round the decay
> Of that colossal wreck, boundless and bare,
> The lone and level sands stretch far away.

In this latter passage, not only the long vowels, but also the *n*'s and *l*'s may be given extra length and sonority, a *legato* effect being thus produced which increases the sense of immensity and desolation. If this method is used self-consciously or to excess, however, it becomes a tiresome mannerism which, instead of enhancing emphasis, weakens it.

Heightening Rhythm.—Sometimes an idea is most effectively emphasized by intensification of the rhythm. The following quotations afford illustrations of this means of emphasis:

> His ram's bell rings 'neath an arch of stars
> Rest, rest, and rest again.

and

> They tolled the one bell only;
> Groom there was none to see;
> The mourners followed after,

> And so to church went she,
> And would not wait for me.

This method also is useful if discriminatingly used, but here, too, there is danger. If rhythm is allowed to become too insistent, all meaning is lost in its lovely, hypnotic music.

4. *Emphasis through Tone Quality*

Tone quality in its wider sense [3] means the general condition of the voice with respect to resonance, clearness, and flexibility. Unless the reader's voice has a good general tone, his reading will never be wholly effective. But in addition to general vocal adequacy, certain particular qualities are necessary in order to give the right value to the more emotional elements in a selection. Fear, hate, love, sorrow, anger, and pity demand corresponding tonal qualities in the voice. Imaginative poetry and prose require a dominant vocal quality suggestive of the prevailing mood, just as they demand a dominant pitch and tempo; but within this general mood, and conditioned by it, there are often decided changes. An illustration of this is found in Walter de la Mare's "Nod." The dominant mood of the poem is that of warm drowsiness, but in the third stanza it is at least half awake—

> The hedge is quick and green with briar,
> From the sands the conies creep,
> And all the birds that fly in heaven
> Flock singing home to sleep.

Not to feel these quick and often subtle changes of mood is to miss the variety and charm that the poet intended. To feel them truly and to express them adequately involve taking the preparation many steps farther. So important is the ability to assume the mood of the author that it is discussed at length in the last section of this chapter.

[3] See Chapter III.

The Rhythmical Approch: through Discovery of the Rhythm of Thought

It must not be inferred that the preparatory work discussed in the preceding section will of itself ensure satisfactory reading of anything but simple, forthright prose, any more than a knowledge of anatomy on the part of a sculptor will automatically give him the ability to make a beautiful statue. No musician would think of playing a composition in public without having carefully studied it as a whole and in all its parts; but both before and after this purely intellectual study, he would play it many times almost passively, trying to hear it as it sounded to the composer, until he had caught the rhythm to which it owed its unity, individuality, and life. Similarly, anyone who wishes to give a satisfactory interpretation of a poem or a fine piece of prose will do well to begin by reading it over several times as if it were a musical composition whose rhythm he was trying to catch.

For those who have a strong natural or acquired sense of rhythm, this rhythmic identification will be easy from the start; for others it may at first be extremely difficult. It will be well to start with verse in which the rhythm is of the strongly marked kind by reason of a predominance of stress over time emphasis. Nursery rhymes and the child poems of Stevenson and A. A. Milne are admirable for acquiring this sense of free, joyous response to natural rhythms. One of the best of these for giving the feeling of a fine free sweep is Robert Louis Stevenson's "The Swing":

> How do you like to go up in a swing,
>   Up in the air so blue?
> Oh, I do think it the pleasantest thing
>   Ever a child can do!

This should be read over and over until all the cells in the body seem to be set vibrating to the rhythm of the swing.

A. A. Milne's "Christopher Robin goes hoppity hoppity" in *When We Were Very Young*, is almost equally good for the purpose. It should be read and reread until the physical pleasure a child feels in hopping and skipping is revived and the body regains the child's sense of lightness and freedom from strain. A poem that expresses a grown person's delight in rhythmical movement is Sorley's "The Ungirt Runners." It does not aim at telling a story or pointing a moral but contents itself with reproducing the joy an athlete feels in running through the rain on a summer day.[4]

Next a poem may be studied in which the rhythm, though based on bodily movement, is used not merely to create a physical sensation, but as the medium for expressing thought. A good choice for this purpose is Browning's "Marching Along," in his collection of "Cavalier Tunes":

> Kentish Sir Byng stood for his King,
> Bidding the crop-headed Parliament swing:
> And, pressing a troop unable to stoop
> And see the rogues flourish and honest folk droop,
> Marched them along, fifty-score strong,
> Great-hearted gentlemen, singing this song.
>
> God for King Charles! Pym and such carles
> To the Devil that prompts 'em their treasonous parles!
> Cavaliers, up! Lips from the cup,
> Hands from the pasty, nor bite take nor sup
> Till you're—
>
> CHORUS.—Marching along, fifty-score strong,
>   Great-hearted gentlemen, singing this song!
>
> Then, God for King Charles! Pym and his snarls
> To the Devil that pricks on such pestilent carles!
> Hold by the right, you double your might;
> So, onward to Nottingham, fresh for the fight,

[4] Charles H. Sorley, a captain in the British Army during the World War, was killed in action at the age of twenty. He was so fond of running in the rain that his fellow officers called a showery day, "Sorley's weather." "The Ungirt Runners" is quoted in Part II.

> CHORUS.—March we along, fifty-score strong,
>   Great-hearted gentlemen, singing this song!

In reading this it is possible to let oneself go almost as completely as in the poems first discussed, for although there is a certain thought content, it is little more than the expression of the contagious enthusiasm of a company of men marching together in a cause for which all are ready to risk their lives.

After catching the quick, joyous rhythm of these marching feet, it may be interesting to contrast this poem with Kipling's "Boots." It would be hard to find a greater contrast than between the spirit of

> Marching along, fifty-score strong,
>   Great-hearted gentlemen, singing this song.

and

> It's foot—slog—slog—slogging over Africa.

or

> Boots, boots, boots, boots, movin' up and down again,
>   And there's no discharge in the war.

This insistent measure beats into the brain the sense of weary and disillusioned men marching through unknown wastes for a cause they do not understand or believe in. Babette Deutsch's "Marseillaise" affords a contrast of the same kind.

The power of quick and sure response to rhythm can be further developed by reading aloud many poems based on fundamental rhythms, such as those of running, dancing, rowing, and working. The sense of freedom and power that primitive man found in his work songs and children find in their work-play songs [5] can be recaptured through this primary rhythm. Several poems of this sort will be found in the selections for practice in oral reading in Part II. The student will perhaps be interested in discovering still others, and in developing his ability to decide whether the rhythm

---

[5] Like, "This is the way we wash our clothes
  So early on Monday morning."

of a given poem is organic—that is, whether it grew out of the thought and is an integral part of the poem or whether it was imitated from some other writer.

When a certain sureness of rhythmical response has been developed, the student can proceed to the study of poems whose rhythm, though equally organic, is less purely physical. Thomas Hardy's "Lyonesse" is just on the border-line between these two types. The tune has, it is true, the confident, swinging stride of the adventurous traveler and is possibly the most important part of the poem. The words, however, not merely relate a particular adventure, but suggest a symbolic and universal meaning. Edna St. Vincent Millay's "The Spring and the Fall," though based on a walking measure, is concerned much less with imitating physical rhythm than with suggesting changes in season and in mood. It follows that the reader, though he must be no less physically conscious of the metrical rhythm of the poem, must concentrate all his powers on the mental and emotional content. If he succeeds in this, he will have gone far toward mastering what is perhaps the most difficult skill in reading, and will have learned to avoid the deadly monotony of sing-song and the equally deadly prosiness of an intellectual but unmusical reading.

Poems like Drinkwater's "Lord Rameses of Egypt" and Mary Coleridge's "Egypt's Might is Tumbled Down" carry us a step farther from primary rhythm. In these there is hardly a suggestion of purely physical movement,[6] the rhythmical setting having sprung somehow from the nature of the thought and emotion it embodies. Such measures, being subtler and less obvious in their nature, require still greater perfection of rhythmical response. This perhaps can be most quickly gained by what has been called the "sing-

---

[6] Though Miss Coleridge's poem was doubtless the result of a memory of the play-song of her childhood, "London Bridge Is Falling Down."

and-say" method. For training of this type a poem that was written as a song is good to begin with. The poems of Burns, except for the difficulty of the dialect, are especially good; "Flow Gently, Sweet Afton," having a beautiful *legato* movement and comparatively little dialect, will probably be best of all. Sing the first stanza,[7] then say it, then sing it, then say it, until your reading represents the poet's rhythm quite as perfectly as your singing. Though not in the same way, mind you. In singing "the *song's* the thing," whereas in reading the problem is to find a nice balance between the rhythmical setting of a poem, which may be called its body, and the thought, its informing spirit. The questions as to which of these elements came first in the order of creation and which should be felt as more important by the reader are still unsettled. It is interesting to observe that English readers, following the example of most of their poets, tend, especially in lyric poetry, to feel that the music of the verse should have primary consideration, or, more accurately perhaps, that the mood of the poem, which was more important to the poet than its purely intellectual content, is best revealed through the rhythm. The power to preserve the metrical rhythm in flawless perfection without in the least sacrificing the thought requires long and intelligent practice. But the delight of the possession is well worth the cost.

After this power has been gained, the next step is to study poems in which the thought has been set to a very definite, predetermined pattern. The extremes of this type are such forms of light verse as the triolet, the villanelle, and the madrigal, in which the form is everything and the thought very little; and the sonnet, in which the thought is so important that it dominates the somewhat rigid and

---

[7] In the privacy of your room it's no great matter if you fail to sing it very handsomely, or even accurately in the matter of pitch, provided you get a sure and satisfying sense of the rhythm.

austere verse form. Each type is excellent for developing a particular ability.

The light forms, mostly imitated from the French and Italian, are delightful as material for practice in achieving perfection of technique. Concentration on the manner is made easier by the unimportance of the matter. Such poems as Lyly's "Cupid and Campaspe" and Dobson's "I Intended an Ode" require almost unbelievable dexterity in articulation, in smoothness, lightness, and variety of tone, in pace, and lastly in ability to achieve the somewhat conversational effect in inflection without in any way sacrificing the lyric flow.

Sonnets are the most difficult form of poetry to read. Here, more than in any other form except the closely related blank verse, the metrical rhythm is subordinated to the thought pattern. Yet, if the underlying music is not strongly and surely present in the reader's consciousness (or unconsciousness), it would have been better for him to have elected to read prose. With the average reader the taste for sonnets develops slowly. Like many other plants of slow growth, however, this taste will be found well worth cultivating.

What will be the result of the attempt to develop, or rather release, a sense of rhythm? It will give a greater interest to the study of poetry and a greater power of discriminating between poetry whose rhythm is organic and that whose tunes are consciously or unconsciously borrowed from other writers. But the most immediate gain lies in the fact that the discovery of the fundamental rhythm of a poem means the discovery of the dynamic principle that gives it what has been called "the spirit of the whole." Finding the rhythm of a poem is thus a valuable contribution to the final synthesis toward which the intellectual analysis was only a preliminary step.

THE NARRATIVE APPROACH: THROUGH IMAGINATIVE RECREATION OF A STORY

Another approach to the interpretation of literature takes advantage of a human trait almost as universal as a sense of rhythm—interest in a story. It has already been pointed out that action is one of the surest means of arousing primary, or involuntary, attention. A story combines this fundamental appeal with others equally compelling—suspense and interest in what happens to one's fellow beings. In learning how to make a piece of narrative literature "come alive" for oneself and one's hearers, it is well to begin with a simple type of narrative—a folk or fairy tale or a ballad.[8] Through such primitive stories or poems one most easily learns to recognize the essential elements in narration and acquires the habit of reliving what is read.

Reduced to their lowest terms, these elements consist of (1) the arousing of interest in a person, whom we may call the hero; (2) the involving of the hero in a situation the outcome of which is uncertain; (3) a chain of events through which the hero's predicament seems alternately to approach solution and to become still further involved; (4) a climax, in which the hero's circumstances, after having gone as far as possible in one direction, take a sudden turn in the opposite direction; and (5) after a moment of final suspense, a resolution of the tangle—a happy or unhappy ending.

In a ballad like "Sir Patrick Spens" this structure is revealed in stark outline:

> The King sits in Dumferling toune
> Drinking the blude-red wine.
> "Now where shall I get guid sailor
> To sail this ship of mine?"

---

[8] This may be studied independently or the whole class may recreate the story with the teacher according to the method so successfully used by Professor Azubah J. Latham of Columbia University.

It is dreary winter in Scotland. Much wine is needed to keep up circulation and spirits in the drafty barracks that were palaces in those days.

> The King has written a braid letter
> And signed it wi' his hand,
> And sent it to Sir Patrick Spens,
> Was walking on the strand.

Some enemy has conspired to get the bold seaman out of the way. He foresees his doom but does not for a moment think of trying to evade it. Events move with the swift inevitableness of a Greek tragedy. There is initial success: the outward-bound ship comes safe to harbor. But now the foretaste of disaster:

> "Late, late yestreen I saw the new moon
> With the auld moon in her arm,
> And I fear, I fear, my dear maister,
> That we shall come to harm."

Then follows catastrophe—the struggle with an overwhelming fate and swift and utter defeat at its hands:

> The Scottish nobles were richt laith
> To wet their cork-heeled shoone,
> But lang ere all the play was played
> Their hats they swam aboone.

Now that the play is played to its tragic end, the ballad singer allows himself a brief touch of pathos which is like the effect of a Greek chorus in reconciling the hearer by its tranquil beauty to this unwarranted destruction:

> O, land, lang may the ladies stand
> Wi' their gold kems in their hair,
> Waiting for their ain dear lords,
> For they'll see them na mair.

Half owre, half owre to Aberdour
'Tis fifty fadom deep,
And there lies guid Sir Patrick Spens
Wi' the Scotch lairds at his feet.

Even in its brief and imperfect form, from which the above stanzas are taken, perhaps more than in the fuller and less primitive versions of the ballad, we find the essence of narrative power and of the magic that arouses the imagination of the reader until he becomes a sharer in the act of creation. Once the whole scene has been relived in all its tragic intensity, the possibility of reading the ballad as mere words becomes unthinkable. Much work will yet be needed before it can be read beautifully, but the danger of reading it dully and lifelessly is past.

Modern ballads, both grave and gay, and short narratives in prose and poetry may also be used to evoke this inborn love of stories and to develop the ability to enter into their spirit. No less than through our common love of rhythm, it will be found that we gain the power to bring life to our reading through our common interest in the affairs of men. It was this interest that inspired one of the greatest of story-tellers to write the line that is sometimes called the most beautiful in all literature: *Sunt lacrimae rerum et mentem mortalia tangunt.* "These are the tears of things and mortal sorrows touch the heart."

THE APPROACH THROUGH IMAGINATIVE RECREATION OF MOOD

Still another approach to interpretation is through an attempt to catch and communicate the mood of the author. This process is closely akin to the objectives of the two approaches first described. Like them, it depends chiefly on the arousing of the imagination through the author's words. But in this case the imagination so functions that the reader actually sees, feels, hears, smells, and tastes what is described; and not only this, but he experiences these sense impressions in the same way as did the author. Moreover, he is able, provided he is not handicapped by lack of an adequate technique, to arouse the imaginations of his hearers to a point where they too share the author's sensory impressions, catch his mood, and relive his total experience.

This, and this only, is true reading—to relive the author's experience and recreate it entire so that one's hearers feel the same release that they would gain from actual participation in the event. This recreation through vicarious experience is what Aristotle had in mind in his well-known definition of tragedy—a spectacle of pity and fear which purges the mind by participation in the same emotions. But it is not merely the emotions of pity and fear that purge the mind. An adequate reading of Keats' "I stood tiptoe on a little hill," can hardly fail to produce the joyous relaxation of body and spirit that a young poet feels when he stands on a hilltop on a May morning.

This process of recreating in the hearer the author's experience, however, is conditioned and must be preceded by a very intense realization on the part of the reader. The black symbols on the printed page must have come to life for him so that "nothing is but what is not." Richard Aldington in his poem "At the British Museum" describes this experience. He is reading an old book of Eastern travel:

I turn the page and read. . . .
The heavy musty air, the black desks,
The bent heads and the rustling noises
In the great dome
Vanish. . . .
And
The sun hangs heavy in the cobalt-blue sky,
The boat drifts over the lake shallows,
The fishes swim like umber shades through the undulating weeds,
The oleanders drop their rosy petals on the lawns,
And the swallows dive and swirl and whistle
About the cleft battlements of Can Grande's castle.

Everyone who passionately loves reading has at one time or another had this experience. Suddenly the words have ceased to be black scrawls and have become magic casements, opening not merely on "the foam of perilous seas, in faery lands forlorn," but on all sorts of alluring vistas. To persons who have this power of imaginative recreation. reading is not a dull and laborious process of self-improvement, but an unfailing source of delight. Like participation in an author's rhythm or in the thrill of his adventures, such sharing of his emotional experiences relaxes the tensions created by our modern mechanized civilization.

How can this power of intense realization be cultivated?

First, by forming the habit of keener observation and more intense appreciation of the beauty of the world, of the amazing variety of human character, of the "tears of things," and the laughter. This deepening of observation and sensibility is necessary for success in the recreation that alone is true reading. The keener our appreciation of what a Scotch writer has called "this queer clamjamfery of a world," the keener will be our enjoyment of its infinite variety in literature.

Secondly, we can increase the power of intense realization by training not merely "that inward eye which is the bliss of solitude," but the responsiveness of all the other senses to the stimuli of the imagination. This can be accomplished in several ways. One of the surest and most pleasant is to form the habit of stopping in silent reading to grasp not merely what the author has said, but also what he has suggested. When we read Chaucer's words, "the smiler with the knife beneath his cloak," we may well ask ourselves a number of questions. Do we really see the man described? Is he tall or short, light or dark, fat or thin? What is the color of his cloak? How does he walk? What sort of eyes has he? What sort of smile? How does Chaucer feel toward him? When Guy de Maupassant says, "He was a little black man who always went through a door first," how complete a picture do we make? An active imagination will make a full-length portrait of the man from those few strokes of the pen.

No less important than this power of filling in details in a given sketch is that of integrating a multitude of details so that a clear picture emerges. In describing a person, for instance, the writer cannot give us the whole picture at once as a painter can do. He can only give us a bit here and a bit there and try by his art to arouse our imagination to such a point of creativeness that it puts these scattered bits together and forms a living portrait. The true artist in words has this power of making his reader an accomplice to complete his work and make it live. Until one has cultivated this collaborative faculty, he should not try to read aloud.

Let us take two or three descriptions and see if we can discover the magics that will make them real. One of these magics is suggestion, a favorite device of the younger school of poets who are almost morbidly afraid of the obvious.

> On a country road
> An old woman walks
> The autumn sun casts her shadow
> Long and thin.

How do we know that the time is either early morning or late afternoon? Notice the condensation and economy— the stage set in the first line, with the additional help of the word *autumn*, which by its symbolism serves to heighten the effect of the whole. Notice too the way in which the short, spare, unbeautiful words and halting metre help to heighten the impression of the old woman's halting and unexpectant walk.

Although this method of depending on suggestion for creating the desired effect is usually spoken of as very mod-

ern, it has always been the habit of poets to depend rather
on the selection of a few suggestive characteristics than on
a careful catalogue of features. This becomes clear if we
compare Rossetti's poem "The Blessed Damosel" with his
painting of the same subject. The poem gives only two
features, her hair and eyes—the latter described not as to
color and size but only as to expression:

> Her eyes were deeper than the depth
> Of waters still'd at even

and

> The wonder was not yet quite gone
> From that still look of hers.

And yet in many ways the poem gives a far more complete
conception of her than does the painting. To discover the
subtle means by which this is accomplished is excellent
training in interpretation.

First of all, the poet appeals to senses other than sight.
He suggests the smoothness of her cheek, the human warmth
of her body, the heavenly music of her voice. Certain details
are more striking when expressed in writing than in painting,
as, for instance, the magic numbers three and seven, especially when they are set into strong relief by the chiastic
order, "*three* lilies" and "stars were *seven*." Besides, her
inner nature is much more definitely suggested in the poem
than is possible in the painting. Furthermore, the poem gives
us the effect of seeing the girl through her lover's eyes, from
the opening lines which express his sense of her inability to
enjoy the delight of heaven without him—"The *blessed*
damozel *leaned out* from the gold bar of Heaven"—to the
final stanza in which he sees her smile and hears her weep.

The first stanzas of Keats' "The Eve of St. Agnes" illustrates a different style, but here also the method is that of
selection and suggestion rather than completeness of information. Let us examine this method for a moment.

St. Agnes' Eve—Ah, bitter chill it was
The owl, for all his feathers, was a-cold;
The hare limped trembling through the frozen grass,
And silent was the flock in woolly fold:
Numb were the Beadsman's fingers, while he told
His rosary, and while his frosted breath,
Like pious incense from a censer old,
Seemed taking flight for heaven, without a death,
Past the sweet Virgin's picture, while his prayer he saith.

His prayer he saith, this patient, holy man;
Then takes his lamp, and riseth from his knees,
And back returneth, meagre, barefoot, wan,
Along the chapel aisle by slow degrees:
The sculptured dead, on each side, seem to freeze,
Emprisoned in black, purgatorial rails:
Knights, ladies, praying in dumb orat'ries,
He passeth by; and his weak spirit fails
To think how they may ache in icy hoods and mails.

A cursory reading of these lines shows that the poet has given the impression of intense cold by telling the effect of silence and aching numbness which it produces everywhere. He secures unity of impression by making the thinly clad beadsman the center of interest and making the old man's suffering seem still greater by telling that even creatures as warmly clothed as the owl, the hare, and the sheep are benumbed with the cold. He still further intensifies the impression by showing that the "holy man" adds to his own misery the imagined suffering of the mortuary statues "in icy hoods and mails."

In both these descriptions the use of figurative language and vivid concrete expressions helps to bring about the coöperation of the reader and hearer:

Her hair that lay along her back
Was yellow like ripe corn,

and

Her voice was like the voice the stars
Had when they sang together,

and
> his frosted breath,
> Like incense from a censer old,
> Seemed taking flight for heaven, without a death.

Perhaps the greatest difference between these two poems and the modern one quoted above is their intense subjectivity.

What does all this mean? Does it not suggest that in real reading, the words through the mechanism of the conditioned reflex act as stimuli to create an echo of the sense impressions that would be aroused by the object of which the words are symbols? Does it not also mean that if in reading aloud one actually feels all these sense impressions, he will be able (granted always a properly trained speech mechanism) to arouse similar sensations in others?

One of the great flaws in the older, elocutionary method of teaching the oral interpretation of literature was that teachers, lacking confidence in their ability to arouse in their students this power of vivid recreation of thought, fell back into the easier way of training through imitation or the mechanical use of tricks by which the various impressions could be counterfeited. All hearers of discrimination could feel the difference, so that the whole technique of elocution became suspect, and persons of real intelligence, hating this artificial reading, fell into the fallacy of "natural" reading.[9] The real solution of the problem of oral interpretation is to train the imagination to recreate the author's experience, the vocal organs to express truly and fully this vicarious experience, and the ear to detect any falseness or feebleness in this expression.

*   *   *

It has seemed advisable to treat thus fully the subject of preparing a passage for oral interpretation because of the

---

[9] See the discussion of this fallacy in the quotation from Corson's *Voice and Spiritual Education* in Part II.

waste of effort that accompanies the student's undirected attempt at such preparation. It is obvious that not all of these steps in preparation will be necessary for every selection or for every student. They represent, however, types of approach which, if properly used, will add greatly to the student's enjoyment of literature and to his ability to arouse this appreciation in others. It is usually the neglect of one or another of these preparatory processes quite as much as the lack of adequate technique that makes most reading aloud so unsatisfactory to the reader and so painful to the hearer.

PART II

MATERIAL FOR PRACTICE

SECTION I

EXERCISES FOR DEVELOPING GOOD HEALTH HABITS

Relating to Chapter I

I. EXERCISES FOR RELAXING THE MUSCLES OF THE BODY

1. Stand easily erect. Droop forward from the hips, relaxing back, shoulders, head, and neck. While in this relaxed position, swing the body to the left and the right several times, keeping the arms hanging loosely and the knees "soft." Then, beginning with extension of the back, shoulders, neck, and finally the head, assume the correct upright position, well balanced and without undue tension in any part of the body.

2. *Arm-Relaxation Exercise.*—Stand easily erect.
  (a) Shake arms freely from the shoulders, being sure to keep the arms and fingers completely relaxed.
  (b) Swing arms forward and backward rhythmically from the shoulders.

3. *Relaxation of Muscles of the Neck and Shoulders.*—Sit easily erect. Drop head forward on chest. Describe a circle with head going left from forward head position around to a position where head is dropped back with eyes facing the ceiling, around right to first position. Repeat twice. Describe circle to the right.

4. *Shoulder-Relaxation Exercise.*—Sit or stand easily erect. Drop arms to sides. Describe circles with the shoulders.

II. EXERCISES FOR DEVELOPING THE MUSCLES OF THE BODY[1]

1. *Stretching.*—Stand erect. Push arms easily upward and rise on toes as far as possible. Let arms sink and heels touch the floor but retain as long as possible the sensation of extension. This is a natural movement which straightens the spine, lifts the chest, and

---

[1] Exercises 1, 2, 3, 5, 6, and 7 are quoted by permission of the author and publisher from Jesse F. Williams, "Health Exercises for Everyday Use," *Teachers College Record*, November, 1918.

overcomes the sagging of the abdominal muscles so commonly seen in adults.

2. *Standing Exercise.*—Stand with the feet parallel to each other and several inches apart. Place one foot three or four inches in front of the other. Have weight on both feet disposed to their outer edges. This position of the feet produces balance, pivot, and control. Push the trunk upward and lift the abdominal wall upward. Retain a feeling of relaxation in the shoulders but secure a sensation of extension and lengthening of the body without contracting or tensing the muscles. Avoid rigidity. Keep the lower half of the abdominal wall constantly flattened.

3. *Throwing.*—Stand with feet about two feet apart and with the left foot about six inches in front of the right. Clasp hands lightly, waist high, shift weight to the right foot, bend the right knee, draw both hands to the right, twist the trunk to the right, and turn the head to the right. The left leg is straight and relaxed and the left heel is off the floor. The trunk is inclined forward. Throw the right hand, twisting the trunk sharply to the left. The left knee is bent and the right knee is straight with the heel off the floor. The body should form a straight line from head to right heel. This is a powerful trunk exercise. It uses the back and side muscles and brings into play the large muscles of both arms and both legs.

4. *Bicycling.*—Lie flat on the back on the floor. Extend knees alternately as in bicycling, describing rhythmical circles in the air. Repeat. This is especially good for strengthening back, chest, and abdominal muscles.

5. *Climbing.*—Stand easily erect. Reach upward with the arms, raise the right knee forward and push the body upward on the ball of the left foot. Secure vigorous stretching upward. Then return to standing position. Repeat in a slow rhythm, accenting the upward movement. This movement is a powerful exercise for the legs and secures strong contraction of the abdominal muscles.

6. *Walking.*—Stand easily erect. Raise the left knee forward and swing the right arm forward, the body remaining poised on the ball of the right foot. Then reverse the position of arms and legs. The rhythmical and continuous walk should be used as soon as the idea of the arm and leg movement is comprehended.

7. *Running.*—Stand easily erect. Swing the right arm forward and thrust the left knee upward and forward, at the same time pushing the body upward on the ball of the right foot. Then

reverse the position of the arms and legs and push the body up on the ball of the left foot. After the coördination is learned, the run should be executed in rhythm. This exercise vigorously stimulates the circulatory and respiratory systems, and will aid in improving all the functions of the organs supplying the body with energy. It should be possible for one to run and enjoy the movement.

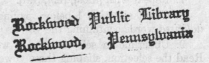

SECTION II

VOICE EXERCISES

Relating to Chapters II and III

I. PRELIMINARY VOWEL PRACTICE

BEAUTY of tone depends chiefly upon good vowels, and good vowels are those which are initiated easily, shaped carefully, and focused forward on the lips. Few students give full value to vowels. The vocalization must be smooth and even deliberate. Speech in which the vowels are scanted is always unmusical.

1. Whisper the vowels [u], [oʊ], [ɔ], [ɑ]—[ɑ], [ɔ], [oʊ], [u] to further develop a sense of correct formation, paying particular attention to lip-shaping and to the feeling of an open throat. *Be sure that the tip of the tongue is behind the lower front teeth for all vowels.*

2. Chant [u], [oʊ], [ɔ], [ɑ]—[ɑ], [ɔ], [oʊ], [u] on the chord tones 1, 3, 5, 8—8, 5, 3, 1.

3. Sing the scale on [u], [oʊ], [ɔ], [ɑ], [i], [eɪ], [aɪ], [ɒɪ].

4. Chant and then say [l] before each vowel and diphthong in the above; [l] after each vowel and diphthong in the above; [l] before and after each vowel and diphthong in the above. Be careful not to insert the vowel [ə] before the [l].

5. Chant on one tone *lu, lu, lu, lu, lu.*

6. Say the same accenting each syllable in turn, as *lú, lu, lu, lu, lu; lu, lú, lu, lu, lu,* etc.

7. Repeat with [moʊ], [nɔ], [taɪ].

8. Chant selection 1 below, paying particular attention to the *italicized* words containing the vowels [u] and [ɔ].

9. Underline in selection 2 the words containing [u] and [oʊ]. Read the selection, shaping these vowels carefully.

252

10. Underline in selections 3 and 4 the words that have special emphasis according to the thought. Read the selections, making these words important by giving extra support to the vowels.

11. Read selection 5, giving special attention to all diphthongs, avoiding a drawl by steady control of the tongue and breath.

12. Look through the exercises for vowel practice in Section III and read one selection for each of the vowels [ʊ], [ɒ], [ɜ], [ə], [ʌ], [æ], [a], [ɛ], [ɪ] and the diphthongs [ɪə], [ɒə], [ʊə], [aʊ], [ɛə].

13. Detect any special sounds in your speech which seem particularly susceptible to nasality. To breathiness. To glottal shock. To drawling. To throatiness.

14. Determine what part the ear plays in vowel practice.

SELECTIONS FOR PRACTICE

1. She left the web, she left the *loom*,
She made three paces *through* the *room*,
She *saw* the water lily *bloom*,
She *saw* the helmet and the *plume*,
She looked down to Camelot.

TENNYSON

2. The moon on the one hand, the dawn on the other·
The moon is my sister, the dawn is my brother.
The moon on my left and the dawn on my right,
My brother, good morning; my sister, good night.

HILAIRE BELLOC

3. Round the cape of a sudden came the sea,
And the sun looked over the mountain's rim:
And straight was a path of gold for him,
And the need of a world of men for me.

BROWNING

4. I saw old Autumn in the misty morn
Stand shadowless, like Silence listening
To silence, for no lonely bird would sing
Into his hollow ear, from woods forlorn,
Nor lowly hedges, nor solitary thorn;
Shaking his languid locks all dewy bright
With tangled gossamer that fell by night.

THOMAS HOOD

5. Deep in the shady sadness of a vale
Far sunken from the healthy breath of morn,
Far from the fiery noon, and eve's one star,
Sat grey-haired Saturn, quiet as a stone,
Still as the silence round about his lair;
Forest on forest hung about his head
Like cloud on cloud.

Keats

II. Exercises for Developing Support of Tone

The following are exercises to develop buoyancy, elasticity, vigor, vitality, and firmness in tone production. The physical conditions for support of tone are, as has been explained, (1) a sympathetic expansion of the whole body, (2) an easy and noiseless intake of breath, and (3) an openness in the vocal passage. This condition will not secure the desired result unless it is brought about through the imagination, which makes the voice seem the natural expression of thinking and feeling.

1. Take an active sitting position:
   (a) Sit easily erect.
   (b) Place hips well back in the chair.
   (c) Swing slightly forward on the hip hinges.
   (d) Place feet flat on floor.
   (e) Take an easy, deep breath, expanding the thorax from under the armpits to the waist line at the side and from front to back, especially at the back.

NOTE: A correct *standing* position for speech was fully described in Chapter III.

2. Place hand lightly on upper chest to be sure that there is a very slight lift in the chest indicating free play of muscles. Repeat the following words, using a buoyant, well-supported tone directed to the lips:

   (a) Fee—fie—fo—fum!
   (b) Boomlay, boomlay, boomlay, boom!
   (c) Ding-dong, ding-dong-bell!
   (d) Ye blocks, ye stones, ye worse than senseless things!
   (e) We take the Golden Road to Samarkand!

(*f*) What, ho! ye weary hunters!

(*g*) Blow, bugles, blow!

(*h*) The King is dead; long live the King!

3. Carry the same buoyant tone quality in repeating the numbers *1 — 2 — 3 — 4 — 5.*

4. Accent each number in turn, as *1́, 2, 3, 4, 5; 1, 2́, 3, 4, 5,* etc.

5. Tell a gay story in ten numbers with a surprise at the end: *1, 2, 3, 4 — 5, 6 — 7 — 8 —— 9 —— 10 !*

6. Read the seven selections below, which have been chosen because of their vigor of thought or feeling. Before you read them aloud be sure you know (*a*) who is talking; (*b*) what he says; (*c*) how he feels about it.

SELECTIONS FOR PRACTICE

1. Waken, lords and ladies gay,
  On the mountain dawns the day;
   And the jolly chase is here
  With hawk and horse and hunting-spear;
  Hounds are in their couples yelling,
  Hawks are whistling, horns are knelling,
  Merrily, merrily mingle they,
    "Waken, lords and ladies gay!"
                              SIR WALTER SCOTT

2. I sprang to the stirrup, and Joris, and he,
  I gallop'd, Dirck gallop'd, we gallop'd all three;
  "Good speed!" cried the watch, as the gate-bolts undrew;
  "Speed!" echoed the wall to us galloping through;
  Behind shut the postern, the lights sank to rest,
  And into the midnight we gallop'd abreast.
                              BROWNING

3. Kentish Sir Byng stood for the King,
  Bidding the crop-headed Parliament swing:
  And, pressing a troop unable to stoop
  And see the rogues flourish and honest folk droop,
  Marched them along, fifty-score strong,
  Great-hearted gentlemen, singing this song.
                              BROWNING

4. Oh, the wild joys of living! the leaping from rock up to rock,
   The strong rending of boughs from the fir-tree, the cool silver
   shock
   Of the plunge in a pool's living water, the hunt of the bear
   And the sultriness showing the lion is couched in his lair.
   How good is man's life, the mere living! how fit to employ
   All the heart and the soul and the senses forever in joy!

   BROWNING

5. Then, welcome each rebuff
   That turns earth's smoothness rough,
   Each sting that bids nor sit nor stand but go!
   Be our joys three-parts pain!
   Strive, and hold cheap the strain;
   Learn, nor account the pang; dare, never grudge the throe!

   BROWNING

6. Fat black bucks in a wine-barrel room,
   Barrel-house kings, with feet unstable,
   Sagged and reeled and pounded on the table,
   Pounded on the table,
   Beat an empty barrel with the handle of a broom,
   Hard as they were able,
   Boom, boom, BOOM,
   With a silk umbrella and the handle of a broom,
   Boomlay, boomlay, boomlay, BOOM.

   VACHEL LINDSAY [1]

7. Look ahead, look a-starn, look the weather and the lee.
   Blow high! blow low! and so sailed we.
   I see a wreck to windward and a lofty ship to lee,
   A-sailing down all on the coasts of High Barbary.

   Then hail her, our captain he called o'er the side:
   Blow high! blow low! and so sailed we.
   O are you a pirate or a man-o'-war, he cried?
   A-sailing down all on the coasts of High Barbary.

   O are you a pirate or man-o'-war, cried we?
   Blow high! blow low! and so sailed we.
   O no! I'm not a pirate but a man-o'-war, cried he.
   A-sailing down all on the coasts of High Barbary.

---

[1] From "The Congo," in *The Congo, and Other Poems*, copyright,
1914, by the Macmillan Company; quoted by permission.

Then pack up your topsails, and heave your vessel to,
Blow high! blow low! and so sailed we.
For we have got some letters to be carried home by you.
A-sailing down all on the coasts of High Barbary.

We'll back up our topsails and heave our vessel to;
Blow high! blow low! and so sailed we.
But only in some harbor and along the side of you.
A-sailing down all on the coasts of High Barbary.

From "The Coasts of High Barbary," an English folk song.

III. Exercises for Developing Projection of Tone

No matter how well a tone is supported, it must be mentally projected in order to possess its full effectiveness and carrying power.

1. Humming exercise. Begin with a hum properly focused on the lips (plucking the lower lip will sometimes help to make sure that the lips vibrate).

(a) Hum—[u]......   [mi], [mi], [mi], [mi]—[mu]
(b)   " —[oʊ]......   [mi], [mi], [mi], [mi]—[moʊ]
(c)   " —[ɔ]......   [mi], [mi], [mi], [mi]—[mɔ]
(d)   " —[ɑ]......   [mi], [mi], [mi], [mi]—[mɑ]
(e)   " —[i]......   [mi], [mi], [mi], [mi]—[mi]

2. (a) Sing [lu] on scale tones, as

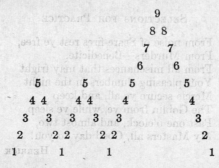

(*b*) Repeat, accenting every other tone, as

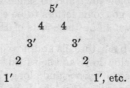

(*c*) Repeat, using various melody patterns with other vowels and diphthongs. Be sure there is no break in the flow of the tone.

3. Project the following syllables across a large room against the opposite wall (give the last syllable with particular firmness and precision of aim):

[lu], [lu], ['lu]   [loʊ], [loʊ], ['loʊ]   [lɑ], [lɑ], ['lɑ]

[lɔ], [lɔ], ['lɔ]   [laʊ], [laʊ], ['laʊ]   [leɪ], [leɪ], ['leɪ]

[laɪ], [laɪ], ['laɪ]   [lɒɪ], [lɒɪ], ['lɒɪ]   [li], [li], ['li], etc.

4. Chant and then say selection 1 below, "The Bellman's Call." (It may be helpful in sensing the rhythm to use the pantomime of the watchman swinging the bell as he walks through the street.)

5. Chant selection 2 as if you were talking through a megaphone.

6. Practice selection 5 for clear, delicate articulation and forward placement to show that a light tone, if well supported and projected, will carry as well as a more vigorous one.

7. In selection 6 indicate the differences in the two voices due to their mental attitudes.

SELECTIONS FOR PRACTICE

1.   From noise of Scare-fires rest ye free,
        From Murders—Benedicite.
        From all mischances that may fright
        Your pleasing slumbers in the night
        Mercie secure ye all, and keep
        The Goblin from ye, while ye sleep.
        Past one o'clock, and almost two,
        My Masters all, Good day to you!

                                    HERRICK

2. Blow trumpet, for the world is white with May!
Blow trumpet, the long night hath roll'd away!
Blow thro' the living world—"Let the king reign!"

TENNYSON

3. Sound, sound the clarion, fill the fife!
To all the sensual world proclaim,
One crowded hour of glorious life
Is worth an age without a name.

SIR WALTER SCOTT

4. Rejoice, you men of Angiers, ring your bells!
King John, your king and England's, doth approach.
Our colors do return in those same hands
That did display them when we first march'd forth;
Open your gates and give the victors way!

SHAKESPEARE

5. Full fathom five thy father lies;
Of his bones are coral made;
These be pearls that were his eyes;
Nothing of him that doth fade
But doth suffer a sea-change
Into something rich and strange.
Sea-nymphs hourly ring his knell;
Hark! now I hear them—ding-dong, bell.

SHAKESPEARE

6. THE MASTER OF THE CARAVAN
Open the gate, O watchman of the night.

THE WATCHMAN

Ho, travellers, I open. For what land
Leave you the dim-moon city of delight?

THE MERCHANTS (*with a shout*)
We make the Golden Journey to Samarkand.

JAMES ELROY FLECKER

IV. Exercises for Developing Smoothness and Purity of Tone

A good tone should be smooth and musical in quality and should have the power to sustain long phrases or long lines of poetry. Indiv'duals vary greatly in their kinæsthetic response to rhythm, and students often require much practice in order to produce sound sequences with the proper tempo, intonation, and stress.

In practicing the following exercises the student should maintain (a) a firm support to the end of syllables and phrases; (b) the tone color that suggests the mood; (c) the proper balance between the verse rhythm and the sense rhythm.

1. Practice combinations of various vowels, being careful to sustain the tone to the end, for example:

[lu] [lu] [lu]　　　　　　[nɔ] [nɔ] [nɔ]

[moʊ] [moʊ] [moʊ]　　　　[tɑ] [tɑ] [tɑ] etc.

2. Sing and then say selection 1 for the purpose of establishing the rhythmical form of the stanzaic structure of this poem. Think of each line as having a wave-like movement.

3. Chant and then say selection 2 below, giving particular emphasis to the verse rhythm. Notice the relative stresses of the strong and weak forms.

4. Read selections 3 and 4, analyzing the rhythmical pattern of each.

5. Read selection 6, working for a perfect association of the sense rhythm with the verse rhythm.

Selections for Practice

1.　　Flow gently, sweet Afton, among thy green braes,
　　　Flow gently, I'll sing thee a song in thy praise,
　　　My Mary's asleep by thy murmuring stream,
　　　Flow gently, sweet Afton, disturb not her dream.

　　　　　　　　　　　　　　　　　　　　　Burns

2.
> And when like her, O Saki, thou shalt pass
> Among the guests star-scattered on the grass,
> And in thy joyous errand reach the place
> Where I made one—turn down an empty glass.
>
> *Rubáiyát of Omar Khayyám*

3.
> O my Luve's like a red, red rose
>   That's newly sprung in June.
> O my Luve's like the melodie
>   That's sweetly play'd in tune!
>
> As fair art thou, my bonnie lass,
>   So deep in luve am I;
> And I will luve thee still, my dear,
>   Till a' the seas gang dry:
>
> Till a' the seas gang dry, my dear,
>   And the rocks melt wi' the sun;
> I will luve thee still, my dear,
>   While the sands o' life shall run.
>
> And fare thee weel, my only Luve,
>   And fare thee weel, a while!
> And I will come again, my Luve,
>   Tho' it were ten thousand mile.
>
> BURNS

4.
> There is a Lady sweet and kind,
> Was never face so pleased my mind;
> I did but see her passing by,
> And yet I love her till I die.
>
> Her gesture, motion, and her smiles,
> Her wit, her voice my heart beguiles,
> Beguiles my heart, I know not why,
> And yet I love her till I die.
>
> Cupid is wingèd and doth range,
> Her country so my love doth change;
> But change she earth, or change she sky,
> Yet will I love her till I die.
>
> THOMAS FORD

5.   Dune and mist and rain-touched lea—
        Spirit on the shore,
        Cool and still you call to me,
            Call me evermore.

EDITH FRANKLIN WYATT

V. EXERCISES FOR DEVELOPING LIGHTNESS AND DELICACY OF TONE

Review your exercises for consonant practice in Section III in order to be sure that each consonant is clearly and accurately formed.

1. Combine the plosives with various vowels, as:

[ti], [taɪ], [toʊ], [tu]
[it], [aɪt], [oʊt], [ut], etc.

2. Combine the lateral with vowels, accenting the last syllable, as:

[laɪ], [laɪ], [laɪ], [laɪ], ['laɪ]
[aɪl], [aɪl], [aɪl], [aɪl], ['aɪl], etc.

3. Combine fricatives with various vowels in a rhythmical order:

['vaɪ], [vaɪ], ['vaɪ], [vaɪ], ['vaɪ]
[zu], ['zu], [zu], ['zu], [zu], etc.

4. Read selection 1 below, bringing out the quality peculiar to plosives. Be sure there is a firm closure and a quick release. Avoid the so-called "flapped" [t], which sounds almost like [r].

5. Practice selection 2 for delicacy of plosives and the liquid quality peculiar to the lateral.

6. Practice selection 3 for plosives, lateral, and the fricatives [f] and [v].

7. Contrast selection 4 with selection 5 as to consonant values. What differences do you note?

8. Practice selection 6 particularly for the assimilations of [k] with [n] and for the [s] and [z] sounds.

9. Practice selections 7, 8, and 9, analyzing the effect of the consonants chosen to interpret the mood.

SELECTIONS FOR PRACTICE

SELECTIONS FOR PRACTICE

1.   Heard melodies are sweet, but those unheard
            Are sweeter; therefore ye soft pipes, play on—
        Not to the sensual ear, but more endeared,
            Pipe to the spirit ditties of no tone!

                                                KEATS

2.   There is sweet music here that softlier falls
        Than petals of blown roses on the grass.

                                                TENNYSON

3.   Under the leaves and the leaves of life
                I met with Virgins seven,
                And one of them was Mary mild,
                Our Lord's Mother of Heaven.

                                            Old song

4.   Over hill, over dale,
                Thorough bush, thorough brier,
                Over park, over pale,
                Thorough flood, thorough fire,
                I do wander everywhere,
                Swifter than the moon's sphere;
                And I serve the fairy queen,
                To dew her orbs upon the green.
                The cowslips tall her pensioners be;
                In their gold coats spots you see,
                Those be rubies, fairy favors,
                In those freckles live their savors:
            I must go seek some dewdrops here,
            And hang a pearl in every cowslip's ear.

                                            SHAKESPEARE

5.   Time flies,
                    Suns rise
                    And shadows fall.
                    Let time go by.
                    Love is forever over all.

                                On an old English sun dial

6.   Music, when soft voices die,
              Vibrates in the memory—
           Odours, when sweet violets sicken,
              Live within the sense they quicken,
           Rose leaves, when the rose is dead,
              Are heap'd for the belovèd's bed;
           And so thy thoughts, when thou art gone,
              Love itself shall slumber on.

                                        SHELLEY

7.   The clouds were pure and white as flocks new-shorn
           And fresh from the clear brook; sweetly they slept
           On the blue field of heaven, and then there crept
           A little noiseless noise among the leaves,
           Born of the very sigh that silence heaves;
           For not the faintest motion could be seen
           Of all the shades that slanted to the green.

                                        KEATS

8.   Golden slumbers kiss your eyes,
           Smiles awake you when you rise,
           Sleep, pretty wantons, do not cry,
           And I will sing a lullaby:
           Rock them, rock them, lullaby.

                                        DEKKER

9.   Come, wait upon him; lead him to my bower.
       The moon, methinks, looks with a watery eye;
       And when she weeps, weeps every little flower,
       Lamenting some enforcèd chastity.
       Tie up my love's tongue, bring him silently.

                                        SHAKESPEARE

VI. EXERCISES FOR DEVELOPING ORAL RESONANCE

Read again the discussion of nasality in Chapter III.
Bear in mind that the throat and the back of the mouth
should be open and free from strain; that the lips, tongue
tip, and soft palate should be flexible, light, and sure in their
action; that the breath should be sustained without effort
and directed well forward *through the mouth*; that the ear

should be trained to recognize and correct the least shade of nasality; and, perhaps most important of all, that a state of mind should be attained which should make nasality seem undesirable and its elimination worth the necessary effort.

If the exercises on vowels have been faithfully and intelligently practiced, the student will by this time have gained the power to make the individual vowels without nasalization. Practice on the following sentences, which contain few nasal consonants, will help to establish his feeling for an oral tone. He should practice them until he can read them in a clear, bell-like voice without nasality.

SELECTIONS FOR PRACTICE

1. There abideth, faith, hope, charity, these three; but the greatest of these is charity.—*I Corinthians*.

2. I gallop'd, Dirck gallop'd, we gallop'd all three.—BROWNING.

3. After life's fitful fever he sleeps well.—SHAKESPEARE.

4. All that glisters is not gold.—SHAKESPEARE.

5. Variety is the very spice of life.—COWPER.

6. Who shall tell of the pleasures of flight?—AMY LOWELL.

7. She is but a story that is told beside the fire.—JAMES STEPHENS.

8. This heavy act with heavy heart relate.—SHAKESPEARE.

9. The woman that deliberates is lost.—ADDISON.

10. Lift up your head, O ye gates; and be ye lifted up ye everlasting doors.—*Psalms*.

11. That he may run that readeth it.—*Habakkuk*.

12. It is not good that man should be alone.—*Genesis*.

13. He clasps the crag with crooked hands.—TENNYSON.

14. Everything comes if a man will only wait.—DISRAELI.

15. Behold, there ariseth a little cloud out of the sea like a man's hand.—*I Kings*.

16. And out of mind as soon as out of sight.—LORD BROOKE.

17. They kept the noiseless tenor of their way.—GRAY.

18. Be there a will, then wisdom finds a way.—CRABBE.

19. There is no new thing under the sun.—*Ecclesiastes*.

20. That which we call a rose by any other name would smell as sweet.—SHAKESPEARE.

21.   Lie lightly on her, gentle earth,
    Her step was light on thee.

                        An Epitaph

22.   He that complies against his will
    Is of his own opinion still.

                        BUTLER

23.   O, that this too, too solid flesh would melt,
    Thaw, and resolve itself into a dew!

                        SHAKESPEARE

24.   Across wide lotus-ponds of light,
    I marked a giant fire-fly's flight.

                        VACHEL LINDSAY [2]

25.   Fair is foul and foul is fair,
    Hover through fog and filthy air.

                        SHAKESPEARE

26.   The fair breeze blew, the white foam flew,
    The furrow followed free.

                        COLERIDGE

27. Oh thou that rollest above, round as the shield of my fathers,
    Whence are thy beams, O Sun—thy everlasting light?

                        OSSIAN

28. For I think that all right use of life, and the sense of life, is to pave ways for the firmer footing of those who succeed us. —MEREDITH.

29. One of the most striking differences between a cat and a lie is that a cat has only nine lives.—MARK TWAIN.

30. What can be expressed in words can be expressed in life.— THOREAU.

---

[2] From "A Chinese Nightingale," in *A Chinese Nightingale, and Other Poems*, copyright, 1917, by the Macmillan Company; quoted by permission.

VII. Exercises for Developing Nasal Resonance and Eliminating Nasal Twang

Full nasal resonance is necessary for beauty of tone. This demands the same freedom from rigidity in the muscles of the soft palate, tongue, throat, and larynx that is necessary in avoiding nasal twang.

The vowels and diphthongs most commonly nasalized are [aʊ], [aɪ], [æ], [ɛ], [eɪ], especially when preceded or followed by a nasal consonant. These vowels are frequently nasalized by persons whose vowels are otherwise quite free from defects.

Perhaps the quickest way to overcome this fault is to train the hearing and the kinæsthetic sense at the same time by consciously directing the tone through the nose and then through the mouth, learning both to hear and feel the difference. The following exercises are suggested for this purpose. In practicing the selections it is important to form every [t] and [d] with great firmness and precision, since this centering of the attention on a firm, forward articulation helps to counteract the natural tendency to allow the breath to pass out through the nose as it does in quiet breathing.

1. Learn to lengthen [m], [n], and [ŋ], with a free, musical quality of tone.

2. Chant [ŋ] — [ŋɑ] – [ŋɑ] – [ŋɑ]—[ɑ]. Feel the vibration of the nostrils on [ŋ] and the freedom from vibration on [ɑ].

3. Practice all vowels and diphthongs preceded by [s] and [z].[3]

4. Separate in the following the nasal from the rest of the word:

[taɪ], [taɪ], [taɪ], [taɪ—m]

[daʊ], [daʊ], [daʊ], [daʊ—n]

[lɒ], [lɒ], [lɒ], [lɒ—ŋ]

---

[3] Since in order to form [s] and [z] satisfactorily, the air must be definitely directed through the mouth, these consonants are least likely to be nasalized and are, therefore, best for establishing the kinæsthetic and auditory sense of an oral tone.

5. Practice with vowels in such combinations as

[mu]—[mu]—[mu]—— [mu]—[mu]—[mu]—— [mu]—[mu]—[mu]
[noʊ]—[noʊ]—[noʊ]— etc.

6. Place [m], [n], [ŋ] after all vowels.

7. Chant all the *italicized* words in selection 1 below for full nasal resonance.

8. Chant the following lines with the purpose of developing full nasal resonance.

(*a*) There is a lonely moorland stream.
(*b*) Blow, west wind, by the lonely mound.
(*c*) My Mary's asleep by thy murmuring stream.
(*d*) That orbèd maiden with white fire laden.
(*e*) Cities drowned in olden time.
(*f*) Ah, Moon of my Delight, that knows no wane.
(*g*) We are the music makers and we are the dreamers of dreams.

Selections for Practice

1.
Blow, west *wind* by the *lonely mound*
And *murmur*, summer *streams*;
There is no *need* of further *sound*
To soothe my lady's *dreams*.

Emily Brontë

2.
We are the music makers,
And we are the dreamers of dreams,
Wandering by lone sea-breakers,
And sitting by desolate streams;
World-losers and world-forsakers,
On whom the pale moon gleams:
Yet we are the movers and shakers
Of the world forever, it seems.

Arthur O'Shaughnessy

3.
Ah, Moon of my Delight, that knows no wane.
The Moon of Heaven is rising once again:
How oft hereafter rising shall she look
Through this same Garden after me—in vain!

Rubáiyát of Omar Khayyám

VIII. Exercises for Developing Depth and Breadth of Tone

These exercises are for the purpose of testing the student's ability to sustain tone and gradually and steadily to increase its intensity and resonance. This should be accomplished with no jerkiness but with a steady accumulation of vocal energy.

1. Repeat the numbers *1, 2, 3, 4, 5*, with cumulative force.
2. Repeat with vowel combinations such as

    [lu], [lu], [lu], [lu], ['lu]

    [noʊ], [noʊ], [noʊ], [noʊ], ['noʊ], etc.

3. Read with cumulative force:
    (*a*) My name is Ozymandias, king of kings.
    (*b*) Earth has not anything to show more fair.
    (*c*) Though much is taken, much abides.
    (*d*) To strive, to seek, to find, and not to yield.
    (*e*) Boomlay, boomlay, boomlay, boom.
    (*f*) Where are the snows of yesteryear?
    (*g*) This was all the harvest that I reaped.
    (*h*) So that wild dog, and wolf, and boar, and bear
      Came night and day, and rooted in the fields,
      And wallow'd in the gardens of the king.
    (*i*)   Sun and moon and beat of sea—
        Great lands stretching endlessly.
        Where be bonds to bind the free?
        All the world was made for me!

4. Read the following selections with firm support, **steady release** of breath, and a forward-flowing tone:

Selections for Practice

1.   "My name is Ozymandias, king of kings:
      Look on my works, ye Mighty, and despair!"
      Nothing beside remains. Round the decay
      Of that colossal wreck, boundless and bare,
      The lone and level sands stretch far away.

      Shelley

2. Though much is taken, much abides; and though
   We are not now that strength which in the old days
   Moved earth and heaven; that which we are, we are;
   One equal temper of heroic hearts,
   Made weak by time and fate, but strong in will
   To strive, to seek, to find, and not to yield.

                                        TENNYSON

3. And thus the land of Cameliard was waste,
   Thick with wet woods, and many a beast therein,
   And none or few to scare or chase the beast;
   So that wild dog and wolf and boar and bear
   Came night and day, and rooted in the fields,
   And wallow'd in the gardens of the king.

                                        TENNYSON

4. My good blade carves the casques of men,
       My tough lance thrusteth sure,
   My strength is as the strength of ten,
       Because my heart is pure.
   The shattering trumpet shrilleth high,
       The hard brands shiver on the steel,
   The splintered spear-shafts crack and fly,
       The horse and rider reel:
   They reel, they roll in clanging lists,
       And when the tide of combat stands,
   Perfume and flowers fall in showers,
       That lightly rain from ladies' hands.

                                        TENNYSON

5. Earth has not anything to show more fair;
       Dull would he be of soul who could pass by
   A sight so touching in its majesty:
   This city now doth like a garment wear
   The beauty of the morning; silent, bare,
       Ships, towers, domes, theatres, and temples lie
       Open unto the fields, and to the sky,
   All bright and glittering in the smokeless air.
   Never did sun more beautifully steep
       In his first splendour valley, rock, and hill;
   Ne'er saw I, never felt, a calm so deep!
       The river glideth at his own sweet will:

Dear God! the very houses seem asleep;
And all that mighty heart is lying still!

WORDSWORTH

IX. EXERCISES FOR DEVELOPING FLEXIBILITY OF TONE

SELECTIONS FOR PRACTICE

1.   As gold
Outvalues dross, light darkness, Abel Cain,
The soul the body, and the church the throne,
I charge thee, upon pain of mine anathema,
That thou obey, not me, but God in me,
Rather than Henry.

SHAKESPEARE

2. Could not this man, who opened the eyes of the blind, have
caused that even this man should not have died?—*Gospel
of St. John.*

3.   We undertook to mediate for the queen.—
To mediate for the queen?—You undertook?—
Wherein concerned it you?

SHAKESPEARE

4.   What shall I say to you?   Should I not say,
Hath a dog money?   Is it possible
A cur can lend three thousand ducats?

SHAKESPEARE

5. Because I live, ye shall live also.—*Gospel of St. John.*

6. IAGO: Did Michael Cassio, when you wooed my lady,
know of your love?

OTHELLO: O, yes; and went between us very oft.

IAGO: Indeed!

OTHELLO: Indeed! ay, indeed.   Discern'st thou ought in
that?   Is he not honest?

IAGO: Honest, my lord?

OTHELLO: Ay, honest.

IAGO: My lord, for aught I know.

OTHELLO: What dost thou think?

IAGO: Think, my lord?

OTHELLO: Think, my lord!   By heaven, he echoes me,
As if there were some monster in his thought
Too hideous to be shown.

SHAKESPEARE

7. Had you rather Caesar were living, and die all slaves, than that Caesar were dead, to live all free men?—SHAKESPEARE.

8.   What! amaz'd
At my misfortunes?   Can thy spirit wonder
A great man should decline?   Nay, an you weep,
I am fallen indeed.

SHAKESPEARE

9.   Think not the king did banish thee,
But thou the king.

SHAKESPEARE

10. NERISSA: Gave it to the judge's clerk!—but well I know
The clerk will ne'er wear hair on's face that had it.

GRATIANO: He will, an if he live to be a man,

NERISSA: Ay, if a woman live to be a man.

SHAKESPEARE

SECTION III

ARTICULATION EXERCISES

Relating to Chapters IV, V, VI, and VII

I. CONSONANTS

THE student is again reminded that exercises are of value, not in themselves, but only as a means of acquiring skills which should then be immediately and permanently incorporated into his everyday speech. He should decide, with the help of the instructor, what are the definite ends towards which he is working and which exercises will be of greatest help in attaining these ends. He should then practice those exercises until he can do them with accuracy and ease, but always with his definite object in view. There are few more wasteful occupations than careless and aimless practice. Before starting to work on any sound the student should be sure that he has gained a clear mental image of the sound and has learned its formation as described in Part I. He should use the mirror to compare his manner of articulation with that there suggested. From the beginning he should train his ear to hear the sound accurately and his muscles to recognize the feeling of the correct articulation. It is well to start with individual sounds and later to practice them in words and sentences.

A. PLOSIVES

[p], [b], [t], [d], [k], [g]

Plosives, more than any other sounds, give firmness and precision to the speech, and anyone who wishes to speak

273

effectively should take care that his plosives are clearly and crisply made. There are no better exercises for the lips and the tip and back of the tongue than practice on plosives, either alone or in combination with other sounds. Furthermore, these exercises help indirectly in overcoming nasality, since vigorous use of the lips and tongue tends to counteract the general sluggishness of articulation which is one of the chief causes of nasality. Practice on lip and teeth-ridge plosives, by concentrating attention on the front of the mouth, helps in directing the tone forward and in avoiding glottal stops. A heavy, labored articulation of the plosives brings too great an element of noise into the language and destroys its smoothness and rhythmic flow.

1. *Individual Plosives*

The following exercise is a good one to begin with, since it not only gives practice in making the sound, but helps to develop a feeling for rhythm and phrasing. Each line should be said on one breath, the time being the same for each. Accent strongly the first [p] in each measure.

The exercise from which this is developed was devised by Joshua Steele a hundred and fifty years ago, not merely as an aid in securing clear articulation, but as a cure for stuttering through the rhythmical control of the breath. The exercise should be practiced with all the plosives until it can be done accurately, easily, quickly, and rhythmically.

2. *Plosives Combined with Vowels*

The plosives may then be practiced in combination with the various vowels and diphthongs, thus:

[pi], [pɪ], [pe], [pɛ], [pæ], [pa], [pɑ], [pɒ], [pɔ], [po], [pʊ], [pu], [pɜ], [pə], [pʌ].

[peɪ], [paɪ], [pɒɪ], [paʊ], [poʊ], [pɪə], [pɛə], [pɒə], [poə], [pʊə].

[ip], [ɪp], [ep], [ɛp], [æp], [ap], [ɑp], [ɒp], [ɔp], [op], [ʊp], [up], [ɜp], [əp], [ʌp].

[eɪp], [aɪp], [ɒɪp], [aʊp], [oʊp], [ɪəp], [ɛəp], [ɒəp], [oəp], [ʊəp].

[bi], [bɪ], [be], etc.

Combinations of plosives with vowels may then be practiced in rhythmical exercises, thus:

['pɑ tə kə]	['pɑ tə kə]	['pɑ tə kə]
[pə 'tɑ kə]	[pə 'tɑ kə]	[pə 'tɑ kə]
[pɑ tə 'kɑ]	[pɑ tə 'kɑ]	[pɑ tə 'kɑ]

and

['poʊ tə koʲ]	['poʊ tə ko]	['poʊ tə ko] etc.

and

['beɪ de pe 'teɪ pe]	['boʊ do po 'toʊ po]
['bi dɪ pɪ 'ti pɪ]	['bu dʊ pʊ 'tu pʊ]

3. *Plosives Combined with Other Consonants*

The plosives [bd] (as in *robbed*) may be practiced in the Steele exercise, thus:

This exercise is exceedingly difficult to do firmly yet lightly without a vowel glide and in perfect rhythm. It should be done very slowly and precisely at first, then with increasing speed as the articulating organs become more adept.

The same or a similar exercise may be practiced with other combinations of two plosives like [pt], [kt], [gd]; with plosive-nasal combinations like [pn], [tn], [dn], [kn], [gn], [tm]; plosive-lateral combinations like [lp], [lb], [lt], [ld], [lg], [lk], and [pl], [bl], [tl], [dl], [kl], [gl] (special care being taken to form the last six pairs without the vowel glide): and the plosive-fricative combinations (or affricates) [ts], [dz], [tʃ], and [dʒ].

4. *Plosives in Words*

The plosives may then be combined in words. It will be seen that the word lists below are planned with several definite purposes in view. In the case of consonants, the first (and sometimes the second) line consists of words in which the sound in question is used initially and is followed by.

various vowels. In the case of [p], for example, the first line consists of words containing the back vowels; the second line, the front and middle vowels. The next line contains words in which the sound is used finally—in some cases, both initially and finally. Then follow groups of words in which it is used medially; then in initial and final combinations; and, lastly, with [l] and [n]. Most students will need considerable practice in order to make the [l], [n] group without the glide consonant. Such practice is invaluable for gaining flexibility of the tongue tip. The lists of words like *pan, ban*, are intended to give practice in distinguishing between voiced and breathed cognates and should be articulated very clearly and yet delicately.

Writing the words in phonetic script is a help in learning to think in terms of sounds rather than of letters.

The word lists should always be regarded as exercises in voice as well as in articulation. They should be practiced in a smoothly initiated, well-sustained and projected tone, and with an increasing sense of rhythm.

[p]

pool, pull, paw, pot, par
path, pan, pet, pink, pea, purr, pun
peep, pip, pep, pap, pipe, pop, pope
happy, pippin, proper, hoping, dumpling
please, pray, preach, speak
rapt, helped, depth, sips, wasps
apple, topple, happen, sharpen

[b]

bay, buy, boy, bough, beau, beer, bear, bore, boor
bib, bab, babe, barb, bob
baby, baboon, amber, somber
bread, bring, bloom, blink
robes, webbed, ribbed, bulb
amble, thimble, tremble, mumble, bubble

[p] *and* [b]

pan, ban	dappled, dabbled
pin, bin	ample, amble
pump, bump	crumpled, crumbled
cap, cab	simple, symbol
sop, sob	harper, harbor
cup, cub	roped, robed
maple, Mabel	ripped, ribbed
staple, stable	disperse, disburse

[t]

tay, tea, tie, toe, too
toot, taught, tart, tot, tight
sit, sat, set
city, mutter, lofty, fifty
state, train, twist, string
slept, tempt, locked, blinked, thatched
lots, posts, faints, faults, acts, insists
actuated, question, future, fixture, structural, mutual, fluctuating [1]
factotum, artist, tacitly, illiterate, practiced
brittle, prattle, shuttle, cotton, kitten
chair (*ch* = tʃ), debt, thyme, receipt, indict, subtle, yacht [2]

[d]

day, Dee, die, dough, do
dear, dare, door, doer
lad, led, lid, lead
could, cod, cad, card, cud, curd
dwell, dread, gem [dʒ]
heads, hedge, width, heard'st, hundredths

---

[1] These words may be pronounced with a [tj] or [tʃ] combination, but in either case the [t] should be firmly made.

[2] This group contains unexpected spellings of the [t] sound.

barbed, fatigued, twanged, wreathed, buzzed, hurled, **singed**
saddle, riddle, muddle; garden, hidden, sadden
huge [dʒ], jest [dʒ], Buddhism, would

[t] *and* [d]

time, dime	but, bud
tame, dame	heat, heed
tome, dome	late, laid
bet, bed	hurt, heard
latter, ladder	fattest, faddist
writer, rider	tight, tide
hearten, harden	shutter, shudder
trip, drip	troll, droll
contented, contended	sweet, Swede
tingle, dingle	tangle, dangle

[k]

key, Kay, car, cow, coo, cur
lick, lake, lack, lock, look, luck
seeking, pockets, trickster, cranking, picnic
creep, cling, skate
socks, asks, asked, pinks, taxed, tucked
picture, fraction, diction, fracture, structure
shackles, sprinkle, crackle
darken, shrunken, Lincoln, Pinkham
Bacchus, soccer, liquor, lacquer, echo, coquette, exercise, **Khan**

[g]

good, goad, god, guard, gad, guide, gird
wig, flag, dug, fog
shaggy, sugar, ragged, tugging, flagrant
gleam, groan
rags, flogged, brag'st
angle, haggle, shingle, wrangle
ghastly, exact, exaggerate, blackguard

[k] *and* [g]

cot, got	tuck, tug
came, game	clocked, clogged
cold, gold	anchor, anger
catarrh, guitar	ankle, angle
curdle, girdle	flocked, flogged
crumble, grumble	crackle, grackle
back, bag	crate, grate
peck, peg	racket, ragged
dock, dog	leaked, leagued

5. *Plosives in Connected Speech*

In practicing the selections below, notice the various ways in which authors use plosives to produce the effect desired. Observe the staccato movement in "Into the street the piper stept" and "Pins and poking sticks of steel." Read "With beaded bubbles winking at the brim" with the delicacy of articulation necessary to suggest the almost inaudible plopping of wine bubbles: and

> Double, double, toil and trouble,
> Fire burn and cauldron bubble

with such heaviness of lip pressure as will suggest the dull bursting of bubbles in the viscous brew of the witches' cauldron. Suggest heaviness also in "Cabin'd, cribb'd, confin'd" and "Sagged and reeled and pounded on the table." Read "Here are sweet peas on tiptoe for a flight" with lightness and delicacy. Notice the difference in the ticking of the clocks in numbers 14 and 15; the sense of solidity that the *b*'s and *d*'s give to the building in number 18; and the effect gained by the alliteration of *st* in number 22.

SELECTIONS FOR PRACTICE

1. She is but a story that is told beside the fire.—JAMES STEPHENS.
2. With beaded bubbles winking at the brim.—KEATS.

3.   Double, double, toil and trouble,
     Fire burn and cauldron bubble.

SHAKESPEARE

4. Into the street the piper stept, smiling first a little smile,
  As if he knew what magic slept in the quiet pipe the while.

BROWNING

5. Good-night, sweet prince, and flights of Angels,
   Speed thee to thy rest.

SHAKESPEARE

6. Of this sad world the loveliest and the best
   Has smiled, and said good-night, and gone to rest.

HILAIRE BELLOC

7. Is this the face that launched a thousand ships
   And burnt the topless towers of Ilium?

MARLOWE

8. Here are sweet peas, on tiptoe for a flight;
   With wings of gentle flush o'er delicate white,
   And taper fingers catching at all things
   To bind them all about with tiny rings.

KEATS

9. But now i am cabin'd, cribb'd, confin'd, bound in
   To saucy doubts and fears.

SHAKESPEARE

10. Your big clock speaks with a deadly sound,
   With a tick and a wail till the dawn comes round.

VACHEL LINDSAY [3]

11.   "Heart," I cried, "How goes it?"
     Heart replied,
   "Right as a ribstone pippin."
     But it lied.

HILAIRE BELLOC

12. And this grey bird, in Love's first spring,
   With its bright-bronze breast and its bronze-brown wing,
   Captured the world with its carolling.

VACHEL LINDSAY [3]

---

[3] From "The Chinese Nightingale," in *The Chinese Nightingale, and Other Poems*, copyright, 1917, by the Macmillan Company; quoted by permission.

13.   Pins and poking sticks of steel;
    What maids lack from head to heel.
    Come buy of me, come; come buy; come buy;
    Buy, lads, or else your lasses cry.
    Come buy.

    SHAKESPEARE

14.   Across the silent stream
         Where the dream-shadows go,
    From the dim blue Hill of Dream
         I have heard the west wind blow.

    FIONA MCLEOD

15.   As the pendulum ticks and ticks, dissecting time,
    Casting piece on piece into the abyss,
    Lost forever.

    CARL HAUPTMANN

16.   She wove a pair of breeches
         Quicker than that;
    She wove a pair of boots
         And a little cocked hat.

    EDNA ST. VINCENT MILLAY

17.   Fat black bucks in a wine-barrel room,
    Barrel-house kings, with feet unstable,
    Sagged and reeled and pounded on the table.

    VACHEL LINDSAY

18.   For an ye heard a music, like enow
    They are building still, seeing the city is built
    To music, and therefore never built at all,
    And therefore built forever.

    TENNYSON

19.   I walk down the patterned garden paths
    In my stiff brocaded gown.

    AMY LOWELL

20.   Whenas in silks my Julia goes
    Then, then, methinks, how sweetly flows
    The liquefaction of her clothes.

    Next, when I turn mine eyes and see
    That brave vibration each way free,
    Oh, how that glittering taketh me.

    ROBERT HERRICK

21.   And the plashing of the water drops
         In the marble fountain
         Comes down the garden paths.
         The dripping never stops.

                          AMY LOWELL

22.   While the cock with lively din
         Scatters the rear of darkness thin,
         And to the stack or the barn door
         Stoutly struts his dames before.

                          MILTON

In your reading look for examples of the artistic use of plosives. The nonsense verses of Edward Lear, Lewis Carroll, and A. A. Milne and the Gilbert and Sullivan operas are rich mines for this sort of treasure.

Practice Milne's "Christopher Robin Goes Hoppity Hoppity" until you can say

         That's why he always goes hoppity, hoppity,
         Hoppity, hoppity,
         Hop

with the firm, light, quick articulation which comes from perfect control of lips and tongue tip. If at the same time you support your breath firmly at the diaphragm, keep your throat free of strain, and round your lips on the [ɒ] to help in focusing the tone forward, you will by this one exercise make appreciable progress toward excellence in voice and speech. Good for plosive practice also are such nursery rhymes as

         Hippity hop to the barber shop
         To buy a stick of candy;
         One for you, and one for me,
         And one for sister Mandy!

These should be practiced first with meticulous accuracy in the formation of every plosive (great care being taken to avoid the substitution of the glottal stop for the proper plosive) and then with increasing rapidity and lightness until they can be said at lightning speed yet with no loss of clearness in articulation.

Excellent for practice also are such rapid narratives as Walter de la Mare's "Off the Ground," Southey's "How the Waters Come Down at Lodore," Scott's "Lochinvar," and Browning's "Pied Piper of Hamelin," "Hervé Riel," "Pheidippides," and "How They Brought the Good News from Ghent to Aix." Vigorous speeches from Shakespeare are also excellent, especially the passages from *Julius Caesar* beginning "Ye blocks, ye stones, ye worse than senseless things!" and "Accoutred as I was, I plunged in."

Having learned the value of plosives in giving clearness and vigor to speech and gained the power of articulating them easily and well, the next step is to incorporate this knowledge and ability into everyday speech. If the necessary labor is regarded as a game to be played with great earnestness and zest, it not only will seem much less onerous, but will be followed by better and more lasting results.

B. NASALS

[m], [n], [ŋ]

So much is said in dispraise of nasality that students sometimes get the idea that nasal consonants, like the sibilants, are essentially ugly sounds to be apologized for and dispatched as quickly as possible. Quite the reverse is true, however. The nasals, when properly made, are the most resonant of the English consonants. Fullness of resonance depends on firm control of air pressure, freedom from all restriction in the throat and nasal passages, and a firm but delicate contact of the articulating organs. It is the tightening of the throat, tongue, and palate muscles that causes the unpleasant twang called nasality. As plosives lend definition and dynamic vigor to speech, nasals give it sustained melody and carrying power. Congestion caused by colds and catarrh, stoppage due to adenoids and malformation, and stricture resulting from nervous tension give a dull, unmusical quality to these sounds. Since a change in the position of the soft palate is necessary in going from nasal to oral sounds, this organ should be so trained as to make the necessary change instantly and accurately without undue tension. Persons who naturally invert the post-dental sounds should take care to make the [n] on the teeth ridge instead of the hard palate; otherwise much of its resonance is lost.

1. *Nasals Alone and in Combination with Other Sounds*

Practice [m], [n], and [ŋ] by the Steele rhythmical exercise on page 274; also [n] and [m] combined with [l], as in *elm* and *stolen.* Exercises in combination with vowels have already been given in the section on voice exercises.

2. *Nasals in Words*

[m]

me, may, my, mow, moo

maim, mime, mum, ma'am, Maugham [mɔm]

summer, simper, murmur, shamming, amber, mumbling, umbrella, chimney

lamps, tombs, glimpse, dumps, benumbs, dreamt, warmth

sample, mumble, elm, chasm, rhythm

[n]

new, no, now, gnaw, nigh, nay, knee

noon, none, non, noun, nine

sinner, shining, anonymous

ant, sound, sense, cents, scans

tunnel, flannel, bundle

burden, heathen, often, stolen, kitten, even, frozen, broken, ripen

knock, gnome

[ŋ]

sing, sang, song, sung
singer, longing, longer, linger, linking
longs, winged, winked
mingle, tangle, bungled, spangled

3. *Nasals in Connected Speech*

Notice the value of nasal consonants (if made without
constricted muscles) in giving musical quality to a passage.
Read the selections below with full resonance and with
legato movement. Bring out the onomatopeia in numbers
3 and 5.

SELECTIONS FOR PRACTICE

1.
Come with me to the meadows,
We'll dance your secret name
With an outside dance in shadows
And an inside dance in flame.

RIDGELY TORRANCE

2.
Mortal though I be, yea ephemeral, if but a moment
I gaze up to the night's starry domain of heaven,
Then no longer on earth I stand; I touch the Creator,
And my lively spirit drinketh immortality.

PTOLEMY THE ASTRONOMER

3.
Five miles meandering with a mazy motion
Through wood and dale the sacred river ran
Then reached the caverns measureless to man
And sank in tumult to a lifeless ocean.

COLERIDGE

4.
Four ducks on a pond,
A grass bank beyond,
A blue sky of spring,
White clouds on the wing;
What a little thing
To remember for years—
To remember with tears.

WILLIAM ALLINGHAM

5.   Myriads of rivulets hurrying thro' the lawn,
      The moan of doves in immemorial elms,
      And murmuring of innumerable bees.

                                        TENNYSON

6.   That orbèd maiden, with white fire laden,
         Whom mortals call the Moon,
      Glides glimmering o'er my fleece-like floor
         By midnight breezes strewn.

                                        SHELLEY

7.   The moving moon went up the sky
         And nowhere did abide;
      Softly she was going up,
         And a star or two beside.

                                        COLERIDGE

Many passages illustrating the use of nasals for securing
melodious effects are given under voice exercises. Find
passages of prose and poetry that owe a great part of their
music to the use of nasals. Carry over into everyday speech
the habit of making [m]'s, [n]'s, and [ŋ]'s with clear nasal
resonance but without nasalizing the adjacent consonants.

C. THE LATERAL

[l]

This consonant resembles the nasals in being produced
without explosion or friction, and in being, therefore, capable
of adding great beauty to the spoken language. But it is
also one of the consonants most frequently ruined by bad
articulation. Reread the warnings on page 95 and be sure
to practice [l] correctly without nasalization, inversion, or
velarization. Remember that the tongue tip should be
lightly pressed against the upper teeth ridge and that the
back of the tongue should not be unduly raised or tensed.
Remember also to give the consonant time. Very few
Americans get anything like the full musical value from the
sonorous consonants, particularly [l], which is often unvoiced

and sometimes entirely eliminated in careless speech.[4] Be especially careful to avoid the drawl produced by a glide vowel before [l] resulting in forms like [skuəl] (*school*), [peɪəl] (*pale*), [koʊəld] (*cold*), and [bætəl] (*battle*). This is particularly unattractive if it is accompanied by inversion and a backward tone resulting from lack of firm breath support.

1. *The Lateral Alone and in Combination with Other Sounds*

Practice the Steele exercise with [l], working for great smoothness of tone. No consonant is better than [l] for securing a legato effect. Practice it preceded and followed by all the vowels, and in combination with other consonants as [lt], [tl], [fl], [vl], [lz], etc. A very good exercise is the French exclamation "La, la!" or "La, la, la!" pronounced very rapidly and in different rhythms and groups of twos, threes, and fours.

2. *The Lateral in Words*

A good way to gain the power of forming a final [l] without the glide is to practice words like *school*, *pole*, and *fall* in which the [l] is preceded by a rounded vowel, keeping the lips firmly rounded for [l] and bringing the tongue smartly from the position of the vowel to that of the [l] and maintaining the sensation of a forward tone.

> loo, lo, law, la, lie, lay, lea
> all, oil, owl, isle, ill, ell, earl
> lily, pulley, sullen, sillier, telephone, island
> flue, clue, flute, gloom, plume, sluice
> fault, shelf, wild, pulls, ells, elves, filth
> file, pale, call, pool, foil, cowl, roll, pull, tall
> thistle, castle, cattle, saddle, trouble, puzzled
> chiseled, prattled, stifled
> tunnel, channel, shingle, mangle, film

---

[4] As, for example, in the pronunciation [ɔɪraɪʔ] for *all right*.

3. *The Lateral in Connected Speech*

SELECTIONS FOR PRACTICE

1.   In the violet-embroidered vale
      Where the love-lorn nightingale
      Nightly to thee his sad song mourneth well.

MILTON

2.   I hear lake water lapping with low sounds by the shore.

YEATS

3.   Across wide lotus-ponds of light,
      I marked a giant fire-fly's flight.

VACHEL LINDSAY

4.   Forlorn! The very word was like a knell,
      To toll me back to my sole self.

KEATS

5.   Why so pale and wan, fond lover?
      Prithee, why so pale?
      Will, when looking well can't move her,
      Looking ill prevail?
      Prithee, why so pale?

SIR JOHN SUCKLING

6.   Look downward in the silent pool:
      The weeds cling to the ground they love,
      They live so quietly, and are so cool;
      They do not need to think or move.

HAROLD MONRO

7.   Lay your cold hands across my brows,
      And I shall sleep, and I shall dream
      Of silver-pointed willow boughs
      Dipping their fingers in a stream.

ELINOR WYLIE

Notice the effect of coolness and quiet especially in the first three and the last two selections. Find other passages illustrating the way in which [l] gives a liquid beauty to the expression of thought. In your daily speech be sure that your [l]'s are a source of beauty rather than of ugliness.

D. FRICATIVES

Fricatives are a mixed and varied group. Some of the so-called fricatives, [w], [v], [r], and [j], if made properly (that is, with a minimum of noise) add much sonority and beauty to the speech. Others, like the sibilants [s], [z], [ʃ], and [ʒ] contain so large an element of noise that they present a definite problem, that of clear articulation which yet does not give too hissing a character to the speech. Complete freedom from throat strain and steady control of the breath stream, as well as very accurate tongue position, are essential in forming these sounds.

i. THE LABIALS

[ʊ] *and* [w]

The bi-labials are excellent for practice in overcoming the American habit of speaking without lip-rounding.

1. *Labials Alone and in Combination with Other Sounds*

Practice both [ʊ] and [w] in fours (the Steele exercise) with the lips well rounded. Use your mirror. Then practice the same exercise with these consonants followed by the rounded vowels.

Practice the owl's [tʊ wɪt tʊ wu] and the sound of the wind [wu, wu, wu].

2. *Labials in Words*

[ʊ]

whew, whoa, why, whey, whirr, where
wheat, whip, when, whale, what
whistle, whisper, whirlpool

[w]

woo, woe, war, wow, wear, way, we, were

dwindle, twinkle, quality, swoon, queer, suite, quorum, one, swan

wash, water, was, waffle, waddle, Waldorf, Washington

[ʊ] *and* [w]

whale, wail	white, wight
whine, wine	whig, wig
whoa, woe	where, wear
while, wile	when, wen

Practice these words before a mirror, making sure that the lips are firmly rounded for the [ʊ] and [w].

3. *Labials in Connected Speech*

Note their power, if well rounded, to focus the tone in the front of the mouth and thus help in securing oral resonance.

SELECTIONS FOR PRACTICE

1.   The water, like a witch's oils,
       Burnt blue and green and white.
                                    COLERIDGE

2.   Why, let the stricken deer go weep,
       The hart ungallèd play;
       For some must watch while some must weep,
       So runs the world away.
                                    SHAKESPEARE

3.   O World, I cannot hold thee close enough!
           Thy winds, thy wide grey skies!
           Thy mists that roll and rise!
       Thy woods this autumn day, that ache and sag
       And almost cry with colour!   That gaunt crag
       To crush!   To lift the lean of that black bluff!
       World, World, I cannot get thee close enough!
                                    EDNA ST. VINCENT MILLAY

4.   Why, what make you here?
Why are you virtuous?   Why do people love you?
O, what a world is this, when what is comely
Envenoms him that bears it.

SHAKESPEARE

ii. THE LABIO-DENTALS

[f] *and* [v]

1. *Labio-Dentals Alone and in Combination with Other Sounds*

Practice on a long, sustained [f] is one of the best ways to gain control of breath and freedom from throat strain. The sound should be smooth and steady. Try [v] in the same way.

Practice both in fours, individually and combined with other sounds, as [fn], [fl], [ft], [fst], [sf].

2. *Labio-Dentals in Words*

[f]

fee, fie, fo, fum
calf, cuff, off, if, oaf
offer, muffin, coffin, affable
flown, fruit, fling, flame, France
soft, proofs, laughed, shelf, twelfth, fifths
shuffle, raffle, muffled, sphinx, enough

[v]

vie, vow, veer
leave, live (verb), live (adj.), love
driving, savior, devil, rendezvous
carves, calves, loved, shelved
drivel, grovel, shovel, striven, shaven

[f] *and* [v]

fat, vat	safe, save	proofs, proves
fail, veil	strife, strive	safer, savor

fine, vine	life, live	shuffle, shovel
fain, vain	fife, five	rifle, rival
	off, of	

Be sure that the [f] is clearly sounded in such words as *twelfth* and *fifths*, and the [v] in such words as *carves, calves.* and *shelved.*

3. *Labio-Dentals in Connected Speech*

SELECTIONS FOR PRACTICE

1. After life's fitful fever he sleeps well.—SHAKESPEARE

2.   Fair is foul and foul is fair,
  Hover through fog and filthy air.

       SHAKESPEARE

3.   The fair breeze blew, the white foam flew,
  The furrow followed free.
  We were the first that ever burst
  Into that silent sea.

       COLERIDGE

4.   Swiftly, swiftly flew the ship
  Yet she sailed softly too:
  Sweetly, sweetly blew the breeze
  On me alone it blew.

       COLERIDGE

Notice the impression of lightness or of insignificance given by [f]. Tennyson, always a very great artist in sound values, has many such phrases as "The flight of birds, the flame of sacrifice." Milton constantly uses [f] to give the effect of scorn, as where he speaks of the earth spinning like a "fretful midge." Bryant is equally felicitous in the expression, "And each shall chase his favorite phantom as before." A critic, in commenting on this line, once spoke of [f] as "the tip-end of nothing" (notice that part of the insignificance of the phrase is due to the preponderance of breathed consonants). In your reading be on the lookout for other examples of the use of [f] to suggest lightness or insignificance.

[v] when well made is a musical consonant. It is too often slighted in American English, the result being a decided loss of beauty as well as of clearness.[5]

iii. The Dentals

[θ] and [ð]

These sounds are somewhat like [f] and [v] in character, the voiceless consonant suggesting lightness or insignificance, its voiced cognate being a reasonably musical sound if well made.

1. *Dentals Alone and in Combination with Other Sounds*

Practice by fours, being careful to make the sounds as dentals and not as intra-dentals. Practice such combinations as [θs], [ðz], [θl], [ðd], [ŋθs], [lθ], [ðm], [ðn]. These are among the most difficult consonant combinations in our language. In careless speech they are often simplified to the point of unintelligibility.

2. *Dentals in Words*

Be particularly careful of the words containing the difficult combinations given above.

[θ]

thigh, thin, thick, thud, thumb, thank
oath, earth, forth, doth
zither, frothing, ether, Ethel, deathly
throb, thwart, fifth, sixth, twelfth, hundredth, health, fourths,
    widths, lengths

---

[5] Often [v] is so inadequately articulated that *shelves* is mistaken for *shells* and *carves* for *cars*.

[ð]

though, thou, thy, thee, there

with, bathe, clothe

father, farthing, further, thither, prithee, rather, either, other, leather

bathed, mouthed, clothes, oaths

rhythm, fathom, heathen

[θ] *and* [ð]

thigh, thy	mouth, mouthe
wreath, wreathe	sheath, sheathe
teeth, teethe	sooth, soothe

3. *Dentals in Connected Speech*

SELECTIONS FOR PRACTICE

1. There was a Door to which I found no Key:
   There was a Veil past which I could not see:
   Some little Talk awhile of Me and Thee
   There seemed—and then no more of Thee and Me.
   Rubáiyát of Omar Khayyám

2. The wind bloweth where it listeth, and thou hearest the sound thereof, but canst not tell whence it cometh or whither it goeth: so is every one that is born of the spirit.—*Gospel of St. John.*

3. If then God so clothe the grass, which today is in the field and tomorrow is cast into the oven, how much more will he clothe you, O ye of little Faith?—*Gospel of St. Luke.*

4. Your Father knoweth that ye have need of these things.— *Gospel of St. Luke.*

5. What, in ill thoughts again? Men must endure
   Their going hence, even as their coming hither.
   Ripeness is all.
   SHAKESPEARE

Because of their archaic forms in *th* the Bible and Shakespeare are good tests of the articulation of dentals.

iv. The Post-Dentals

THE TIP POST-DENTAL

[r]

This sound, like [l], is often very poorly articulated, but, also like [l], it is one of the most liquid and beautiful of English sounds when well made. Practice making the two sounds alternately and decide how the best resonance for each is secured.

You will perhaps find that the chief difference between the two sounds, when this most favorable articulation is secured, is that for [l] the edge of the tongue tip is firmly pressed against the upper teeth ridge so that the air stream is divided and escapes at each side of the tongue, while for [r] the *under side* of the tip is placed *near enough* to the teeth ridge so that the air in passing over produces a slight murmuring sound, or else is brought to that position and then so quickly changed to the position for the following vowel that it is rather a glide or semi-vowel than a real consonant. As with the other post-dentals, its beauty depends on its being made very far forward in the mouth and with relaxation of all the tongue except the tip.

1. [r] *Alone and in Combination with Other Sounds*

Practice the Steele exercise with [r] alone and with [r] followed by various vowels and in the consonant groups [br], [dr], [fr], [kr], [pr], and [tr]. These latter are not easy to make delicately yet firmly. The combination [wr] is so difficult that modern English has simplified it to [r] as in *wring* and *write*.

2. [r] *in Words*

Be especially careful to make medial [r] clear and well forward in the mouth.

rue, roe, row, rah, Roy, rye, rare, rear

hurry, currant, serene, every, horror, sorry, verily, torrid, reiterate

terrify, merrier, charity, corroborate

brass, cream, drive, freeze, grow, prow, try, scrape, strange

rhetoric, rhubarb, wrangle

3. [r] *in Connected Speech*

Try to make the [r]'s in the following passages contribute definitely to the legato effect intended.

SELECTIONS FOR PRACTICE

1.   Rarely, rarely comest thou,
            Spirit of delight.

                                        SHELLEY

2.   From you have I been absent in the spring,
            When proud pied April, dressed in all his trim,
            Hath put a Spirit of youth in everything,
            That heavy Saturn laughed and leaped with him.

                                        SHAKESPEARE

3.   The Rainbow comes and goes,
            And lovely is the Rose,
            The Moon doth with delight
            Look round her when the heavens are bare;
            Waters on a starry night
            Are beautiful and fair;
            The sunshine is a glorious birth;
            But yet I know, where'er I go,
            That there hath pass'd away a glory from the earth.

                                        WORDSWORTH

4.   Brighter than the blossom
            On the rose's bough
            Sits the wizened, orange,
            Bitter berry now.

                    EDNA ST. VINCENT MILLAY

THE SIBILANTS AND THE AFFRICATES

[s], [z], [ʃ], *and* [ʒ]   [ts], [dz], [tʃ], *and* [dʒ]

These sounds are so often lisped or hissed or otherwise obtrusively articulated that they have a bad reputation. One of the most frequent criticisms of our language on the part of foreigners is that it has such a preponderance of sibilants. But the extent to which poets deliberately use them to obtain special effects of slight musical sounds proves that if they are made accurately and delicately, they are not to be feared. Persons who have any difficulty with these sounds should practice making them before the mirror to make sure (1) that the tongue does not protrude between the teeth and (2) that it does not lie passive on the floor of the mouth, relying on the jaw to do the work. In making [s] and [z] care should be taken that the tongue has a narrow groove and that the breath is emitted through this groove in a thin stream which is perfectly controlled at the diaphragm and allowed to pass through the throat without interference. In making [ʃ] and [ʒ], as has been said, the lip action, as well as that of the tongue and the diaphragm, should be firm and decisive. Although these sounds are continuants, they should not be prolonged. The more briefly they are sounded, the better, *so long as they are clearly articulated.* Some persons in attempting to correct a hissing [s] or [z] omit it altogether; this always suggests careless articulation and sometimes makes the meaning unclear.

1. *Sibilants and Affricates Alone and in Combination*

Like [f], a prolonged [s] is often used by singing teachers to test breath control. Some teachers question the wisdom of this exercise, fearing that it may tend to develop the habit of unduly prolonging the sound in ordinary speech. With intelligent students, however, there should be little danger of this, and the exercise is valuable in testing not only breath control but also the position of the tongue. The same exercise with the voiced cognate is good practice for persons who are inclined to unvoice final [z]'s.

Because vowels are less apt to be nasalized when used with [z] than with most other consonants, teachers often use it in combination with vowels in such exercises as [zu], [zɑ], [zu], [zɑ], [zu], [zɑ], [zu], [ɑ], [eɪ], [i], [oʊ], [u]; and [mɑ], [zɑ], [skɑ], [ɑ]. For gaining lightness and precision the Steele exercise is excellent for all four of these sibilants alone and in combination with other vowels and consonants. Special attention should be given to the affricates [ts], [dz], [tʃ] and [dʒ] since they occur so frequently in plural forms and in words which end in *-tion*, *-sion*, *-ture*, *-age*, and similar suffixes.

2. Sibilants and Affricates in Words

[s]

see, say, sigh, so, Sue
miss, mess, mace, mice, mouse, moss, moose
passing, sister, senseless, disinterested
skate, sluice, smokes, snakes, spice, stone, sweet
tracks, frosts, sixths, widths, tasks, tastes, fourteenths
rustle, castle, fasten, listen
lax, mice, expect

[z]

zoo, zone, zest, zinc, zeal
his, has, haze, whose, hose
hazy, using, business, praises
dogs, robs, carves, lags, cabs
dazzle, puzzle, sizzled, prison, chasm, prism

[s] *and* [z]

sink, zinc,	hearse, hers	ceased, seized
seal, zeal	sinks, sings	racer, razor
base, bays	pricing, prizing	looser, loser

[ʃ]

she, shay, shy, show, shoe
hush, harsh, wish, wash, crash
fissure, tissue, session, pressure, cushion, precious, ocean
election, pension, partial, Russia, caption, specie
shrill, washed

[ʒ]

rouge, garage, prestige, mirage
azure, seizure, pleasure, casual, decision, explosion, usual
vision, usurer, glazier, intrusion

[ts] *and* [dz]

cats, cads	clots, clods	pots, pods
cots, cods	coats, codes	parts, pards
cents, sends	pats, pads	bits, bids
founts, founds	watts, wads	Burt's, birds
newts, nudes	knots, nods	bites, bides
	heats, heeds	

[tʃ] *and* [dʒ]

rich, ridge	chest, jest	chokes, jokes
match, Madge	chain, Jane	chunk, junk
catcher, cadger	chin, gin	cherry, jerry
catching, cadging	char, jar	h (aitch), age
cheering, jeering	choose, Jews	aitchless, ageless

3. *Sibilants and Affricates in Connected Speech*

SELECTIONS FOR PRACTICE

1. Is this the face that launched a thousand ships,
    And burnt the topless towers of Ilium?

    MARLOWE

2. Softly sweet in Lydian measures,
    Soon he soothed his soul to pleasures.

    DRYDEN

3. The clouds were pure and white as flocks new shorn
   And fresh from the clear brook; sweetly they slept
   On the blue fields of heaven, and there crept
   A little noiseless noise among the leaves,
   Born of the very sigh that silence leaves,
   For not the faintest motion could be seen
   Of all the shades that slanted o'er the green.

   KEATS

4.   Sleep is a reconciling,
           A rest that peace begets;
           Shall not the sun rise smiling
           When fair at even it sets?

   Elizabethan song

5. Listen;
   With faint, dry sound,
   Like steps of passing ghosts,
   The leaves, frost-crisped, break from the trees
   And fall.

   ADELAIDE CRAPSEY

6. A flock of sheep that leisurely pass by,
   One after one; the sound of rain and bees
   Murmuring; the fall of rivers, winds and seas,
   Smooth fields, white sheets of water, and pure sky:
   I have thought of all by turns, and yet do lie
   Sleepless! and soon the small birds' melodies
   Must hear, first uttered from my orchard trees;
   And the first cuckoo's melancholy cry.

   WORDSWORTH

7. Often I think of the beautiful town
       That is seated by the sea;
   Often in thought go up and down
   The pleasant streets of that dear old town,
       And my youth comes back to me.
           And a verse of a Lapland song
           Is haunting my memory still:
       'A boy's will is the wind's will,
   And the thoughts of youth are long, long thoughts.'

   LONGFELLOW

8. With sloping masts and dipping prow,
As who pursued with yell and blow
Still treads the shadow of his foe,
And forward bends his head,
The ship drove fast, loud roared the blast,
And southward aye we fled.

COLERIDGE

9. *Hush, ah, hush, the Scythes are saying,*
Hush, and heed not, and fall asleep;
Hush they say to the grasses swaying;
Hush they sing to the clover deep!
Hush—'tis the lullaby Time is singing—
Hush and heed not for all things pass;
Hush, ah, hush! and the Scythes are swinging
Over the clover, over the grass!

ANDREW LANG

v. THE PALATAL FRICATIVE

[j]

This vowel-like consonant presents little difficulty to the average speaker, except that it is sometimes produced with too great tension in the throat or too much pressure of the tongue. Either of these articulations brings an added element of noise into what is otherwise a musical sound.

1. *The Palatal Fricative in Words*

ye, yea, you, year, your, yore, use, utility, Europe, United States
pure, beauty, muse, few, view, dew, cue, hue
lawyer, clothier, canyon, arduous, actual, furniture

2. *The Palatal Fricative in Connected Speech*

SELECTIONS FOR PRACTICE

1. Better fifty years of Europe than a cycle of Cathay.

TENNYSON

2.   And where, I pray you, is the Queen
        Who willed that Buridan should steer
    Sewed in a sack's mouth down the Seine?
    But where are the snows of yesteryear?

*   *   *

    Nay, never ask this week, fair lord,
        Where they are gone, nor yet this year,
    Except with this for an over-word,
    Where are the snows of yesteryear?

FRANÇOIS VILLON

3.   Then sing, ye birds, sing, sing a joyous song!
        And let the young lambs bound
        As to the tabor's sound!
    We in thought would join your throng,
        Ye that pipe and ye that play,
        Ye that through your hearts today
    Feel the gladness of the May!

WORDSWORTH

vi. THE GLOTTAL FRICATIVE

[h]

This consonant also offers little difficulty to Americans.

1. *The Glottal Fricative in Words*

    who, hoe, haw, ha, he, her, how, high, hair, hear
    hate, hit, hot, hat, height
    rehearse, inhale, inherit, incoherent
    haha, ahem, oho, harbinger, wholly, whose

2. *The Glottal Fricative in Connected Speech*

SELECTIONS FOR PRACTICE

1.   Sing, heigh ho, the holly!
        This life is most jolly.

SHAKESPEARE

2.   O horror! horror! horror! tongue nor heart
        Cannot conceive nor name thee!

SHAKESPEARE

3.   Him the Almighty power hurled headlong
Flaming from the ethereal sky.

                       MILTON

4.   Here he lies where he longed to be;
Home is the sailor, home from the Sea,
And the hunter home from the hill.

                    STEVENSON

WORD LISTS FOR PRACTICE ON CONSONANT COMBINATIONS

acts, expects, directs, facts, ducts, edicts
shafts, gifts, lifts, sifts, thefts, tufts
hosts, posts, fists, wrists, costs, lists, insists
helps, yelps, alps, scalps, pulps
melts, bolts, colts, tilts, wilts, dolts
adepts, adopts, excerpts
hints, tents, dents, punts, scents, vents
wasps, wisps, lisps, clasps, asps
stamps, scamps, lamps, imps, limps
desks, asks, risks, masks, husks
thinks, thanks, blinks, winks, sinks
sulks, silks, balks, elks
nymphs, gulfs, golf's, sylphs

fifths, health's, wealth's, stealth's, sixths, hundredths
widths, breadths, lengths, strengths

prince, prints, sense, cents, tense, tents
mince, mints, dense, dents, chance, chants

asked, masked, tusked, risked, balked, sulked, milked, skulked

helped, scalped, yelped
stamped, camped, pumped

fixed, mixed, hoaxed
lanced, rinsed, against
repulsed, convulsed, waltzed
hitched, hatched, patched

bands, hounds, hands, mends, bends, bonds
shields, builds, fields, colds, moulds, holds
seasons, basins, opens, chickens
prisms, elms, dazzles, battles, gurgles, stifles
stables, bulbs, elves

squabbled, bridled, ruffled, haggled, trickled, steepled
rustled, tattled, reveled, puzzled, filmed, beckoned, happened
chastened, reasoned, delved, judged, bronzed

samples, uncles, bundles, spangles, tingles, sprinkled
filched, flinched, twelfths, bulged, changed

The following are words which occur in the plays of
Shakespeare and other Elizabethan writers.

robbed'st, hugged'st, fold'st, harmed'st, earned'st
wronged'st, wreathed'st, engraved'st, raised'st, milk'st
think'st, ask'st, trouble'st, handl'st, stifl'st, haggl'st
buckl'st, people'st, rustl'st, battl'st, revel'st, puzzl'st
reckon'st, open'st, chasten'st, reason'st, help'st, waft'st
remark'st, tilt'st, dreamt'st, spent'st, hoped'st, insist'st
crushed'st

troubled'st, trifled'st, suckled'st
peopled'st, rustled'st, reveled'st, puzzled'st, reckoned'st

EXERCISES FOR PRACTICE ON DIFFICULT CONSONANT COMBINATIONS

1. Thou'rt not thyself
    For thou exist'st on many thousand grains
    That issue out of dust, happy thou art not
    For what thou hast not, still thou strivest to get,
    And what thou hast forget'st.   Thou art not certain
    For thy complexion shifts to strange effects after the morn.

                                        SHAKESPEARE

2. A casement high and triple-arched there was,
    All garlanded with carven imag'ries
    Of fruits, and flowers, and bunches of knot-grass,
    And diamonded with panes of quaint device,
    Innumerable of stains and splendid dyes,
    As are the tiger-moth's deep-damasked wings;
    And in the midst, 'mong thousand heraldries,
    And twilight saints, and dim emblazonings,
    A shielded scutcheon blushed with blood of queens and
       kings.   KEATS

3. Music to hear, why hear'st thou music sadly?
    Sweets with sweets war not, joy delights in joy.
    Why lov'st thou that which thou receiv'st not gladly,
    Or else receiv'st with pleasure thine annoy?

SHAKESPEARE

4. Yet better thus, and known to be contemn'd,
    Than, still contemn'd and flattered, to be worst.
    The lowest and most dejected thing of fortune
    Stands still in esperance, lives not in fear,
    The lamentable change is from the best;
    The worst returns to laughter. Welcome, then,
    The unsubstantial air that I embrace!
    The wretch that thou hast blown unto the worst
    Owes nothing to thy blasts.

SHAKESPEARE

5.   I have ventured,
    Like little wanton boys that swim on bladders,
    This many summers on a sea of glory
    Far beyond my depth; my high blown pride
    At length broke under me; and now has left me,
    Weary and old with service, to the mercy
    Of the rude stream, that must forever hide me.

SHAKESPEARE

6.   What thou seest, when thou dost wake,
        Do it for thy true love take;
        Love and languish for his sake:
        Be it ounce, or cat, or bear,
        Pard, or boar with bristled hair,
        In thy eye that shall appear
        When thou wak'st it is thy dear.
        Wake when some vile thing is near.

SHAKESPEARE

7. Art is nothing less than the world as we ourselves make
    it, the world remolded nearer to the heart's desire. In this
    construction of a world around us in harmonious response to
    all our senses, we have at once a healthy exercise for our motor
    activities, and the restful satisfaction of our sensory needs.
    Art as no mere passive hyperæsthesia to external impressions,
    or exclusive absorption in a single sense, but as a many-sided
    and active delight in the wholeness of things, is the great

restorer of health and rest to the energies distracted by our turbulent modern movements. Thus understood, it has the firmest of scientific foundations; it is but the reasonable satisfaction of the instinctive cravings of the organism, cravings that are not the less real for being often unconscious. Its satisfaction means the presence of joy in our daily life, and joy is the prime tonic of life. It is in the gratification of the art instinct that repose becomes joyous.

HAVELOCK ELLIS, *The New Spirit*

8. Praise waiteth for thee, O God, in Sion; and unto thee shall the vow be performed:

O Thou that hearest prayer, unto thee shall all flesh come.

Iniquities prevail against me: as for our transgressions, thou shalt purge them away.

Blessed is the man whom thou choosest, and causest to approach unto thee that he may dwell in thy courts: we shall be satisfied with the goodness of thy house, even of thy holy temple.

By terrible things in righteousness wilt thou answer us, O God of our salvation; who art the confidence of all the ends of the earth, and of them that are afar off upon the sea.

Which by his strength setteth fast the mountains; being girded with power:

Which stilleth the noise of the seas, the noise of their waves, and the tumult of the people.

They also that dwell in the uttermost parts are afraid at thy tokens: thou makest the outgoings of the morning and evening to rejoice.

Thou visitest the earth, and waterest it; thou greatly enrichest it with the river of God which is full of water; thou preparest them corn, when thou has so provided for it.

Thou waterest the ridges thereof abundantly; thou settlest the furrows thereof; thou makest it soft with showers; thou blessest the springing thereof.

Thou crownest the year with thy goodness; and thy paths drop fatness.

They drop upon the pastures of the wilderness; and the little hills rejoice on every side.

The pastures are clothed with flocks; the valleys also are covered over with corn; they shout for joy, they also sing.

Psalm LXV

II. VOWELS

Compared with consonants, vowels are relatively unimportant in conveying thought. The meaning of a sentence could often be made clear if all the vowels were omitted or leveled to the neutral [ə]. But a sentence made up entirely of vowels would convey nothing. They are important chiefly in giving carrying power and beauty of tone.[6] In studying the vowels, therefore, we should be careful to form them in the way that will give them the greatest degree of resonance without interfering with the characteristic quality of each.

The first requirement for this is a knowledge of the general theory of vowel formation. This includes adequate breath support, correct initiation of tone, freedom from undue tension in the muscles of the throat, and such control of the tongue, soft palate, and lips as will enable these organs to take each of the various positions quickly and surely and then to pass smoothly to the position for the following sound. The next requirement is a knowledge of the position that is theoretically considered most favorable to give at the same time the characteristic quality of each vowel and its best resonace. The last and perhaps the most important requisite is an ear sufficiently trained to enable the speaker to find for each vowel the position that is best suited to the contour of his vocal passage. *Since no two mouths are shaped exactly alike, each individual will need to experiment until he finds the position that will give maximum clearness of vowel quality with maximum resonance.*

---

[6] Vowels have been called the texture of the language, consonants the joints which shape the texture into the desired form. But consonants, as we have learned, may give comeliness as well as form to the language. They are relatively dynamic and give the effect of life and vigor, while vowels chiefly contribute smoothness and beauty of tone.

Practice on Individual Vowels

When the most favorable position for each vowel has been found, it should be practiced before the mirror until the muscles have formed the habit of taking the correct position promptly and decisively, maintaining it unchanged for an instant, and then passing smoothly to the position for the next sound. This practice forms a large part of the elementary training in singing; it is equally necessary in speech training. Poor speaking voices are often largely the result of poorly formed vowels.

The chief faults to be guarded against are:

1. *Drawling.*—This fault is partly a matter of instability in the articulating organs and partly of inadequate breath support.

2. *Nasalization.*—This is due partly to failure to direct the breath through the mouth, partly to lack of control of the soft palate (either through rigidity or through flabbiness of the muscles) and partly to restriction of the walls of the resonators.

3. *Inversion.*—This is due to turning back the tip of the tongue toward the hard palate because of the proximity of an inverted consonant. (Practically the same vowel quality is produced by retracting the tongue toward the soft palate.)

4. *Flatness.*—This is due to wrong position of the vocal organs and to muscle strain, which result in the reinforcement of unpleasant upper partials. It is apt to be accompanied by nasality and drawl.

5. *General Lack of Definition.*—This is due partly to lack of firmness in tongue position, but still more to lack of proper lip formation, the stretching of the lips against the teeth in forming the front vowels, and the failure to round them properly for the back vowels. This stretching and unrounding of the lips diminishes the front resonator and

greatly detracts from the resonance of the tone,[7] as well as from the distinct vowel quality.

After learning to take each vowel position with ease and precision, it is helpful to make the front series beginning with [i], watching in the mirror the gradual change in the position of jaw, lips, and tongue, learning to feel muscular adjustments and determining what adjustment gives the clearest resonance for each vowel. Especially important is it to direct the air consciously through the mouth till the ear learns to recognize and check nasalization. In this exercise great care should be taken not to lessen the resonance by stretching the lips and holding them tightly against the teeth.

Similarly, the back vowels should be made slowly and carefully before the mirror, with accurate lip formation and with attention to the matter of resonance. Particular attention should be given to the fact that the accurate rounding of these vowels is of great importance, not only in giving the characteristic quality to each, but also in giving greater resonance to the voice and decreasing the tendency to nasalization by directing the attention to the front of the mouth. Anything that does this tends to prevent the passage of air through the nose.

The middle vowels should be practiced in the same way, with particular care to avoid inversion and too great tension at the back of the tongue.

The diphthongs should then be practiced, care being taken to avoid drawling, as well as overtensing of the second element. Exercises for practice on the vowels individually and in combination with resonant consonants will be found in this section.

---

[7] It can readily be seen that stretching the lips and drawing them tightly against the teeth is unfavorable to resonance in two ways: it reduces the size of the resonator and forms an opening less capable of focusing the sound waves. (Notice the projecting lips of the Helmholtz resonator.)

Practice on Vowels in Words and Connected Speech

There follow classified word lists and connected passages for practice on vowels and diphthongs. Be careful to pronounce the words with proper tone production. It is helpful to transcribe them in phonetic script, comparing your habitual pronunciation with the one suggested by the classification. *Remember that the form suggested is in many cases only one of a number of acceptable pronunciations.*

Having learned to form each vowel in words with its unmistakable resonance and without drawling, nasalization, or inversion, practice the passages containing it. Be especially careful of the following points:

1. Smooth initiation of tone.

2. Adequate breath support (this is particularly important since in most cases the sound in question occurs at the end of the line and will not be given with proper resonance unless the tone is sustained to the end).

3. Full resonance.

4. Clear enunciation of all sounds, especially of the particular vowel illustrated.

5. Special care in avoiding nasalization, particularly of the vowels [ɛ], [æ], [eɪ], [aɪ], [aʊ].

6. Avoidance of the glottal stop, especially in words beginning with a vowel and in words containing plosives.

7. Sufficient attention to the thought and mood of the passage to bring out the organic rhythm instead of a monotonous singsong.

A. FRONT VOWELS

[i]

eat, she, mead, beet, thief, piece, clique
deceive, cease, grieve, police, leisure
reel, feel, seal, heal, ceiling
meat, neat, theme, seen, leaning, beaming, kneeling, **mean**

My Mary's asleep by thy murmuring stream,
Flow gently, Sweet Afton, disturb not her dream.

BURNS

Sun and moon and beat of sea—
Great lands stretching endlessly.
Where be bonds to bind the free?
All the world was made for me!

ADELAIDE CRAPSEY

Sand-strewn caverns, cool and deep,
Where the winds are all asleep;
Where the spent lights quiver and gleam;
Where the salt weed sways in the stream;
Where the sea-beasts, ranged all round,
Feed in the ooze of their pasture ground.

MATTHEW ARNOLD

Waking or asleep,
    Thou of death must deem
Things more true and deep
    Than we mortals dream,
Or how could thy notes flow in such a crystal stream?

SHELLEY

Down by the salley gardens my love and I did meet,
She passed the salley gardens with little snow-white feet,
She bid me take love easy as the leaves grow on the tree,
But I, being young and foolish, with her would not agree.

YEATS

[I]

it, bid, lip, tick, pity, pretty, busy

terrible, business, civilization, spirit, civility, women,

respite, gibbet, bicycle, syrup, stirrup, Syracuse, syndicate,
    Italian

ill, fill, still, miller, willing

myth, mint, since, Latin, fountain, minister

I remember the black wharves and the ships
    And the sea-tides tossing free;
And Spanish sailors with bearded lips,
And the beauty and mystery of the ships,
    And the magic of the sea.

LONGFELLOW

Here are sweet peas, on tip-toe for a flight:
With wings of gentle flush o'er delicate white,
And taper fingers catching at all things,
To bind them all about with tiny rings.

KEATS

The moving finger writes; and, having writ,
Moves on: nor all your piety or wit
Shall lure it back to cancel half a line,
Nor all your tears wash out a word of it.

Rubáiyát of Omar Khayyám

Here note especially the use of [ɪ] in prefixes and suffixes:

A casement high and triple-arched there was,
All garlanded with carven imag'ries
Of fruits, and flowers, and bunches of knot-grass,
And diamonded with panes of quaint device,
Innumerable of stains and splendid dyes,
As are the tiger-moth's deep-damasked wings;
And in the midst, 'mong thousand heraldries,
And twilight saints, and dim emblazonings,
A shielded scutcheon blushed with blood of kings and queens.

KEATS

[ɛ]

met, bed, fed, wreck, steady, deaf

pleasure, weather, very, verily, sherry

Shelley, fell, teller, bell, selling

Thames, measure, merry, men, extemporaneous, nemesis,
    many, energize

A lad went piping through the Earth,
    Gladly, madly, merrily,
With a tune for death and a tune for birth
    And a tune for lover's revelry.

JAMES ELROY FLECKER

Sleep is a reconciling,
A rest that peace begets,
Shall not the sun rise smiling
When fair at even it sets?

Elizabethan song

Under the leaves and the leaves of life
I met with virgins seven,
And one of them was Mary mild,
Our Lord's Mother of heaven.

Old song

[æ]

at, sad, catch, shall, flat, gas

fallacy, Aphrodite, adverse, attic, albumen, pastel, asthma, altitude

marry, maritime, Paris, garrulous, marrow, guarantee, parasol

caravan, charity, Harris, carriage, paramount, caramel

band, ant, mat, Annie, stand, slam, rant, mandatory, slander, cant, fanned, fancy, mass

A tap at the pane, the quick sharp scratch
And blue spurt of a lighted match.

Browning

Lo, in yon brilliant window-niche
How statue-like I see thee stand,
The agate lamp within thy hand;
O, Psyche, from the regions which
Are holy land.

Poe

Then I saw the Congo, creeping through the black,
Cutting through the jungle with a golden track.

Vachel Lindsay

In Xanadu did Kubla Khan
A stately pleasure-dome decree:
Where Alph, the sacred river, ran
Through caverns measureless to man,
Down to a sunless sea.

Coleridge

[a] *or* [æ] *or* [ɑ]

asks, pass, clasp, grass, fast, path, shaft, calf, lath, laugh, last

bath, glass, asked, clasped, mast, craft

dance, France, advancing, glance, grant, chance, demand

And when like her, O Saki, thou shalt pass
Among the guests star-scattered in the grass,
And in thy joyous errand reach the place
Where I made one—turn down an empty glass.

Rubáiyát of Omar Khayyám

And all my days are tranoes,
And all my nightly dreams
Are where thy grey eye glances
And where thy footstep gleams—
In what ethereal dances,
By what eternal streams.

POE

For the good are always the merry,
Save by an evil chance,
And the merry love the fiddle
And the merry love to dance.

YEATS

B. BACK VOWELS

Be particularly careful to round the back vowels [u], [ʊ],
[o], [ɔ], and [ɒ].

[u]

ooze, flew, blue, rude, zoo
root, roof, hoop, fool, pool, stool
souvenir, trousseau, ruler, schooling
loom, boom, loon, soon, croon, moon, luminous, plumed

Death will come when thou art dead,
     Soon, too soon—
Sleep will come when thou art fled;
Of neither would I ask the boon
I ask of thee, beloved Night—
Swift be thine approaching flight,
     Come soon, soon!

SHELLEY

She left the web, she left the loom,
She made three paces through the room,
She saw the water lily bloom,
She saw the helmet and the plume,—
She looked down to Camelot.

TENNYSON

And I shall find some girl perhaps,
And a better one than you,
With eyes as wise, but kindlier,
And lips as soft, but true,
And I dare say she will do.

RUPERT BROOKE

It ceased: yet still the sails made on
A pleasant noise till noon
A noise like of a hidden brook
In the leafy month of June,
That to the sleeping woods all night
Singeth a quiet tune.

COLERIDGE

[ʊ]

put, foot, book, took, soot, today, sugar, cook, look, bosom,
butcher

corrugated, pull, full, pulley, pulpit

And this our life, exempt from public haunt,
Finds tongues in trees, books in the running brooks,
Sermons in stones, and good in everything.

SHAKESPEARE

My only books were women's looks
And folly all they taught me.

BYRON

All the pretty things put by—
Wait upon the children's eye,
Sheep and shepherds, trees and crooks,
In the picture story-books.

STEVENSON

[o]

See under "Diphthongs"

[ɔ]

awe, awl, saw, call, fall

laud, lord, fraught, fought, sort, sought, short

water, fortune, because, paltry, Launfal, Salisbury, recalled, falcon, waltz, scrawled

gnaw, norm, lawn, forlorn, dawning

> I rose from dreamless hours and sought the morn
> That beat upon my window, from the sill
> I watched sweet lands, where autumn light unborn
> Strayed through the trees and lingered on the hill.
>
> JAMES ELROY FLECKER

> Light your footsteps fall for me
>   Walking on the shore.
> Cool and still you call to me,
>   Call me evermore.
>
> EDITH FRANKLIN WYATT

[ɒ]

odd, sod, rock, dog, got, shock, loss

God, chops, lock, pop

horror, botany, coral, foreign, orange, sophomore, officer

torrid, Boston, forest, authority, laurel

wan, watch, swan, want, wallet, was, wash

quality, squash, yacht

mock, moss, pomp, comma, not, song, long, wrong, tongs

> Like young Shakespearian kings,
>   He won the adoring throng,
> And, as Apollo sings,
>   He triumphed with a song;
> Triumphed, and sang, and passed along.
>
> LIONEL JOHNSON

Pack, clouds, away! and welcome, day!
  With night we banish sorrow.
Sweet air, blow soft; mount, lark, aloft
  To give my Love good-morrow!
Wings from the wind to please her mind,
  Notes from the lark I'll borrow:
Bird, prune thy wing! nightingale, sing!
  To give my Love good-morrow!
To give my Love good-morrow
  Notes from them all I'll borrow.

                    THOMAS HEYWOOD

[ɑ]

ah, alms, ark, ha, heart
father, farther, Arthur, park, hard, Harvard
shah, harp, darling, garden, afar, partner, artistic
dart, tardy, articulation, particle, department
psalm, farm, charm, calm, almond, disarmanent

There are maidens in Scotland more lovely by far,
That would gladly be bride to young Lochinvar.

                              SCOTT

Come, secret sleep, with thy unuttered psalm,
Come, heavy dreamless sleep, and close and press
Upon mine eyes thy fingers dropping balm.

                    CHRISTINA ROSSETTI

  In common things that round us lie
  Some random truths we can impart,—
  The harvest of a quiet eye
  That broods and sleeps on his own heart.

                    WORDSWORTH

  My spirit beats her mortal bars,
  As down dark tides the glory slides,
  And, star-like, mingles with the stars.

                          TENNYSON

C. Middle, Neutral, or Mixed Vowels

[ʌ]

up, ruff, rough, duct, pluck, judge
putter, suffer, fussing, hurry, courage, cover, plover, covet
thumb, mumble, money, humble

> The isles of Greece!   The isles of Greece!
>   Where burning Sappho loved and sung,
> Where grew the arts of war and peace,
>   Where Delos rose, and Phœbus sprung!
> Eternal summer gilds them yet,
> But all, except their sun, is set.
>
> BYRON

> This is the bricklayer; hear the thud
> Of his heavy load dumped down on a stone.
> His lustrous bricks are brighter than blood,
> His smoking mortar whiter than bone.
>
> ELINOR WYLIE

> And childish fears I have outgrown
> Into my eyes are thrust
> Till my dull tears go dropping down
> Like lead into the dust.
>
> EDNA ST. VINCENT MILLAY

> Fear no more the heat of the Sun
> Nor winter's rages;
> Thou thy worldly task hast done,
> Home art gone and ta'en thy wages;
> Golden lads and girls all must,
> Like chimney sweepers, come to dust.
>
> SHAKESPEARE

[ə]

err, earth, myrrh, fir, fur
dirt, curb, purr, curt, worth
hurl, pearl, furl, swirl, world
worm, burn, yearns, turned, nurse

and in the accented syllables of the following:

murmur, perverse, irksome, interment, incur, refer, furry, guerdon, furnish

> Rejoice that man is hurled
> From change to change unceasingly,
> His soul's wings never furled.
>
> BROWNING

> O blithe Newcomer!   I have heard,
> I hear thee and rejoice.
> O Cuckoo, shall I call thee Bird,
> Or but a wandering Voice?
>
> WORDSWORTH

> By the rude bridge that arched the flood,
>   Their flag to April's breeze unfurled,
> Here once the embattled farmers stood,
>   And fired the shot heard round the world.
>
> EMERSON

> Then to the lips of this poor earthen urn,
> I leaned, the secret of my life to learn;
> And lip to lip it murmured, "While you live,
> Drink! for once dead you never shall return!"
>
> *Rubáiyát of Omar Khayyám*

> Sweet white lilac
>   With blooms that stir
> White and cool
>   As the breast of her;
> Hill girl, hill girl,
>   Why do you creep
> Back through the lilac·
>   Can't you sleep?
>
> ROSE MILLS POWERS

[ə]

In the unaccented syllables of the following:

murmur, perverse, irksome, cupboard, firmament, permanent, purser, surprise, supportable, patient, monarch, porpoise, method, afterwards

Some of the most common prefixes and suffixes in which [ə] occurs are: *-ar, -er, -ir, -or, -ur, -yr, -tion, -ment, -ous, -able, -ence, -ary, -ory, -ery, -acy, a-, ab-, ac-, ad-, af-, an-, ap-, as-, at-, ob-, per-, par-*; for example:

pillar, proper, tapir, debtor, femur, satyr, portion, garment, porous

portable, prominence, alimentary, sensory, machinery, supremacy

sofa, around, absorb, acquire, adjourn, affairs, announce, appoint

assert, attest, observe, persist, partake

> From you, Ianthe, little troubles pass
> Like little ripples down a sunny river,
> Your pleasures spring like daisies in the grass,
> Cut down, and up again as blithe as ever.
>
> LANDOR

> The moon on the one hand, the dawn on the other:
> The moon is my sister, the dawn is my brother.
> The moon on my left hand, the dawn on my right,
> My brother, Good morning; my sister, Good night.
>
> HILAIRE BELLOC

> A damsel with a dulcimer
> In a vision once I saw;
> It was an Abyssinian maid,
> And on a dulcimer she played,
> Singing of Mount Abora.
>
> COLERIDGE

> She is so proper and so pure
> Full steadfast, stable and demure
> There is none such, ye may be sure,
> As my swete sweting.
>
> Old song

> Ah, happy, happy bough! that cannot shed
> Your happy leaves, nor ever bid the spring adieu;
> And happy melodist, unwearied,
> Forever piping songs forever new.
>
> KEATS

D. DIPHTHONGS

[eɪ]

ate, save, day, aid, ale, ace, rake
fable, stay, amiable, data, status, gratis, apparatus
male, jail, whale, fail, daily, sailing
may, sane, vain, nay, maimed, remain

> Why, let the stricken deer go weep,
> The hart ungallèd play;
> For some must watch while some must weep,
> So runs the world away.
>
> SHAKESPEARE

> The glories of our blood and state
> Are shadows, not substantial things;
> There is no armor against fate;
> Death lays his icy hand on kings:
> Sceptre and crown
> Must tumble down
> And in the dust be equal made
> With the poor crooked scythe and spade.
>
> JAMES SHIRLEY

> Poor soul, the center of my sinful earth—
> Starved by these rebel powers that thee array,
> Why dost thou pine within and suffer dearth,
> Painting thy outward walls so costly gay?
>
> SHAKESPEARE

> When that I was and a little tiny boy,
> With hey, ho, the wind and the rain
> A foolish thing was but a toy,
> For the rain it raineth every day.
>
> SHAKESPEARE

[aɪ]

eye, ice, ride, fly, side, cries, bright
pliant, prying, priory, flying, biology, geyser, sleight, biennial,
allies, defy

isle, tiles, wiles, defiles
lime, dine, time, wine, mine, nine

> Music that gentlier on the spirit lies
> Than tired eyelids upon tired eyes.
>
> TENNYSON

> Tiger, Tiger, burning bright
> In the forests of the night,
> What immortal hand or eye
> Could shape thy fearful symmetry?
>
> BLAKE

Ho, giant!   This is I!
I have built me a beanstalk into your sky.
La, but it's lovely up so high!

EDNA ST. VINCENT MILLAY

> Sweet day, so cool, so calm, so bright,
> The bridal of the earth and sky,
> The sky shall weep thy fall to-night,
> For thou must die.
>
> HERRICK

The whole of the world was merry,
One joy from the vale to the height,
Where the blue woods of twilight encircled
The lovely lawns of the light.

Æ

> Golden slumbers kiss your eyes,
> Smiles awake you when you rise,
> Sleep pretty wantons, do not cry
> And I will sing a lullaby:
> Rock them, rock them, lullaby.
>
> DEKKER

I shall desire and I shall find
The best of my desires;
The autumn road, the mellow wind
That soothes the darkening shires,
And laughter, and inn fires.

RUPERT BROOKE

She walks in beauty, like the night
Of cloudless climes and starry skies;
And all that's best of dark and light
Meet in her aspect and her eyes.

BYRON

Drink to me only with thine eyes,
  And I will pledge with mine;
Or leave a kiss but in the cup
  And I'll not look for wine.
The thirst that from the soul doth rise
  Doth ask a drink divine;
But might I of Jove's nectar sup,
  I would not change for thine.

BEN JONSON

[DI]

oil, poise, boy, doit
avoid, rejoice, cloying, destroyer
coil, foil, toiling, spoiler, oiled, turmoil, soil
join, coin, noisome, annoying, groin, appoint

Another said—why ne'er a peevish Boy
Would break the bowl from which he drank in Joy:
Shall he that made the Vessel in pure Love
And Fancy, in an after Rage destroy?

Rubáiyát of Omar Khayyám

Hence vain deluding joys,
  The brood of folly without father bred!
How little you bested
  Or fill the fixed mind with all your toys.

MILTON

Year after year beheld the patient toil
That built that lustrous coil.

HOLMES

[Iə]

ear, ears, idea, fears, sheer, tier, seer
arrears, real, ideal, really

Reflected in a mirror clear
That hangs before her all the year,
Shadows of the world appear;
Here she sees the highway near
Winding down to Camelot.

TENNYSON

Long have I loved what I beheld
The night that calms, the day that cheers:
The common growth of mother earth
Suffices me—her tears, her mirth,
Her humblest mirth and tears.

WORDSWORTH

[ɛə]

air, airs, wares, fair
share, dare, there, pare, pear, aware
barely, fairy, Mary, various, vary
tearing, sharing, wearing, fared

Fair is foul and foul is fair,
Hover through fog and filthy air.

SHAKESPEARE

Had I but plenty of money, money enough and to spare,
The house for me, no doubt, were a house in a city square,
O such a life, such a life, as one leads at the window there!

BROWNING

[ɛə] *and* [eɪ]

Sabrina fair,
Listen where thou art sitting
Under the glassy, cool, translucent wave,
In twisted braids of lilies knitting
The loose train of thy amber-dropping hair.

Listen for dear honor's sake,
Goddess of the silver lake;
Listen and save.

MILTON

[oə] *or* [ɒə]

oar, oars, more, floors, bore, pour, shores
four, roared, boring, fort, floors, pouring, more

Helen, your beauty is to me
Like those Nicean barks of yore,
That gently, o'er a perfumed sea,
The weary, way-worn traveler bore
To his own native shore.

Poe

[ʊə]

lured, poor, sure, fury, tour, boor
ensured, alluring, mooring

She is so proper and so pure
Full steadfast, stable and demure
There is none such, ye may be sure,
As my swete sweting.

Old song

[aʊ]

out, cow, proud, rouse, vows, flout, pout
hour, flower, power, shower
cowl, prowl, foul, howling
round, town, sound, mound, ounce, now, noun, flounder

Merrily, merrily shall I live now,
Under the blossom that hangs on the bough.

Shakespeare

You wear the morning like your dress
And are with mastery crowned;
Whenas you walk your loveliness
Goes shining all around.
Upon your secret, smiling way
Such contents were found,
The Dancing Loves made holiday
On that delightful ground.

There is a silence where has been no sound,
There is a silence where no sound may be,
 In the cold grave—under the deep, deep sea,
 Or in wide desert where no life is found,
Which has been mute, and still must sleep profound.

THOMAS HOOD

And when he fell in whirlwind, he went down,
As when a kingly cedar green with boughs
Goes down with a great shout upon the hills,
And leaves a lonesome place against the sky.

EDWIN MARKHAM

Silence is scattered like broken glass,
 The minutes prick their ears and run about,
 Then one by one subside again and pass
 Sedately in, monotonously out.

HAROLD MUNRO

[oʊ]

oh, ode, rote, flow, rope, nose, soap, boat, goes
open, flowing, negotiable, pro-English
slowly, coterie, copious, precocious
slower, showing, rower, flowing
hole, pole, told, shoals, slowly
prone, note. most, tone, foam, moan, gloaming

Banners yellow, glorious, golden,
 On its roof did float and flow;
This, all this, was in the olden
 Time, long ago.

POE

We shall walk in velvet shoes:
 Wherever we go.
Silence will fall like dews
 On white silence below
We shall walk in the snow.

ELINOR WYLIE

Most holy night, that still dost keep
The keys of all the doors of sleep,
To me when my tired eyelids close
Give thou repose.

HILAIRE BELLOC

Small busy flames play through the fresh laid coals,
And their faint cracklings o'er our silence creep
Like whispers of the household gods that keep
A gentle empire o'er fraternal souls.

KEATS

EXERCISES FOR ELIMINATION OF THE GLOTTAL STOP

I, I'm, end, every, exit, am, Anna, earn, earth, ark, ask, eager, ether, ember, aster, anxious, old, oath, Easter, Indian, otter, emit, alike, all, ought, owl, oil, ale, aim, ate, air, idea, it, eat, each, our, ear, art, any, other, in, easy, along, ooze, earl, under, ore.

the East, the inn, the art, the otter, the other, the author, the aster, the earth, the exit, the ooze, the air, the aim, the eye, the oath, the oil, the owl the earl, the unused the ear, the oar, the hour, the ire.

button, bitten, kitten, mitten, fatten, beaten, cotton.

what with, that will, it would, Kate wants, that which, sat where, got one, what will, that would

that man, what matter, department, deportment, apartment, Dartmouth, it makes.

EXERCISES FOR PRACTICE IN PRONOUNCING TWO CONSECUTIVE VOWELS WITHOUT USING AN INTRUSIVE [r], [w], [j], OR [ʔ]

oasis	ideal	clawing
drawing	geography	zoölogy
iota	the olive	raw eggs
three Indians	Edna and I	china eggs
go on	how awful	reincarnate
the ordeal	the artichoke	two apples
the attribute	the eagles	put a comma after it
the area of the isosceles triangle	to awe and majesty blowing	the idea of it the altitude,
I saw an elephant	high altar	seeing
preëminent	flower	reiterate

SENTENCES FOR VOWEL AND DIPHTHONG REVIEW

(Also to be used for phonetic transcription)

[i]

She weeps when she sees that there is no redeeming him from his double dealing.

[ɪ]

It is not the easiest thing in the world to look beneath the surface to the intricate and elusive realities of this excitable and restless twentieth century.

[ɛ]

They met casually but very soon fell into the way of spending many merry hours together.

[æ]

After a passably comfortable crossing they arrived at Paris where the young man who had taken a fancy to Alice was often seen standing at the door with a large bouquet of asters in his hand.

[a] *or* [ɑ] *or* [æ]

As he passed down the pathway, she glanced up and saw him laughing at a little calf that was frisking over the short grass of the meadow.

[u]

In the cool blue heavens the moon hung pale and luminous.

[ʊ]

He put his right foot on the pulley, took the rope in his hand, and was soon in full view of the druid stones on Pulpit Rock.

[o]

Poetry teaches obedience to inner law; not to scholastic precept nor prohibitory legislation.

[ɔ]

At dawn he heard the lonely call of the loon over the water and saw that a cold rainy morning was before him.

[ɒ]

He got some laurel in the forest but did not break long branches or destroy the moss growing on the rocks.

[ɑ]

The farther he went through the park in the evening calm the more artistic the landscape gardening seemed to him.

[ɜ]

The erring man spoke to him so curtly that it did not seem worth while to hurl at him the hot words that whirled through his mind.

[ə]

The farmers stood around absorbed in their personal affairs and no one seemed observant or intelligent enough to question the data of the charlatan.

[ʌ]

Up, up they went over the rough Surrey hills till they reached the coveted plum tree.

[eɪ]

With the aid of the pale but amiable warden of the jail they saw the maimed man every day until he was sane and well again.

[aɪ]

They fly over the ice between the islands, defying one another with sharp cries, and promptly at nine file into the house for wine and cake.

[ɔɪ]

In all the turmoil and rejoicing the boys were careful not to spoil the furniture nor annoy their hostess.

[aʊ]

In that dark hour the proud man called out for help against this foul play, but the silence around him was unbroken except for the distant howling of the wolves and the hooting of an occasional owl.

[oʊ]

All night the snow fell on the open fields and drifted over the roads, and in the morning the bell tolled slowly for the death of an unknown traveler.

[ɪə]

He that hath ears to hear let him hear.

[ɛə]

The cool morning air awakened Mary before she realized that she had slept at all. She said her prayers, dressed carefully, and wished she could share her breakfast with a fieldfare or a March hare.

[oə] *or* [ɔə] *(often simplified to* [ɔ]*)*

He took some more money from the drawer, picked out four or five of the Rector's best cigars, opened the door quietly, and went forth into the pouring rain.

[ʊə]

The poor child will surely feel the lure of the rocks and moors and mountain lakes.

SELECTIONS FOR PRACTICE ON ALL VOWELS AND CONSONANTS

1

HAMLET: Speak the speech, I pray you, as I pronounc'd it to you, trippingly on the tongue; but if you mouth it, as many of your players do, I had as lief the town-crier spoke my lines. Nor do not saw the air too much with your hand, thus, but use all gently; for in the very torrent, tempest, and, as I may say, the whirlwind of passion, you must acquire and beget a temperance that may give it smoothness. O, it offends me to the soul to see a robustious periwig-pated fellow tear a passion to tatters, to very rags, to split the ears of the groundlings, who for the most part are capable of nothing but inexplicable dumb-shows and noise. I could have such a fellow whipp'd for o'erdoing Termagant. It out-herods Herod. Pray you, avoid it.

1ST PLAYER: I warrant your honour.

HAMLET: Be not too tame neither, but let your own discretion be your tutor. Suit the action to the word, the word to the action; with this special observance, that you o'erstep not the modesty of nature. For anything so overdone is from the purpose of playing, whose end, both at the first and now, was and is, to hold, as 'twere, the mirror up to nature; to show virtue her own feature, scorn her own image, and the very age and body of the time his form and pressure. Now this overdone, or come tardy off, though it make the unskilful laugh, cannot but make the judicious grieve; the censure of the which one must, in your allowance, o'erweigh a whole theatre of others. O, there be players that I have seen play, and heard others praise, and that highly, not to speak it profanely, that, neither having the accent of Christians nor the gait of Christian, pagan, nor man, have so strutted and bellowed that I have thought some of Nature's journeymen had made men and not made them well, they imitated humanity so abominably.

2

Thus the Mayne glideth
Where my Love abideth;
Sleep's no softer: it proceeds
On through lawns, on through meads,
On and on, whate'er befall,
Meandering and musical,
Though the niggard pasturage
Bears not on its shaven ledge
Aught but weeds and waving grasses
To view the river as it passes,
Save here and there a scanty patch
Of primroses too faint to catch
A weary bee. . . . And scarce it pushes
Its gentle way through strangling rushes
Where the glossy kingfisher
Flutters when noon-heats are near,
Glad the shelving banks to shun,
Red and steaming in the sun,
Where the shrew-mouse with pale throat
Burrows, and the speckled stoat;
Where the quick sandpipers flit
In and out the marl and grit
That seems to breed them, brown as they:
Naught disturbs its quiet way,
Save some lazy stork that springs,
Trailing it with legs and wings,
Whom the shy fox from the hill
Rouses, creep he ne'er so still.

BROWNING

3

VIOLA: If I did love you in my master's flame,
With such a suffering, such a deadly life,
In your denial I would find no sense,
I would not understand it.

OLIVIA: Why, what would you?

VIOLA: Make me a willow cabin at your gate,
And call upon my soul within the house;
Write loyal cantons of contemned love
And sing them loud even in the dead of night;
Halloo your name to the reverberate hills
And make the babbling gossip of the air
Cry out "Olivia," O, you should not rest
Between the elements of air and earth,
But you should pity me!

SHAKESPEARE

4

That ancient Beadsman heard the prelude soft;
And so it chanced, for many a door was wide,
From hurry to and fro. Soon, up aloft,
The silver, snarling trumpets 'gan to chide:
The level chambers, ready with their pride,
Were glowing to receive a thousand guests:
The carved angels, ever eager-eyed,
Stared where upon their heads the cornice rests,
With hair blown back, and wings put crosswise on their breasts.

KEATS

5

Surely there is a vein for the silver, and a place for gold where they fine it.

Iron is taken out of the earth, and brass is molten out of the stone.

He setteth an end to darkness, and searcheth out all perfection: the stones of darkness, and the shadow of death.

The flood breaketh out from the inhabitant; even the waters forgotten of the foot: they are dried up, they are gone away from men.

Book of Job

The following selection, because of the extraordinarily rapid tempo which it demands, serves as an excellent test of proficiency in articulation:

6

CATHERINE: What are you doing, my dear? You seem busy. You work too much. (*She goes to the window-seat and takes up her embroidery.*) Aren't you afraid it will make you ill? You must rest once in a while. Why don't you tell me what you are doing, dear?

LEONARD: I am examining a case and preparing to draw up a verdict on it.

CATHERINE: Is drawing up a verdict so very important?

LEONARD: Most certainly it is.

CATHERINE: Then write out your verdict. I shan't say another word.

LEONARD: That's right. (*Reading, and making notes.*) "Now, the guardian of the said young lady, namely, Hugo Thomas of Piedeloup, gentleman, stole from the said young lady her—"

CATHERINE: My dear, if one were to believe the wife of the Chief Justice of Montbadon, the world has grown very corrupt; it is going to the bad; young men nowadays don't marry; they prefer to hang about rich old ladies; and meanwhile the poor girls are left to wither on their maiden stalks. Do you think it's as bad as all that? Do answer me, dear.

LEONARD: My darling, won't you please be silent one moment? Or go and talk somewhere else? I'm all at sea.

CATHERINE: There, there, dear; don't worry. I shan't say another word! Not a word!

LEONARD: Good! (*Writing.*) "The said Piedeloup, gentleman, counting both hay crops and apple crops . . . "

CATHERINE: My dear, we shall have for supper to-night some minced mutton and what's left of that goose one of your suitors gave us. Tell me, is that enough? Shall you be satisfied with it? I hate being mean, and like to set a good table, but what's the use of serving courses which will only be sent back to the pantry untouched? The cost of living is getting higher all the time.

Chickens, and salads, and meats, and fruit have all gone up so, it will soon be cheaper to order dinner sent in by a caterer.

LEONARD: I beg you . . . (*Writing.*) "An orphan by birth . . . "

CATHERINE: Yes, that's what we're coming to. No home life any more. You'll see. Why, a capon, or a partridge, or a hare, cost less all stuffed and roasted than if you buy them alive at the market. That is because the cook-shops buy in large quantities and get a big discount; so they can sell to us at a profit. I don't say we ought to get our regular meals from the cook-shop. We can do our everyday plain cooking at home, and it's better to; but when we invite people in, or give a formal dinner party, then it saves time and money to have the dinner sent in. Why, at less than an hour's notice, the cook-shops and cake-shops will get you up a dinner for a dozen, or twenty, or fifty people; the cook-shop will send in meat and poultry, the caterer will send galantines and sauces and relishes, the pastry-cook will send pies and tarts and sweets and desserts; and it's all so convenient. Now, don't you think so yourself, Leonard?

LEONARD: Please, please! (*Leonard tries to write through the following speech, murmuring:* "An orphan by birth, a capon by birth, an olla podrida," etc.)

CATHERINE: It's no wonder everything goes up. People are getting more extravagant every day. If they are entertaining a friend, or even a relative, they don't think they can do with only three courses, soup, meat, and dessert. No, they have to have meats in five or six different styles, with so many sauces, or dressings, or pasties, that it's a regular olla podrida. Now, don't you think that is going too far, my dear? For my part I just cannot understand how people can take pleasure in stuffing themselves with so many kinds of food. Not that I despise a good table; why, I'm even a bit of an epicure myself. "Not too plenty, but dainty," suits *my* taste. Now, what I like best of all is capons' kidneys with artichoke hearts. But you, Leonard, I suspect you have a weakness for tripe and sausages. Oh, fie! Oh, fie! How can anyone enjoy sausages?

LEONARD: (*His head in his hands.*) I shall go mad! I shall go mad!

ANATOLE FRANCE, *The Man Who Married a Dumb Wife*,
translated by Curtis Hidden Page

III. PHONETIC TRANSCRIPTIONS

Selections for General Practice

The following fifty short selections are given to enable the student to gain facility in reading phonetic symbols with accuracy and ease.

The reader must be careful to reproduce exactly the pronunciations indicated, noticing differences between those pronunciations and his own. Particular attention should be given to weak forms, assimilations, and consonant combinations. The student should remember that the purpose of the authors is not to dictate a standard to him, but to give him opportunity for training his ear to make fine distinctions in sound so that he will be able to improve his speech according to his own standards. In some cases, optional readings are given. It will be easily seen, however, that if all the correct forms were given the transcription would be too difficult to print or read.

Note. The following modifiers are used in some of the transcriptions: ', |, ||, |·| mark phrasing; ˑ and ː are length marks; ˈ stresses the syllable following; ʔ indicates the glottal stop, ~ nasality, and · (under a sound) inversion. Symbols in parentheses indicate optional pronunciations.

1

ʍɒt ɪz maɪnd? noʊ mætə(r).
ʍɒt ɪz mætə(r)? nɛvə(r) maɪnd.
ʍɒt ɪz spɪrɪt? ðæts ɪm͜mətɪərɪəl.

2

ðɪ oʊld foʊgɪ {hu / hʊ} θrʌst {ɪz / hɪz} hɛd aʊt frəm {bəhaɪnd / bɪhaɪnd}

ðə taɪmz, hæd ɪt {nɑkt / nɒkt} {ɔf / ɒf} baɪ ə p {æ / a / ɑ} sɪŋ {əvɛnt / ɪvɛnt}

3

θri meɪ kip kɑʊnsəl ɪf tu bɪ ˈəweɪ.

4

ðə tʌŋ siks ðɪ eɪkɪŋ tuθ.

5

ðɪ aɪ əv ðə mastə(r) fætnz ðə hɔ(r)s.

6

ɪf ɔl kændlz bɪ ɑʊt ɔl kæts bɪ greɪ.

7

ðə lʌvd tʃaɪld hæz menɪ neɪmz.

8

ðɪ aɪz ər əv lɪtl jus ɪf ðə maɪnd bɪ blaɪnd.

9

$$\left.\begin{array}{l} \text{foə(r)} \\ \text{fʊə(r)} \\ \text{fɔə(r)} \\ \text{fɔ} \end{array}\right\}$$ θɪŋz kænɒt bi brɔt bæk; ə wɜ(r)d spoʊkn, ən

æroʊ dɪstʃɑ(r)dʒd, ðə dɪvaɪn dɪkri, ənd past taɪm.

10

ðɪs ɪz bət ə smɔl wɪndoʊ, maɪ mastə(r)z, bət ɪt oʊpnz ɒn ə greɪt wɜ(r)ld.

11

ðɪ esəns əv gʊd ənd ivɪl ɪz ɪn ə sɜ(r)tn dɪspəsɪʃən əv ðə wɪl.

12

ə frentʃ steɪtsmən wʌns kɔld spitʃ ðə fækəltɪ baɪ hʊɪtʃ wɪ haɪd ɑʊə(r) θɔts.

13

truθ ɪz ɪstæblɪʃt baɪ dɪleɪ, fɔlshʊd prɒspə(r)z baɪ ræʃ heɪst.
—tæsɪtəs.

14

ʰwen ðə laɪtnɪŋ əv gɒd flæʃɪz ɪn menz hɑ(r)ts ðeɪ du
ɪmpɒsɪbl θɪŋz.—hɪndu prɒvə(r)b.

15

θri men ə(r) maɪ frendz: hi hʊ heɪts mi, hi hʊ lʌvz mi,
ənd hi hʊ ɪz ɪndɪfərənt tʊ mi.

16

ɪf ju kip jʊə(r) feɪs tə(r)nd tʊ ðə sʌn, ʃædoʊz wɪl ɔlwɪz
fɔl bɪhaɪnd ju.

17

hi hʊ ɪts wɪð ðə devɪl ʃʊd hæv ə lɒŋ spun.

18

ʰwɒt wʊd jʊ hæv? kwoʊθ gɒd—peɪ fɒr ɪt ənd teɪk ɪt.
—emə(r)sn.

19

aɪrɪʃ prɒvə(r)bz: ə sɔ(r)d, ə speɪd, ənd ə θɔt ʃʊd nevə(r)
bɪ əlaʊd tʊ rʌst.

ə kɪŋz sʌn ɪz noʊblə(r) ðən hɪz fud.

ðə best kjʊə(r)z ɪn ðə dɒktə(r)z bʊk ɑ(r) ə gʊd laf ənd ə
lɒŋ slip.

fɑ(r) hɪlz ə(r) grin ənd fɑ(r) seɪlz ə(r) ʰwaɪt.

ðə mɪlə(r)z pɪgz ɑ(r) fæt, bət gɒd noʊz huz mil ðeɪ eɪt.

ɪts ðə fɜ(r)st drɒp ðət dɪstrɔɪd mi.   ðə(r)z noʊ hɑ(r)m
ət ɔl ɪn ðʊ ḷast.

20

nɪsesɪti ɪz nɒt soʊ mʌtʃ ðə mʌðər əv ɪnventʃən æz ɪt ɪz ðə
tʃaɪld əv ʌnrɪsɒ(r)sfəlnɪs.

21

saɪəns həz gɪvn mæn, ɪn ðɪs twentɪəθ sentʃʊrɪ, ðə paʊə(r)
tə spik tʊ ɔl ðə kɔ(r)nə(r)z əv ðɪ ɜ(r)θ, ənd bɪhoʊld! hi həz
nʌθɪŋ wɜ(r)θ lʊaɪl tə seɪ.

22

nʌθɪŋ dʌz məə(r) hɑ(r)m | ɪn ʌnnə(r)vɪŋ men fə(r) ðɛə(r)
djutɪz ɪn ðə prezənt | ðən ðɪ ətenʃn dɪvoʊtɪd tə ðə pʊɪnts əv
ɛksələns ɪn ðə past | əz kəmpɛə(r)d wɪð ðɪ ævərɪdʒ feɪljər əv
ðə prezənt deɪ |·|

23

kənsit | lʊɪtʃ ɔl tu ɒfn mɑ(r)z pə(r)sənælɪtɪ | ɪz bət ə
kənfeʃn əv ðə groʊsɪst kaɪnd əv ɪgnərəns |·|

24

ə pə(r)sn hʊ ɪz waɪz | ɔlwɪz hæz sʌtʃ ə vɪstə | əv θɪŋz hi
noʊz nʌθɪŋ əbaʊt ɪn frʌnt əv hɪm | ðət hi groʊz mɒər ənd
mɒə(r) hʌmbl | əz hɪz wɪzdəm ɪnkrisɪz |·|

25

tʊ spik əv ðə lɪmɪteɪʃənz' əv ðɪ ɪndɪvɪdjʊəl | ɪz blæsfəmɪ
ənd sʊɪsaɪd |·| ðə spɪrɪt əv ðə hoʊl' ɪz ɪnkɑ(r)nɪt ɪn ɛvrɪ
pɑ(r)t |·|—nɪtʃə.

26

laɪf minz fər ʌs | tə transfɔ(r)m ɪntʊ laɪt ənd fleɪm | ɔl
ðət wɪ ɑr ɔ(r) mit wɪð.—nɪtʃə.

27

mʌs tʊ miʃən ɔl nɒlɪdʒ ɪz ə grasp əv truθ ‖ ən ɪnsaɪt ɪntʊ sʌm
$\left\{\begin{array}{l}\text{poə(r)ʃn}\\\text{pə(r)ʃn}\end{array}\right\}$ əv rɪælɪtɪ |·| nʌθɪŋ ɪz nɒlɪdʒ | lʊɪtʃ ɪz nɒt beɪst
ɒn evɪdəns səfɪʃnt tə pruv ɪt ‖ ðæt ɪz | lʊɪtʃ ɪz nɒt faʊnd tə
bi | ə pɑ(r)t əv ðɪ ɔ(r)dər əv ðə wɜ(r)ld |·|

28

ʰwən jʊ hæv ə peɪnfəl djutɪ tə pə(r)fɔ(r)m ‖ dʒʌst meɪk
ə pʌblɪk steɪtmənt | ðət jʊ ə(r) goʊʊŋ tə pə(r)fɔ(r)m ɪt |·|
praɪd meɪ kærɪ jʊ θru |·|

29

ʰwɒt aɪ laɪk əbɑʊt klaɪv |
ɪz ðət hiz noʊ lɒŋgər əlaɪv |·|
ðə(r)z ə greɪt dil tə bi sed |
fə(r) biɪŋ ded |·|

30

dʒɒn stjuə(r)t mɪl |
baɪ ə maɪtɪ ɛfə(r)t əv ðə wɪl |
oʊvə(r)keɪm hɪz nætʃərəl bɒnɒmi |
ənd roʊt prɪnsɪplz əv pəlɪtɪkl ɪkɒnəmɪ |·|

31

sə(r) krɪstəfə(r) ren |
sed | aɪm goʊʊŋ tə daɪn wɪð səm men |·|
ɪf ɛnɪwən kɔlz |
seɪ | aɪm dɪzaɪnɪŋ sənt pɔlz.

32

ðɛə(r) wɒz ən oʊld mæn wɪð ə bɪə(r)d |
hu sed | ɪt ɪz dʒʌst əz aɪ fɪə(r)d ‖
tu ɑʊlz ənd ə hen |
fʊə(r) lɑ(r)ks ənd ə ren |
həv ɔl bɪlt ðɛə(r) nests[1] ɪn maɪ bɪə(r)d |·|

33

ðɛə(r) wɒz ən oʊld mæn əv keɪp hɒ(r)n |
hu wɪʃt (h)i (h)əd nɛvə(r) bɪn bɒ(r)n ‖
soʊ (h)i sæt ɒn ə tʃɛə(r) |
tɪl (h)i daɪd əv dɪspeə(r) |
ðæt dɒlərəs mæn frəm keɪp hɒ(r)n |·|

34

ðɛə(r) wɒz ən oʊld mæn hu sed¹ hʌʃ |
aɪ pɜ(r)siv ə jʌŋ bɜ(r)d ɪn ə bʊʃ ||
ʰʋɛn ðeɪ sed | ɪz ɪt smɒl |
hi rɪplaɪd | nɒt æt ɒl ||
ɪt ɪz fɒə(r) taɪmz əz bɪg əz ðə bʊʃ |·|

35

ən æs felt ɪt (h)ɪz djutɪ | tə dɪstrɒɪ sjupə(r)stɪʃən || soʊ
(h)ɪ went ʌp tə ðə bras aɪdl¹ ɪn ðə mɑ(r)kɪt pleɪs | ənd geɪv
ɪt ə vɪgərəs kɪk |·|

ə dɒg keɪm tʊ (h)ɪm, əz (h)i leɪ groʊnɪŋ ɒn ðə graʊnd |
nɜ(r)sɪŋ (h)ɪz broʊkən leg | ənd sed || wel | dɪd ju pruv
ɛnɪθɪŋ? ||

nʌθɪŋ | sed ðɪ ʌðə(r) || ɪksept ðət aɪ əm ən æs |·|

36

ðɛə(r) wɒz ə jʌŋ bɑ(r)d əv dʒəpæn |
hu roʊt vɜ(r)sɪz¹ ðət noʊwʌn kʊd skæn |·|
ðeɪ toʊld (h)ɪm twəz soʊ ||
hi rɪplaɪd || jes | aɪ noʊ ||
bət aɪ ɔlwɪz traɪ tə get əz mɛni wɜ(r)dz ɪntʊ ðə last laɪn
əz aɪ pɒsɪblɪ kæn |·|

37

aɪ əm hɪz haɪnɪs dɒg | əv kju ||
preɪ tɛl mi | sɜ || huz dɒg ə ju? |·|

38

ðə wɒz ən oʊld mæn ɪn ə tri |
hu wəz hɒrɪblɪ bɒəd baɪ ə bi |·|
ʰʋɛn ðeɪ sed | dəz ɪt bʌz? ||
hɪ rɪplaɪd | jes ɪt dʌz ||
ɪts ə regjələ brut əv ə bi |·|

39

ju bit jʊə peɪt | ənd fænsɪ wɪt wɪl kʌm ||
nɒk əz jʊ pliz || ðɛz noʊbədɪ ət hoʊm |·|

40

ə fʊks' lʊkt ət (h)ɪz ʃædoʊ' ət sʌnraɪz | ənd sɛd | aɪ wɪl
hæv ə kæməl fə lʌntʃ | tədeɪ || ənd lɛ mɒnɪŋ hɪ went əbaʊt'
lʊkɪŋ fə kæməlz |·| bət ət nun' hɪ sɔ ɪz ʃædoʊ əgen | ənd
sɛd | ə maʊs wɪl du |·|

41

ən eɪnʃənt fɪlɒsɪfə' həz sɛd ðət ə mænz preɪz' həz verɪ
mjuzɪkl ənd tʃamɪŋ æksents' ɪn ənʌðəz maʊθ || bət ɪt ɪz
verɪ flæt ənd ʌntjunəbl' ɪn hɪz oʊn |·|

42

bət ðɛər ɪz ə kaɪnd əv lʌkʃərɪ əv leɪzɪnɪs' ɪn ridɪŋ | ɥɪtʃ
ɪz pəhæps ðə best θɪŋ ɪn ɔl ðə wɜld |·| ɪt ɪz tə bi kæptʃəd
oʊnlɪ | aɪ θɪŋk | θru ðɪ oʊld bʊks || bʊks ðət ju noʊ soʊ wel |
ðət ðeɪ stɛp aʊt' ənd mit ju |·|

43

məsjə bɒsweɪz səmɛn

məsjə bɒsweɪ | bɪʃəp əv moʊ | ət eɪt jɪəz əv eɪdʒ pritʃt
wɪð greɪs |·| hi dɪlɪvəd ə səmən ət ðæt eɪdʒ' ət ðə hotəl
də ræmbujeɪ |·| ɪt wəz nɪəlɪ mɪdnaɪt lʊɛn (h)ɪ kloʊzd || ənd
vwatjʊə | hu wəz prezənt | rɪmakt əz (h)ɪ roʊz tə goʊ ||
"aɪ əv nevə həd ə səmən pritʃt soʊ ɜlɪ || ə soʊ leɪt" |·|

44

dʌblɪŋ daʊn ə peɪdʒ

ɪt biɪŋ rɪpətɪd' ðət leɪdɪ kærəlaɪn læm' hæd | ɪn ə moʊ-
mənt əv pæʃn | nɒkt daʊn wʌn əv (h)ə peɪdʒɪz wɪð ə stul | ðə

poʊɪt mɒə | tə hum ðɪs wəz toʊld baɪ ləd stræŋfəd | əbzɛvd
"oʊ nʌθɪŋ ɪz mɒə nætʃərəl fər ə lɪtərɛrɪ leɪdɪ | ðən tə dʌbl
daʊn ə peɪdʒ" |·| "aɪ wəd raðə" | rɪplaɪd (h)ɪz lədʃɪp | "ədvaɪz
leɪdɪ kærəlaɪn tə tɛn oʊvər ə nju lɪf" |·|

45
kərekʃən əv ɛrəs

i(h) ze tɔʌz ɡʒæn dʊktə bɑtn wəz ɪn kʌmpənɪ wɪð dʊktə næʃ dʒʌst əz (h)i
wəz goʊɪŋ tə pʌblɪʃ (h)ɪz wɜk ɒn ði æntɪkwɪtɪz əv wʊstəʃɪə ||
"aɪ fɪə" | sed dʊktə bɑtn | "ðə wɪl bi ə ɡreɪt mɛnɪ ɪnækjʊrəsɪz
ɪn jʊə bʊks ʰʊen ðeɪ kʌm aʊt" |·| " hɑʊ ər ɛrəz tə bi əvɒɪ-
dɪd?" | sed dʊktə næʃ |·| " ə ju nɑʊ ə dʒʌstɪs əv pis?" |·| "aɪ
æm" |·| "ʰʊaɪ ðen" | rɪplaɪd ðɪ oʊld wɒdn | "juv nʌθɪŋ tə du
bət tə send jʊ bʊks tə ðə hɑʊs əv kərekʃən" |·|

46
bək pʊt tə flaɪt

mɪstə bək | ɒn wʌn əkeɪʒn | həd dʒʌst rɪzn ɪn ðə hɑʊs əv
kɒmənz | wɪð səm peɪpəz ɪn (h)ɪz hænd | ɒn ðə sʌbdʒɪkt əv
ʰʊɪtʃ hi ɪntendɪd tə meɪk ə moʊʃən || ʰʊen ə rʌfhjun membə |
hu həd noʊ ɪə fə ðə tʃɑmz əv ɛlokwəns | rudlɪ stɑtɪd ʌp ənd
sed || "mɪstə spɪkə | aɪ hoʊp ðɪ ɒnərəbl dʒentlmən dʌznt min
tə rid ðæt lɑdʒ bʌndl əv peɪpəz || ənd tə bɒər ʌs wɪð ə lɒŋ
spitʃ ɪntʊ ðə bɑɡɪn" |·| mɪstə bək wəz soʊ ənreɪdʒd əz tə
bi ɪnkeɪpəbl əv ʌtərəns || ənd æbsəlutlɪ ræn aʊt əv ðə
hɑʊs |·| ɒn ðɪs əkeɪʒən dʒɒdʒ selwɪn rɪmɑkt | ðæt ɪt wəz ðɪ
oʊnlɪ taɪm hi ɛvə sɒ ðə feɪbl rɪəlaɪzd || ə laɪən pʊt tə flaɪt[1] baɪ
ðə breɪŋ əv ən æs |·|

47
raɪtɪŋ hɪstərɪ

ʰʊen letɪ | ðə hɪstɔrɪən | wəz wʌn deɪ ətendɪŋ ðə levɪ əv
tʃɑlz ðə sekənd | hɪ sed tə hɪm | "letɪ | aɪ hɪə ðət ju ə raɪtɪŋ
ðə hɪstərɪ əv ðə kɒt əv ɪŋɡlənd" |·| "sə | aɪ (h)əv bɪn fə sʌm

taɪm prɪpɛərɪŋ mətɪrɪəlz fə sʌtʃ ə hɪstərɪ" |·| "teɪk kɛə
ðət jʊə wɜk gɪv noʊ əfɛns" || sɛd ðə prɪns |·| lɛtɪ rɪplaɪd ||
"sɜ | aɪ wɪl du hʊɒt aɪ kæn || bət ɪf ə mæn wɜr əz waɪz əz
sɒləmən | hi wəd skɛəslɪ bi eɪbl tʊ əvɔɪd gɪvɪŋ əfɛns" |·|
"hʊaɪ ðɛn" | rɪdʒɔɪnd ðə prɪns | " bi əz waɪz əz sɒləmən || raɪt
prɒvəbz || nɒt hɪstərɪz" |·|

48

truθ ɪn fɪkʃən

"hi nju" || sɛz leɪ hʌnt | spikɪŋ əv tʃɑlz læm || " haʊ menɪ
fɒls kənkluʒənz ənd prɪtenʃənz | ə meɪd baɪ mɛn hu prəfɛs
tə bɪ gaɪdɪd baɪ fækts oʊnlɪ || əz ɪf fækts kəd nɒt bɪ
mɪskənsɪvd | ə fɪgmənts teɪkn fə ðəm || ənd ðefʊə wʌn
deɪ | hʊɛn sʌmbədɪ wəz spikɪŋ əv ə pɜsn | hu praɪdɪd (h)ɪm-
self ɒn biɪŋ ə mætər-əv-fækt mæn || læm sɛd 'aɪ vælju maɪself
ɒn biɪŋ ə mæn əv ðə greɪtɪst vəræsɪtɪ' ɪn ði ɒdənərɪ sɛns əv
ðə wəd || bət truθ ɪz preʃəs | ənd nɒt tə bɪ weɪstɪd ɒn ɛvrɪ-
bɒdɪ'" |·|

49

elokwəns

ə wɪtɪ frentʃwʊmən həd bɪn prezənt ət ə səmən | fʊl əv
faɪər ənd elokwəns | bət lækɪŋ ɪn səlɪdɪtɪ ənd əreɪndʒmənt |·|
wʌn əv (h)ə frendz askt hə' haʊ ʃɪ laɪkt ɪt |·| wɒz ɪt nɒt
fʊl əv spɪrɪt? | sɛd ʃi |·| soʊ fʊl | rɪplaɪd ðɪ ʌðə | ðət aɪ kʊd
nɒt si ɛnɪ bɒdɪ |·|

50

ju rɪmembə | hʊɛn jʊ wə tʃɪldrɪn | lʊkɪŋ oʊvə ðɪ oʊld
storɪbʊk' hændɪd daʊn tə ju baɪ ðə pjʊərɪtn faðəz | ðət
wʌn əv ðə kənʌndrəmz wɪð hʊɪtʃ ðə geɪtɪŋ əv ðɛə taɪmz wəz
ɪlʌstreɪtɪd | wɒz || hu wəz ðə ʃɒtɪst mæn ɪn ðə baɪbl? |·| ðɪ
ansə wɒz || bɪldæd ðə ʃuhaɪt || bət naʊ | ɪn ðə rɪvaɪzd tekst |
ɪt ɪz pitə | bɪkɒz pitə sed | sɪlvə ənd goʊld hæv aɪ nʌn |
ənd noʊwən kəd bi ʃɒtə ðən ðæt.

SELECTIONS ILLUSTRATING VARIOUS STYLES

There follow a number of phonetic transcriptions arranged according to their speech levels.

In the first division have been placed the more formal types of poetry and prose. Such selections contain more strong forms and fewer assimilations and omissions than other types of discourse.

The later groups represent increasingly informal style and illustrate slight differences in method of transcribing. In some cases variant forms (as for instance the use or omission of [h] and [r]) are indicated, in others, only the pronunciation of the transcriber is given.

A. FORMAL STYLE

1

sʌnɪt — ʃeikspɪə(r)

frəm ju hæv ai bin æbsənt in ðə sprɪŋ ‖
wen praud-paid eiprɪl | drest in ɔːl hiz trɪm |
hæθ pʊt ə spɪrɪt əv juːθ in evrɪθɪŋ ‖
ðət hevɪ sætə(r)n laft ənd liːpt wið him |—|
jet nʌə(r) ðə leiz əv bɜː(r)dz ‖ nʌə(r) ðə swiːt smel
əv difərənt flavə(r)z in ovdə(r) ænd in hju |
kʊd meik mi enɪ sʌmə(r)z stɔrɪ tel ‖
və(r) frəm ðeə(r) praud læp plʌk ðəm hreə(r) ðei gru ‖
nʌə(r) did ai wʌndə(r) æt ðə lilɪz hwait ‖
nʌə(r) preiz ðə diːp və(r)miljən in ðə rovz ‖
ðei wɜː(r) bət swiːt ‖ bət figjə(r)z əv dilait|
drɔːn æftə(r) ju ‖ ju | pætə(r)n əv ɔːl ðovz|—|
jet siːmd it wintə(r) stɪl ‖ ænd ju əwei |
æz wið jʊə(r) ʃædov | ai wið ðiːz did plei |—|

2

briːdn hil — ei iː havsmən

in sʌmə taim ʌn briːdn |
ðə belz ðei saund sou kliə ‖
raund bouθ ðə ʃaiəz ðei riŋ ðəm |
in stiːplz faːr ənd niə ‖
ə hæpi nɔiz tu hiə |—|

miːniːm 'idʌvə ə və reiə
mai lʌv ənd ai wud lai |
ənd siː ðə kʌləd kauntiz |
ənd hiə ðə laːkə sou hai
əbaut ʌs in ðə skai |—|

ðə belz wəd riŋ tə kɔːl hə |
in væliz mailz əwei ‖
"kʌm ɔːl tu tʃɜtʃ | gud piːpl ‖
gud piːpl | kʌm ənd prei" ‖
bət hiə mai lʌv wud stei |—|

ənd ai wud tɜːn ənd ansə |
əmʌŋ ðə spriŋiŋ taim |
"ou piːl əpən auə wedin |
ənd wi wil hiə ðə tʃaim |
ənd kʌm tu tʃɜːtʃ in taim |—|

bət hwen ðə snouz ət krisməs
ʌn briːdn hil wə stroun |
mai lʌv rouz ʌp sou ɜːli |
ənd stoul aut ʌnbinoun ‖
ənd went tu tʃɜːtʃ əloun |—|

briːdn hil — kəntinjuə

ðei tovld ðə wʌn bɛl ovnli ‖
qruːm ðə wəz nʌn tv siː ‖
ðə mɔːnəz fɒlovd aftə |
ənd sov tv tʃɜːtʃ went ʃʋ ‖
ənd wʋd nɒt weit fə miː |—|

ðə bɛlz ðei savnd ɒn briːdn |
ənd stil ðə stiːplz hʌm ‖
"kʌm ɔːl tv tʃɜːtʃ | qʋd piːpl̩" ‖
ɒv nɔizi bɛlz bi dʌm ‖
ai hiə ʃu ‖ ai wil kʌm |—|

3

hɜːd ' mɛlodiz ' a swiːt | bət ðovz ʌnhɜːd |
ə swiːtə ‖ ðeəfɔ | ji sɒft paips ' plei ɒn ‖
nɒt tv ðə sensjvəl iə | bət mɔr endiəd |
paip tv ðə spirit | ditiz əv nov tovn ‖
feə ʃuːθ | biːniːθ ðə triːz | ðav kænst nɒt liːv |
ðai sɒŋ ‖ nɒr ɛvə kæn ðovz triːz bi beə ‖
bovld lʌvə | nevə ' nevə ' kænst ðav kis |
ðov winiŋ niə ðə qovl ‖ jɛt du nɒt griːv ‖
ʃi kænʌt feid | ðov ðav hæst nɒt ðai blis ‖
fɔr ɛvə ' wilt ðav lʌv | ænd ʃiː ' bi feə |—|

4

ɔr ɛvə ðə silvə kɔːd bi luːst ‖ ɔ ðə qovldn.
bovl bi brovkn ‖ ɔ ðə pitʃə bi brovkn æt ðə
favntin ‖ ɔ ðə hwiːl bi brovkn æt ðə sistən |—|

5

ʃeɪkspɪə(r)

ʌðəz əbaɪd aʊə kwestʃən |·| ðaʊ at fri |·|
wi ask' ənd ask || ðaʊ smaɪlɪst' ənd ɑt stɪl ||
aʊttʊpɪŋ nʊlɪdʒ |·| fə ðə lɒftɪɪst hɪl |
hu tʊ ðə stɑz' ʌnkraʊnz hɪz mædʒəstɪ |
plantɪŋ hɪz stedfast fʊtsteps' ɪn ðə si |
meɪkɪŋ ðə hevn əv hevn' hɪz dwelɪŋ pleɪs |
speəz bet ðə klaʊdɪ bədər əv hɪz beɪs'
tʊ ðə fʊɪld sətʃɪŋ əv mətælɪtɪ ||
ənd ðaʊ | hu dɪdst ðə stɑz ənd sʌnbimz noʊ |
selfskuld | selfskænd | selfnʊnəd | selfsɪkjʊə ||
dɪdst tred ðɪ əθ ʌngest æt |·| betə soʊ |·|
əl peɪnz' ðə mətəl [8] spɪrɪt mʌst ɪndjʊə
| əl wiknɪs' hʊɪtʃ ɪmpeəz | əl grifs hʊɪtʃ baʊ |
faɪnd ðeə soʊl spɪtʃ' ɪn ðæt vɪktʊrɪəs braʊ |·|
—mæθju anəld

B. Informal Style

1

æləs nʊkt ' ənd ræŋ ɪn veɪn ' fər ə lɒŋ
taɪm || bət ət last ' ə vɛrɪ ʊvld frɒg ' hʊ wəz
sɪtɪŋ ʌndər ə tri | gʊt ʌp ' ənd hʊbld sloʊvlɪ
tʊəd hə || hi wəz drest ɪn braɪt jeloʊ |ənd
hæd ɪnʊməs buts ʊn ||
  "hweəz ðə səvənt ' huz bɪznəs ɪt ɪz ' tʊ ænsə
ðə dʊə?" | ʃɪ bɪgæn æŋgrɪlɪ ||
  ðə frɒg lʊkt ət ðə dʊə wɪð hɪz ladʒ
dʌl aɪz ' fər ə mɪnət || "tʊ ænsə ðə dʊə? |
hɪ sed 'hwʊt dɪd ɪt ask ju?" ||

---

[8] Pronounced [mətəl] here on account of the rhythm.

2

ən ɪntruːʒən

mɒræliti pʊt hə(r) tou ɪntu ɪntə(r)næʃənəl
pɒlɪtɪks ənd ɪt wəz prɒmptli tʃɒpt ɒf |—| ə
θauzənd θæŋks" | sed diploumæsi wɪð ən ɪŋgeɪdʒɪŋ
bau | "wiːl kiːp ɪt ɪn memərɪ əv ə moust dɪs-
tɪŋgwɪʃt vnə(r)" |—| ənd mɒræliti həz lɪmpt ə
lɪtl ɛvə(r) sɪns |—|

3

kræb ənd sʌn

ə lɒdʒɪkəl kræb sed tu hɪz sʌn | "hwaɪ du
ju nɒt wɔːk streɪt fɔː(r)wə(r)d? ‖ juə(r) saɪdlɒŋ
geɪt ɪz sɪŋgjulə(r)li ʌŋgreɪsfəl" |—|
"hwaɪ dount ju wɔːk streɪt fɔː(r)wə(r)d ' jə(r)self?‖
sed ðə sʌn |—|
"ɜːrɪŋ juːθ" ‖ sed ðə lɒdʒɪkəl kræb ‖ juə(r)
ɪntrədjuːsɪŋ njuː ənd ɪreləvənt mætə(r)" |—|

4

ə tʃeɪnd iːgl

ə provɪnʃl steɪtsmən | njuːli ələktɪd tə ðə
paː(r)ləmənt əv despəteɪmɪə | dɪkleə(r)d ðət hi wəd
ɪntrədjuːs ə resəluːʃən sensərɪŋ ðə kɪŋ |—| əz hi left
ðə paː(r)ləmənt-haus | hi met ə streɪndʒə(r)· hu
wɔː(r)nd hɪm ðət ɪf hi pə(r)sɪstɪd ɪn (h)ɪz dɪslɔɪəl
dɪzaɪn | hi wəd luːz hɪz hed |—|
"ðæt" | sed hi ‖ "wəd bi ə smɔːlə(r) praɪveɪ-
ʃən | ðən ðə lɒs əv maɪ lɪbə(r)ti" |—|
"aɪ dount nou ðæt" ‖ sed ðə streɪndʒə(r)‖
"lɪbə(r)ti ɪz sʌmθɪŋ ðət aɪ kant raɪtli əpreɪz | nevə(r)
hævɪŋ hæd ɪt ‖ aɪ əm ðə kɪŋ" |—|

5

dɪsəpɔɪntmənt

ə dɒg ðət (h)əd bɪn ɪngeɪdʒd ɪn ðə pə(r)-
ʃuːt əv (h)ɪz oʊn teɪl | əbændənd ðə tʃeɪs |
ənd laɪɪŋ daʊn | kɜː(r)ld ʌp fə(r) rɪpoʊz |—|
ɪn (h)ɪz nʲu poʊtʃə(r) | hɪ faʊnd (h)ɪz teɪl
wɪðɪn iːzɪ riːtʃ əv (h)ɪz tiːθ | ənd siːzd ɪt
wɪð əvɪdɪtɪ ‖ bət ɪmiːdɪətlɪ rɪliːst ɪt | wɪnsɪŋ
wɪð peɪn |—|

"aftər ɔːl" ‖ hɪ sɛd ‖ "ðɛə(r)z moə(r) dʒɔɪ
ɪn pə(r)ʃuːt | ðən ɪn pəzɛʃən" |—|

6

ðə rɪzn soʊ mɛnɪ ɑ(r)tɪsts həv lɪvd tə bi verɪ oʊld ənd
həv bɪn soʊ jʌŋ ət ə greɪt eɪdʒ ɪz ðət ðeɪ həv lɪvd lɪvɪŋ,
ʍɛræz moʊst pɪpl həv lɪvd daɪŋ.

7

lɛktʃəz ər ə səvaɪvl əv ðə mɪdl eɪdʒɪz, djuː tʊ ðə fækt ðət
junɪvɜsɪtɪz həv nɒt jɛt ədæptɪd ðəmsɛlvz tə prɪntɪŋ.

8

əmʌŋ əl prevələnt taɪps əv heroɪn ‖ ðə wə(r)stʹ ɪz wʌn
əpærəntlɪ faʊndɪd ɒn poʊps feɪməs dɪktəm | ðət moʊst
wɪmɪn hæv noʊ kærɪktə(r)z ət əl ‖ ə dɪktəm ʍɪtʃ wɪ wəd
dɪnaʊns wɪð skɔ(r)n | ɪf soʊ əkjut ən əbzɜvər əz dɪkwɪnsɪ
dɪd nɒt stægər əs baɪ dɪfendɪŋ ɪt |·| hɪ dɪfendz ɪt tʊ ətæk
poʊp |·| poʊp | sez dɪkwɪnsɪ | dɪd nɒt si ðət ʍɒt hɪ ədvansɪz əz
ə rɪproʊtʃʹ əgenst wɪmɪn | kɒnstɪtjuts ðə verɪ bjutɪ əv
ðəm |·| ɪt ɪz ɪð æbsəns əv ɪnɪ defɪnɪt kærɪktə(r) | ʍɪtʃ
əneɪblz ðəə(r) kærɪkte(r) tə bi moʊldɪd baɪ ʌðə(r)z ‖ ənd ɪts
ðɪs sɒft plæstɪsɪtɪ, ʍɪtʃ rendə(r)z ðəm sʌtʃ tʃɑ(r)mɪŋ kəmpænj-
ənzʹ əz waɪvz |·| ɪt meɪ bi soʊ |·| ænd ɪt meɪ bi pærɪ-
dɪzaɪɪkl blɪsʹ tu hæv ə waɪfʹ hʊm jʊ kn kʌt aʊt ɒn ə peɪpe(r)

pætə(r)n |·| pə(r)snəlɪ' wi ʃəd prɪfɜ(r) tə kip ə dɒg || ɪt wəd
bi lɛs ɪkspɛnsɪv |·|—fransɪs tɒmpsən.

9

wʌns mɒə(r) || spik klɪə(r)lɪ | ɪf jʊ spik ət ɔl ||
ka(r)v ɛvrɪ wɜ(r)d | bɪfɔ(r) jʊ lɛt ɪt fɔl |·|
doʊnt | laɪk ə lɛktʃərər | ɔ(r) drəmætɪk sta(r) |
traɪ oʊvə(r)-ha(r)d | tə roʊl ðə brɪtɪʃ a(r) |·|
du pʊt jʊə(r) æksɛnts ɒn ðə prɒpə(r) spɒt |·|
doʊnt' lɛt mɪ bɛg ju' doʊnt seɪ | "haʊ?" | fə(r) "lʊʊt?" ||
ənd lʊɛn jʊ stɪk ɪn kɒnvə(r)seɪʃənz bə(r)z |
doʊnt stru ðə paθweɪ | wɪð ðoʊz drɛdfəl ə(r)z |·|

10

ðər ɪz noʊ bɛtə(r) weɪ tʊ oʊpn ə tʃaɪldz maɪnd' tʊ ðə
bjutɪ əv ðə wɜ(r)ld əraʊnd hɪm | ðən θru ðə stʌdɪ əv pɔɪtrɪ |·|
ɪn rɪdɪŋ pɔɪtrɪ ʌndə(r)stændɪŋlɪ | ðə tʃaɪldz sɛnsɪz ə(r)
ʃa(r)pnd || hɪz ɪmædʒɪneɪʃn stɪmjʊleɪtɪd || hɪz sɪmpəθɪz
brɒdənd |·| hɪ məst si | ənd fil | ənd θɪŋk wɪð ðə pɔɪt |·|

11

ði atɪst ənd ðə ʃɒpkipə

moʊst atɪsts | lʊɛðɜ‹ ɪn rɪlɪdʒən | mjuzɪk | lɪtərətʃə |
peɪntɪŋ | ə lʊʊt nɒt | ə ʃɒpkipəz ɪn dɪsgaɪz |·| ðeɪ haɪd ðɛə
ʃɒʃ əz mʌtʃ əz ðeɪ kæn | ənd kip prɪtɛndɪŋ ðət ɪt dəz nɒt
ɪgzɪst | bət ðeɪ ər ɪsɛnʃəlɪ ʃɒpkipəz ənd nʌθɪŋ ɛls |·| lʊaɪ
du aɪ traɪ tə sɛl maɪ bʊks' ənd fil rɪgrɛt | nɛvə siŋ ðɛm peɪ
ðɛər ɪkspɛnsɪz | ɪf aɪ əm nɒt ə ʃɒpkipə? |·| əv kəs aɪ æm ||
oʊnlɪ aɪ kip ə bæd ʃɒp || ə ʃɒp ðət dʌznt peɪ |·|

ɪn laɪk mænə | ðə prəfɛst ʃɒpkipə həz dʒɛnərəlɪ ə teɪnt
əv ði atɪst sʌmlʊɛər əbaʊt (h)ɪm | ʃtʊʃ (h)ɪ traɪz tə kənsɪl'
əz mʌtʃ əz ðə prəfɛst atɪst traɪz tə kənsɪl (h)ɪz ʃɒpkipɪŋ |·|

ðə bɪznɪs mæn ənd ði atɪst' ə laɪk mætər ənd maɪnd ||
wi kən nɛvə get iðə pjʊə' ənd wɪðaʊt sʌm əlʊɪ əv ði ʌðə |·|

12

maɪ rændəm pæsɪdʒɪz

ət ðə sentʃərɪ klʌb | ə frend verɪ kaɪndlɪ ənd hezɪteɪtɪŋlɪ
ventʃəd tə sədʒest tə mi | ðət aɪ ʃəd get sʌm wʌn tə goʊ
oʊvə maɪ mænjuskrɪpt bɪfʋə prɪntɪŋ |·| ə dʒudɪʃəs edɪtə | hi
sed | wʋd əv prɪventɪd mi frəm prɪntɪŋ mʌnɪ ə hʋɪtʃ | ɪt siːmd
tə hɪm | wə rɪtn tu reklɪslɪ ənd əfhændɪ |·| ðə fækt ɪz | ðət
ðə mʋə reklɪs ənd rændəm ə pæsɪdʒ əpɪəz tə bi | ðə mʋə
keəfəlɪ ɪt (h)əz bɪn səbmɪtɪd tə frendz¹ ənd kənsɪdəd ənd
rɪkənsɪdəd |·| wɪðaʋt ðə səpət əv frendz aɪ ʃʋd nevər əv
deəd tə prɪnt wʌn haf əv hʋɒt aɪv prɪntɪd |·|

aɪ əm nʋt wʌn əv ðoʋz hu kən rɪpit ðə dʒenərəl kənfeʃn
ʌnrɪzəvɪdlɪ || aɪ ʃʋd seɪ raðə ||

aɪ (h)əv left ʌnsed ðət aɪ əm sʋrɪ ðət aɪ dɪd nʋt seɪ |
bʌt aɪ (h)əv sed verɪ lɪtl ðət aɪ əm sʋrɪ fə hævɪŋ sed || ənd
ɪa ɪə əm prɪtɪ wel ʋn ðə hoʋl | θæŋk ju |·|

13

ɪf ə tɪtʃə(r) ɪz mʋər ɪntərəstɪd ɪn kənvə(r)ʃən | ðən ɪn
ɪnkwaɪərɪ || mʋər ɪntərəstɪd ɪn truθ | ðən ɪn ðə prʋses əv
faɪndɪŋ truθ | hi ɪz feɪlɪŋ ɪn hɪz wə(r)k |·| hi ɪz wə(r)kɪŋ
tʋ ɪmprɪzən ðə maɪnd ɪnsted əv tə lɪbəreɪt ɪt || tə fə(r)nɪʃ
ɪt wɪð (h)ɪz predʒudɪsɪz | ɪnsted əv treɪnɪŋ ɪt tə rɪzɪst
predʒudɪsɪz |·|

14

laɪbrərɪ ə(r) dʒɪm

stændɪŋ ʋn ðə kæmpəs |

bælənst ʋn ðə brɪm |

ʋn ðə raɪt ðə laɪbrərɪ |

ʋn ðə left ðə dʒɪm ||

fɪsɪkl ə(r) mentl |

betə(r) breɪn ə(r) lɪmb? |

pə(r)spəreɪʃn? | kʋnsəntreɪʃn? |

laɪbrərɪ ə(r) dʒɪm? |·|

wel | aɪl hæv tə tʃuz wʌn |
tʃant mɪ | kwaɪə(r) | ə hɪm |
doʊnt bɪ sɪlɪ | laɪbrərɪ |
aɪm goʊɪŋ tə ðə dʒɪm |·|

15

ə pʊə(r) lesgɪən [9] wʌns oʊnd ə dɒŋkɪ hʊɪtʃ fə(r) sʌm riːzn
gru sɪk ənd daɪd. hwerəpɒn ðɪ oʊnə(r) bɪkeɪm verɪ melənkəlɪ
ənd ɔlmoʊst wept fə(r) grif.

"doʊnt fil bæd," sed wʌn əv (h)ɪz neɪbə(r)z knsoʊlɪŋlɪ,
"gɒd wɪl gɪv ju ənʌðə(r) dɒŋkɪ."

"noʊ, brʌðə(r)" rɪplaɪd ðə lesgɪən wɪð ə sɒb, "aɪ noʊ
gɒd betə(r) ðən ju du—hi woʊnt gɪv mi ə dɒŋkɪ fə(r) les
ðən twelv rublz."

C. Rapid Colloquial Style

1

ə lesgɪən maʊntənɪə(r) wʌns went tʊ ə neɪbə(r)—ən
oʊld greɪhedɪd mæn—ənd askt tə bɒroʊ hɪz dɒŋkɪ. "maɪ
dɒŋkɪ ɪznt ət hoʊm," rɪplaɪd ðɪ oʊld mæn. dʒʌst ət ðæt
mɪnɪt, haʊevə(r), ə prəlɒŋd breɪ wəz ʌnfɔ(r)tʃʊnətlɪ hə(r)d
frəm ðɪ ədʒeɪsənt steɪbl.

"ðɛə(r)" sed ðə maʊntənɪə(r), "aɪ θɒt jʊ sed jə(r) dɒŋkɪ
wɒznt ət hoʊm—ðæts hɪm naʊ."

"oʊ, hʊt ə ful jʊ a(r)" rɪplaɪd ðɪ oʊld mæn, "jul bɪliv ə
dʒækæs, bət ju woʊnt bɪliv mi, ɔlðoʊ aɪv gɒt ə greɪ bɪə(r)d."

2

teɪkɪŋ ðə beɪbɪz pɪktʃə

ti wəz oʊvə(r), ə klɪərɪŋ wəz meɪd əv ðɪ a(r)tɪklz əv
mɒə(r) frædʒɪl və(r)tʃu, ənd tɪməθɪ, ɛnterɪŋ ɪn steɪt, wəz
ɒfloʊdɪd frəm (h)ɪz nə(r)sɪz a(r)mz ɪntʊ (h)ɪz mʌðə(r)z.

[9] membər əv ə prɪmɪtɪv traɪb ɪn nɔ(r)ðə(r)n saɪbɪərɪə.

"ɪznt (h)ɪ lʊkɪŋ swit tədeɪ?" sɛd sʊzæn. "ɪts rɪəlɪ taɪm
wɪ hæd (h)ɪm fʊʊtəgraft."

" hʊaɪ? " aɪ askt.

" wɛl, hʊaɪ du pipl əz ə rul gɛt fʊʊtəgraft? "

" ðæt," aɪ sɛd, "ɪz ə kwɛstʃən aɪv ɒfn askt maɪsɛlf, bət
wɪðaʊt faɪndɪŋ ə sætɪsfæktərɪ ansə(r). hʊɒt də jʊ prəpoʊz
tə du wɪð ðə kɒpɪz? "

3

aɪm soʊ ɪksaɪtɪd | sɛd mɪsɪz hædək | əz ðə taɪm fə(r)
dɪpa(r)tʃə(r) dru nɪə(r) |·| aɪv nɛvə(r) bɪn ɒn ə bʊʊt
bɪfoə(r) |·|

jul bi vɛrɪ sɪsɪk | səd ant flɒrə |·| ðə kwɛtʃɪz wə(r)ˌ
nɛvə(r) gʊd seɪlə(r)z | ɪksɛpt jə(r) haf brʌðə(r) ɛdmənd | hʊ
wəz draʊnd ət ðæt pɪknɪk | θɜ(r)tin jɪə(r)z əgoʊ nɛkst
dʒulaɪ foə(r)θ |·|

draʊnd pipl kn bɪ reɪzd tə ðə sɜ(r)fɪs | baɪ faɪərɪŋ gʌnz
oʊvər ə rɪvə(r) | səd lɪtl mɪldrɪd |·|

pipl hʊ ə(r) draʊnd ət si | səd ant flɒrə | ə(r) nɛvə(r)
rɪkʌvə(r)d |·|

aɪ ʃəd θɪŋk | səd lɪtl mɪldrɪd | ðət ɪf jʊ faɪə(r)d ə bɪg mʌf
gʌn oʊvə(r) ðɪ ətlæntɪk oʊʃən | jʊ kəd brɪŋ ə lɒt əv ɪntərɪstɪŋ
θɪŋz tə ðə sɜ(r)fɪs |·|

4

" ju ʃəd lə(r)n nɒt tə meɪk pə(r)sənəl rɪma(r)ks," ælɪs
sɛd wɪð sʌm səvɛrɪtɪ: " ɪts vɛrɪ rud."

ðə hætər oʊpənd (h)ɪz aɪz vɛrɪ waɪd ɒn hɪərɪŋ ðɪs; bət
əl hɪ sɛd wəz, " hʊaɪ ɪz ə reɪvn laɪk ə raɪtɪŋ dɛsk? "

kʌm, wɪ ʃəl hæv səm fʌn naʊ! θɒt ælɪs. aɪm glæd ðeɪv
bɪgʌn askɪŋ rɪdlz—" aɪ bɪliv aɪ kn gɛs ðæt," ʃɪ ædɪd əlaʊd.

" du jʊ min ðət jʊ θɪŋk jʊ kn faɪnd aʊt ðɪ ansə(r) tʊ ɪt?"
sɛd ðə ma(r)tʃ heə(r).

" ɪgzæktɪlɪ soʊ," sɛd ælɪs.

" ðɛn jʊ ʃəd seɪ hʊət jʊ min."

" aɪ du. ət lïst aɪ min ʰʊət aɪ seɪ—ðæts ðə seɪm, jʊ noʊ."

" nɒt ðə seɪm θɪŋ ə bɪt," sɛd ðə hætə. " ʰʊaɪ jʊ maɪt
dʒʌst əz wɛl seɪ ðət aɪ si ʰʊət aɪ it ɪs ðə seɪm θɪŋ əz aɪ it ʰʊət
aɪ si! "

5

" aɪ min, ʰʊɒt ɪz ən ʌnbɜ(r)θdeɪ prɛzənt? "

" ə prɛzənt gɪvn ʰʊɛn ɪt ɪsnt jʊə(r) bɜ(r)θdeɪ, əv kɔ(r)s."
ælɪs kənsɪdəd ə lɪtl. " aɪ laɪk bɜ(r)θdeɪ prɛzənts bɛst,"
ʃɪ sɛd ət last.

" ju doʊnt noʊ ʰʊət jʊə(r) tɔkɪŋ əbaʊt," kraɪd hʌmptɪ
dʌmptɪ. " haʊ mɛnɪ deɪz ɑ(r) ðɛə(r) ɪn ə jɪə(r)? "

"θri hʌndrɪd ənd sɪkstɪ faɪv," sɛd ælɪs.

" ənd haʊ mɛnɪ bɜ(r)θdeɪz hæv jʊ? "

" wʌn. "

" ənd ɪf jʊ teɪk wʌn frəm θri hʌndrɪd ənd sɪkstɪ faɪv,
ʰʊɒt rɪmeɪnz? "

" θri hʌndrɪd ənd sɪkstɪ fʊə(r), əv kʊə(r)s."

hʌmptɪ dʌmptɪ sɛd geɪlɪ, " ðæt ʃoʊz ðət ðɛə(r) ə(r) θri
hʌndrɪd ənd sɪkstɪ fʊə(r) deɪz ʰʊɛn jʊ maɪt gɛt ʌnbɜ(r)θdeɪ
prɛzənts! "

D. Careless Colloquial Style

1

sæ̃ʊθ θri foʊər θri |·| seɪ | əpəreɪtər | wʌ? ðə dɪkənz z
ðə trʌbəl? |·| kæ̃ntʃə gɛʔ mɪ sæ̃ʊθ θri foʊər θri? |·| waɪ
sɜ̃rʔnli ðeɪl æ̃nsər |·| oʊ hɛlo | θri foʊər θri? |·| wɒntə
spik mɪst rɪzlɪŋ || mɪst bæ̃bɪt təkɪn |·| jɛ̃ʌ || lo | pəəl? |·|
sdʒɔrdʒ spikɪn? |·|
jɛ̃ʌ |·|
hæ̃ʊz ol saks? |·|
fɛər t mɪdlɪn |·| hæ̃ʊərju? |·|
faɪ̃n, pəlitʌs |·| wɛl ʰʊʌ̃dʒəno? |·|

o | nᴧ̃θən mᴧ̃tʃ |·|

ʰʋeər jə bɪn kɪpɪn jərsɛlf? |·|

o | dʒᴧs stɪkɪn əræ̃ʋn |·| ʰʋᴧ?s ᴧ̃p dʒɔrdʒɪ? |·|

hæ̃ʋ bæ̃ʋ? lɪl lᴧntʃ s nun? |·|

bi ə raɪ? wɪ mi | aɪ gɛs |·| klᴧb? |·|

jɛᴧ̃ || mitʃᴧ ðeəɹ ↓ twɛlv θɜrtɪ |·|

ə raɪ? || twɛlv θɜrtɪ |·| slɔ̃ŋ dʒɔ̃rdʒɪ |·|

2

lɔ̃ flɔ̃rɛ̃nts |·| aɪ fəgᴧ̃ tə æ̃stʃə ə kwɛ̃ʃn | læ̃s taɪ̃m aɪ̃ kəld ᴧp |·|

wᴧ? wᴧz ɪ? ? |·|

ɪt wəz əbæ̃ʋ ə pɜɪmnɪ̃n? || wʋdʒᴧ ədvaɪ̃z mɪ tə ge? wᴧn? |·|

rɪlɪ | mə̃ɪbᴧl | aɪ̃də nɔ̃ʋ wᴧdə seɪ || ɪf ə pɜɪmnɪ̃n? kᴧ̃mz æ̃ʋ? oraɪ̃? | sʋəraɪ? || bᴧt ɪf ɪt dɔ̃ʋn? | nᴧ̃? so gʋd |·|

3

ʰʋᴧ? dʒə seɪ? fə(r) ðə lᴧv əv mɜ(r)sɪ lɛtʃə slɪp? mɜ(r)sɪ ɪndɪd! oʋ jɛs aɪ du nɔ̃ʋ ʰʋᴧt mɜ(r)sɪ minz bət ðæts noʋ risn ʰʋaɪ aɪ ʃt goʋ ʃʋpɪŋ ə bɪt ɜ(r)lɪə(r) ðən aɪ du.

ʰʋᴧts ᴧðər piplz əfeəɹ(r)z tə ju? ɪf jʋ wər ɪn trᴧbl ðə(r) ɪznt ə soʋl əd kəm nɪə(r) jə. jɛs, aɪʃt ɪndʒɔɪ ðæt, dʒᴧs tə ʃoʋ jə ðət aɪm əlwɪz raɪt.

aɪm ʃʋər aɪ dənoʋ hʋd bi ə wʋmən. ə waɪf məs steɪ ət hoʋm ən drᴧdʒ ʰʋaɪl ə mæn kn goʋ ɛnɪʰʋeə(r). jʋd nɛvər əv gɒt mi tə mæɹɪ jə ɪf aɪd noʋn wᴧ ə dɪspəsɪʃn jə hæd, ən wᴧd ə laɪf aɪd lɪd.

4

ðɪ ævərɪdʒ mæn

næ̃ʋ ðət ðɪ ævərɪdʒ mæn hæz bɪn fæ̃ʋnd wi bɪlɪv ðət æʋər rɪdərz ʃəd bɪ toʋld dʒᴧs? ʰʋᴧ? kaɪn əv ə feloʋ hi ɪz.

hi ɪz fɒnd əv æθəletɪk spoəṛts.

hɪ gɛts ət lɪst wʌn bʊk ə wik frəm ðə pʌblɪk ḷaɪbɛ̣rɪ.

hɪ lʌvz kɔfi ðæt hæz bɪn meɪd ɪn ə pərkjʊleɪtər.

ɪn sʌmər hɪ hæz ə smɔl gɑ̣rdʌ̣n ɪn wɪtʃ hɪ reɪzɪz ṛ̣ediʃɪz,
kɔ̣lʌflæʊər ənd sʌtʃ vɛdʒətʌblz.

ɪn wɪntər hɪ sʌmtaɪmz sʌfərz frəm brʌnɪkɔ̣ḷ ətæks.

hɪ goʊz tə si əl ðə gʊd fɪləmz.

hɪ noʊz ðæt ði ịḷɛktọ̣rịəḷ kɔ̣lədʒ dɪsaɪdz hu hæz bɪn ịḷɛktəd
prɛzʌdʌ̣nt.

hɪz waɪf waʃɪz ənd aɪə̣rnz hɪz ʃɜrts, bət hɪ hæz (h)ɪz
kɔ̣lə̣rs lɔ̣ndə̣rd.

ju hæv mɛt hɪm, əv kɔə̣rs.

TRANSCRIPTIONS OF THE SPEECH OF SOUTHERN ENGLAND

Notice the difference between this English standard and
American speech.

1

ði ˈʌðə ˈdeɪ aɪ hæd ˈlʌtʃ wɪð ə ˈverɪ ˈtʃɑːmɪŋ ˈæktrɪs ɪn ə
ˈplɛznt ˈrɛstrɔ̃.

ʺ ˈraɪðər ə ˈfʌnɪ ˈθɪ̣ŋ ˈhæpṇd ðə ˈlɑ̣ɪst ˈtaɪm aɪ wəz hɪə,ʺ
ʃɪ rɪˈmɑkt.

ʺ ˈjɛs?ʺ aɪ rɪˈplaɪd ˈlæŋgwɪdlɪ.

ʺ əˈbaʊt ˈju:ʺ

ʺ ˈoʊ!ʺ aɪ ˈsɛd wɪð ænɪˈmeɪʃn̩. ʺ ˈduː ˈtɛl mi.ʺ

ʺ ɪt wəz ˈɔlsoʊ ət ˈlʌtʃ,ʺ ʃɪ ɪksˈpleɪmd. ʺ ðə ˈpipl ət
ðəˈnɛkst ˈteɪbl wə ˈtɔkɪŋ əˈbaʊt ju. aɪ ˈkʊdnt ˈhɛlp ˈhɪərɪŋ
ə lɪtl. ə ˈmæn ˈðcə ˈsɛd hid ˈmɛt ju ɪn ˈʃæŋˈhaɪ.ʺ

ʺ ˈnɒt ˈrɪəlɪ!ʺ aɪ ɪksˈkleɪmd.

ʺ ˈjɛs. hi ˈmɛt ju ɪn ˈʃæŋˈhaɪ.ʺ

ʺ ˈðæts ˈfraɪtfʊlɪ ˈɪntrəstɪŋ,ʺ aɪ ˈsɛd. ʺ ˈwɒt dɪd hɪ ˈseɪ
əbaʊt mi?ʺ

ʺ ðæts ˈwɒt aɪ ˈkʊdnt ˈhɪə,ʺ ʃɪ rɪplaɪd. ʺ ju si, aɪ hæd
tə ˈpeɪ ˈsʌm əˈtɛnʃn tʊ maɪ ˈoʊn ˈkraʊd. aɪ ˈoʊnlɪ ˈkɔɪt ðə
ˈwɜɪd ˈdɪˈlaɪtfʊl.ʺ

'evə 'sıns ʃi 'toʊld mi 'ðıs, aıv bin 'tənıŋ ıt 'oʊvər ın
maı 'maınd; ænd ıt ız pə'tıkjʊləlı 'veksıŋ 'nɒt tə noʊ 'mə.
" dı'laıtfʊl " kən bi 'sʌtʃ 'dʒɑıgən ənd 'miːn nʌθıŋ, ɔr ət 'enı
reıt, 'nʌθıŋ 'məː ðən eımjə'bılıtı, 'ivın wen 'miːtıŋ 'streındʒəz.
ɒn ði 'ʌðə hænd, ıt 'maıt bi, frəm 'ðıs 'mæn, ðə 'haıəst 'preız.

ðə 'hoʊl 'θıŋ 'nætʃrəlı 'liːdz tə 'θıɪt. bıkɒz aıv 'nevə
biːn 'fɑıðər 'iːst ðən 'æθənz ın maı 'laıf. wɒt dıd ðə mæn
'miːn? kən wi 'pɒsıblı 'vızıt 'ʌðə 'sıtız ın aʊə 'slip? hæz
'ıtʃ əv əs ən 'æltər 'ego hu kən 'rıəlı bı'heıv, 'els'weə?

weðə wi 'hæv ɔ 'nɒt, aı 'noʊ ðət 'ðıs ınfə'meıʃn ə'baʊt
maı 'ʃæŋ'haı 'dʌbl ız goıŋ tə bi ə 'greıt 'njusns tə mi. ıts
goıŋ tə 'tʃeındʒ maı 'kærəktə. ın 'fækt, ıt hæz ɔ'l'redı bı-
'gʌn tə tʃeındʒ ıt. 'let mi 'giv ju ən ıg'zɑımpl.

'oʊnlı 'jestədeı aı wəz ə'baʊt tə bi 'verı 'æŋgrı wıð ə
'telıgraf bɔı hu 'brɔ·t 'bæk ə 'telıgræm aı həd dıs'pætʃt
əbaʊt 'tuː 'aʊəz, 'ɜːlıə, bıkɒz ıt wəz 'ınsə'frıʃəntlı ə'drest.

'ɒbvıəslı ıt wəz 'nɒt ðə 'bɔız fɔılt, fə hi bı'lɒŋd tʊ 'aʊə
'kʌntrı 'poʊstɒfıs, ənd ðə 'telıgræm həd bin 'sent tə 'lʌndən
ənd wəz rı'tɜːnd frəm 'ðeə; ənd jet aı 'stɑ·tıd tʊ ə'bjuːz
'ðæt 'bɔı əz ðoʊ hi wə 'nɒt 'oʊnlı ðə 'poʊstmaıstə 'dʒenrəl
hım'self, bət ði ın'ventər əv 'red 'teıp ıntʊ ðə 'bɑıgən. ənd
'ɔıl fər ə 'piːs əv 'keəlısnıs əv maı 'oʊn.

ənd ðen 'sʌdnlı aı rı'membəd 'ʃæŋ'haı, ənd 'haʊ dı'laıtfʊl
aı 'wɒz 'ðeə. ənd aı 'ʃʌt 'ʌp 'ınstəntlı, ənd ə'pɒlədʒaızd,
ənd 'ri'roʊt ðə 'mesıdʒ, ən 'geıv ðə 'bɔı ə 'ʃılıŋ fə hım'self.
ıf wʌn kʊd bi dı'laıtful ın 'ʃæŋ'haı, wʌn məst bi dı'laıtful
ət 'hoʊm 'tuː.

From *Maître Phonétique; transcribed by* A. Lloyd James

2

" 'ju hævnt biːn tə roʊm, 'hæv ju? " aı ınkwaıəd.
" 'rɑıðə," hi rıplaıd· 'briːflı: " aı 'lıv ðeə."
'ðıs wəz 'tu 'mʌtʃ, ənd maı 'dʒɔı 'drɒpt əz aı 'strʌgld tə
'grɑ·sp ðə 'fækt ðət aı wəz 'sıtıŋ 'ðeə 'tɔːkıŋ tʊ ə 'feloʊ hu
'lıvd ın 'roʊm. ət 'lɑ·st aı 'mænıdʒd tə 'get 'aʊt, " bət ju

'doʊnt 'rɪəlɪ lɪv ðɛə, 'duː ju?" 'nɛvə 'daʊtɪŋ ðə fækt, bət 'wɒntɪŋ tə 'hɪər ɪt rɪ'piˈtɪd.

" 'wɛl," hi sɛd 'gʊd-'neɪtʃədlɪ, "aɪ 'lɪv 'ðɛər əz 'mʌtʃ əz aɪ lɪv 'ɛnɪwɛə; əbaʊt 'hɑːf ðə 'jɜː sʌm'taɪmz. aɪ vɪ gɒt ə sɔˈt əv 'ʃæntɪ ðɛə. ju mʌst kʌm ənd 'siː ɪt 'sʌm deɪ."

" bət 'duː ju lɪv ɛnɪwɛər 'ɛls əz 'wɛl?" aɪ wɛnt ɒn.

" oʊ 'jɛs—'ɔːl oʊvə ðə 'pleɪs," wəz hɪz 'veɪg rɪ'plaɪ. "ənd aɪ gɒt ə 'dɪgɪŋz 'sʌmwɛər ɒf 'pɪkə'dɪlɪ.

" wɛəz 'ðæt?" aɪ ɪnkwaɪəd.

" wɛəz 'wɒt?" sɛd hi. " 'oʊ, 'pɪkə'dɪlɪ! ɪts ɪn 'lʌndən."

" 'hæv ju ə 'laɪdʒ 'gɑɪdn?" aɪ ɑskt; "ənd 'haʊ mɛnɪ 'pɪgz hæv ju gɒt?"

" aɪv 'noʊ 'gɑɪdn ət 'ɔɪl," hi rɪ'plaɪd 'sædlɪ, "ənd ðeɪ doʊnt ə'laʊ mi tə 'kip 'pɪgz, ðoʊ aɪd 'laɪk tʊ, 'ɔɪflɪ. ɪts vɛrɪ 'hɑɪd."

From *Maître Phonétique; transcribed by* L. E. ARMSTRONG

MATERIAL FOR TRANSCRIPTION AND EAR TRAINING

1. Write the following selections in phonetic script. Before transcribing a sentence, read it aloud several times at your normal rate, then read it phrase by phrase *at this same rate and with the same assimilations and weak forms* and write it as you say it thus naturally. *Remember to write what you say* and not what you think from the spelling that you should say. Do not use capitals. Indicate phrasing. Study the formation of the symbols in the phonetic script on pages 83, 345–47, and 348–50.

Other material for transcription may be taken from the selections for oral reading in Section IV.

1.   For we are all, like swimmers in the sea,
       Poised on the top of a huge wave of fate,
       Which hangs uncertain to which side to fall.

2. On Fortune's cap we are not the very button.

3. If I were an American, as I am an Englishman, I would never lay down my arms—never—never—never!

4. A man's religion is that which gives him a secret and permanent escape from the eternal present.

5. Everything flows, said the philosopher, and even as he spoke, time had flowed on.

6.   Little Robin Redbreast
           Sat on a rail,
      Niddle-noddle went his head
      Wiggle-waggle went his tail.

7.   America, I do not vaunt my love for you,
      I have what I have.

8. By experience, says Roger Ascham, we find a short way by long wandering.

9. There is one medium in which Nature does her best work. It is fearlessness. Apprehension halts Nature, fear fetters her. We profess to believe this, but our conduct belies our profession. "God is not manifested unto cowards."

10.   Cowards die many times before their death;
      The valiant die but once.

11. But the tongue no man can tame, it is an unruly evil full of deadly poison. My brethren, these things ought not so to be. Who is a wise man and endued with knowledge among you? Let him show out of a good conversation his works with meekness of wisdom.—*Third Chapter of the General Epistle of James.*

12. A seventeenth century writer says: "A woman's voice should be like the music of the spheres—sweet and charming, but not to be heard at a distance."

13. The essence of art is not to bestow upon the universe a new aspect, but upon the beholder a new enthusiasm.

14. "Reading is not acting, and the point cannot be too strongly insisted upon," says Amy Lowell in "The Dial." "In a play the audience is intended to see the march of events with its physical eye. In reading, the audience must see nothing with the eyes that detracts from the mental vision."

15. Your figure is a good one; you have no natural defects in the organs of your speech; your address may be engaging and your manner of speaking graceful, if you will; so that if they are not so neither I nor the world can ascribe it to anything but your want of parts. Words were given us to communicate our ideas by, and there must be something inconceivably absurd in uttering them in such a manner as that either people cannot understand them or will not desire to understand them.—*Lord Chesterfield's Letters to His Son.*

THE FOX

16. A fox looked at his shadow at sunrise and said,
   "I will have a camel for lunch today."
   And all morning he went about looking for camels.
   But at noon he saw his shadow again—and he said,
   "A mouse will do."

17. An ancient philosopher has said that "A man's praise has very musical and charming accents in another's mouth, but it is very flat and untunable in his own."

18. But there is a kind of luxury of laziness in reading which is perhaps the best thing in all the world; it is to be captured only, I think, through the old books, books that you know so well that they step out and meet you.—HUGH WALPOLE.

2. Write the following in phonetic script, being sure that you give the right value to the letter *n* in every case.

singing	phalange	infringing
singeing	languid	inkling
English	clangor	inked
linger	length	syncopation
singer	plunger	incompatible
longer	danger	twinkling
finger	dangling	anxiety
wringer	Lincoln	dingy
springing	sprinkle	dinghy
angular	shingling	tinkling
income	anxious	tingling
nightingale	anguish	fingering
engage	malingering	lunging

Retreating and beating and meeting and sheeting,
Delaying and straying and playing and spraying,
Advancing and prancing and glancing and dancing,
Recoiling, turmoiling and toiling and boiling,
And gleaming and streaming and steaming and beaming,
And rushing and flushing and brushing and gushing,
And flapping and rapping and clapping and slapping,
And curling and whirling and purling and twirling,
And thumping and plumping and bumping and jumping,
And dashing and flashing and splashing and clashing;
And so never ending, but always descending,
Sounds and motions for ever and ever are blending
All at once and all o'er, with a mighty uproar,—
And this way the water comes down at Lodore.

SOUTHEY

3. Write phonetically your customary pronunciation of
the following words. Compare your pronunciation with
any others you may have heard and decide which you prefer.
Try to discover why you prefer one to the others. Remember to allow for a perfectly natural bias in favor of the one to
which your ears are accustomed, and for an equally natural
bias in favor of that used by some person whose speech you
admire. Try as far as possible to cultivate an objective
attitude toward speech.

man   (Do you say [mæn], [man], [mæ̃n], or [mæ̃ən]?)

farm   (Do you say [fɑrm], [fɑərm], [fɑɪm], [farm], [fɑərm],
      [fɑəm], [fam], [fãm], or [fãrm]?)

room   } (Is your pronunciation of *room* the same in
dining room }   both cases?)

ask	glibly	schedule	clapboard
current	village	new	blackguard
school	fitted	Tuesday	thyme
cow	saddest	paths	luxurious
soot	axes	mattress	indict
carry	axis	plover	subtle

hoop	rhythm	garage	subtile
reel	mutton	corps	chestnut
real	heaven	corpse	exactly
behind	athletic	hiccough	mustn't
daisies	helm	warmth	perfectly

Arctic	idea	government
data	effect	probably
culinary	gentleman	Latin
clique	colonel	family
biography	flower	secretary
athlete	flour	hundred
amenable	coffee	world
aeronautics	chocolate	cloud
financier	laurel	because
version	coral	arduous
thither	course	sergeant
solace	root	departure
prithee	mutilation	artistry
recluse	enthusiasm	diaphragmatic
juvenile	adjoining	fortune
lineament	adjourning	question
liniment	dromedary	soldier
grovel	vaudeville	grandeur
grievous	hygiene	whooping cough
patriot	library	forehead
patronize	laboratory	annihilate
salutary	every	which
youths	history	quality
zoology	horseshoe	water
statue	compact	wash
stature	detail	Greenwich
avenue	envelope	pumpkin
exactly	abstract	breeches
cleanly	contract	remembrance
marry	futile	profile
merry	insists	gradual
Mary	texts	structural
vary	ax	kindling
very	acts	height
pass	naturally	kitchen
passable	subject	pantomime

parasol	restless	schedule
passage	kept	mutual
hearth	clawing	diphtheria
drama	across	shelves
directly	garage	anxiety

4. Transcribe phonetically the following words, indicating the syllable you accent:

despicable	precedence	illustrate
indisputable	detail	address
inhospitable	exquisite	vehement
condolence	extant	irreparable
decorative	grimace	prestige
inexplicable	lamentable	deficit
rudimentary	impious	contemplate
confiscatory	mischievous	clematis
extraordinarily	piquant	gladiolus
advertisement	prestige	combatant
chastisement	resources	authoritatively
indissolubly	respite	disingenuous
construe	harass	interpolate
vehement	incomparable	chauffeur
vagary	lyceum	coadjutor
exemplary	nomenclature	alias
exigency	obligatory	necessarily
exponent	placard	abdomen

5. Which of the following pronunciations do you prefer?

1. [græs], [gras], or [grɑs]; [klæs], [klas], or [klɑs]
   [pæθ], [paθ], or [pɑθ]
   [ænt], [ant], or [ɑnt] (*aunt*)
2. [kloʊz] or [kloʊðz]
3. [waʃɪŋtn], [wɔːʃɪŋtn], or [wɒʃɑŋtn]
4. [kwalɪtɪ] or [kwɒlɪtɪ]
5. [pə(r)su] or [pə(r)sju]
6. [nuɪz] or [njuɪz]; [suɪt] or [sjuɪt]; [tuɪzdɪ] or [tjuɪzdɪ]; [duɪk] or [djuɪk]
7. [sɛns] or [sɛnts] (*sense*)
8. [æks] or [ækts] (*acts*)

9. [ænkʃes], [ænʃəs], [æŋkʃəs], or [æŋʃəs]
10. [əsoʊʃɪeɪʃən] or [əsoʊsɪeɪʃən]; [əpriːsɪeɪʃən] or [əpriːʃɪeɪʃən]
11. [vɜɪ(r)tju] or [vɜɪ(r)tʃu]
12. [ɪŋlɪʃ] or [ɪŋglɪʃ]
13. [soʊsɪɒlədʒɪ] or [soʊʃɪɒlədʒɪ]
14. [wɑʃ] or [wɒʃ]; [wɑtə(r)], [wɒtə(r)], or [wɔɪtə(r)]
15. [æktjuəlɪ], [æktʃəlɪ], or [æktʃuəlɪ]
16. [tiːdʒəs] or [tiːdjəs] or [tiːdɪəs]
17. [juːnɪvɜɪ(r)stɪ] or [juːnɪvɜɪ(r)sɪtɪ]
18. [naɪtɪngeɪl] or [naɪtɪŋgeɪl]
19. [bəliːv], [biːliːv] or [bɪliːv]
20. [ædəd], [ædɛd], or [ædɪd]
21. [lɪtərətjʊə(r)], [lɪtərətjə(r)], [lɪtrətjə(r)], [lɪdərədʒʊə(r)], [lɪt(ə)rətʃə(r)], or [lɪt(ə)rətʃʊə(r)]
22. [ɛdjʊˈkeɪʃ(ə)n], [ɛdjəˈkeɪʃn], [ɛdʒʊkeɪʃ(ə)n], [ɛdʒəkeɪʃ(ə)n], [ɛdʒkeɪʃn], [ɛdʒəkeɪʃʌn], [ɛdjuːˈkeɪʃ(ə)n], or [ɛdʒuːˈkeɪʃ(ə)n]
23. [wɪtθ] or [wɪdθ]
24. [fɪf], [fɪθ], or [fɪfθ]
25. [ɪsju], [ɪʃu], or [ɪʃju]
26. [plɛntɪəs], [plɛntʃəs], or [plɛntjəs]
27. [sɪt daʊn], [sɪddaʊn], or [sɪtdaʊn]
28. [tliːn dlʌvz] or [kliːn glʌvz]
29. [dʒʌssoʊ] or [dʒʌst soʊ]
30. [doʊntʃə], [doʊntʃʊ], or [doʊnt jʊ]
31. [dɪdnjʊ], [dɪdntʃʊ], or [dɪdnt jʊ]
32. [mɪs jʌŋ] or [mɪʃjʌŋ]
33. [θriːeɪts], [θriːeɪθs], or [θriːeɪtθs] (three-eighths)
34. [hædʒə], [hædʒn], or [hæd jn]
35. [haʊd jʊ du], [haʊdʒudu], [haʊdədu], [haʊ du ju du], or [haʊddu]
36. [aɪ mʌs goʊ] or [aɪ mʌst goʊ]
37. [wi ɔɪdəgoʊ], [wi ɔɪt tə goʊ], or [wi ɔɪtə goʊ]
38. [aɪ juzd tə goʊ], [aɪ ʒuztə goʊ], or [aɪ justə goʊ]
39. [hæsʃi kʌm], [hæzʃi kʌm], [hæʒikʌm], or [hæz ʃi kʌm]
40. [ðæs əraɪ], [ðæʔs ɔɪraɪʔ], [ðæʔz əraɪʔ], or [ðæts ɔɪlraɪt]

SECTION IV

SELECTIONS FOR PRACTICE IN ORAL READING

(*Relating to Chapters IX, X, and XI*)

For convenience this material has been arranged according to the four methods of approach discussed in Chapter X. Many of the selections could have been placed in some other division quite as appropriately as the one in which they appear. This is a matter of slight importance, however, since an adequate reading of practically all of the passages will require more than the one kind of preparation. Questions and exercises follow in Section V.

A. SELECTIONS ILLUSTRATING MAINLY THE INTELLECTUAL APPROACH

Numbers 1–20 are short selections, chiefly expositional; numbers 21–30 illustrate various types of public address; numbers 31–42 illustrate various theories of speech education.

1

aɪ sɛd ðət ' "lɪtərɛrɪ skʊlə(r)ʃɪp " ɪz ə mɪslidɪŋ freɪz |·| tʊ bi skʊlə(r)lɪ ɪn lɪtərətʃʊə(r) | aɪ ʃəd θɪŋk | wəd bi tʊ noʊ lɪtərətʃʊə(r) θərəlɪ | ənd tʊ noʊ ɪt æz ən ɑ(r)t | —tʊ bi sɛnsɪtɪv tə ðə laɪf ɪt ɛksprɛsɪz | tʊ bi waɪz ɪn ðə saɪkʊlədʒɪ əv ðə raɪtər ənd ðə ridə(r) | tʊ ʌndə(r)stænd ðə kaɪnd əv truθ ' ðət kən bɪ sɛd ɪn wə(r)dz | ənd ðə kaɪnd əv bjutɪ ' læŋgwɪdʒ kən krieɪt |·|

2

ɪt ɪz nɒt miːtə(r)z | bət ə miːtə(r) meɪkɪŋ ɑ(r)gjumənt | ðət meɪks ə poʊɪm || ə θɔɪt soʊ pæʃənɪt ənd əlaɪv | ðət laɪk ðə spɪrɪt əv ə plænt ' ər ən ænɪml | ɪt hæz ən ɑ(r)kɪtɛktʃər əv ɪts oʊn | ənd

ədɔɪ(r)nz neɪtʃə(r) wɪð ə nju biɪŋ |·| ðə θɪcθ ənd ðə fɔɪ(r)m ɪr
ɪːkwəlˡ ɪn ðɪ ɪːcθ(r)dər əv taɪm || bət ɪn ðɪ ɪɔ(r)dər əv dʒenɪsɪs | ðə
θɪcθ ɪz praɪə(r) tə ðə fɔɪ(r)m |·|

3

ju wɪl teɪk keə(r) tʊ ovpɒn jʊə(r) tiːθ ʰ ʍen ju spiːk | tʊ aɪ(r)tɪk-
jʊleɪt ɛvrɪ wɜɪ(r)d dɪstɪŋktlɪ | ənd tə beg əv mɪstə(r) ha(r)t |
mɪstə(r) sleɪə | ə(r) hʊɪʍəv(r) ju spiːk tu | tə rɪmaɪnd ənd stɒp
ju ɪf ɛvə(r) ju fɔɪl ɪntʊ ðə ræpɪd ənd ʌnɪntelɪdʒɪbl mʌtə(r) |·| ju
wɪl iːvn riːd əlaʊd tə jʊə(r)self | ənd tjuːn jʊər ʌtərəns tə jʊər ovn
ɪə(r) || ənd rɪɪd ət fɜɪ(r)st | mʌtʃ mɒə(r) sloʊlɪ ðən ju niːd tə du | ɪn
ɔɪðə(r) tə kərekt jʊə(r)self əv ðæt ʃeɪmfəl trɪk əv spiːkɪŋ fastə(r)
ðən ju ɔɪt |·|

—lə(r)d tʃestə(r)fiːldz letə(r)z tə(h)ɪz sʌn.

4

tɔɪkɪŋ ɪz wʌn əv ðə krɪeɪtɪv a(r)ts | fə(r) baɪ ɪt ju bɪld ʌp θɪŋz
ðət hæv | ʌntɪl tɔɪkt əbaʊt | noʊ ɪgzɪstəns || sʌtʃ əz skændlz |
siːkrɪts | kwɒrəlz | lɪtərɪɪ ənd a(r)tɪstɪk stændə(r)dz | ɔɪl kaɪndz əv
pɒɪnts əv vjuː əbaʊt pɜɪ(r)snz ənd θɪŋz |·|

let ʌs tɔɪk | wɪ seɪ | miːnɪŋ | let ʌs si: hʊʊ wɪ kən krɪeɪt | ər ɪn
hʊʊ weɪ wɪ meɪ trænsmjuɪt ðə fækts ðət aɪ(r) | ɪntə fækts ðət
aɪ(r) nɒt jet || ɪt ɪz wʌn əv ðə mædʒɪk aɪ(r)ts |·| ðə trʌbl əbaʊt
ɪt ɪz ðət | iːvn mɒə(r) ðən ðɪ ʌðə aɪ(r)ts | ɪt ɪz præktɪst baɪ ðə
stjuːpɪd | hu kən krɪeɪt nʌθɪŋ wə(r)θ krɪeɪtɪŋ |·|

5

tʊ bi | ɔ nɒt tʊ bi || ðæt ɪz ðə kwestʃn||
hʊðʒ tɪz noʊblər ɪn ðə maɪnd | tʊ sʌfə
ðə stɪŋz ənd ærʊʊz əv aʊtreɪdʒəs fɔtjun ||
ɔ tʊ teɪk amz əgenst ə si əv trʌblz |
ənd baɪ əpoʊzɪŋ | end ðəm? |·| tʊ daɪ || tʊ slip ʰ
noʊ mɒə || ænd baɪ ə slip | tʊ seɪ wɪ end
ðə hateɪk | ənd ðə θaʊzənd nætʃʊrəl ʃɒks
ðə fleʃ ɪz eə tu || tɪz ə kɒnsʊmeɪʃən¹
dɪvaʊtlɪ tʊ bɪ wɪʃt |·| tʊ daɪ || tʊ slip |·|
tʊ slip || pətʃəns tʊ drim || aɪ | ðeəz ðə rʌb ||
fɔr ɪn ðæt slip əv deθ | hʊʊt drimz meɪ kʌm |
hʊen wi hæv ʃʌfld ɒf ðɪs mɒtl kɒɪl |
mʌst gɪv ʌs pɒz |·|

6

Cromwell, I did not think to shed a tear
In all my miseries; but thou hast forc'd me,
Out of thy honest truth, to play the woman.
Let's dry our eyes: and thus far hear me, Cromwell;
And, when I am forgotten, as I shall be,
And sleep in dull cold marble, where no mention
Of me more must be heard of, say, I taught thee;
Say, Wolsey, that once trod the ways of glory,
And sounded all the depths and shoals of honour,
Found thee a way, out of his wreck, to rise in;
A sure and safe one, though thy master miss'd it.

SHAKESPEARE, *Henry VIII*

7

The regret we have for our childhood is not wholly justifiable; so much a man may lay down without fear of public ribaldry; for although we shake our heads over the change, we are not unconscious of the manifold advantages of our new state. What we lose in generous impulse, we more than gain in the habit of generously watching others; and the capacity to enjoy Shakespeare may balance a lost aptitude for playing at soldiers. Terror is gone out of our lives, moreover; we no longer see the Devil in the bed-curtains nor lie awake to listen to the wind. We go to school no more; and if we have only exchanged one drudgery for another (which is by no means sure), we are set free forever from the daily fear of chastisement. And yet a great change has overtaken us; and although we do not enjoy ourselves less, at least we take our pleasures differently. We need pickles nowadays to make Wednesday's cold mutton please our Friday's appetite; and I can remember the time when to call it red venison, and tell myself a hunter's story, would have made it more palatable than the best of sauces. To the grown person, cold mutton is cold mutton all the world over; not all the mythology invented by man will make it better or worse to him; the broad fact, the clamant reality, of the mutton carries away before it such seductive figments. But for the child it is still possible to weave an enchantment over eatables; and if he has but read of a dish in a story book, it will be heavenly manna to him for a week.

ROBERT LOUIS STEVENSON, "Child's Play"

8

The place was worthy of such a trial. It was the great hall of William Rufus, the hall which had resounded with acclamations at the inauguration of thirty kings, the hall which had witnessed the just sentence of Bacon and the just absolution of Somers, the hall where the eloquence of Strafford had for a moment awed and melted a victorious party inflamed with just resentment, the hall where Charles had confronted the High Court of Justice with the placid courage which has half redeemed his fame. Neither military nor civil pomp was wanting. The avenues were lined with grenadiers. The streets were kept clear by cavalry. The peers, robed in gold and ermine, were marshalled by the heralds under Garter King-at-arms. The judges in their vestments of state attended to give advice on points of law. Near a hundred and seventy lords, three fourths of the Upper House as the Upper House then was, walked in solemn order from their usual place of assembling to the tribunal. The gray old walls were hung with scarlet. The long galleries were crowded by an audience such as has rarely excited the fears or the emulations of an orator. There were gathered together, from all parts of a great, free, enlightened, and prosperous empire, grace and female loveliness, wit and learning, the representatives of every science and of every art. There the Ambassadors of Great Kings and Commonwealths gazed with admiration on a spectacle which no other country in the world could present.

MACAULAY, *Essay on Warren Hastings*

9

A foolish consistency is the hobgoblin of little minds, adored by little statesmen and philosophers and divines. With consistency a great soul has simply nothing to do. He may as well concern himself with his shadow on the wall. Speak what you think now in hard words and to-morrow speak what to-morrow thinks in hard words again, though it contradict everything you said to-day—'Ah, so you shall be sure to be misunderstood.'—Is it so bad, then, to be misunderstood? Pythagoras was misunderstood, and Socrates, and Jesus, and Luther, and Copernicus, and Galileo, and Newton, and every pure and wise spirit that ever took flesh. To be great is to be misunderstood . . .

EMERSON, "Self-Reliance"

10

To a homeless man, who has no spot on this wide world which he can truly call his own, there is a momentary feeling of something like independence and territorial consequence when, after a weary day's travel, he kicks off his boots, thrusts his feet into his slippers, and stretches himself before an inn fire. Let the world go as it may; let kingdoms rise or fall; so long as he has the wherewithal to pay his bill, he is, for the time being, the very monarch of all he surveys. The armchair is his throne, the poker his scepter, and the little parlor, of some twelve feet square, his undisputed empire. It is a morsel of certainty snatched from the midst of the uncertainties of life; it is a sunny moment gleaming out of a cloudy day. Shall I not take mine ease in mine inn? thought I, as I gave the fire a stir, lolled back in my elbowchair, and cast a complacent look about the little parlor of the Red Horse at Stratford-on-Avon.

IRVING, *Sketch Book*

11

The Moslem quarter of a city is lonely and desolate; you go up and down, and on, over shelving and hillocky paths, through narrow lanes walled in by blank, windowless dwellings; you come out upon an open space strewn with the black ruins that some late fire has left; you pass by a mountain of castaway things, the rubbish of centuries, and on it you see numbers of big, wolf-like dogs torpid under the sun, with limbs outstretched to the full, as if they were dead; storks, or cranes, sitting fearless upon the low roofs, look gravely down upon you; the still air that you breathe is loaded with the scent of citron and pomegranate rinds scorched by the sun, or (as you approach the Bazaar) with the dry, dead perfume of strange spices. You long for some signs of life, and tread the ground more heavily, as though you would wake the sleepers with the heel of your boot; but the foot falls noiseless upon the crumbling soil of an Eastern city, and Silence follows you still. Again and again you meet turbans, and faces of men, but they have nothing for you—no welcome—no wonder—no wrath— no scorn—they look upon you as we do upon a December's fall of snow—as a "seasonable," unaccountable, uncomfortable work of God that may have been sent for some good purpose—to be revealed hereafter.

A. W. KINGLAKE. *Eöthen*

12

"A clear fire, a clean hearth, and the rigour of the game." This was the celebrated "wish" of old Sarah Battle (now with God) who, next to her devotions, loved a good game at whist. She was none of your lukewarm gamesters, your half and half players, who have no objection to take a hand, if you want one to make up a rubber; who affirm that they have no pleasure in winning; that they like to win one game and lose another; that they can while away an hour very agreeably at a card-table, but are indifferent whether they play or no; and will desire an adversary, who has slipt a wrong card, to take it up and play another. These insufferable triflers are the curse of a table. One of these flies will spoil a whole pot. Of such it may be said, that they do not play at cards, but only play at playing at them.

CHARLES LAMB, "Mrs. Battle's Opinions on Whist"

13

Poetry is the breath and finer spirit of all knowledge, it is the impassioned expression which is in the countenance of all Science. . . .

In spite of difference of soil and climate, of language and manners, of laws and customs—in spite of things silently gone out of mind, and things violently destroyed, the Poet binds together by passion and knowledge the vast empire of human society, as it is spread over the whole earth and over all time. . . . Poetry is the first and last of all knowledge—it is as immortal as the heart of man.

WORDSWORTH, Preface to *Lyrical Ballads*

14

The Iliad is from two to three thousand years older than *Macbeth*, and yet it is as fresh as if it had been written yesterday. We have there no lessons save in the emotions which rise in us as we read. Homer had no philosophy; he never struggles to impress on us his views about this or that; you can scarcely tell indeed whether his sympathies are Greek or Trojan; but he represents to us faithfully the men and women among whom he lived. He sang the Tale of Troy, he touched his lyre, he drained the golden beaker in the halls of men like those on whom he was conferring immortality. And thus, although no Agamemnon, king of men, ever led a Grecian fleet to Ilium; though no Priam sought the midnight tent of Achilles; though Ulysses and Diomed and Nestor were but names, and Helen but a dream, yet through Homer's power of representing men and women those old Greeks will still stand out from amidst the darkness of the ancient world with a sharpness of outline which belongs to no period of history except the most recent.

FROUDE, *Short Studies on Great Subjects*

15

The awakening of the personality, or, more accurately expressed, the dawning consciousness of dormant personal creative powers and personal prerogatives in the individual, is perhaps the most fundamental and novel feature of the Renaissance. Without such a prerequisite, at any rate, the "age of discoveries" would be unthinkable. The adventurous quest for distant lands was shared by the men of the Middle Ages; the Crusades had aroused it, world-commerce had powerfully fostered it. Had it been only a matter of *wanderlust*, some Columbus might have accidentally discovered America in the twelfth or thirteenth century. But it is one thing to be accidentally cast upon some shore, and another to find what you have sought—and to seek it where you were sure you would find it. The noteworthy feature of Columbus's achievement is precisely that he was not accidentally driven upon a western coast, but that he found the land, unknown but assumed by him to exist, because he had consciously steered for it. Columbus had trusted his strong judgment. And it is the Renaissance in him that enabled him to say to himself: "My own understanding possesses the power to envisage something that my eye cannot yet see. But even though I cannot see it, it exists: I can figure out that it exists, just as certainly as I can calculate an unknown quantity from two that are known." Even this method would have been inconceivable to the medieval mind. For the Middle Ages were unaware of the possibility of determining the actuality of an unknown by the power of reasoning. The discovery of this creative power of the understanding was in itself perhaps the greatest discovery of the new age. On this discovery (and on all that derives from it) our whole philosophy is based; it accounts for Galileo, Copernicus, Kant, and Einstein.

OSCAR HAGEN, *Art Epochs and Their Leaders*

16

When, in disgrace with Fortune and men's eyes,
I all alone beweep my outcast state,
And trouble deaf heaven with my bootless cries,
And look upon myself, and curse my fate,
Wishing me like to one more rich in hope,
Featur'd like him, like him with friends possess'd,
Desiring this man's art, and that man's scope,
With what I most enjoy contented least;
Yet in these thoughts myself almost despising,
Haply I think on thee; and then my state,
Like to the lark at break of day arising
From sullen earth, sings hymns at heaven's gate;
  For thy sweet love rememb'red such wealth brings
  That then I scorn to change my state with kings.

SHAKESPEARE

17

NIGHT

    Swiftly walk over the western wave,
        Spirit of Night!
    Out of the misty eastern cave,—
    Where, all the long and lone daylight,
    Thou wovest dreams of joy and fear
    Which make thee terrible and dear,—
        Swift be thy flight!

    Wrap thy form in a mantle grey,
        Star-inwrought!
    Blind with thine hair the eyes of Day;
    Kiss her until she be wearied out.
    Then wander o'er city and sea and land,
    Touching all with thine opiate wand—
        Come, long-sought!

    When I arose and saw the dawn,
        I sigh'd for thee;
    When light rode high, and the dew was gone,
    And noon lay heavy on flower and tree,

And the weary Day turn'd to her rest,
Lingering like an unloved guest,
        I sigh'd for thee.

Thy brother Death came, and cried,
        'Wouldst thou me?'
Thy sweet child Sleep, the filmy-eyed,
Murmur'd like a noontide bee,
'Shall I nestle near thy side?
Wouldst thou me?'—And I replied,
        'No, not thee!'

Death will come when thou art dead,
        Soon, too soon—
Sleep will come when thou art fled.
Of neither would I ask the boon
I ask of thee, belovèd Night—
Swift be thine approaching flight,
        Come soon, soon!

                                        SHELLEY

18

ULYSSES

It little profits that an idle king,
By this still hearth, among these barren crags,
Matched with an aged wife, I mete and dole
Unequal laws unto a savage race,
That hoard, and sleep, and feed, and know not me.
I cannot rest from travel; I will drink
Life to the lees. All times I have enjoyed
Greatly, have suffered greatly, both with those
That loved me, and alone; on shore, and when
Through scudding drifts the rainy Hyades
Vexed the dim sea. I am become a name;
For always roaming with a hungry heart
Much have I seen and known,—cities of men,
And manners, climates, councils, governments,
Myself not least, but honored of them all,—
And drunk delight of battle with my peers,
Far on the ringing plains of windy Troy.

I am a part of all that I have met;
Yet all experience is an arch wherethrough
Gleams that untravelled world, whose margin fades
Forever and forever when I move.
How dull it is to pause, to make an end,
To rust unburnished, not to shine in use!
As though to breathe were life! Life piled on life
Were all too little, and of one to me
Little remains: but every hour saved
From that eternal silence is something more,
A bringer of new things; and vile it were
For some three suns to store and hoard myself,
And this gray spirit yearning in desire
To follow knowledge like a sinking star,
Beyond the utmost bound of human thought.
        This is my son, mine own Telemachus,
To whom I leave the sceptre and the isle—
Well-loved of me, discerning to fulfil
This labor, by slow prudence to make mild
A rugged people, and through soft degrees
Subdue them to the useful and the good.
Most blameless is he, centred in the sphere
Of common duties, decent not to fail
In offices of tenderness, and pay
Meet adoration to my household gods,
When I am gone. He works his work, I mine.
        There lies the port; the vessel puffs her sail;
There gloom the dark, broad seas. My mariners,
Souls that have toiled, and wrought, and thought with me,—
That ever with a frolic welcome took
The thunder and the sunshine, and opposed
Free hearts, free foreheads,—you and I are old;
Old age hath yet his honor and his toil.
Death closes all; but something ere the end,
Some work of noble note, may yet be done,
Not unbecoming men that strove with Gods.
The lights begin to twinkle from the rocks;
The long day wanes; the slow moon climbs; the deep
Moans round with many voices. Come, my friends,
'Tis not too late to seek a newer world.
Push off; and sitting well in order smite
The sounding furrows; for my purpose holds

To sail beyond the sunset, and the baths
Of all the western stars, until I die.
It may be that the gulfs will wash us down;
It may be we shall touch the Happy Isles,
And see the great Achilles, whom we knew.
Though much is taken, much abides; and though
We are not now that strength which in old days
Moved earth and heaven; that which we are, we are;
One equal temper of heroic hearts,
Made weak by time and fate, but strong in will
To strive, to seek, to find, and not to yield.

TENNYSON

19

What do we know today? We are certain of our common
ancestry with the anthropoid apes. Our brains show the same
form and convolutions, our dentition follows the same formula,
our hands with their power of grasp and the inestimable advantage
of a thumb that can be opposed to the other fingers are the
direct inheritance of a tree-dwelling ancestry. As for the foot,
that most highly evolved, most human character, the elements
are all present in orang-utan, gorilla, and chimpanzee. All can
walk to a limited extent. The orang-utan and chimpanzee walk
on their knuckles, but the gorilla, the most terrestrial and the
possessor of the best heel, walks flat upon his foot. On the physiological side, owing to the difficulty and danger in obtaining living
apes and their rapid death in captivity, we know less. Certain
things, however, are clear, such as the susceptibility of the anthro-
poids to human diseases and the identity of the constituents of
their blood with that of man which no other animals share. . . .

There are two features, however, that set man apart from his
simian cousins, the proportion of the upper to the lower limbs and
the relation of jaw to brain. Among the great apes, legs, comparatively speaking, are poor, short, weak things. . . . The condition of the skull is even more strikingly different from the human
type. The small brain case, lost behind the enormous bars of bone
over the eyes and the central skull crest, and the gigantic, out-
standing jaws with their projecting canine teeth give the impression that has made many a would-be scientist say secretly with
Benjamin Disraeli, "My Lord, I am on the side of the angels."

RUTH OTIS SAWTELL and IDA TREAT,
Primitive Hearths in the Pyrenees

20

After dark vapours have oppress'd our plains
    For a long dreary season, comes a day
    Born of the gentle South, and clears away
From the sick heavens all unseemly stains.
The anxious month, relievèd of its pains,
    Takes as a long-lost right the feel of May,
    The eyelids with the passing coolness play,
Like rose-leaves with the drip of summer rains.
And calmest thoughts come round us—as of leaves
    Budding,—fruit ripening in stillness,—autumn suns
Smiling at eve upon the quiet sheaves,—
    Sweet Sappho's cheek,—a sleeping infant's breath,—
    The gradual sand that through an hour-glass runs,—
A woodland rivulet,—a Poet's death.

KEATS

21

. . . My hold of the Colonies is in the close affection which grows from common names, from kindred blood, from similar privileges, and equal protection. These are ties which, though light as air, are as strong as links of iron. Let the Colonists always keep the idea of their civil rights associated with your Government;— they will cling and grapple to you; and no force under heaven will be of power to tear them from their allegiance . . . As long as you have the wisdom to keep the sovereign authority of this country as the sanctuary of liberty, the sacred temple consecrated to our common faith, wherever the chosen race and sons of England worship freedom, they will turn their faces towards you. The more they multiply, the more friends you will have; the more ardently they love liberty, the more perfect will be their obedience. Slavery they can have anywhere. It is a weed that grows in every soil. They may have it from Spain, they may have it from Prussia. But until you become lost to all feeling of your true interest and your natural dignity, freedom they can have from none but you. This is the commodity of price of which you have the monopoly. . . . It is the spirit of the English Constitution, which, infused through the mighty mass, pervades, feeds, unites, invigorates, vivifies every part of the empire, even down to the minutest member . . .

All this, I know well enough, will sound wild and chimerical to the profane herd of those vulgar and mechanical politicians, who have no place among us; a sort of people who think that nothing exists but what is gross and material; and who therefore, far from being qualified to be directors of the great movement of empire, are not fit to turn a wheel in the machine. But to men truly initiated and rightly taught, these ruling and master principles, which in the opinion of such men as I have mentioned, have no substantial existence, are in truth everything, and all in all. Magnanimity in politics is not seldom the truest wisdom; and a great empire and little minds go ill together. If we are conscious of our station and glow with zeal to fill our places as becomes our situation and ourselves, we ought to elevate our minds to the greatness of that trust to which the order of Providence has called us. By adverting to the dignity of this high calling, our ancestors have turned a savage wilderness into a glorious empire; and have made the most extensive, and the only honourable conquests, not by destroying, but by promoting the wealth, the number, the happiness, of the human race.

EDMUND BURKE, *Speech on Conciliation with America*

22

There is only one cure for the evils which newly acquired freedom produces; and that cure is freedom. When a prisoner first leaves his cell he cannot bear the light of day; he is unable to discriminate colours, or recognise faces. But the remedy is, not to remand him into his dungeon, but to accustom him to the rays of the sun. The blaze of truth and liberty may at first dazzle and bewilder nations which have become half blind in the house of bondage. But let them gaze on, and they will soon be able to bear it. In a few years men learn to reason. The extreme violence of opinion subsides. Hostile theories correct each other. The scattered elements of truth cease to contend, and begin to coalesce. And at length a system of justice and order is educed out of the chaos.

Many politicians of our time are in the habit of laying it down as a self-evident proposition, that no people ought to be free till they are fit to use their freedom. The maxim is worthy of the fool in the old story, who resolved not to go into the water till he had learned to swim. If men are to wait for liberty till they become wise and good in slavery, they may indeed wait forever.

MACAULAY, *Essay on Milton*

23

Now, in this your accepted time, now, in this your day of salvation, take counsel, not of prejudice, not of party spirit, not of the ignominious pride of a fatal consistency, but of history, of reason, of the ages which are past, of the signs of this most portentous time. Pronounce in a manner worthy of the expectations with which this great debate has been anticipated, and of the long remembrance which it will leave behind. Renew the youth of the state. Save property, divided against itself. Save the multitude, endangered by its own unpopular power. Save the greatest, and fairest, and most highly civilized community that ever existed, from calamities which may in a few days sweep away all the rich heritage of so many ages of wisdom and glory.

MACAULAY, *Speech on the Reform Bill*

24

By the "mud-sill" theory it is assumed that labor and education are incompatible, and any practical combination of them impossible. According to that theory, a blind horse upon a treadmill is a perfect illustration of what a laborer should be—all the better for being blind, that he may not kick understandingly. According to that theory, the education of laborers is not only useless but pernicious and dangerous. In fact, it is, in some sort, deemed a misfortune that laborers should have heads at all. Those same heads are regarded as explosive materials, only to be safely kept in damp places, as far as possible from that peculiar sort of fire which ignites them. A Yankee who could invent a strong-handed man without a head would receive the everlasting gratitude of the "mud-sill" advocates.

But free labor says, "No." Every head should be cultivated and improved by whatever will add to its capacity for performing its charge. In one word, free labor insists on universal education.

ABRAHAM LINCOLN, *Address before the Wisconsin Agricultural Society, 1859*

25

In conclusion, I am asked to say in a few words what application my experiment may have to college education in the United States. To college education as such it can hardly have any application. But I do think that its example can be of value all the same. My impression is that America believes much too much in education, institutions, programs, and the like. It believes much too much in measures, not in men. It is a fact that everything great in this world has been accomplished by personalities and not by institutions; by single individuals, and not by collectivities. The whole value of anything alive depends upon the quality of its uniqueness. Indeed, it is the uniqueness-quality which differentiates what is alive from what is not alive. Take the uniqueness-quality away and only superficial and not really vital forces remain. This is the reason why the quality of a crowd is always much lower than that of its individual constituents: a crowd has no self, its so-called soul is only the sum or the resulting force of empirical elements; to acquire intrinsic value, they need be ensouled by a spirit—and "spirit" is always unique and personal. It is therefore inevitable that collective ideals level downward.

COUNT HERMANN KEYSERLING, "The School of Wisdom"

26

But this property, we are told, is not to be questioned on account of its long duration. "Two hundred years of legislation have sanctioned and sanctified negro slaves as property." Nothing but respect for the speaker could repress criticism on this unhappy phraseology. We will trust it escaped him without thought. But to confine ourselves to the argument from duration; how obvious the reply! Is injustice changed into justice by the practice of ages? Is my victim made a righteous prey because I have bowed him to the earth till he cannot rise? For more than two hundred years heretics were burned, and not by mobs, not by lynch law, but by the decrees of the councils, at the instigation of theologians, and with the sanction of the laws and religions of nations; and was this a reason for keeping up the fires, that they had burned two hundred years?

WILLIAM ELLERY CHANNING, *Remarks on the Slavery Question*

27

It follows that the test of the teacher is not whether he believes in one creed or another, but how he believes in it. If he believes in it as an unexamined premise, he is no teacher, though he wears a conservative or a progressive label. If he is more interested in conversion than in inquiry, more interested in his truth than in the process of finding truth, he is failing in his work. He is working to imprison the human mind instead of to liberate it, to furnish it with his prejudices instead of training it to resist prejudices. The teacher is human, of course, and will have his convictions. But if he is a real teacher he will love those pupils best who learn most quickly to stand alone. That for him is the climax, the point of graduation. It is the time when the pupil no longer leans on, or submits to authority. The moment of the teacher's triumph is the moment when the pupil can demonstrate that he has acquired the essentials of the art of thinking for himself. Then the true teacher rejoices. For he wishes his acorns to grow into oaks, not into clinging vines.

The New Republic

28

How to live?—that is the essential question for us. Not how to live in the mere material sense only, but in the widest sense. The general problem which comprehends every special problem is—the right ruling of conduct in all directions under all circumstances. In what way to treat the body; in what way to treat the mind; in what way to manage our affairs; in what way to bring up a family; in what way to behave as a citizen; in what way to utilize those sources of happiness which nature supplies—how to use all our faculties to the greatest advantage of ourselves and others—how to live completely? And this, being the great thing needful for us to learn, is, in consequence, the great thing which education has to teach. To prepare us for complete living is the function which education has to discharge.

HERBERT SPENCER, *Education*

29

Now, the spirit of the scholar in a country like ours must be a spirit related to the national life. It cannot, therefore, be a spirit of pedantry. I suppose that this is a sufficient working conception of pedantry to say that it is knowledge divorced from life. It is knowledge so closeted, so desecrated, so stripped of the significances of life itself, that it is a thing apart and not connected with the vital processes in the world about us.

There is a great place in every nation for the spirit of scholarship, and it seems to me that there never was a time when the spirit of scholarship was more needed in affairs than it is in this country at this time.

We are thinking just now with our emotions and not with our minds; we are moved by impulse and not by judgment. We are drawing away from things with blind antipathy. The spirit of knowledge is that you must base your conclusions on adequate grounds. Make sure that you are going to the real sources of knowledge, discovering what the real facts are, before you move forward to the next process, which is the process of clear thinking. By clear thinking I do not mean logical thinking. I do not mean that life is based upon any logical system whatever. Life is essentially illogical. The world is governed now by a tumultuous sea of commonalities made up of passions, and we should pray God that the good passions should outvote the bad passions. But the movement of impulse, of motive, is the stuff of passion, and therefore clear thinking about life is not logical, symmetrical thinking, but it is interpretative thinking, thinking that sees the secret motive of things, thinking that penetrates deepest places where are the pulses of life.

Now scholarship ought to lay these impulses bare just as the physician can lay bare the seat of life in our bodies. That is not scholarship which goes to work upon the mere formal pedantry of logical reasoning, but that is scholarship which searches for the heart of a man. The spirit of scholarship gives us catholicity of thinking, the readiness to understand that there will constantly swing into our ken new items not dreamed of in our systems of philosophy, not simply to draw our conclusions from the data that we have had, but that all this is under constant mutation, and that therefore new phases of life will come upon us and a new adjustment of our conclusions will be necessary. Our thinking must be detached and disinterested thinking.

The particular objection that I have to the undergraduate forming his course of study on his future profession is this: that from start to finish, from the time he enters the university until he finishes his career, his thought will be centered upon particular interests. He will be immersed in the things that touch his profit and loss, and a man is not free to think inside that territory. If his bread and butter is going to be affected, if he is always thinking in the terms of his own profession, he is not thinking for the nation. He is thinking for himself, and whether he be conscious of it or not, he can never throw these trammels off. He will only think as a doctor, or a lawyer, or a banker. He will not be free in the world of knowledge and in the circle of interests which make up the great citizenship of the country. It is necessary that the spirit of scholarship should be a detached, disinterested spirit, not immersed in a particular interest. That is the function of scholarship in a country like ours, to supply not heat, but light, to suffuse things with the calm radiance of reason, to see to it that men do not act hastily, but that they act considerately, that they obey the truth whether they know it or not. The fault of our age is the fault of hasty action, of premature judgments, of a preference for ill-considered action over no action at all. Men who insist upon standing still and doing a little thinking before they do any acting are called reactionaries. They want actually to reach to a state in which they can be allowed to think. They want for a little while to withdraw from the turmoil of party controversy and see where they stand before they commit themselves and their country to action from which it may not be possible to withdraw.

The whole fault of the modern age is that it applies to everything a false standard of efficiency. Efficiency with us is accomplishment, whether the accomplishment be by just and well-considered means or not; and this standard of achievement it is that is debasing the morals of our age, the intellectual morals of our age. We do not stop to do things thoroughly; we do not stop to know why we do things. We see an error and we hastily correct it by a greater error; and then go on to cry that the age is corrupt.

And so it is, gentlemen, that I try to join the function of the university with the great function of the national life. The life of this country is going to be revolutionized and purified only when the universities of this country wake up to the fact that their only reason for existing is intellect, that the objects that I have set forth, so far as undergraduate life is concerned, are the only legitimate objects. And every man should crave for his university primacy in these things, primacy in other things also if they may be brought in without enmity to it, but the sacrifice of everything that stands in the way of that.

For my part, I do not believe that it is athleticism which stands in the way. Athletics have been associated with the achievements of the mind in many a successful civilization. There is no difficulty in uniting vigor of body with achievement of mind, but there is a good deal of difficulty in uniting the achievement of the mind with a thousand distracting social influences, which take up all our ambitions, which absorb all our thoughts, which lead to all our arrangements of life, and then leave the university authorities the residuum of our attention, after we are through with the things that we are interested in. We absolutely changed the whole course of study at Princeton and revolutionized the methods of instruction without rousing a ripple on the surface of the alumni. They said those things are intellectual, they were our business. But just as soon as we thought to touch the social part of the university, there was not only a ripple, but the whole body was torn to its depths. We had touched the real things. These lay in triumphal competition with the province of the mind, and men's attention was so absolutely absorbed in these things that it was impossible for us to get their interest enlisted on the real undertakings of the university itself.

Now that is true of every university that I know anything about in this country, and if the faculties in this country want to recapture the ground that they have lost, they must begin pretty soon, and they must go into the battle with their bridges burned behind them so that it will be of no avail to retreat. If I had a voice to which the university men of this country might listen, that is the endeavor to which my ambition would lead me to call.

WOODROW WILSON, "The Training of the Intellect"

30

But now I shall be asked: Would you substitute these activities for the studies—give up the classroom for the lounging room and the union? Of course not. The very excellence of these activities is that fundamentally they are the fruits of the classroom. But the point is that by these fruits the work of the classroom shall be known. We need not forget that these activities are only accidental and that the real values lie in the studies and the teaching. But none the less it is true that these activities reveal to us, far better than any examinations can do, the success or failure of the classroom itself. They are, as it were, mirrors in which we can see ourselves and our work. If we want to know the effects of what we are doing in the classroom, let us look to see what the students are doing outside of it, when they are free to follow their own desires. If they do not, on their own initiative, carry on activities springing out of their studies, then you may count on it that, however well the tests are met, the studies are of little value. Show me a college in which literature is taught, but in which the boys do not band together to read and write and criticize, in which they do not yearn to be themselves "literary." However well literature may be taught in that college, it is not well learned. What would you say of the teaching of philosophy which did not send boys off into quarreling, puzzling groups, determined each to give to his fellows the solutions of the problems that have baffled human thinking? What will you say of the teaching of history, economics, or social science which ends in the passive appropriation of a book? Surely if it is vital, you will find the young men stimulated by it eagerly reforming and reshaping in idea the society about them, and perhaps going out to do some work to bring their ideals to fulfillment. And if in these and other cases it does appear that the studies in the classroom have no outside effect, lead to no outside activities, what expectation can you have that they will lead to activity after the college days are done? If studies do not stimulate to spontaneous, free outside activities, if they are the learning of lessons and giving them back, then the results of our training are typically small; we may send out good, well-meaning boys, who will do what they are told, and refrain from doing anything else, but we shall not send out men of intellectual power and grip who are able to learn for themselves the life which the intellect opens before them.

ALEXANDER MEIKLEJOHN, *The Liberal College*

31

American college education ought to substitute for much of the present muddlement of the pseudo-sciences, sociological, psychological, pedagogical, or what-not, that now dissipate the student's attention and confuse his thinking, a more critical and intensive study of the logic of debate and discussion, or rhetoric in the broader meaning, . . . the rhetoric which is the chief reliance of faddists, pseudo-scientists and propagandists for the tyrannical imposition of their ideas by the hypnotizing of democracy with words. . . .

So far as we teach rhetoric, logic, and the arts of debate at all we should teach them with a view to redeeming the educated classes, at least, from thraldom to this excessive natural susceptibility, and so establishing a coercive public opinion that will make unfair logic and the misuse of rhetoric fatal to the reputation of any statesman or publicist. It is only by the educated conscience of trained minds that this can be accomplished. For the uneducated, so far as they listen to words at all, will always be at the mercy of words.

PAUL SHOREY

32

Debating is the most essentially academic of all the extracurricular activities in which college students engage, for it necessitates clear thinking and intensive study. It provides excellent training as well in reasoning,—for a debater must be able to think logically. . . .

Debating develops the ability to formulate arguments quickly, to see the fallacy in an opponent's logic, and to marshal one's own points in the most effective manner. In addition to this it fosters poise and ease of bearing in public speaking. The debater who reasons well, however, is not necessarily successful; he must also present his arguments convincingly. Thus, to a certain degree, oratory and other rhetorical devices enter as elements in debating.

Debating is no pastime for the lazy student; but for him who is willing to work there is something fascinating in this contest of wits. Intramural debates should hold, therefore, an important place among collegiate activities.

Teachers College Record

33

Next to those whose elocution is absorbed in action, and who converse chiefly with their arms and legs, we may consider the professed "speakers" and, first, the emphatical, who squeeze and press and ram down every syllable with excessive vehemence and energy. These orators are remarkable for their distinct elocution and force of expression; they dwell on the important particles *of* and *the,* and the significant conjunction *and,* which they seem to hawk up, with much difficulty, out of their own throats, and to cram, with no less pain, into the ears of their auditors. I must confess that I am equally offended with the whisperers, or low speakers, who seem to fancy all their acquaintance deaf, and come up so close to you that they may be said to measure noses with you. I would have a speaking trumpet, or apply their lips to the walls of a whispering gallery. The wits, who will not condescend to utter anything but a bon mot, and the whistlers, or tune-hummers, who never talk at all, may be joined very agreeably together in a concert; and to these "tinkling cymbals" I would also add the "sounding brass," the bawler, who inquires after your health with the bellowing of a town crier.

The Spectator, "Habits of Expression"

34

"Enter into the *spirit* of what you read, *read naturally,* and you will read well," is about the sum and substance of what Archbishop Whateley teaches on the subject, in his "Elements of Rhetoric." Similar advice might with equal propriety be given to a clumsy, stiff-jointed clodhopper in regard to dancing: "Enter into the spirit of the dance, dance naturally, and you will dance well." The more he might enter into the spirit of the dance, the more he might emphasize his stiff-jointedness and his clodhopperishness. . . .

"Nature," says the Archbishop, "or custom, which is a second nature, suggests spontaneously the different modes of giving expression to different thoughts, feelings, and designs, which are present to the mind of any one who, without study, is speaking in earnest his own sentiments. Then, if this be the case, why not leave nature to do her own work? Impress but the mind fully with the sentiments, etc., to be uttered; withdraw the attention from the sound, and fix it on the sense; and nature, or habit, will spontaneously suggest the proper delivery."

Such instruction as this is not unlike that which Hamlet gives to Guildenstern, for playing upon a pipe, and would be, in the majority of cases, hardly more efficacious: "Govern these ventages with your fingers and thumb, give it breath with your mouth, and it will discourse most excellent music. Look you, these are the stops." Guildenstern replies: "But these cannot I command to any utterance of harmony; *I have not the skill.*" The last sentence tells the whole story. The Archbishop, with all his great abilities, had not the requisite *skill* in oratorical delivery.

So this may be said to be the conclusion of the whole matter: the main result which can be secured in teaching reading, and in training the voice, is technique and elocutionary *skill* of various kinds—a skill which the student can bring into his service, when voicing his intellectual appreciation and spiritual assimilation of a poem or any other form of spiritualized thought; the illumination of the subject-matter, intellectual and spiritual, must come from the *being* of the reader. He can't give to his hearers what he doesn't possess. . . . An attempt to express what is beyond the range of his spiritual life and experience, at once betrays his deficiency. And no amount of mere vocal training will compensate for this deficiency.

HIRAM CORSON, *The Voice and Spiritual Education* [1]

35

As courage and intelligence are the two qualities best worth a man's cultivation, so it is the first part of intelligence to recognize our precarious estate in life, and the first part of courage to be not at all abashed before the fact. A frank and somewhat headstrong carriage, not looking too anxiously before, not dallying in maudlin regret over the past, stamps the man who is well armored for this world.

And not only well armored for himself, but a good friend and a good citizen to boot. We do not go to cowards for tender dealing; there is nothing so cruel as panic; the man who has least fear for his own carcass, has most time to consider others. That eminent chemist who took his walks abroad in tin shoes, and subsisted wholly on tepid milk, had all his work cut out for him in considerate dealings with his own digestion. So soon as prejudice has begun to grow up in the brain, like a dismal fungus, it finds its first expression in a paralysis of generous acts. The victim begins to shrink spiritually; he develops a fancy for parlors with a regulated temperature, and takes his morality on the principle of tin shoes and tepid milk. The care of one important soul or body becomes so engrossing, that all the noises of the outside world begin to come thin and faint into the parlor with the regulated temperature; and the tin shoes go equably forward over blood and rain. To be overwise is to ossify; and the scruple-monger ends by standing stockstill.

Now the man who has his heart on his sleeve, and a good whirling weathercock of a brain, who reckons his life as a thing to be dashingly used and cheerfully hazarded, makes a very different acquaintance of the world, keeps all his pulses going true and fast, and gathers impetus as he runs, until, if he be running toward anything better than wildfire, he may shoot up and become a constellation in the end. Lord look after his health, Lord have a care of his soul, says he; and he has at the key of the position, and swashes through incongruity and peril toward his aim. Death is on all sides of him with pointed batteries, as he is on all sides of all of us; unfortunate surprises gird him round; mim-mouthed friends and relations hold up their hands in quite a little elegiacal synod about his path: and what cares he for this? Being a true lover of living, a fellow with something pushing and spontaneous in his inside, he must, like any other soldier, in any other stirring, deadly warfare, push on at his best pace until he touch the goal.

ROBERT LOUIS STEVENSON, "Aes Triplex"

36

But one can imagine only with difficulty the complete voice. It should range throughout life and life's mysteries, crudities, solemnities, noble rages, ignoble terrors; and as the sound races in our ears, it should be so much larger a fancy than our own, so incalculably dominant, that we too are on foot and away, illimitable ourselves, at the moment. Controlled it must be, yet thereby no stranger to life. He that rides all day from dawn to the gray of evening has heard many a crossroad cry and many a Philomena. He has faltered and fallen. He is knight and rescuer, slow plodder under storm, willing traveller beside ambulant pilgrim or priest. Betrayed, succored, never betraying, never quite losing kerchief or shield, he wanders near at last, bringing the world to our ears through his voicing of its medley. . . .

Curious the effect of many voices in a crowd. The sibilance and reiteration of similar sounds rattle at last in the ear, hiss, and subside, and roar again hydra heads. And suddenly a single voice is born out of this tumult. You are instantly quite secure in a little special peaceful atmosphere of your own and some one else's, produced entirely by the key of tone to which your own sensitiveness is attuned, and which in some mysterious way, under all its dailiness, says Beautiful! to you. And the voice heard from a distance, the owner quite invisible, is the veritable voice reduced to its own merits; no lift of eyebrow, no familiar flicker of the lips, no laughter below the crumpling eyes. Swiftly adaptive and flexible, the supple throat follows the convolutions of its deft mind, and you stand as if with eyes closed, hearing the soul play close to unseen lips, they translating all sorts of hidden languages and folk lore and loveliness to you, though bare words themselves are unheard.

LUCY SCARBOROUGH CONANT, *Voices*[1]

37

We learn on unimpeachable authority that a certain group of amateur athletes have been offered free board for life at the training-table of their home organization. A new road has been built into their home town by which they alone may enter it. The most expensive sculptors of their time have been engaged to perpetuate their forms, and the most esteemed poets to record their achievements in deathless verse. It is even whispered that their images have been set up in places of worship, and that before them religious ceremonies have been performed. Where and when, you ask, did these fantastic absurdities take place? According to the *Encyclopædia Britannica*, in Greece of the days of Pericles, that golden age of time when man led an intellectual life of sanity, measure, and harmony now forgotten in this, his latter end of folly.

Cornell Alumni News

38

For citizens of an English-speaking country, English is the foundation of all education. It is not only the study which deals with the language used in teaching the facts and ideas of other studies, but it is also that which fits a man for every kind of intercourse with his fellowmen. An imperfect command of English hinders him from telling other people what he thinks, from letting them know how he feels, from converting them to his plans and ideas; and, on the other hand, from learning their thoughts, feelings, and information. A good knowledge of the mother tongue is the most important instrument for success in business, in studies, and in society.

Most people are likely to assume that since they speak English every hour there is no need for them to study it as a spoken language, yet this is a great mistake. The rules of pronunciation are the result of habit. They are not logical and they cannot be arrived at by reasoning, though pronunciation like spelling can

---

[1] Copyright, Little, Brown & Company; reprinted by permission.

ısually be explained when we know the history of words. Rules
of pronunciation are much less exact than those of grammar for
they vary much more from place to place; and there is no one
place that makes the laws of pronunciation for the whole English-speaking world. If this is so, you may ask why you should
trouble about it, why your natural way of speaking a word is
not as good as that of any one else. The answer to that appears
when you consider that, since you speak in order to be understood, you cannot let your way of speaking vary too much from
that of other people. The special way in which a language is
spoken in a particular district is called a dialect; and there
are some dialects so special and peculiar that they are very hard
for people from other districts to understand. But as civilization
goes on there is less and less difference between dialects; and
pronunciation approaches more and more to a standard which
all use and understand. For the purpose of speech, then, we
ought to bring our own pronunciation as near the standard as
possible, and to avoid making ourselves ridiculous by personal or
local peculiarities.

The standard of which I have spoken is not the form of speech
used by the largest number of people; it is rather that of the
best educated and the most refined. These are the people who
can go from state to state and from one English speaking country
to another and be intelligible everywhere without difficulty and
without appearing provincial, that is, without showing the marks
and limitations of their own little part of the world.

WILLIAM ALLAN NEILSON

39

In America, education occupies the attention of everyone;
and this is one of the most hopeful things that can be said
about our outlook. We are beginning to wonder what education
is, and what part of it is connected with schoolbooks.

There has, within the last generation, grown up a scattered
class of enthusiasts who are interested in speech. It was revealed to them, perhaps by some deep semi-religious instinct,—
one of those impulses by which Nature saves herself,—that a
person who could *articulate* was a civilized being. They discovered, as it were, by a miracle, that the brain, the heart, the attention, the muscular system, the soul and body, were drawn to
a focus in the act of speech, and that education began here.

Perhaps, also, the danger that threatened our language through the influx of foreigners, and which was reflected in the speech of our own children and their intimates, frightened these new prophets. Perhaps the suspicion flashed through their minds that, unless they bestirred themselves, they would soon not understand the lingo that was being spoken in their own neighborhood.

Certain it is that many minds among us have been awakened to the importance of articulate speech. This is a matter that has never been neglected in Europe, where people have always taught their children to speak carefully, as a matter of course, and in the same spirit in which they put a spoon in the hands of a baby who is old enough to feed itself.

But the effort to improve our speech in America must be self-conscious and dogmatic; because a large part of our population believes that babies will find spoons for themselves, and that good speech comes by nature, and is at best a foolish thing.

The problem of reforming the speech of America would seem ghastly and hopeless, but for the fact that such a reform is mimetic rather than rational. Many a man has reformed his own speech in middle life through contact with someone whose voice and utterance he admired. His ears became sharpened.

As for the young, they need only a model and good-will to show a change for the better in a week. Give a shock to a certain portion of their consciousness, and they become aware of their own deficiencies; they hear their own horrors: the rest is easy. There will, no doubt, be many dogmas, many methods, and every one of them will act as a stimulus and a step in advance. When our people shall come to understand the importance of Articulate Speech, the first province of Learning will have been conquered.

It makes little difference what pronunciation is adopted, so long as the vocalization is good. The Scotch utterance is to my mind beautiful, and reveals the remarkable intellect of that people as clearly as anything they have accomplished. Should America develop a pronunciation totally different from the British pronunciation, there would be nothing to regret so long as it was good.

But if you slur and gargle your mother-tongue, I question whether your mother-wit will ever do much for literature. The voice is so much a part of the brain, that you can hardly think clearly and yet speak in a gibberish; and this is the great and wonderful discovery that America is making.

JOHN JAY CHAPMAN, *A Glance toward Shakespeare*

40

What I feel to be English therefore may not and need not arouse a similar experience in my neighbors. In all probability it will, for the large sense of unity in the language comes from the fact that under like circumstances, various persons will have approximately the same reactions. In the end the sum of these approximate similars in the speech habits of the group may come to exert a far-reaching control over the linguistic actions of individuals through the establishment of a kind of moral tone for the use of the language. But the exercise of this control is subtle and diffused, and it is like speech itself, one of the general social possessions of the group.

The extraordinary vitality and variability of the language come home to us when we reflect on the millions of the users of the language, each with his own individual sense of the life of the native idiom, each sure of himself within his own circle, and yet each at the same time genuinely living only because his little circle is part of the great circle of the language. The life of the language thus has a double aspect, and like all life, we can know it only because we experience it. But the unity of linguistic feeling by which one realizes the greater circle of the language does not necessarily imply approval of all within the circle. There are empires within the great empire. We may agree to call many uses idiomatic English which we do not commend or propose to put into practice. Approval and disapproval are minor aspects and moods of the all-embracing life of the language. But in the dispassionate observation of this life, there is a world of interesting matters to reward the student of our mother tongue. Custom cannot stale her infinite variety. Only the pedantry of narrow precisianists can do that. When our native speech sits close to the hearts of the English people, as all speech should, it is quick and manifold in its changes. It is a great ocean of speech, closed within its own shores, but never twice the same in the many forms which its moving waters are constantly taking.

* * *

A moment ago, in speaking of the professional diction of actors and actresses, the question of the value of a disciplined and trained pronunciation was touched upon. The actor, the orator, or any person who addresses a large audience from a platform undoubtedly must have a technique of his own that can be developed and mastered only by assiduous application. Does a similar necessity rest upon every person, even in the more intimate associations of cultivated conversation, or should speech on this level be left to take care of itself? In effect this is the old question of nature and nurture, and we need not dwell again upon the fact that no person has language, English or any other language, as a direct gift of nature. The child is disciplined in the formation of the sounds of speech from his earliest speaking moments, partly self-disciplined through the impulse to imitate, partly through the definite direction he receives from his parents. Normally this discipline is continued until the child learns to recognize the sounds of English speech and to produce them in their proper places. Sometimes, however, the discipline is remitted too soon, and the child then carries over to his adult years some of his childish imperfections, lisping, for example, or a tendency to confuse the sound of *tl* with *kl*, causing him to say something like *brickle* for *brittle*, or of *th* and *f*, resulting in *fing* for *thing*, or of *s* and *sh*, producing a mushy kind of pronunciation, *yesh* for *yes*, *thish* for *this*, not infrequent even among educated adults. That these defects, and others of a more pathological nature, like stuttering and stammering, should be corrected by discipline, as most of them can be, goes without saying. The main question at present, however, is not whether manifest defects should be corrected by training, but whether positive virtues, not merely a normal but a super-normal, a best pronunciation should be inculcated in the same way. This question can be answered most readily by drawing a parallel between speech and certain other aspects of personal deportment—carriage of the body, for example. If left to themselves children and others may carry themselves well, easily and unconsciously. Such persons are said to have a natural grace, the best kind, possibly, that anyone could have. Yet such persons seem to be unfortunately the exceptions, not the rule. Every parent knows how insistently children must be directed to sit straight, not to shuffle, shamble, and slouch. It has been said that the final test of good breeding is the ability to walk gracefully across the floor before the eyes of an assemblage. A supremely unconscious person might do this, or a supremely self-conscious person, that is, one who by training has acquired complete control of the motions of the body. So also in speech, a well bred, natural undisciplined pronunciation may be the gift of the fortunate few, but ordinarily, and in whatever associations one's type of speech is formed, a certain amount of training is necessary to secure that certainty and fineness of control in speech which distinguishes the speech of the cultivated person from that of the boor. Just when this training should stop is a matter to be determined by observation of the subtle properties of cultivated speech. Certainly it should stop before it produces an impression of professionalism. Carrying the body well for the average person does not mean carrying it with a military carriage. So also training in pronunciation and the use of the voice should stop before it turns cultivated conversational speech into an elocutionary, or theatrical, or any other kind of professional diction. The highly trained manner of speaking which is so highly trained that it calls attention to itself is out of place on the plane of colloquial use. It may arouse admiration, but admiration is a poor substitute for the sense of intimate sympathy which a merely adequate use of speech may enable two speakers to attain. Good taste demands that speech shall be as unobtrusive as dress and as any other form of social conduct. To find the proper balance between carelessness and uncouthness in speech, on the one hand, and a finical precision or florid amplitude on the other is not always easy. It can be found only when the true character of cultivated speech is kept in mind as neither a self-determining natural growth nor a fine art, with a technique like that of singing or acting, to be cultivated as an end in itself, but rather as a social convention of many adaptations, all the demands of which are satisfied when each fits its own circumstances. A single best pronunciation is therefore not to be expected, but many bests, conversation being always at its best when human minds are brought into intelligible and kindly relations to each other, "without heat and without vulgarity," through the forms of human speech.

GEORGE PHILIP KRAPP, *The Knowledge of English*

41

The four types of conflict above discussed—conflict between emotional states within the individual, conflict between nations, between capital and labor, and between races—are not staged by us for our own pleasure. They arise, somehow; and we do the best we can with them. To be sure, our best has been fairly inadequate; but it can hardly be said that we have deliberately set about to wish these conflicts upon ourselves. It is different, however, with the type of conflict which we are now to discuss. We deliberately create it, and come out in crowds—fathers and mothers and sisters and aunts and all the rest of the noble citizenry—to admire our handiwork! Nay, more than that, we solemnly instruct our young folk that to engage in such a conflict—we call it a debate—and to come forth victorious is to be well on the way toward success.

It is only in a very special field that we are still able to continue this thing. If we go into the chemical laboratory and ask that a public combat be staged on the possible outcome of radical research, the chemical professor will shake his head: "We don't stage combats here. We try to find things out." If we go into the biological laboratory, we get the same subtly ironic answer. The biologist will admit, if pressed, that there are indeed conflicting views in biology—between mechanists and vitalists, for example. "Ah, then," we say, "let us stage a combat—a great public combat—affirmative and negative; with judges to decide who wins and who gets defeated; and an audience to go wild with enthusiasm at the oratory." The biologist will shake his head. "That is not the way we scientists do things. Long ago, when science was still learned out of Aristotle, scientific men argued themselves hoarse;—disputations, they called such verbal orgies. No more of that now. Our task, as scientists, is not to see who can argue the most cleverly, but who can really find things out." Then, if he is a good friend, he may whisper in our ear: "Go to those who deal in social questions. They still do that mediæval thing!" . . .

As one writer has recently expressed it: "Now what kind of process is this? Students meet, and agree to discuss a problem. The latter is generally of a political, sociological, ethical or philosophical nature, and one they know little or nothing about. Whatever it is, they have yet to make a careful, thorough and systematic study of it. But their ignorance does not prevent them from determining that this or that proposed solution is or is not practicable. Having come to a conclusion, they proceed to find the facts and justify it!

"As a process, this is the very reverse of that dictated by logic and by science. Yet it is one of the objects of our schools to train students in the art of approaching problems with minds free of any bias toward a preconceived solution. It is also the object of the science courses in particular to impress upon the pupils the importance and the necessity of arriving at even tentative conclusions, or rather hypotheses, only after a careful, thorough, systematic and impartial examination of all the available data relating to a given problem."

Debate, then, is deeply in conflict with the scientific spirit of our age. It is militarism in the intellectual life. It is mediævalism in modernity. By teaching young minds to start with their conclusions and then find the facts to justify them, it is the great aider and abettor of the noble art of rationalizing.

But it is always a little dangerous to cast out the baby with the bath. Perhaps there is something that can be salvaged out of this verbal bellicosity. Let us recall our hypothesis about conflict. Conflict, we said, was civilizing when it was accepted as an opportunity (1) to understand the opposed side; (2) to find a new way out. Debate, as hitherto conducted has been carried on like war, namely, with the deliberate refusal to understand the other side, and with the sole aim, not of a creative way out, but of a smashing victory.

Let us suppose, however, that we keep in mind our creative view of conflict. Let us also grant to our debating friends that there are social, economic and political problems with reference to which, in a more or less general way, two opposed stands can be taken. Suppose now that we say to our young minds, "It is fair to give each side its strongest defense: let us first do that. It makes no difference whether you believe in the affirmative or not. If you defend it valiantly, we all know you are simply doing your chivalric best to say what can be said in its favor. But now, after we have done our best for the affirmative and the negative, let us take off our disputatious habits and don the habit of the scientists. Let us in short now consider together what we are going to do with the whole question. We shall not now debate; we shall discuss. We shall try honestly to understand each other. Above all, we shall hope not to end with the affirmative-negative deadlock with which we began; we shall rather hope to find a new way out."

We might call this "constructive debate," implying by the term the spirit of the upbuilding scientist rather than the spirit of the down battering militarist . . .

All this is in line with our more civilized techniques. Open diplomacy, the leaguing of all nations, international conferences, fact-finding agencies, boards of adjustment—all these operate in terms of the hypothesis above expressed for the handling of conflicts. The militaristic mind is the either-or mind; the black-white, god-devil mind. It is essentially, therefore, the static and destructive mind. The new type that is increasingly developing in our social affairs is the neither-and-both mind; the gradations-of-color; the neither-you-nor-I-am-God-or-devil; the come-let-us-reason-together mind. It is therefore essentially the evolving, creative mind.

Some day we shall doubtless realize, more than we now do, the profound psychological significance of the biblical sentence: "Where two or three are gathered together in My name there am I in their midst." That has hitherto been taken only in a religiously mystical sense. Psychologically interpreted, however, it means that in every coming together of minds that are serious in the effort to understand, there is something more than the sum of minds. There is the Creative Plus which no one mind by itself could achieve. And even when the two or three are in conflict together, if the intent to understand and to find a new way out is there, something creatively new emerges.

This is the secret of civilized conflict which is slowly but quite certainly being learned in our times. The day of destructive fight is passing; the day of constructive fight is ahead of us.

H. A. OVERSTREET, *Influencing Human Behavior*

42

THE CHAIRMAN AS SOCIAL TECHNICIAN

One party to the discussion ought to be charged with a special concern for its integrity as a social process. The appropriate member for this role is the chairman. Better than the others he can keep his mind on the points already noted as making for progress in debate, and can pilot the discussion clear of rocks, shallows and aimless circling. As a chart of the normal course of really profitable group thinking he should memorize the following little scheme of procedure:—

1. The controversial situation sharply presented.
2. The essential problem discovered and analyzed in a way to invite suspended judgment.
3. Data (from authorities and from experience) offered and compared as a basis for suggestions.

4. A plan evolved by exploring the possibilities of action and critically testing the workableness of some course as a solution.

5. New issues arising from action on the plan stated as projects for experiment and further inquiry.

The success of a chairman depends on his attitude towards the discussion group, on his preparation for the meeting, and on his alertness, during the speaking, to the changes that take place in the controversial situation.

Where the discussion is one between the parties to a contentious dispute, the chief requisite in the chairman's attitude is an open-minded interest in getting all the points of view accurately understood. He should display a generous faith in the sincerity of the disputants, and see that the case does not get weighted one way or another by mere differences among them in fluency and assurance. While he may interject questions or explanatory comments at any time to ensure the full statement of a point, he should avoid making speeches himself, or letting his remarks for the purpose of transition or summary suggest a note of approval for views that chime in with his own.

Where the discussion is one between members of a study-group the chairman's attitude is more like that of a stage manager towards the cast of a play. The play here is a drama not of persons but of interests, the speakers representing a small cross-section of public opinion, and the leader an impressario of group-thinking. To get the best out of his speakers he should stimulate their self-confidence. Average people feel their information to be scanty, and will not "talk up" until they realize that the discussion group is not a lecture-class but a little power-plant for influence, where the ideas that boil up from every-day experience must count. The chairman can remind them that profitable thinking is a matter not only of information but of method, that the group is here using a method which gets the most out of what they know, and that what they know includes not only the "active" information which springs to mind but a good deal of submerged information which counts in their mental attitudes.

The chairman should prepare to bring to the meeting both some fact-material and some carefully phrased questions. Fact material that serves a discussion is of two sorts: facts that *supplement* experience—that is, data drawn from the studies of specialists—and facts that *stir memories of* experience. By marking a few thought-provoking passages to be read aloud in the meeting

he assures himself of having something worth-while to produce
at opportune moments. The question he prepares should apply
the scheme of thought-procedure (see above) to the problem
under discussion. Two kinds of questions are needed: analysis
questions, which bring out the *nature* of the problem, and solution
questions, which call for workable measures for action. The chairman will treat his questions as approaches to the subject which
may prove serviceable, but which he is ready to change or drop as
the discussion takes its own course. When he is tempted to pre-
judge a debate as conforming to one type of procedure, he should
remember the words of Von Moltke: "I have generally found that
there are exactly three courses open to the enemy—and that he
takes the fourth!"

When the meeting begins, the chairman's alertness to the situation is likely to be needed at once. Nobody is disposed to "break
the ice" in speaking. Rather than allow an awkward pause the
chairman should put a question likely to get a "rise" out of a good
speaker, calling on him by name, if necessary. Or, he can ask to
have read aloud one or two of the quotations that he has brought.
These he should have placed in the hands of shy members, who
would otherwise take little part.

It is not necessary to make much of parliamentary rules, but
the leader should not let speakers drop into the way of addressing
one another without securing recognition from "the chair." Mon-
opolizing talkers should find it hard to catch his eye, while the
hesitant should get encouraging glances. In interjecting remarks
to draw people out the chairman should offer what he says as
something implied or called for by what others have been saying,
not as something *he* wants to have discussed. Half-jokingly he
may even interpret a member's silence, or the expression on his
face, in a way to make everybody look to that member for remarks.

In addition the chairman can deal with the speaking in ways
to soften combativeness, to save time, and to register agreement
point by point.

Combativeness in discussion usually springs from over-state-
ment and "crowd" words—that is, words emotionally charged with
old prejudices. The chairman should get them translated into
language more accurate and temperate, rephrasing them himself,
if necessary.

Time is lost when speakers indulge in preambles and fall into
repetitions. Much talk, also, springs from the speakers' uncon-

scious egotism. In various ways they consume time in conveying that their opinions do their hearts credit, or that they are not really backing down. The chairman can avert much of this by dropping reassuring intimations that the face-saving is unnecessary. Again, the average member tends to lose the drift of the group-thought. His "span of attention" reaches only a speech or two back. The chairman should take sketchy notes that will help remind the meeting of what has been said and what seems to be called for. Such notes will give him confidence in challenging speakers who tend to ramble.

Agreement in the end should ideally take expression in something like a consensus. But the group can approach this only by registering assent on one point at a time. The chairman can hold the speaking to the point, and ask a decision when it seems to have got its due. Each stage of the meeting will thus end with some statement that the group will agree upon as showing where they now stand. Either the chairman or someone acting informally as secretary should write such statements down, so that they can be accurately cited when the group arrives at discussing what kinds of *action* will carry the agreements out. Much of the success of a discussion in marking an orderly advance in group thinking turns on the chairman's sense of tactical sequence for the points discussed. The guiding maxim here is: *Register a maximum of agreement where agreement comes easily before passing to matters where agreement costs pains.* Practically this invites something like the following order of dealing with a discussion topic:—

1. *Report of the situation that gives rise to dispute.*

This means the stating first of the undisputed facts in the case, and then of any items, likely to be invoked as evidence, that are open to doubt as to their truth or their bearing. The statement should bring out sharply the points of conflict in the situation, so as to show where the problem lies.

2. *Discovery and appraisal of the interests at stake in the situation.*

The situation is a controversial one because the parties to it are making claims and displaying activities that conflict. This means that the interests, the ends which they pursue, and the agencies or methods by which they pursue them, are clashing interests and activities *in the form in which these are now professed and displayed.* By getting the partisans to state what interests (aims, objectives, "values," rights) they have at heart, the chairman

man invites the first steps in discovering and analyzing the problem. In its essentials the problem is to find a plan of action that will harmonize these interests. But the interests, more than likely, are neither accurately professed nor mutually understood. Partisans naturally overstate their claims, just as they pursue them by methods that carry further consequences than they strictly intend. Obviously, therefore, the group is not ready to appraise any plan of action involving methods for attaining and safeguarding interests until it agrees on *precisely what interests* to safeguard. The chairman can help the speakers to start right by preserving two distinctions:—

(*a*) By distinguishing between *what* the parties to the conflict want to get, and *the way* they want to get it (suspending judgment as to the latter).

(*b*) By distinguishing between what they profess and pursue as their interests *under the present conditions of conflict* and what they might accept as fair interpretations of their interests *if their present opponents would accept them too.*

The questions which the chairman puts for discussion at this stage should be confined—

To getting any interests which are challenged *as their partisans first profess them* so interpreted that all parties admit their claim to some respect.

Any agreement here (as to precisely what interests are socially justifiable) has only the provisional value of clearing the way for discussion upon specific features in plans for joint action. The chairman should challenge agreements that rest on mere vague words, as where people agree to respect "liberty of speech but not license." (Real agreement here involves either an agreed *definition* of license or an agreed *way to settle* what license is).

3. *Explanation of the available agencies or methods by which the various partisans are expecting to secure their interests.*

Having agreed as to what ends are socially justifiable, the group stands committed to agree upon *some* means to those ends. If a plan of action is being proposed, the group is now ready to hear any data from authorities and from experience that show its bearing upon the interests at stake. Possible alternatives of action should here be offered. The speaking at this stage should still be kept, so far as possible, in the mood of explaining—of displaying facts as to organization, resources, technique, conduct, which point to ways and means by which the various parties to the situation may expect to get things done. Particular attention should be paid to terms requiring definition and to any precedents and analogies that will afford a basis for constructive suggestions.

4. *Questions that explore and test the possibilities of action that will bring the conflicting interests into some coöperative plan.*

Dispute is now narrowed down to the really crucial matters, and it can proceed with a general understanding of the problem taken for granted. Since the questions arise from definite points of view, the chairman knows where to turn for responses that may express fresh advances of the opposed interests. The aim of all questions here is to get some developing plan of action critically tested.

When conflict on a crucial point comes to a deadlock, the chairman should turn back to whatever agreement has been registered so far, and set the group to thinking *what activities can start on the basis of that.* The change of mood from combating to contriving loosens up the situation, and the suggested activities, however slight as an approach to coöperation, may yet open the way to a larger agreement. Ideally, of course, what is sought from the various parties is agreement *to do something together,* with definite arrangements by which the doing shall *be kept up through the further situations that are likely to develop.*

Any approach to an agreed plan or solution the chairman should clearly state at the end of the discussion, so that the group can feel itself to have achieved progress. At the same time he should remark where new issues seem to be budding out of the discussion and inviting further inquiry.

ALFRED DWIGHT SHEFFIELD, "A Coöperative Technique for Conflict"

B. SELECTIONS ILLUSTRATING MAINLY THE RHYTHMICAL APPROACH

43

ɑ(r)tⁱ æt ɪts bestⁱ ɪz nɒt ən əskeɪp frəm laɪf | nɔr ə krɪtɪsɪzm əv laɪf | bət ən ɪkspænʃən əv laɪfⁱ ɪntʊ ridʒənzⁱ ɪntʊ hʊɪtʃ ɔ(r)dɪnərɪ hjumən ɪkspɪərɪənsⁱ kænʊt ʌðə(r)waɪz ritʃ |·|

44

ɔl ðət ə junɪvɜ(r)sɪtɪ | ɔ(r) faɪnəl haɪɪst skul | kn du fɒr ʌs | ɪz
stɪl bət ləʊt ðə fɜ(r)st skul bɪgæn dʊɪŋ || tɪtʃ əs tə rid |·| wi lɜ(r)n
tə ridˈ ɪn veərɪəs læŋgwɪdʒɪz | ɪn veərɪəs saɪənsɪz || wɪ lɜ(r)n
ðɪ ɪmpɔ(r)tns ənd leɪtə(r)zˈ əv wɪ mænər əv bʊks || bət ðə pleɪs lʊeə(r)
wɪ ə(r) tə get nɒlɪdʒ | ivn θɪərətɪk nɒlɪdʒ | ɪz ðə bʊks ðəmselvz |·|

45

mæn ɪz ðə lafɪŋ ænɪməl | ðə tɪmfɪ ænd ɪʃ ɪ tə bnd əv te bnd | ðə fɪlɒsəfə
faɪndz hɪmself klɪŋɪŋ tə laftər | əz ðə bəst əv hjumən frut || pjʊə
hjumən | ənd seɪn | ənd kʌmfətɪŋ |·| soʊ təl əs bi kɒdʒəlɪ θæŋkfəl |
tə ðoʊz hu fənɪʃ mætə fə saʊnd ɪmbreɪʃɪŋ laftə |·|

46

lʊen ðə plaʊmən (h)əz plaʊd (h)ɪz fərəʊ | lʊen ðə hʌntə həz
kɪld (h)ɪz kwɒrɪ | lʊen ðə wivəz lum ɪz stɪl | ɪtʃ wʌn sɪts ət rest
bɪfʊə hɪz kɒtɪdʒˈ ənd gɪvz weɪ tə drimz |·| ðɪs ɪz ðə frutfəl aʊəˈ
lʊen ɪtʃ ɪz lɪvɪŋ hɪz tru laɪf |·|

47

kalaɪl wəz ə mæn tə hum ðə rɪælɪtɪz əv laɪfˈ wə sɒləʊ mesɪv θɪŋə | ənd
hi dɪd nɒt noʊ | hi kʊd nɒt si | ðət ðə flɪpənsɪ ənd bæntəˈ hi dɪtestɪdˈ
wə læmz weɪ əv meɪkɪŋ ðoʊz rɪælɪtɪz ɪndʒʊərəbl |·|

48

ðə medʒɒrɪtɪ mæn əv aʊə lʌŋ poʊɪtsˈ həv noʊ θiɪt bət ðɪs || ðət ðeə θɔt
sʌbdʒektɪvɪtɪ ɪz nɒt ɪmpɔ(r)tənt || ənd ðət ðeɪ kænət faɪnd mætər ɪn ðɪ
ɒbdʒektɪv |·|

49

if ðeə wə drimz tə sel |
lʊɒt wʊd jʊ baɪ?||
sʌm kɒst ə pasɪŋ bel |
sʌm ə laɪt saɪˈ
ðət ʃeɪks frəm laɪfs freʃ kraʊnˈ
oʊnlɪ ə roʊz-lif daʊn |·|

| ɪf ðɛə wə drimz tʊ sɛl |
| mɛrɪ ənd sæd tʊ tɛl |
| ænd ðə kraɪə ræŋ ðə bɛl |
| hʊt wʊd jʊ baɪ?|·|

ə kɒtɪdʒ' loʊn ənd stɪl |
wɪð baʊəz naɪ |
ʃædoʊɪ' maɪ woʊz tə stɪl'
ʌntɪl aɪ daɪ |·|
sʌtʃ pəl' frəm laɪfs frɛʃ kraʊn |
feɪn' wʊd aɪ ʃeɪk mi daʊn ||
wə drimz tʊ hæv ət wɪl |
ðɪs wʊd bɛst hil maɪ ɪl ||
ðɪs' wʊd aɪ baɪ |·|

50

DREAM PEDLARY

If there were dreams to sell,
  What would you buy?
Some cost a passing bell;
  Some a light sigh,
That shakes from Life's fresh crown
Only a rose-leaf down.

If there were dreams to sell,
  Merry and sad to tell,
And the crier rang the bell,
  What would you buy?

A cottage lone and still,
  With bowers nigh,
Shadowy, my woes to still,
  Until I die.
Such pearl from Life's fresh crown
Fain would I shake me down.
Were dreams to have at will,
This would best heal my ill,
  This would I buy.

THOMAS LOVELL BEDDOES

51

The Song of the Ungirt Runners

We swing ungirded hips,
And lightened are our eyes.
The rain is on our lips,
We do not run for prize.
We know not whom we trust
Nor whitherward we fare,
But we run because we must
    Through the great wide air.

The waters of the seas
Are troubled as by storm.
The tempest strips the trees
And does not leave them warm.
Does the tearing tempest pause?
Do the tree-tops ask it why?
So we run without a cause
    'Neath the big bare sky.

The rain is on our lips,
We do not run for prize.
But the storm the water whips
And the wave howls to the skies.
The winds arise and strike it
And scatter it like sand,
And we run because we like it
    Through the broad, bright land.

CHARLES HAMILTON SORLEY

52

When I Set Out for Lyonnesse[1]

When I set out for Lyonnesse,
    A hundred miles away,
    The rime was on the spray,
And starlight lit my lonesomeness
When I set out for Lyonnesse
    A hundred miles away.

[1] Copyright by the Macmillan Company; reprinted by permission.

What would bechance at Lyonnesse
　While I should sojourn there
　No prophet durst declare,
Nor did the wisest wizard guess
What would bechance at Lyonnesse
　While I should sojourn there.

When I came back from Lyonnesse
　With magic in my eyes,
　All marked with mute surmise
My radiance rare and fathomless,
When I came back from Lyonnesse
　With magic in my eyes!

THOMAS HARDY

53

VELVET SHOES

Let us walk in the white snow
　In a soundless space;
With footsteps quiet and slow,
　At a tranquil pace,
　Under veils of white lace.

I shall go shod in silk,
　And you in wool,
White as a white cow's milk,
　More beautiful
　Than the breast of a gull.

We shall walk through the still town
　In a windless peace;
We shall step upon white down,
　Upon silver fleece,
　Upon softer than these.

We shall walk in velvet shoes:
　Wherever we go
Silence will fall like dews
　On white silence below.
　We shall walk in the snow.

ELINOR WYLIE

54

THE SPRING AND THE FALL

In the spring of the year, in the spring of the year,
I walked the road beside my dear.
The trees were black where the bark was wet.
I see them yet, in the spring of the year.
He broke me a bough of the blossoming peach
That was out of the way and hard to reach.

In the fall of the year, in the fall of the year,
I walked the road beside my dear.
The rooks went up with a raucous trill.
I hear them still, in the fall of the year.
He laughed at all I dared to praise,
And broke my heart, in little ways.

Year be springing or year be falling,
The bark will drip and the birds be calling.
There's much that's fine to see and hear
In the spring of a year, in the fall of a year.
'Tis not love's going hurts my days,
But that it went in little ways.

                              EDNA ST. VINCENT MILLAY

55

WHITE WAVES ON THE WATER

White waves on the water,
Gold leaves on the tree,
As Mananan's daughter
Arose from her sea.

The bud and the blossom,
The fruit of the foam
From Ocean's dark bosom
Arose, from the home.

She came at your calling,
O winds of the world,

When the ripe fruit was falling
And the flowers unfurled.

She came at your crying,
O creatures of earth,
And the sound of your sighing
Made music and mirth.

She came at your keening,
O dreamers of doom,
And your sleep had new dreaming
And splendor and bloom.

JOSEPH MARY PLUNKETT

56

MARSEILLAISE

With stones in your boots and the head of a clod,
Your throat full of mist,
Plod
In a wind with the thrust of a fist.
Plod   plod   plod   plod.

Lie on your belly and bed with the damp,
Rise in the dark.
Tramp
Over streets that are fanged like a shark.
Tramp   tramp   tramp   tramp.

Shiver the bridge and sunder the arch,
Move like a glacier that threatens the town,
March
Till you trample it down.
March   march   march   march.

March like a slow and devouring rust
On a town, on a land, on a world that is doomed.
Dust
Is the portion you shall have consumed.
MARCH AS YOU MUST.

BABETTE DEUTSCH

57

A Wave of the Sea

I am a wave of the sea
And the foam of the wave
And the wind of the foam
And the wings of the wind.

My soul's in the salt of the sea
In the weight of the wave
In the bubbles of foam
In the ways of the wind.

My gift is the depth of the sea
The strength of the wave
The lightness of foam
The speed of the wind.

JOSEPH MARY PLUNKETT

58

The Dead Dancer

On youthful dancers
I can't look now;
She lies so quiet
Who taught them how.

Each step and gesture
Reminds of her
Whom earthly music
Will no more stir.

Surely, somewhere
She will be found,
Swaying to sweet
Melodious sound,

Who, loving rhythm,
So gently drew
Little children
To learn the clue.

ROSE MILLS POWERS

59

THE LISTENERS

"Is there anybody there?" said the Traveller,
    Knocking on the moonlit door;
And his horse in the silence champed the grasses
    Of the forest's ferny floor:
And a bird flew up out of the turret,
    Above the Traveller's head:
And he smote upon the door again a second time;
    "Is there anybody there?" he said.
But no one descended to the Traveller;
    No head from the leaf-fringed sill
Leaned over and looked into his grey eyes,
    Where he stood perplexed and still.
But only a host of phantom listeners
    That dwelt in the lone house then
Stood listening in the quiet of the moonlight
    To that voice from the world of men:
Stood thronging the faint moonbeams on the dark stair,
    That goes down to the empty hall,
Hearkening in an air stirred and shaken
    By the lonely Traveller's call.
And he felt in his heart their strangeness,
    Their stillness answering his cry,
While his horse moved, cropping the dark turf,
    'Neath the starred and leafy sky;
For he suddenly smote on the door, even
    Louder, and lifted his head:—
"Tell them I came, and no one answered,
    That I kept my word," he said.
Never the least stir made the listeners,
    Though every word he spake
Fell echoing through the shadowiness of the still house
    From the one man left awake:
Ay, they heard his foot upon the stirrup,
    And the sound of iron on stone,
And how the silence surged softly backward
    When the plunging hoofs were gone.

WALTER DE LA MARE

60

When men were all asleep the snow came flying,
In large white flakes falling on the city brown,
Stealthily and perpetually settling and loosely lying,
    Hushing the latest traffic of the drowsy town;
Deadening, muffling, stifling its murmurs failing;
Lazily and incessantly floating down and down:
    Silently sifting and veiling road, roof and railing;
Hiding difference, making unevenness even,
Into angles and crevices softly drifting and sailing.
    All night it fell, and when full inches seven
It lay in the depth of its uncompacted lightness,
The clouds blew off from a high and frosty heaven;
    And all woke earlier for the unaccustomed brightness
Of the winter dawning, the strange unheavenly glare:
The eye marvelled—marvelled at the dazzling whiteness;
    The ear hearkened to the stillness of the solemn air;
No sound of wheel rumbling nor of foot falling,
And the busy morning cries came thin and spare.

ROBERT BRIDGES, "London Snow"

61

There is sweet music here that softer falls
Than petals from blown roses on the grass,
Or night-dews on still waters between walls
Of shadowy granite, in a gleaming pass;
Music that gentlier on the spirit lies
Than tired eyelids upon tired eyes;
Music that brings sweet sleep down from the blissful skies.

TENNYSON, "Song of the Lotus Eaters"

62

THE LITTLE WAVES OF BREFFNY

The grand road from the mountain goes shining to the sea,
    And there is traffic on it, and many a horse and cart;
But the little roads of Cloonagh are dearer far to me,
    And the little roads of Cloonagh go rambling through my heart.

A great storm from the ocean goes shouting o'er the hill,
  And there is glory in it, and terror on the wind;
But the haunted airs of twilight are very strange and still,
  And the little winds of twilight are dearer to my mind.

The great waves of the Atlantic sweep storming on their way,
  Shining green and silver with the hidden herring shoal;
But the little waves of Breffny have drenched my heart in
  spray,
  And the little waves of Breffny go stumbling through my
  soul.

EVA GORE-BOOTH

63

EGYPT'S MIGHT IS TUMBLED DOWN

Egypt's might is tumbled down,
  Down-adown the deeps of thought;
Greece is fallen and Troy town,
Glorious Rome has lost her crown,
  Venice' pride is nought.

But the dreams their children dreamed,
  Fleeting, unsubstantial, vain,
Shadowy as the shadows seemed,
Airy nothings, as they deemed—
  These remain.

MARY COLERIDGE

64

THERE BE NONE OF BEAUTY'S DAUGHTERS

There be none of Beauty's daughters
  With a magic like thee;
And like music on the waters
  Is thy sweet voice to me:
When, as if its sound were causing
The charmed ocean's pausing,
The waves lie still and gleaming,
And the lulled winds seem dreaming:

And the midnight moon is weaving
　　Her bright chain o'er the deep,
Whose breast is gently heaving
　　As an infant's asleep:
So the spirit bows before thee
　To listen and adore thee;
With a full but soft emotion,
Like the swell of Summer's ocean.

BYRON

65

BIRTHRIGHT

Lord Rameses of Egypt sighed
Because a summer evening passed;
And little Ariadne cried
　That summer fancy fell at last
To dust; and young Verona died
　When beauty's hour was over-cast.

Theirs was the bitterness we know
Because the clouds of hawthorn keep
So short a state, and kisses go
　To tombs unfathomably deep,
Where Rameses and Romeo
　And little Ariadne sleep.

JOHN DRINKWATER

66

AGAINST OBLIVION

Cities drowned in olden time
Keep, they say, a magic chime
Rolling up from far below
When the moon-led waters flow.

So within me, ocean-deep,
Lies a sunken world asleep.
Lest its bells forget to ring,
Memory, set the tide aswing!

SIR HENRY NEWBOLT

67

SWAN WOMAN

Helen is a name for me
Of beauty fraught with mystery;

Just to say the word will stir
Shining memories of her,

Leda's daughter, white upon
The waters of oblivion;

Swan child of Olympian Jove
Whom the fateful Moira drove

To be Sparta's ringing joy
And the bright despair of Troy.

Helen, you have come to mean
All of beauty ever seen;

Men will dream forevermore
Of that brooding smile you wore,

It is you their arms embrace
Looking on another's face,

And your swan-call still is heard
In all music, woman-bird.

Starting up as if a wing
Brushed them when they heard you sing,

Men will haunt all streams nor know
That they seek you as they go;

Supernaturally fair,
Born of water and of air,

Magical, mysterious
Swan child of immortal Zeus.

ROSE MILLS POWERS

68

She Walks in Beauty

She walks in beauty, like the night
  Of cloudless climes and starry skies;
And all that's best of dark and bright
  Meet in her aspect and her eyes:
Thus mellow'd to that tender light
  Which heaven to gaudy day denies.

One shade the more, one ray the less,
  Had half impaired the nameless grace
Which waves in every raven tress,
  Or softly lightens o'er her face;
Where thoughts serenely sweet express
  How pure, how dear their dwelling-place.

And on that cheek, and o'er that brow,
  So soft, so calm, so eloquent,
The smiles that win, the tints that glow,
  But tell of days in goodness spent,
A mind at peace with all below,
  A heart whose love is innocent!

Byron

69

To Helen

Helen, thy beauty is to me
  Like those Nicæan barks of yore,
That gently, o'er a perfumed sea,
  The weary, wayworn wanderer bore
  To his own native shore.

On desperate seas long wont to roam,
  Thy hyacinth hair, thy classic face,
Thy Naiad airs have brought me home
  To the glory that was Greece
  And the grandeur that was Rome.

Lo! in yon brilliant window-niche
How statue-like I see thee stand,
The agate lamp within thy hand!
Ah, Psyche, from the regions which
Are Holy Land!

POE

70

THE SHEPHERD

How sweet is the shepherd's sweet lot!
From the morn to the evening he strays;
He shall follow his sheep all the day,
And his tongue shall be fillèd with praise.

For he hears the lambs' innocent call,
And he hears the ewes' tender reply;
He is watchful while they are in peace,
For they know when their shepherd is nigh.

WILLIAM BLAKE

71

WHEN I WAS ONE AND TWENTY

When I was one-and-twenty
I heard a wise man say,
'Give crowns and pounds and guineas
But not your heart away;
Give pearls away and rubies
But keep your fancy free.'
But I was one-and-twenty,
No use to talk to me.

When I was one-and-twenty
I heard him say again,
'The heart out of the bosom
Was never given in vain;
'Tis paid with sighs a-plenty
And sold for endless rue.'
And I am two-and-twenty,
And, oh, 'tis true, 'tis true.

A. E. HOUSMAN

72

HARVESTING A-SINGING

All ye that lovely lovers be,
Pray you for me:
Lo, here we come a-sowing, a-sowing,
And sow sweet fruits of love;
In your sweet hearts well may it prove!

Lo, here we come a-reaping, a-reaping,
To reap our harvest-fruit!
And thus we pass the year so long,
And never be we mute.

GEORGE PEELE

73

THE PEDLAR

Lend me, a little while, the key
    That locks your heavy heart, and I'll give you back—
Rarer than books and ribbons and beads bright to see,
    This little Key of Dreams out of my pack.

The road, the road, beyond men's bolted doors,
    There shall I walk and you go free of me,
For yours lies North across the moors,
    And mine South. To what sea?

How if we stopped and let our solemn selves go by,
    While my gay ghost caught and kissed yours, as ghosts
        don't do,
And by the wayside this forgotten you and I
    Sat, and were twenty-two?

Give me the key that locks your tired eyes,
    And I will lend you this one from my pack,
Brighter than coloured beads and painted books that make
        men wise:
    Take it. No, give it back!

CHARLOTTE MEW

74

Out Upon It, I Have Loved

Out upon it, I have loved
    Three whole days together!
And am like to love three more,
    If it prove fair weather.

Time shall moult away his wings
    Ere he shall discover
In the whole wide world again
    Such a constant lover.

But the spite on't is, no praise
    Is due at all to me:
Love with me had made no stays,
    Had it any been but she.

Had it any been but she,
    And that very face,
There had been at least ere this
    A dozen dozen in her place.

              Sir John Suckling

75

Mending Wall

Something there is that doesn't love a wall,
That sends the frozen-ground-swell under it,
And spills the upper boulders in the sun;
And makes gaps even two can pass abreast.
The work of hunters is another thing:
I have come after them and made repair
Where they have left not one stone on a stone,
But they would have the rabbit out of hiding,
To please the yelping dogs. The gaps I mean,
No one has seen them made or heard them made,
But at spring mending-time we find them there.
I let my neighbour know beyond the hill;
And on a day we meet to walk the line

And set the wall between us once again.
We keep the wall between us as we go.
To each the boulders that have fallen to each.
And some are loaves and some so nearly balls
We have to use a spell to make them balance:
"Stay where you are until our backs are turned!"
We wear our fingers rough with handling them.
Oh, just another kind of out-door game,
One on a side. It comes to little more:
There where it is we do not need the wall:
He is all pine and I am apple orchard.
My apple trees will never get across
And eat the cones under his pines, I tell him.
He only says, "Good fences make good neighbours."
Spring is the mischief in me, and I wonder
If I could put a notion in his head:
"*Why* do they make good neighbors? Isn't it
Where there are cows? But here there are no cows.
Before I built a wall I'd ask to know
What I was walling in or walling out,
And to whom I was like to give offence.
Something there is that doesn't love a wall,
That wants it down." I could say "Elves" to him,
But it's not elves exactly, and I'd rather
He said it for himself. I see him there
Bringing a stone grasped firmly by the top
In each hand, like an old-stone savage armed.
He moves in darkness as it seems to me,
Not of woods only and the shade of trees.
He will not go behind his father's saying,
And he likes having thought of it so well
He says again, "Good fences make good neighbours."

ROBERT FROST

76

A SONG OF WALES

Oh, some men pine for the South Country,
And some for the mellow West,
And some fare out on the wide sea
For the dreams that bring them rest,

But give to me the old road that winds through town
    and shire
Across the bar of the Severn Sea to the land of my
    desire.

And some men sing of a cloudless sky
And the blue of a Southern day,
But—oh—for me the wind's cry
At night by a lonely bay,
With wreathing mists on the high hills that laugh above
    the rain
Away in the land of the golden heart that I must see
    again.

Oh, some men go to the ends of earth
For a heritage proud and fine,
But give to me the deep mirth
Of the songs that flow like wine,
The old, thatched farm and the peat-fires that glimmer
    through the night
In the land of the little fairy-folk, the land of my de-
    light.

And there shall I find harping strings
And silver rhymes and old,
And precious, half-forgotten things,
And hearts which grow not cold,
And the healing peace of the mountains, and the gleam of
    the lowland corn,
And the voices out of the twilight—in the land where
    I was born.

A. G. Prys-Jones

77

Autumn Days

The dizzy wind of ambient autumn days
Blows o'er the hills. It seeks me in byways
And lanes, and rushes on me unaware.
It sets the whirlwind dancing with bright leaves,
And sends the robin headlong through the purple air.

It calls to the heart in cheery tones.
　　It shouts with a rollicking glee.
Then it pauses to whisper of fairer zones
　　That lie o'er a fairer sea,
Charming the bird from its withered nest
　　With a wondrous melody.
It paints a red on the sumach's vest,
And gives to the fields a golden crest
　　To tempt the laggard bee.
　　　　　Heigho!

The circle of the year is almost done.
The days have been too gladding swift to run
From springtime back to autumn, too quick to crown
　　The sower's faith with harvest. Come, a dance,
A giddy, whirling dance, before the frost steals down.
Underneath the maple trees,
　　Underneath the oak,
Breaking through the brambles
　　Into dells that cloak
The haw and ripened hazel-nut
　　And milk-weed's feathery smoke.
Up a bank and o'er a ditch
　　And down a winding way
To come upon a flock of crows
　　When each would have his say,
To chase a squirrel through the fence
　　And fright a chattering jay.
So past a field, across a brook,
　　And up a little hill.
Then for a moment pause for breath,
　　But not for want of will.
　　　　　Heigho!

For I am drunk with joy of life and limb.
The summer's store is garnered to the brim,
The yesterdays of toil are past, and give
A respite brief. Another draft! Drink deep
While autumn pours its wine, so rare, so fugitive!
　　　Drink deep!

CARY F. JACOB

78

Alas, that Spring should vanish with the Rose!
That Youth's sweet-scented Manuscript should close!
    The Nightingale that in the Branches sang,
Ah, whence, and whither flown again, who knows!

Ah, Love! could thou and I with Fate conspire
To grasp this sorry Scheme of Things entire,
    Would not we shatter it to bits—and then
Re-mould it nearer to the Heart's Desire!

Ah, Moon of my Delight who know'st no wane,
The Moon of Heav'n is rising once again:
    How oft hereafter rising shall she look
Through this same Garden after me—in vain.

And when Thyself with shining Foot shall pass
Among the Guests Star-scatter'd on the Grass,
    And in thy joyous Errand reach the Spot
Where I made one—turn down an empty Glass!

Rubáiyát of Omar Khayyám

79

Behold, a king shall reign in righteousness, and princes shall rule in judgment.

And a man shall be as an hiding place from the wind, and a covert from the tempest; as rivers of water in a dry place, as the shadow of a great rock in a weary land.

Isaiah, xxxi

80

But where shall wisdom be found? and where is the place of understanding?

Man knoweth not the price thereof; neither is it found in the land of the living.

The depth saith, It is not in me: and the sea saith, It is not with me.

It cannot be gotten for gold, neither shall silver be weighed for the price thereof.

It cannot be valued with the gold of Ophir, with the precious onyx, or the sapphire.

The gold and the crystal cannot equal it: and the exchange of it shall not be for jewels of fine gold.

No mention shall be made of coral, or of pearls: for the price of wisdom is above rubies.

The topaz of Ethiopia shall not equal it, neither shall it be valued with pure gold.

Whence then cometh wisdom? and where is the place of understanding?

Seeing it is hid from the eyes of all living, and kept close from the fowls of the air.

Destruction and death say, We have heard the fame thereof with our ears.

God understandeth the way thereof, and he knoweth the place thereof.

For he looketh to the ends of the earth, and seeth under the whole heaven;

To make the weight for the winds; and he weigheth the waters by measure.

When he made a decree for the rain, and a way for the lightning of the thunder:

Then did he see it, and declare it; he prepared it, yea, and searched it out.

And unto man he said, Behold, the fear of the Lord, that is wisdom; and to depart from evil is understanding.

Job, xxviii

81

A thousand years in thy sight are but as yesterday when it is past, and as a watch in the night.

Psalm XC

82

And Ahimaaz called, and said unto the king, All is well. And he fell down to the earth upon his face before the king, and said, Blessed be the Lord thy God, which hath delivered up the men that lifted up their hand against my lord the king.

And the king said, Is the young man Absalom safe? And

Ahimaaz answered, When Joab sent the king's servant, and me thy servant, I saw a great tumult, but I knew not what it was.

And the king said unto him, Turn aside, and stand here. And he turned aside, and stood still.

And behold, Cushi came; and Cushi said, Tidings my lord the king: for the Lord hath avenged thee this day of all them that rose up against thee.

And the king said unto Cushi, Is the young man Absalom safe? And Cushi answered, The enemies of my lord the king, and all that rise against thee to do thee hurt, be as that young man is.

And the king was much moved, and went up to the chamber over the gate, and wept: and as he went, thus he said, O my son Absalom, my son, my son, Absalom! would God I had died for thee, O Absalom, my son, my son!

II Samuel, xviii

83

On, on, on, over the countless miles of angry space roll the long heaving billows. Mountains and caves are here, and yet are not; for what is now the one, is now the other; then all is but a boiling heap of rushing water. Pursuit, and flight, and mad return of wave on wave, and savage struggle, ending in a spouting-up of foam that whitens the black night; incessant change of place, and form, and hue; constancy in nothing, but eternal strife; on, on, on, they roll, and darker grows the night, and louder howls the wind, and more clamorous and fierce become the million voices in the sea, when the wild cry goes forth upon the storm, "A ship!"

Onward she comes, in gallant combat with the elements, her tall masts trembling, and her timbers starting from the strain; onward she comes, now high upon the curling billows, now low down in the hollows of the sea, as hiding for the moment from its fury; and every storm-voice in the air and water cries more loudly yet, "A ship."

DICKENS, *Martin Chuzzlewit*

84

Yet day by day Tristan's sorrow grew heavier; he desired but one Iseult, Iseult of Ireland; and Iseult of the white hand, she

would have none but Tristan. Her heart and soul were his, his
grief was hers, and she saw him grow pale and sigh for sorrow,
so she herself sighed and grew pale, till at length she shewed
her love to him so openly, in sweet gestures, looks, and words,
that he scarce knew what he might do, and his heart was tossed
on a sea of doubt.

And as time passed on, and never word or message came from
Queen Iseult, he began to think whether his sorrow and his faith
were not all in vain. . . .

Thus his doubt of Iseult of Ireland, and the love shewn him
by Iseult of the white hand, wrought on Tristan's heart, and
vexed him day and night, till at last, for the friendship he bare
to her brother, and for the sweetness and beauty of Iseult the
maiden, he determined to wed her. So the duke proclaimed a
great feast, and the folk came from far and wide, and Iseult
of the white hand and Tristan were made man and wife by
the bishop of the land, in the Minster at Karke. And yet, for
the love which he bare to Iseult of Ireland, which might not be
stilled, was she but his wife in name. . . . [Here follows an
account of how Tristan was wounded with a poisoned arrow in
combat with a traitor knight.]

Iseult of the white hand dressed Tristan's wound, and bade
the leeches of the land do what they might to heal him, but
nought that they might do was of any avail, for the venom was
so potent their skill might not prevail against it.

Then Tristan saw well how it stood with him, and he said
to himself: "Now might I but send to my lady Iseult, methinks
she would cure me now, even as her mother did aforetime, otherwise must I die of this hurt." Then secretly he sent for Kurwenal,
and prayed him to go with all speed to Tintagel and seek out
Iseult the queen. "Bear with thee this ring, and shew it to her
as a token from me, and say how that I lie sorely wounded, and
must needs die an she come not to mine aid. And if for love
of me she will come, then I pray thee to set a white sail to
the ship; but if she cometh not, then let the sail be black, for
I shall know she loveth me no more."

Then Kurwenal departed, even as Tristan bade him, and
came to Tintagel, and told Iseult the queen secretly all that
Tristan had bade him say. She made ready in haste, and wrapped
her in her veil, and stole to the harbour, and sailed away ere
any might know of it.

Now Tristan bade them bear him day by day to the shore

that he might watch for the ship from Cornwall till his weakness grew so great he might do so no longer; then he bade his wife, Iseult, watch from the window of his chamber and bear him tidings when Kurwenal should return.

But Iseult of the white hand had hearkened secretly when her husband spake to Kurwenal, and her heart was hot within her for anger 'gainst the other Iseult, for she knew well who it was that Tristan loved. So when at last she spied the ship that bare Iseult the queen thither, she said to her husband: "Yonder cometh the ship wherein Kurwenal sailed hence."

"What manner of sail doth it bear?" spake Tristan.

" 'Tis black as night," answered Iseult of the white hand, yet she lied, for the sail was white as snow.

Then Tristan spake no word, but turned his face to the wall, and said in his heart: "God keep thee, my love Iseult, for I shall look on thee no more," and with that he loosed his hold of the life he had held till then, and his soul departed.

Tristan and Iseult

85

La Gioconda is, in the truest sense, Leonardo's masterpiece, the revealing instance of his mode of thought and work. In suggestiveness, only the Melancholia of Dürer is comparable to it; and no crude symbolism disturbs the effect of its subdued and graceful mystery. We all know the face and hands of the figure, set in its marble chair, in that circle of fantastic rocks, as in some faint light under sea. Perhaps of all ancient pictures time has chilled it least. (Yet for Vasari there was some further magic of crimson in the lips and cheeks, lost for us.) As often happens with works in which invention seems to reach its limit, there is an element in it given to, not invented by, the master. In that inestimable folio of drawings, once in the possession of Vasari, were certain designs by Verrocchio, faces of such impressive beauty that Leonardo in his boyhood copied them many times. It is hard not to connect with these designs of the elder, by-past master, as with its germinal principle, the unfathomable smile, always with a touch of something sinister in it, which plays over all Leonardo's work. Besides, the picture is a portrait. From childhood we see this image defining itself on the fabric of his dreams; and but for express historical testimony, we might fancy that this was but his ideal lady, embodied and beheld at last. What was the relationship of a living Florentine to this creature of his thought? By what strange affinities had the dream and the person grown up thus apart, and yet so closely together? Present from the first incorporeally in Leonardo's brain, dimly traced in the designs of Verrocchio, she is found present at last in Il Giocondo's house. That there is much of mere portraiture in the picture is attested by the legend that by artificial means, the presence of mimes and flute-players, that subtle expression was protracted on the face. Again, was it in four years and by renewed labour never really completed, or in four months and as by stroke of magic, that the image was projected?

The presence that rose thus so strangely beside the waters, is expressive of what in the ways of a thousand years men had come to desire. Hers is the head upon which all the ends of the world are come, and the eyelids are a little weary. It is a beauty wrought out from within upon the flesh, the deposit, little cell by cell, of strange thoughts and fantastic reveries and exquisite passions. Set it for a moment beside one of those white Greek goddesses or beautiful women of antiquity, and how would they be troubled by this beauty, into which the soul with all its maladies has passed! All the thoughts and experience of the world have etched and moulded there, in that which they have of power to refine and make expressive the outward form, the animalism of Greece, the lust of Rome, the mysticism of the middle age with its spiritual ambition and imaginative loves, the return of the Pagan world, the sins of the Borgias. She is older than the rocks among which she sits; like the vampire, she has been dead many times, and learned the secrets of the grave; has been a diver in deep seas, and keeps their fallen day about her; and trafficked for strange webs with Eastern merchants; and, as Leda, was the mother of Helen of Troy, and, as Saint Anne, the mother of Mary; and all this has been to her but as the sound of lyres and flutes, and lives only in the delicacy with which it has moulded the changing lineaments, and tinged the eyelids and the hands. The fancy of a perpetual life, sweeping together ten thousand experiences, is an old one; and modern philosophy has conceived the idea of humanity as wrought upon by, and summing up in itself, all modes of thought and life. Certainly Lady Lisa might stand as the embodiment of the old fancy, the symbol of the modern idea.

WALTER PATER

86

On First Looking into Chapman's Homer

Much have I travell'd in the realms of gold,
    And many goodly states and kingdoms seen;
    Round many western islands have I been
Which bards in fealty to Apollo hold.
Oft of one wide expanse had I been told
    That deep-brow'd Homer ruled as his demesne;
    Yet did I never breathe its pure serene
Till I heard Chapman speak out loud and bold:
Then felt I like some watcher of the skies
    When a new planet swims into his ken;
Or like stout Cortez, when with eagle eyes
    He stared at the Pacific—and all his men
Look'd at each other with a wild surmise—
    Silent, upon a peak in Darien.

Keats

87

On the Road to Tchi-Li

I sit by the wayside on a fallen tree,
and gaze along the road
that stretches before me to Tchi-Li.

This morning
the blue satin of my shoes glistened like steel,
and one could see the black-embroidered traceries;
but now my shoes are covered with dust.

When I set out
the sun was laughing in the sky,
the butterflies hovered around me,
and I counted the white daisies,
scattered through the grass
like handfuls of pearls.

It is evening now,
and there are no daisies.

Swallows dart by swiftly at my feet;
crows are calling each other to rest,
and labourers are entering the villages near by,
with their plaits wrapped round their heads.

But for me there are many miles to go;
I will compose a poem,
as full of sadness as my lonely heart,
and with a rhythm so difficult
that the road to Tchi-Li will seem too short.

TIN-TUN-LING

88

SONNET PREFACED TO HIS TRANSLATION OF DANTE

Oft have I seen at some cathedral door
A laborer, pausing in the dust and heat,
Lay down his burden, and with reverent feet
Enter, and cross himself, and on the floor
Kneel to repeat his paternoster o'er;
Far off the noises of the world retreat;
The loud vociferations of the street
Become an undistinguishable roar.
So, as I enter here from day to day,
And leave my burden at this minster gate,
Kneeling in prayer, and not ashamed to pray,
The tumult of the time disconsolate
To inarticulate murmurs dies away,
While the eternal ages watch and wait.

LONGFELLOW

89

When I have seen by Time's fell hand defaced
The rich-proud cost of outworn buried age;
When sometime lofty towers I see down-razed
And brass eternal slave to mortal rage;
When I have seen the hungry ocean gain
Advantage on the kingdom of the shore,
And the firm soil win of the watery main,
Increasing store with loss and loss with store;

When I have seen such interchange of state,
Or state itself confounded to decay;
Ruin hath taught me thus to ruminate,
That Time will come and take my love away.
This thought is as a death, which cannot choose
But weep to have that which it fears to lose.

SHAKESPEARE

C. SELECTIONS ILLUSTRATING MAINLY THE NARRATIVE APPROACH

90

pliːz gʊd

wʌn naıt ðə koʊdʒə wəz tʃætıŋ wıð (h)ız waıf | ənd sed ‖
təmɒroʊ | ıf ðə weðər ız wet | aım goʊıŋ aʊt tə kʌt wʊd ‖ bət ıf
ıts faın | aı ʃəl wɜː(r)k ın maı vınjə(r)d |·|

seı¹ pliːz gʊd | ɪʋen ju tɔːk laık ðæt ‖ səd ʃiː |·|
nɒt ət ɔːl | səd (h)i ‖ aı ʃəl sɜː(r)tnlı du wʌn ə(r) ðı ʌðə(r) |·|
æz hi wəz liːvıŋ ðə taʊn¹ nekst mɒː(r)nıŋ | tə goʊ tʊ (h)ız
vınjə(r)d | hı met ə truːp əv soʊldʒə(r)z |·| wʌn əv ðəm kɔːld tʊ
(h)ım ‖ oʊld mæn | kəm hıə(r) ənd ʃoʊ əs ðə weı tə kærəbæʃ |·|

ðə koʊdʒə ansə(r)d rʌflı ‖ aı doʊnt noʊ ıt |·|
haı ‖ ðeı kraıd | ju ımpjudənt feloʊ |·| ənd bıfʋə(r) (bıfoə(r))
ðə koʊdʒə kəd faınd taım tə spiːk | ðeı bıgæn tə biːt (h)ım |·|
ðæt wıl tiːtʃ ju ə lesn |·| naʊ ʃoʊ əs ðə weı |·| ənd ðeı droʊv
(h)ım əlɒŋ¹ əz (h)i ræn beə(r)fʊt ın frʌnt əv ðəm |·|

ıt bıgæn tə reın | ənd hi wəz kwaıt wet bıfʋə(r) hi riːtʃt ðə
vılıdʒ |·| hi gɒt hoʊm ət mıdnaıt | fʊtsʋə(r) | tɜː | ənd koʊld |·|
ɪʋen hi nɒkt ət ðə dʋə(r) | hız waıf kɔːld aʊt | huːz ðeə(r) |·|
hi ansə(r)d | maı lıtl waıf | pliːz gʊd | ıts aı |·|

—ðə koʊdʒə—transleıtıd frəm ðə pɜː(r)ʒən baı henrı baı(r)nəm.

91

soʊʃəl səkses

ðə sɜː(r)vənt geıv mi maı koʊt ənd hæt | ənd ın ə gloʊ əv self-
sætısfækʃən | aı wɔːkt aʊt ıntʊ ðə naıt |·|
ə dılaıtfəl iːvnıŋ | aı rıflɛktıd ‖ ðə naısıst kaınd əv piːpl |·| hʋɒt
aı sed əbaʊt fınans | ənd frenʒ fılɒsʋfı | ımprest ðəm ‖ ənd haʊ ðeı
laft ɪʋen aı ımıteıtıd ə pıg skwiːlıŋ |·|
bət suːn aftə(r) ‖ oʊ | ıts ɔıfəl | aı mʌtə(r)d ‖ aı wıʃ aı wə(r) dɛd |·|

92

ðə koʊdʒəz driːm

wʌn naɪt ðə koʊdʒə dremt¹ ðət ə mæn geɪv (h)ɪm naɪn goʊld
piːsɪz ‖ ənd ðə næt hɪ bɪgæn tʊ hægl ‖ ənd sed tʊ (h)ɪm ‖ ju maɪt ət
liːst əv meɪd ɪt ten |·|

ət ðɪs pɔɪnt hɪ woʊk ʌp | ənd faɪndɪŋ ðət (ðeə(r) wəz nʌθɪŋ ɪn ðe
(h)ɪz hænd | hi ʃʌt (h)ɪz aɪz verɪ taɪt | ənd riːtʃt tʊ (h)ɪz hænd |
seɪɪŋ ‖ verɪ wel | brɪŋ ðəm hɪə(r) ‖ aɪl teɪk naɪn |·|

93

ðə koʊdʒə æz ə letə(r) raɪtə(r)

ə mæn keɪm tʊ ðə koʊdʒə | ənd sed | du mi ə feɪvə(r) ‖ aɪ wɒnt
ju tə raɪt ə letə(r) fə(r) mi¹ tʊ ə frend ɪn bægdæd |·|

oʊ doʊnt bʊðə(r) mi | sed (h)i |·| aɪv noʊ taɪm nɑʊ tə goʊ tə
bægdæd |·|

hi wəz wɜːkɪŋ ʃf | lʊen ðə mæn ræn aftər | ənd stʊpt (h)ɪm |·|

maɪ dɪə(r) koʊdʒə | sed (h)i ‖ lʊaɪ ʃəd jʊə(r) raɪtɪŋ ðɪs letə(r)
meɪk ɪt nesəserɪ (nesəserɪ) tə goʊ tə bægdæd? |·|

ðə koʊdʒə ansə(r)d ‖ ðeə(r)z nʌθɪŋ streɪndʒ əbaʊt ɪt |·| maɪ
hændraɪtɪŋ ɪz verɪ bæd |·| aɪm ðɪ oʊnlɪ pɜː(r)sn¹ hu kn riːd ɪt |·|
soʊ ðət ɪf aɪ raɪt ə letə(r) fə(r) ju | aɪ məst bi ðeə(r) tə riːd ənd
ɪkspleɪn ɪt |·|

94

tuː men keɪm bɪfʊə ðə dʒʌdʒ ənd pliːdɪd əz fɒloʊz ‖

pleɪntɪf ‖ ″ jʊər ɒnə | θɪs mæn hæd ə loʊd əv wʊd ɒn (h)ɪz bæk |
ənd əz (h)ɪ wəz wɜːkɪŋ əlɒŋ | hɪz fʊt slɪpt ‖ hi fel ‖ ənd iː ðə wʊd
keɪm dɑʊn wɪð (h)ɪm |·| hi begd mi tə pʊt ɪt ɒn (h)ɪz bæk əgen |
ənd aɪ askt (h)ɪm lʊɒt (h)ɪ wʊd peɪ mɪ fə duːɪŋ ɪt |·| hi ansəd |
′nʌθɪŋ′ ‖ aɪ sed | ɔɪl raɪt | aɪ əgriː tə du ɪt fə ′nʌθɪŋ′ ‖ ənd aɪ
pʊt ðə wʊd ɒn (h)ɪz bæk |·| aɪ ðen askt (h)ɪm fə peɪmənt əv
′nʌθɪŋ″ | ənd (h)ɪ wɪl nɒt gɪv ɪt mi |·| jʊər ɒnə | aɪ dɪmand maɪ
raɪts ‖ let (h)ɪm peɪ mi ′ nʌθɪŋ ′hɪər ənd nɑʊ″ |·|

ðə dʒʌdʒ ɔɪlwɪz hændɪd oʊvə delɪkət kwestʃənz laɪk θɪs | tu ɑʊə
frend ðə koʊdʒə | hu | hævɪŋ lɪsənd ətentɪvlɪ | sed | ″ jʊə kleɪm ɪz
dʒʌst | hi mʌst kiːp (h)ɪz wɜːd | hi ʃæl peɪ ″ |·|

ðɛn pɔɪntɪŋ tə ðə rʌg ɒn ðə dɪvæn¹ hi sɛd tə ðə kleɪmənt |
" dʒʌst lɪft ðæt rʌg ə bɪt ənd tɛl mi hʊɒt ɪz ʌndər ɪt " |·|

ðə mæn lʊkt ənd ansəd || " nʌθɪŋ " |·|

" hʋaɪ " | sɛd hi | " ðæt ɪz hʊɒt ju wɒnt || teɪk ɪt ənd goʊ " |·|

95

ðə skɔɪldɪŋ suɪp

wʌn deɪ ðə koʊdʒəz waɪf | biːɪŋ ɪn ə bæd tɛmpə | pʊt ðə suɪp
ɒn ðə teɪbl skɔɪldɪŋ hɒt |·|

aftər ə hʋaɪ ʃɪ fəgʊt ðət ɪt wəz soʊ hɒt ənd swɒloʊd ə spuːnfʊl |·|
ðə peɪn meɪd ər aɪz fɪl wɪð tɪəz |·|

ðə koʊdʒə askt hə hʋaɪ ʃɪ wəz kraɪɪŋ wɪðaʊt əpeərənt riːzn ||
ənd ʃɪ sɛd | " maɪ pʊə mʌðə wəz vɛrɪ fɒnd əv ðɪs suɪp || aɪ rɪmɛmbəd
ɪt ənd ðæt meɪd mi kraɪ " |·|

ðə koʊdʒə ət wʌns tʊk ə spuːnfʊl wɪð greɪt rɪspɛkt | ənd swɒloʊd
ɪt || ənd hɪz aɪz ɔɪlsoʊ fɪld wɪð tɪəz |·|

" hʋɒt ɪz rɒŋ? " | sɛd (h)ɪz waɪf | " hʋaɪ ə juː tuː kraɪɪŋ? " |·|

" aɪ əm kraɪɪŋ " | sɛd (h)i | " ðət jʊər ʌnlʌkɪ mʌðə ʃəd əv daɪd |
ənd ə retʃ laɪk ju bɪ stɪl əlaɪv " |·|

96

ðə paɪpɪŋ fɪʃə(r)mən

ən edɪtə(r) hu wəz ɔːlwɪz vɔɪntɪŋ ðə pjʊərɪtɪ | entə(r)praɪz | ənd
fɪə(r)lɪsnɪs | əv (h)ɪz peɪpə(r) | wəz peɪnd tʊ əbzəːt(r)v ðət hɪ gɒt
noʊ səbskraɪbə(r)z |·| wʌn deɪ ɪt əkəːr(r)d tʊ hɪm tə stɒp seɪɪŋ ðət
hɪz peɪpə(r) wəz pjʊə(r) | ənd entə(r)praɪzɪŋ | ənd fɪə(r)lɪs || ənd
meɪk ɪt soʊ |·| ɪf ðɪz ə(r) nɒt gʊd kwɒlɪtɪz | hi riːznd || ɪt ɪz fɒlɪ
tə kleɪm ðəm |·|

ʌndə(r) ðə nju: pɒlɪsɪ | hɪ gɒt soʊ mɛnɪ səbskraɪbə(r)z | ðət hɪz
raɪvəlz əndevə(r)d tə dɪskʌvə(r) ðə siːkrɪt əv hɪz prɒsperɪtɪ || bət
hɪ kɛpt ɪt || ənd hʋɛn (h)i daɪd | ɪt daɪd wɪð (h)ɪm |·|

97

ðə dɒlz haʊs

'ðɛə 'stʊd ðə 'dɒlz 'haʊs | ə 'daɪk | 'hɪlɪ | 'spɪnɪdʒ 'griːn | 'pɪkt
'aʊt wɪð brait 'jɛloʊ |·| ɪts 'tuː 'sɒlɪd 'lɪtl 'tʃɪmnɪz | 'gluɪd 'ɒntʊ ðə

ˈruːf | wə ˈpeɪntɪd ˈrɛd ənd ˈʰwaɪt || ənd ðə ˈdɒə | ˈgliːmɪŋ wɪð ˈjeloʊ
ˈvɑːnɪʃ | wəz ˈlaɪk ə ˈlɪtl ˈslæb əv ˈtɒfɪ |·| ˈfɔə ˈwɪndoʊz || ˈrɪəl ˈwɪn-
doʊz || wə dɪˈvaɪdɪd ɪntə ˈpeɪnz baɪ ə ˈbrɔːd ˈstriːk əv ˈgriːn |·|ˏðə
wəz ˈæktʃʊəlɪ ə taɪnɪ ˈpɔətʃ | ˈtuː | ˈpeɪntɪd ˈjeloʊ | wɪð ˈbɪg ˈlʌmps
əv ˈkəndʒiːld ˈpeɪnt ˈhæŋɪŋ əˈlɒŋ ðɪ ˈɛdʒ |·|

ðə ˈhʊk ət ðə ˈsaɪd wəz ˈstʌk ˈfast |·| ˈpæt ˈpraɪd ɪt ˈoʊpn wɪð ɪz
ˈpɛnnaɪf || ənd ðə ˈhoʊl ˈhaʊsˈfrʌnt ˈswʌŋ ˈbæk || ənd | ˈðɛə jʊ
ˈwɜɪ | ˈgeɪzɪŋ ət ˈwʌn ənd ðə ˈseɪm ˈmoʊmənt | ɪntʊ ðə ˈdrɔɪŋrum
ənd ˈdaɪnɪŋrum | ðə ˈkɪtʃən ənd ˈtuː ˈbedrumz |·| ˈðæts ðə ˈweɪ fər
ə ˈhaʊs tʊ ˈoʊpn! |·| ˈʰwaɪ doʊnt ˈɔːl ˈhaʊzɪz ˈoʊpn laɪk ˈðæt? |·|
haʊ ˈmʌtʃ mər ˈɪksaɪtɪŋ ðən ˈpɪərɪŋ ðru ðə ˈslɪt əv ə dʊər ɪntʊ ə
miːn ˈlɪtl ˈhɔːl | wɪð ə ˈhætˈstænd ənd ˈtuː ʌmˈbrɛləz! || ˈðæt ɪz |
ˈɪznt ɪt? || ˈhʊʊt jʊ ˈlɒŋ tə ˈnoʊ əˈbaʊt ə haʊs | ˈhʊen jʊ ˈpʊt jə ˈhænd
ɒn ðə ˈnɒkə |·| pəˈhæps ɪts ðə ˈweɪ ˈgɒd ˈoʊpnz ˈhaʊzɪz | ət ˈded
əv ˈnaɪt | ʰʊen (h)ɪz ˈteɪkɪŋ ə ˈkwaɪət ˈtɜɪn wɪð ən ˈeɪndʒəl |·|

When dear Old Mrs. Hay went back to town after staying
with the Burnells she sent the children a doll's house. It was so
big that the carter and Pat carried it into the court yard, and
there it stayed, propped up on two wooden boxes beside the
feed-room door. No harm could come to it; it was summer.
And perhaps the smell of paint would have gone off by the
time it had to be taken in. For, really, the smell of paint coming
from that doll's house (Sweet of old Mrs. Hay, of course, most
sweet and generous!)—but the smell of paint was quite enough
to make any one seriously ill, in Aunt Beryl's opinion. Even before the sacking was taken off. And when it was . . .

There stood the doll's house, a dark, oily, spinach green,
picked out with bright yellow. Its two solid little chimneys
glued on to the roof, were painted red and white, and the door,
gleaming with yellow varnish, was like a little slab of toffee.
Four windows, real windows, were divided into panes by a broad
streak of green. There was actually a tiny porch, too, painted
yellow, with big lumps of congealed paint hanging along the
edge.

But perfect, perfect little house! Who could possibly mind the
smell? It was part of the joy, part of the newness.

"Open it quickly, some one!"

The hook at the side was stuck fast. Pat pried it open with
his penknife, and the whole house-front swung back, and—

there you were, gazing at one and the same moment into the drawing-room and dining-room, the kitchen and two bedrooms. That is the way for a house to open! Why don't all houses open like that? How much more exciting than peering through the slit of a door into a mean little hall with a hatstand and two umbrellas! That is—isn't it?—what you long to know about a house when you put your hand on the knocker. Perhaps it is the way God opens houses at dead of night when He is taking a quiet turn with an angel . . .

"O-oh!" The Burnell children sounded as though they were in despair. It was too marvelous. All the rooms were papered. Red carpet covered all the floors except the kitchen; red plush chairs in the drawing-room, and green in the dining-room; tables, beds with real bedclothes, a cradle, a stove, a dresser with tiny plates and one big jug.

But what Kezia liked more than anything, what she liked frightfully was the lamp. It stood in the middle of the dining-room table, an exquisite little amber lamp with a white globe. It was even filled all ready for lighting, though, of course, you couldn't light it.

The father and mother dolls, who sprawled very stiff as though they had fainted in the drawing-room, and their two little children asleep upstairs, were really too big for the doll's house. They didn't look as though they belonged. But the lamp was perfect. It seemed to smile at Kezia, to say, "I live here"; the lamp was real.

The Burnell children could hardly walk to school fast enough the next morning. They burned to tell everybody, to describe, to—well—to boast about their doll's house before the school-bell rang.

"I'm to tell," said Isabel, "because I'm the eldest. And you can join in after. But I'm to tell first." There was nothing to answer. Isabel was bossy, but she was always right.

KATHERINE MANSFIELD, "The Doll's House"

99

PROUD MAISIE

Proud Maisie is in the wood,
   Walking so early;
Sweet Robin sits on the bush,
   Singing so rarely.

"Tell me, thou bonny bird,
  When shall I marry me?"
"When six braw gentlemen
  Kirkward shall carry ye."

"Who makes the bridal bed,
  Birdie, say truly?"
"The gray-headed sexton
  That delves the grave duly.

"The glow-worm o'er grave and stone
  Shall light thee steady;
The owl from the steeple sing,
  Welcome, proud lady!"

SIR WALTER SCOTT

100

BREDON HILL

In summertime on Bredon
  The bells they sound so clear;
Round both the shires they ring them
  In steeples far and near,
  A happy noise to hear.

Here of a Sunday morning
  My love and I would lie,
And see the coloured counties,
  And hear the larks so high
  About us in the sky.

The bells would ring to call her
  In valleys miles away:
"Come all to church, good people;
  Good people, come and pray."
  But here my love and I would stay.

And I would turn and answer
  Among the springing thyme,
"Oh, peal upon our wedding,
  And we will hear the chime,
  And come to church in time."

But when the snows at Christmas
  On Bredon top were strown,
My love rose up so early
  And stole out unbeknown
  And went to church alone.

They tolled the one bell only,
  Groom there was none to see,
The mourners follow'd after,
  And so to church went she,
  And would not wait for me.

The bells they sound on Bredon,
  And still the steeples hum,
"Come all to church, good people,"—
  Oh, noisy bells, be dumb;
  I hear you, I will come.

A. E. Housman

101

Helen of Kirconnell

I wish I were where Helen lies,
Night and day on me she cries;
O that I were where Helen lies,
  On fair Kirconnell lea!

Curst be the heart that thought the thought,
And curst the hand that fired the shot,
When in my arms burd Helen dropt,
  And died to succour me!

O think na ye my heart was sair,
When my Love dropp'd and spak nae mair!
There did she swoon wi' meikle care,
  On fair Kirconnell lea.

As I went down the water side,
None but my foe to be my guide,
None but my foe to be my guide,
  On fair Kirconnell lea;

I lighted down my sword to draw,
I hackèd him in pieces sma',
I hackèd him in pieces sma',
    For her sake that died for me.

O Helen fair, beyond compare!
I'll mak a garland o' thy hair,
Shall bind my heart for evermair,
    Until the day I dee!

O that I were where Helen lies!
Night and day on me she cries;
Out of my bed she bids me rise,
    Says, "Haste, and come to me!"

O Helen fair! O Helen chaste!
If I were with thee, I'd be blest,
Where thou lies low and taks thy rest,
    On fair Kirconnell lea.

I wish my grave were growing green,
A winding-sheet drawn owre my e'en,
And I in Helen's arms lying
    On fair Kirconnell lea.

I wish I were where Helen lies!
Night and day on me she cries;
And I am weary of the skies,
    For her sake that died for me.

102

CUPID AND CAMPASPE

Cupid and my Campaspe play'd
At cards for kisses; Cupid paid:
He stakes his quiver, bow, and arrows,
His mother's doves, and team of sparrows;
Loses them too; then down he throws
The coral of his lip, the rose
Growing on's cheek (but none knows how);

With these, the crystal of his brow,
And then the dimple on his chin;
All these did my Campaspe win.
At last he set her both his eyes—
She won, and Cupid blind did rise.
O Love! has she done this to thee?
What shall, alas! become of me?

JOHN LYLY

103

LUCY

She dwelt among the untrodden ways
    Beside the springs of Dove,
A Maid whom there were none to praise
    And very few to love:

A violet by a mossy stone
    Half hidden from the eye!
Fair as a star, when only one
    Is shining in the sky.

She lived unknown, and few could know
    When Lucy ceased to be;
But she is in her grave, and oh,
    The difference to me!

WORDSWORTH

104

THE ARRIVAL OF BLACKMAN'S WARBLER

I am become an Authority on Birds. It happened in this way.
The other day we heard the cuckoo in Hampshire. (The next
morning the papers announced that the cuckoo had been heard
in Devonshire—possibly a different one, but in no way superior
to ours except in the matter of its press agent.) Well, everybody in the house said, "Did you hear the cuckoo?" to everybody else, until I began to get rather tired of it; and, having
told everybody several times that I *had* heard it, I tried to
make the conversation more interesting. So, after my tenth "Yes"
I added quite casually:

"But I haven't heard the tufted pipit yet. It's funny why it should be so late this year."

"Is that the same as the tree pipit?" said my hostess, who seemed to know more about birds than I had hoped.

"Oh, no," I said confidently.

"What's the difference exactly?"

"Well, one is tufted," I said, doing my best, "and the other —er—climbs trees."

"Oh, I see."

"And of course the eggs are more speckled," I added, gradually acquiring confidence.

"I often wish I knew more about birds," she said regretfully. "You must tell us something about them now we've got you here."

And all this because of one miserable cuckoo!

"By all means," I said, wondering how long it would take to get a book about birds down from London.

However, it was easier than I thought. We had tea in the garden that afternoon, and a bird of some kind struck up in the plane-tree.

"There, now," said my hostess, "what's that?"

I listened with my head on one side. The bird said it again.

"That's the lesser bunting," I said hopefully.

"The lesser bunting," said an earnest-looking girl; "I shall always remember that."

I hoped she wouldn't, but I could hardly say so. Fortunately, the bird lesser-bunted again, and I seized the opportunity of playing for safety.

"Or is it the Sardinian white-throat?" I wondered. "They have very much the same note during the breeding season. But, of course, the eggs are more speckled," I added casually.

And so on for the rest of the evening. You see how easy it is.

However, the next afternoon a most unfortunate occurrence occurred. A real Bird Authority came to tea. As soon as the information leaked out I sent up a hasty prayer for bird-silence until we had got him safely out of the place; but it was not granted. Our feathered songster in the plane-tree broke into his little piece.

"There," said my hostess—"there's that bird again." She turned to me. "What did you say it was?"

I hoped that the Authority would speak first, and that the

others would then accept my assurance that they had misunderstood me the day before; but he was entangled at that moment in a watercress sandwich, the loose ends of which were still waiting to be tucked away.

I looked anxiously at the girl who had promised to remember, in case she wanted to say something, but she also was silent. Everybody was silent except that miserable bird.

Well, I had to have another go at it. "Blackman's warbler," I said firmly.

"Oh, yes," said my hostess.

"Blackman's warbler; I shall always remember that," lied the earnest-looking girl.

The Authority, who was free by this time, looked at me indignantly.

"Nonsense," he said; "it's the chiff-chaff."

Everybody else looked at me reproachfully. I was about to say that "Blackman's warbler" was the local name for the chiff-chaff in our part of Flint, when the Authority spoke again.

"The chiff-chaff," he said to our hostess with an insufferable air of knowledge.

I wasn't going to stand that.

"So *I* thought when I heard it first," I said, giving him a gentle smile.

It was now the Authority's turn to get the reproachful looks.

"Are they very much alike?" my hostess asked me, much impressed.

"Very much. Blackman's warbler is often mistaken for the chiff-chaff, even by so-called experts"—and I turned to the Authority and added, "Have another sandwich, won't you?"—"and particularly so, of course, during the breeding season. It is true that the eggs are more speckled, but——"

"Bless my soul," said the Authority, but it was easy to see that he was shaken, "I should think I know a chiff-chaff when I hear one."

"Ah, but do you know a Blackman's warbler? One doesn't often hear them in this country. Now in Switzerland——"

The bird said "chiff-chaff" again with an almost indecent plainness of speech.

"There you are!" I said triumphantly. "Listen," and I held up a finger. "You notice the difference? *Obviously* a Blackman's warbler."

Everybody looked at the Authority. He was wondering how

long it would take to get a book about birds down from London, and deciding that it couldn't be done that afternoon. Meanwhile "Blackman's warbler" sounded too much like the name of something to be repudiated. For all he had caught of our mumbled introduction I might have been Blackman myself.

"Possibly you're right," he said reluctantly.

Another bird said "chiff-chaff" from another tree, and I thought it wise to be generous. "There," I said, "now that *was* a chiff-chaff."

The earnest-looking girl remarked (silly creature) that it sounded just like the other one, but nobody took any notice of her. They were all busy admiring me.

Of course I mustn't meet the Authority again, because you may be pretty sure that when he got back to his books he looked up Blackman's warbler and found that there was no such animal. But if you mix in the right society and only see the wrong people once it is really quite easy to be an authority on birds— or, I imagine, on anything else.

A. A. MILNE

105

DJADDESDÉ

Djaddesdé is a favorite game in the harem. I am told it is also played in the West. A player who accepts any object from his or her opponent without saying Djaddesdé! ("I think of it!") loses. Of course, such a game can last for weeks and months; indeed, I played it once for a year and a half, and even then it was not ended by an oversight, but because the man who was my opponent grew tired and irritated at its interminable duration.

Once upon a time a wise man, who had thoroughly fortified himself against the wiles of women, was journeying through a desert. Suddenly he saw a white tent standing in the shade of a date tree. Before the tent was spread a gorgeous carpet. As he approached, a woman arose from this carpet and invited him courteously to enter the tent. Since it would be impolite to refuse, he complied.

However, the husband of the woman was absent. The wise man had scarcely seated himself on the soft and sumptuous carpets inside the tent before the woman had placed fresh dates before him. As she did so, he observed the wonderful delicacy and softness of her hands.

Thereupon he took alarm, for he recalled the proverb: "A woman's hands are a devil's claws"; and in self-defense he drew from his girdle a book he himself had written that recorded partly his own experience. It was entitled, "The Thousand Enticements, Beguilements, and Tricks of Women." The fair hostess observed with wonder the conduct of her guest, and said to him, in a voice sweeter and more melodious than he had ever heard before: "This must be a very important book, since you feel that you must read it instead of talking with me. What is the science or wisdom that it contains?"

The wise man replied: "It treats of a philosophy of life that does not concern women."

Naturally the young woman secretly resented this reply; but unconcernedly lighting a cigarette, and stretching a foot clad in a tiny gold-embroidered slipper forth from beneath her gown, she moved closer to him and, glancing over his shoulder at the manuscript, said: "I should awfully like to know what kind of book it is."

Thereupon he told her what the volume contained.

"Ah," she said, "and have you really learned all these enticements and beguilements and solved completely the puzzle of woman?"

"All," he said.

"Ah, then you are nine times a wise man. For I truly thought the subject was inexhaustible."

"No," said the wise man; "there are only one thousand, and they are all here."

When he said this, the woman stared at him with a gaze of such challenging surprise and teasing and impertinent incredulity that he almost lost his composure. But just then she sprang to her feet, turned deathly pale, and listening intently said: "Allah, save us! Do you hear that horseman? My husband has come. If he should find you here we are both lost. Where shall I put you? There—in that chest!"

The cover stood open. The nine-times-wise man sprang into the chest and crouched down. She closed the cover, turned the key, and taking it from the lock hastened to meet her husband.

"Allah be praised that He has sent you!"

"What then has happened to my gazelle?" asked the rider and wrapped her in his arms.

"While you were away, a philosopher arrived, a wise man. He assured me he knew all the enticements and beguilements of woman and began to make love to me."

"Where is the scoundrel?" exclaimed the Arab wrathfully.

"At first I was frozen with terror. But he spoke so passionately——"

"No! No!"

"But just then you came—You have saved me!"

"Where is the dog? Let me kill him!"

"There in the chest. I locked him in and here is the key!"

The man snatched the key from her in a fury and rushed toward the chest, whereupon the young woman shrieked with laughter.

"Djaddesdé!" she shouted, and clapped her hands with you. "You have taken the key without saying 'Djaddesdé!'"

Her husband looked at her for a moment in bewilderment. Then, throwing the key to one side with a gesture of irritation, he said: "How could you be so cruel as to anger me like that just to win the game!"

But the woman put her arms gently around her husband's neck and inquired pleadingly: "When do I get the gold chain I have won?"

Thereupon he laughed aloud.

"Right off," he said. "I'll go to town at once and get it."

And he mounted his horse and rode away. Thereupon the wife cautiously picked up the key from where her husband had thrown it, opened the chest, and released the nine-times-wise man more dead than alive. Smiling quizzically, she sped him on his way with the question: "Is this trick also in your book?"

MELEK HANUM

106

In a pool of serene radiance Grandmother sat. A black velvet cloak, lined with crimson silk, had been thrown about her; her hands, glittering with rings, rested on the top of her gold-headed ebony stick. Boney, chained to his perch, had been brought out to the terrace at her command, that he might bask in the light of the birthday conflagration. But his head was under his wing. He slept, and paid no heed to lights or music.

She was very tired. The figures moving about the lawn looked like gyrating, gesticulating puppets. The jigging of the fiddles, the moaning of the flute, beat down upon her, dazed her. She was sinking lower and lower in her chair. Nobody looked at her. One hundred years old! She was frightened suddenly by the stupendousness of her achievement. The plumes of the bonfire were drooping. The sky loomed black above. Beneath her the solid earth, which had borne her up so long, swayed with her, as though it would like to throw her off into space. She blinked. She fumbled for something, she knew not what. She was frightened.

She made a gurgling sound. She heard Ernest's voice say, "Mama, must you do that?"

She gathered her wits about her. "Somebody," she said, thickly, "somebody kiss me—quick!"

They looked at her kindly—hesitated to determine which should deliver the required caress; then from their midst Pheasant darted forth, flung herself before the old lady, and lifted up her child's face.

Grandmother peered, grinning, to see which of them it was; then, recognizing Pheasant, she clasped her to her breast. From that hug she gathered new vitality. Her arms grew strong. She pressed the young body to her and planted warm kisses on her face. "Ha," she murmured, "that's good!" And again, "Ha!"

MAZO DE LA ROCHE, *Jalna*[1]

107

Telemachus had seen no such house as this. The roof was high, and somehow the smoke got out and the light got in; you would think the sun or moon was shining. The size and wealth of it embarrassed him. He remembered that his father had more brains, but the thought didn't bring ease of manner. They took him to the marble baths, where the attendants embarrassed him still further by the thorough washing they gave him, and they oiled his hair, and put on him better clothes than he was accustomed to. Menelaos came to welcome him, a tall man with beautiful, long, dark locks, which needed no oil to make them shine. He wasn't so impressive as his house. It occurred to Telemachus that he was missing his daily exercise at Troy; he was of full habit. At the feast which Menelaos ordered for his guest, he showed that loss of exercise does not diminish appetite.

"I've never seen a house like this," said Telemachus, "and

though I haven't traveled far, I doubt if there's another such in the world. All this bronze and gold and amber, to say nothing of the silver and ivory! The court of Zeus himself on Olympus must be like this—it can't be much finer."

Menelaos put on a sober air, and said no one ought to compare himself to the gods, but it certainly was a satisfactory house. That is, the building.

"But I would exchange a large part of my wealth," he said, "to have back the years I spent away from this house, and the friends of mine who died at Troy, or were lost on the way home. Of course, we all have to die sometime, and I dare say many of them would be in their graves anyway, even if there had been no Troy. But I'm sorry for one friend in particular— for Odysseus. You must have heard the name. He did more than any of the others for me, and here am I home again, and nobody knows where he is, or whether he is alive at all. I dare say his old father has a broken heart, and his wife, and that infant son of his, who must be growing up now."

The mention of his father brought sudden anguish to Telemachus, sudden because he had had his thoughts on Menelaos's fine house. He was about to reveal his name and his errand, when Helen entered from her vaulted room. How could it be? Yet it could be no other! His mother had been careful to tell him how old Helen was, and he knew what she had been through. He had expected Aphrodite, a sophisticated goddess, charming as sin. As she walked toward him he saw that she was young and maidenly, and he knew what Artemis must be like. With her came a girl who seemed older but probably wasn't. They called her Adraste. She set a chair for Helen, with a footstool, and brought her the wool for spinning in a golden basket set on wheels. Telemachus forgot his father, forgot his mother, forgot the suitors. All his life he tried to be sorry he forgot, but he never was.

Helen greeted him, and took the wool in her hands, and entered into the conversation as though Telemachus were a very old friend, or as though she hadn't really noticed him yet. Then she let her hands fall in her lap.

"Menelaos, I suppose we shouldn't ask the stranger who he is before he is ready to tell us, but if he is willing, I'd like to make a guess at his name."

She looked straight at Telemachus. and he was so happy he felt foolish.

"I did not know," she said, "that two people could be so much alike. Of course, you see the resemblance, Menelaos."

"No, I don't," said Menelaos.

"Oh, you must have, the moment he appeared!"

"Perhaps I must, but I didn't," said Menelaos.

"I'll have to tell you, then—Odysseus," said Helen.

"Upon my word, I do see it now!" said Menelaos. "And I spoke to him of his father, just before you joined us; I noticed his interest in what I was saying. Upon my word! There's no mistake, is there?"

Menelaos looked at him, and he looked at Menelaos, and he noticed an expression on the older man's face which hadn't been there before his wife came in. A suggestion of serenity, or almost that; of satisfaction, let us say. Telemachus admitted that he was himself. But he wasn't quite himself. They talked for hours, or Menelaos did, and since there was no word of his father, Telemachus listened politely and watched Helen and her weaving hands, and his soul went out of him utterly. Then Helen said there had been talk enough, and Menelaos looked slightly rebuked, but used to it, and he asked Helen if there wasn't to be something for supper.

Helen came to the young man with a goblet of wine in her hand, and said,

"Who drinks of this wine, they say, forgets all his sorrows forever. It comes from Egypt, where they know the secrets of herbs and drugs and charms, and there's a magic in it!"

He took it from her, his hand touched hers, and she smiled at him. It was as she had said; he forgot all his sorrows—as it seemed, forever. But the magic, he knew, was not in the wine.

Menelaos was busy with his food on the other side of the table.

JOHN ERSKINE, *The Private Life of Helen of Troy* [1]

108

Between two and three o'clock the *Ariel* sailed out of harbour almost at the same moment with two feluccas. Trelawny re-anchored sullenly, furled his sails, and with a ship's glass watched the progress of his friends. His Genovese mate said to him, "They should have sailed this morning at three or four A. M. instead of three P. M. She is standing too much in shore; the current will fix her there."

Trelawny replied, "She will soon have the land-breeze."

"Maybe she will soon have too much breeze," remarked the mate. "That gaff top-sail is foolish in a boat with no deck and no sailor on board. . . . Look at those black lines and the dirty rags hanging on them out of the sky, look at the smoke on the water! The Devil is brewing mischief."

Standing on the end of the mole Captain Roberts also kept the boat in view. When he could see her no longer, he got leave to ascend the lighthouse-tower whence he could again discern her about ten miles out at sea. A storm was visibly coming from the Gulf, and he perceived that the *Ariel* was taking in her top-sail. Then the haze of the storm hid her completely.

In the harbour it was oppressively sultry. The heaviness of the atmosphere and an unwonted stillness benumbed the senses Trelawny went to his cabin and fell asleep in spite of himself. He was aroused by noises overhead: the men were getting up a chain cable to let go another anchor. There was a general stir amongst the shipping, getting-down yards and masts, veering out cables, letting-go anchors. It was very dark. The sea looked as solid and smooth as a sheet of lead and was covered with an oily scum: gusts of wind swept over it without ruffling it, and big drops of rain fell on its surface rebounding as if they could not penetrate it. Fishing-craft under bare poles rushed by in shoals running foul of the ships in the harbour. But the din and hubbub made by men and their shrill pipings were suddenly silenced by the crashing voice of a thunder-squall that burst right overhead.

When, twenty minutes later, the horizon was in some degree cleared, Trelawny and Roberts looked anxiously seaward in the hopes of descrying Shelley's boat amongst the many small craft scattered about. No trace of her was to be seen.

ANDRÉ MAUROIS, *Ariel*

109

From the middle of the transept in which the archbishop [Thomas à Becket] was standing a single pillar rose into the roof. On the eastern side of it opened a chapel of St. Benedict, in which were the tombs of several of the old primates. On the west, running parallel to the nave, was a lady chapel. Behind the pillar, steps led up into the choir, where voices were already singing vespers. A faint light may have been reflected into the transept from the choir tapers, and candles may perhaps have been burning before the altars in the two chapels—of light from without through the windows at that hour there could have been scarcely any. Seeing the knights coming on, the clergy who had entered with the archbishop closed the door and barred it. "What do you fear?" he cried in a clear, loud voice. "Out of the way, you cowards! The Church of God must not be made a fortress." He stepped back and reopened the door with his own hands, to let in the trembling wretches who had been shut out. They rushed past him, and scattered in the hiding places of the vast sanctuary, in the crypt, in the galleries or behind the tombs. All, or almost all, even of his closest friends, William of Canterbury, Benedict, John of Salisbury himself, forsook him to shift for themselves, admitting frankly that they were unworthy of martyrdom. The archbishop was left alone with his chaplain Fitzstephen, Robert of Merton his old master, and Edward Grim, the stranger from Cambridge—or perhaps with Grim only, who says that he was the only one that stayed, and was the only one certainly who showed any signs of courage. A cry had been raised in the choir that armed men were breaking into the cathedral. The vespers ceased; the few monks assembled left their seats and rushed to the edge of the transept, looking wildly into the darkness.

The archbishop was on the fourth step beyond the central pillar ascending into the choir when the knights came in. The outline of his figure may have been just visible to them, if the light fell upon it from the candles in the lady chapel. Fitzurse passed to the right of the pillar, De Morville, Tracy and Le Breton to the left. Robert de Broc and Hugh Mauclerc, an apostate priest, remained at the door by which they entered. A voice cried, "Where is the traitor? Where is Thomas à Becket?" There was silence; such a name could not be acknowledged. "Where is the archbishop?" Fitzurse shouted. "I am here," the archbishop replied, descending the steps, and meeting the knights full in the face. "What do you want with me? I am not afraid of your sword. I will not do what is unjust."

The knights closed round him. "Absolve the persons whom you have just excommunicated," they said, "and take off the suspensions."

"They have made no satisfaction," he answered; "I will not."

"Then you shall die as you have deserved," they said.

They had not meant to kill him—certainly not at that time and in that place. One of them touched him on the shoulder with the flat of his sword and hissed in his ears, "Fly, or you are a dead man." There was still time; with a few steps he would have been lost in the gloom of the cathedral, and could have concealed himself in any one of a hundred hiding places. But he was careless of life and he felt that his time had come. "I am ready to die," he said. "May the Church through my blood obtain peace and liberty! I charge you in the name of God that you hurt no one here but me." The people from the town were now pouring into the cathedral; De Morville was keeping them back with difficulty at the head of the steps from the choir, and there was danger of a rescue. Fitzurse seized hold of the archbishop, meaning to drag him off as a prisoner. He had been calm so far; his pride rose at the indignity of an arrest. "Touch me not, Reginald!" he said, wrenching his cloak out of Fitzurse's grasp. "Off, thou pander, thou!" Le Breton and Fitzurse grasped him again, and tried to force him upon Tracy's back. He grappled with Tracy and flung him to the ground, and then stood with his back against a pillar, Edward Grim supporting him He reproached Fitzurse with ingratitude for past kindness; Fitzurse whispered to him again to fly. "I will not fly," he said, and then Fitzurse swept his sword over him and dashed off his cap. Tracy, rising from the pavement, struck at his head. Grim raised his arm and caught the blow. The arm fell broken and the one friend found faithful sank back disabled against the wall. The sword, with its remaining force, wounded the archbishop above the forehead, and the blood trickled down his face. Standing firmly with his hands clasped, he bent his neck for the death-stroke, saying in a low voice, "I am prepared to die for Christ and His Church." These were his last words. Tracy again struck him. He fell forward upon his knees and hands. In that position Le Breton dealt him a blow which severed the scalp from the head and broke the sword against the stone, saying, "Take that for my Lord William." Le Broc or Mauclerc—the needless ferocity was attributed to both of them—strode forward from the cloister door, set his foot on the neck of the dead lion, and spread his brains upon the pavement with his sword's point. "We may go," he said; "the traitor is dead, and will trouble us no more."

FROUDE, *Short Studies on Great Subjects*

110

SIR GAWAIN AND THE GREEN KNIGHT

King Arthur lay at Camelot upon a Christmas-tide, with many a gallant lord and lovely lady, and all the noble brotherhood of the Round Table. There they held rich revels with gay talk and jest; one while they would ride forth to joust and tourney, and again back to the court to make carols; for there was the feast holden fifteen days with all the mirth that men could devise, song and glee, glorious to hear, in the daytime, and dancing at night. Halls and chambers were crowded with noble guests, the bravest of knights and the loveliest of ladies, and Arthur himself was the comeliest king that ever held a court. For all this fair folk were in their youth, the fairest and most fortunate under heaven, and the king himself of such fame that it were hard now to name so valiant a hero.

Now the New Year had but newly come in, and on that day a double portion was served on the high table to all the noble guests, and thither came the king with all his knights, when the service in the chapel had been sung to an end. And they greeted each other for the New Year, and gave rich gifts, the one to the other (and they that received them were not wroth, that may ye well believe!), and the maidens laughed and made mirth till it was time to get them to meat. Then they washed and sat them down to the feasting in fitting rank and order, and Guinevere the queen, gaily clad, sat on the high dais. Silken was her seat, with a fair canopy over her head, of rich tapestries of Tars, embroidered, and studded with costly gems; fair she was to look upon, with her shining gray eyes, a fairer woman might no man boast himself of having seen.

But Arthur would not eat till all were served, so full of joy and gladness was he, even as a child; he liked not either to lie long, or to sit long at meat, so worked upon him his young blood and his wild brain. And another custom he had also, that came of his nobility, that he would never eat upon an high day till he had been advised of some knightly deed, or some strange and marvelous tale, of his ancestors, or of arms, or of other ventures. Or till some stranger knight should seek of him leave to joust with one of the Round Table, that they might set their lives in jeopardy, one against another, as fortune might favor them. Such was the king's custom when he sat in hall at each high feast with his noble knights; therefore on that New Year tide, he abode, fair of face, on the throne, and made much mirth withal.

Thus the king sat before the high tables, and spake of many things. . . .

As the sound of the music ceased, and the first course had been fitly served, there came in at the hall door one terrible to behold, of stature greater than any on earth; from neck to loin so strong and thickly made, and with limbs so long and so great that he seemed even as a giant. And yet he was but a man, only the mightiest that might mount a steed; broad of chest and shoulders and slender of waist, and all his features of like fashion; but men marveled much at his color, for he rode even as a knight, yet was green all over.

For he was clad all in green, with a straight coat, and a mantle above; all decked and lined with fur was the cloth and the hood that was thrown back from his locks and lay on his shoulders. Hose had he of the same green, and spurs of bright gold with silken fastenings richly worked; and all his vesture was verily green. Around his waist and his saddle were bands with fair stones set upon silken work, 'twere too long to tell of all the trifles that were embroidered thereon—birds and insects in gay gauds of green and gold. All the trappings of his steed were of metal of like enamel, even the stirrups that he stood in stained of the same, and stirrups and saddle-bow alike gleamed and shone with green stones. Even the steed on which he rode was of the same hue, a green horse, great and strong, and hard to hold, with broidered bridle, meet for the rider.

The knight was thus gaily dressed in green, his hair falling around his shoulders; on his breast hung a beard, as thick and green as a bush, and the beard and the hair of his head were clipped all round above his elbows. The lower part of his sleeves was fastened with clasps in the same wise as a king's mantle. The horse's mane was crisp and plaited with many a knot folded in with gold thread about the fair green, here a twist of the hair, here another of gold. The tail was twined in like manner, and both were bound about with a band of bright green set with many a precious stone; then they were tied aloft in a cunning knot, whereon rang many bells of burnished gold. Such a steed might no other ride, nor had such ever been looked upon in that hall ere that time; and all who saw that knight spake and said that a man might scarce abide his stroke.

MALORY, *Le Morte d'Arthur*

D. Selections Illustrating Mainly the Approach through Mood

111

wʌns əpɒn ə taɪm ðɛə wəz ə peɪntə | hu dɪvaɪdɪd (h)ɪz laɪf ɪntʊ
tu havz |·| ɪn ðə wʌn haf (h)i peɪntɪd pɒtbɒɪləz fə ðə makɪt |
setɪŋ ɛvrɪ kənsɪdəreɪʃən əsaɪd ɪksept ðæt əv duɪŋ fər ɪz mastə |
ðə pʌblɪk | sʌmθɪŋ fə lʊɪtʃ (h)i kəd get peɪd ðə mʌnɪ ɒn lʊɪtʃ (h)i
lɪvd |·| hi wəz greɪt ət flʌdz | ənd nevə lʊkt ət neɪtʃər | ɪksept ɪn
ədə tə si lʊɒt wəd meɪk mɒʊst ʃɒʊ wɪð lɪst ɪkspens |·|

ðɪ ʌðə haf əv ɪz taɪm (h)i stʌdɪd ənd peɪntɪd wɪð ðə sɪnsɛrɪtɪ
əv dʒʊvanɪ belini | rembrant | hɒlbaɪn | ɔ də hug |·| hi wəz ðen
(h)ɪz oʊn mastə | ənd θɒt oʊnlɪ əv duɪŋ (h)ɪz wək əz wel əz (h)i
kʊd | rɪgadlɪs əv lʊeðər ɪt wʊd brɪŋ ɪm ɛnɪθɪŋ bət det ənd əbjus |
ə nɒt |·| hi geɪv (h)ɪz best | wɪðaʊt rɪsɪvɪŋ soʊ mʌtʃ əz θæŋks |·|
hi əvɒɪdɪd ðə tempteɪʃn əv telɪŋ iðə haf əbaʊt ðɪ ʌðə |·|

112

Light was wasted on Persephone's hair. Even when the wind
lifted the heavy coils and tangled them into a net to catch the
light, they turned the gold into a pale-moon silver. It was a color
one never sees, except out of the corner of one's eyes: in the
heart of dead trees, flaking in a dazzling cream-gray; in starlight
on yellow leaves; in the last gleaming hint of color before fire
strips the pine-cone to a white skeleton; in noonday glare on a
field of ripened grain. In the sun it was a cool, smothered gold,
and it smoldered at night like hot golden ashes.

Her face burned white under this restless heavy flame of hair;
burned honey-pale, with an intense light, from the sharp little
chin up to the brow, broad and untroubled. Beneath dark arches
her gray eyes were wide-set portals to a contradictory world;
a world of vain, warm promises, where flowers withered in over-
eager hands, and barren places blossomed for despairing eyes.
She walked as if she had learned dancing first; danced as if she
had never at all learned to walk—slowly, like dim smoke weaving
a pattern through mist; madly, as fire yields itself to the shape
of the wind. And in all her movements, even in the tall arrogance
of her pauses, there was a childlike, hesitant quality of fear, as if
she knew her happiness to be only a torch-lit entrance on darkness.

Eleanor Chilton, *Shadows Waiting*

113

Over there on the weed-hung rocks that looked at low tide like shaggy beasts come down to the water to drink, the sunlight seemed to spin like a silver coin dropped into each of the small rock pools. They danced, they quivered, and minute ripples laved the porous shores. Looking down, bending over, each pool was like a lake with pink and blue houses clustered on the shores; and oh! the vast mountainous country behind those houses—the ravines, the passes, the dangerous creeks and fearful tracks that led to the water's edge. Underneath waved the sea-forest—pink thread-like trees, velvet anemones, and orange berry-spotted weeds. Now a stone on the bottom moved, rocked, and there was a glimpse of a black feeler; now a thread-like creature wavered by and was lost. Something was happening to the pink, waving trees; they were changing to a cold moonlight blue. And now there sounded the faintest "plop." Who made that sound? What was going on down there? And how strong, how damp the seaweed smelt in the hot sun.

KATHERINE MANSFIELD, "At the Bay"

114

Perhaps the true way to toboggan is alone and at night. First comes the tedious climb, dragging your instrument behind you. Next a long breathing space, alone, with snow and pine woods, cold, silent, and solemn to the heart. Then you push off; the toboggan fetches way; she begins to feel the hill, to glide, to swim, to gallop. In a breath you are out from under the pine-trees, and a whole heavenful of stars reels and flashes overhead. Then comes a vicious effort, for by this time your wooden steed is speeding like the wind, and you are spinning round a corner, and the whole glittering valley and the lights in all the great hotels lie for a moment at your feet; and the next you are racing once more in the shadow of the night, with close shut teeth and beating heart. Yet a little while and you will be landed on the highroad by the door of your own hotel. This, in an atmosphere tingling with forty degrees of frost, in a night made luminous with stars and snow, and girt with strange white mountains, teaches the pulse an unaccustomed tune, and adds a new excitement to the life of man upon his planet.

From a letter of ROBERT LOUIS STEVENSON, quoted in Balfour's *Life*

115

THE POPLAR

There is a great tree in Sussex, whose cloud of thin foliage floats high in the summer air. The thrush sings in it, and blackbirds, who fill the late, decorative sunshine with a shimmer of golden sound. There the nightingale finds her green cloister; and on those branches sometimes, like a great fruit, hangs the lemon-coloured Moon. In the glare of August, when all the world is faint with heat, there is always a breeze in those cool recesses, always a noise, like the noise of water, among its lightly hung leaves.

But the owner of this Tree lives in London, reading books.

LOGAN PEARSALL SMITH, *Trivia*

116

UNDER AN UMBRELLA

From under the roof of my umbrella I saw the washed pavement lapsing beneath my feet, the news-posters lying smeared with dirt at the crossings, the tracks of the busses in the liquid mud. On I went through this dreary world of wetness. And through how many rains and years shall I still hurry down wet streets—middle-aged, and then, perhaps, very old? And on what errands?

Asking myself this cheerless question I fade from your vision, Reader, into the distance, sloping my umbrella against the wind.

LOGAN PEARSALL SMITH, *Trivia*

117

His uncle had had him taught Latin and Greek of an evening; he had taken kindly to these languages and had rapidly and easily mastered what many boys take years in acquiring. I suppose his knowledge gave him a self-confidence which made itself felt whether he intended it or not; at any rate, he soon began to pose as a judge of literature, and from this to being a judge of art, architecture, music and everything else, the path was easy. Like his father, he knew the value of money, but he was at once more ostentatious and less liberal than his father; while yet a boy he was a thorough little man of the world, and did well rather upon principles which he had tested by personal experiment, and recognised as principles, than from those profounder convictions which in his father were so instinctive that he could give no account concerning them.

His father, as I have said, wondered at him and let him alone. His son had fairly distanced him, and in an inarticulate way the father knew it perfectly well. After a few years he took to wearing his best clothes whenever his son came to stay with him, nor would he discard them for his ordinary ones till the young man had returned to London. I believe old Mr. Pontifex, along with his pride and affection, felt also a certain fear of his son, as though of something which he could not thoroughly understand, and whose ways, notwithstanding outward agreement, were nevertheless not as his ways. Mrs. Pontifex felt nothing of this; to her George was pure and absolute perfection, and she saw, or thought she saw, with pleasure, that he resembled her and her family in feature as well as in disposition rather than her husband and his.

SAMUEL BUTLER, *The Way of All Flesh*

118

Girls of fifteen are always laughing. They laugh when Mr. Binney helps himself to salt instead of sugar. They almost die of laughing when old Mrs. Tomkins sits down upon the cat. But they are crying the moment after. They have no fixed abode from which they see that there is something eternally laughable in human nature, some quality in men and women that for ever excites our satire. They do not know that Lady Greville who snubs, and poor Maria who is snubbed, are permanent features of every ballroom. But Jane Austen knew it from her birth upwards. One of those fairies who perch upon cradles must have taken her a flight through the world directly she was born. When she was laid in the cradle again she knew not only what the world looked like, but had already chosen her kingdom. She had agreed that if she might rule over that territory, she would covet no other. Thus at fifteen she had few illusions about other people and none about herself. Whatever she writes is finished and turned and set in its relation, not to the personage, but to the universe. She is impersonal; she is inscrutable.

VIRGINIA WOOLF, *Jane Austen*

119

The scene was a plain, bare, monotonous vault of a school-room, and the speaker's square forefinger emphasized his observations by underscoring every sentence with a line on the schoolmaster's sleeve. The emphasis was helped by the speaker's square wall of a forehead, which had his eye-brows for its base, while his eyes found commodious cellarage in two dark caves, overshadowed by the wall. The emphasis was helped by the speaker's mouth, which was wide, thin, and hard-set. The emphasis was helped by the speaker's voice, which was inflexible, dry, and dictatorial. The emphasis was helped by the speaker's hair, which bristled on the skirts of his bald head, a plantation of firs to keep the wind from its shining surface, all covered with knobs, like the crust of a plum pie, as if the head had scarcely warehouse-room for the hard facts stored inside. The speaker's obstinate carriage, square coat, square legs, square shoulders,—nay, his very neck-cloth, trained to take him by the throat with an unaccommodating grasp, like a stubborn fact, as it was,—all helped the emphasis."

DICKENS, *Hard Times*

120

Mr. George Ormerod stepped from the drawing-room window of Sedbury House, Gloucestershire, wearing a tall furry hat and white trousers strapped under his instep; he was closely, though deferentially, followed by a lady wearing a yellow-spotted dress over a crinoline, and behind her, singly and arm in arm, came nine children in nankeen jackets and long white drawers. They were going to see the water let out of a pond.

The youngest child, Eleanor, a little girl with a pale face, rather elongated features, and black hair, was left by herself in the drawing-room, a large sallow apartment with pillars, two chandeliers, for some reason enclosed in holland bags, and several octagonal tables some of inlaid wood and others of greenish malachite. At one of these little Eleanor Ormerod was seated in a high chair.

"Now, Eleanor," said her mother, as the party assembled for the expedition to the pond, "here are some pretty beetles. Don't touch the glass. Don't get down from your chair, and when we get back little George will tell you all about it."

VIRGINIA WOOLF, *The Lives of the Obscure*

121

Toward the end of September, when school-time was drawing near and the nights were already black, we would begin to sally from our respective villas, each equipped with a tin bull's-eye lantern. The thing was so well known that it had worn a rut in the commerce of Great Britain; and the grocers, about the due time, began to garnish their windows with our particular brand of luminary. We wore them buckled to the waist upon a cricket belt, and over them, such was the rigour of the game, a buttoned top-coat. They smelled noisomely of blistered tin; they never burned aright, though they would always burn our fingers; their use was naught; the pleasure of them merely fanciful; and yet a boy with a bull's-eye under his top-coat asked for nothing more. The fishermen used lanterns about their boats, and it was from them, I suppose, that we had got the hint; but theirs were not bull's-eyes, nor did we ever play at being fishermen. The police carried them at their belts, and we had plainly copied them in that; yet we did not pretend to be policemen. Burglars, indeed, we may have had some haunting thoughts of; and we had certainly an eye to past ages when lanterns were more common, and to certain story-books in which we had found them to figure very largely. But take it for all in all, the pleasure of the thing was substantive; and to be a boy with a bull's-eye under his top-coat was good enough for us.

When two of these asses met, there would be an anxious "Have you got your lantern?" and a gratified "Yes!" That was the shibboleth, and very needful too; for, as it was the rule to keep our glory contained, none could recognise a lantern-bearer, unless (like the pole-cat) by the smell. Four or five would sometimes climb into the belly of a ten-man lugger, with nothing but the thwarts above them—for the cabin was usually locked, or choose out some hollow of the links where the wind might whistle overhead. There the coats would be unbuttoned and the bull's-eyes discovered; and in the chequering glimmer, under the huge windy hall of the night, and cheered by a rich steam of toasting tinware, these fortunate young gentlemen would crouch together in the cold sand of the links or on the scaly bilges of the fishing-boat, and delight themselves with inappropriate talk. Woe is me that I may not give some specimens—some of their foresights of life, or deep inquiries into the rudiments of man and nature, these were so fiery and so innocent, they were so richly silly, so romantically young. But the talk, at any rate, was but a condiment; and these gatherings themselves only accidents in the career of the lantern-bearer. The essence of this bliss was to walk by yourself in the black night; the slide shut, the top-coat buttoned; not a ray escaping, whether to conduct your footsteps or to make your glory public; a mere pillar of darkness in the dark; and all the while, deep down in the privacy of your fool's heart, to know you had a bull's-eye at your belt, and to exult and sing over the knowledge.

ROBERT LOUIS STEVENSON, "The Lantern-Bearers"

122

"I'm so excited," said Mrs. Haddock, as the time for departure drew near. "I've never been on a boat before."

"You'll be very seasick," said Aunt Flora. "The Quetches were never good sailors except your half-brother Edmund who was drowned at that picnic thirteen years ago next July fourth."

"Drowned people can be raised to the surface by firing guns over the river," said little Mildred.

"People who are drowned at sea," said Aunt Flora, "are never recovered."

"I should think," said little Mildred, "that if you fired a big enough gun over the Atlantic Ocean you could bring a lot of interesting things to the surface."

That was the way little Mildred's mind worked and she was already becoming known among the simple folk of the town as the Joan of Arc of 453 Crestview Ave.

The last week before sailing was full of problems. There was first of all the question of whether or not to take Mr. Haddock's winter pajamas.

"It might turn cold," said Mrs. Haddock, who, man and boy, had had forty-nine years of experience with weather and ought to have known what she was talking about.

"Nonsense," said Mr. Haddock. "It won't turn cold in June."

"It was in June," said Aunt Flora, "that your brother Samuel took pneumonia and died—June twenty-sixth."

"That wasn't in Europe," said Mr. Haddock, who had once thought of taking up the law.

"Weather is the same the world over," said Mrs. Haddock.

"It isn't," said Mildred. "In Abyssinia the average mean rainfall is 13.4 inches."

"But we aren't going to Abyssinia," said Mr. Haddock plaintively.

"We might," said Mrs. Haddock, and so she packed the pajamas rather triumphantly (for pajamas) and asked Mr. Haddock to sit on the lid.

"I don't see why you packed my dress suit," said Mr. Haddock, "I'm not going to any banquets."

"At the opera in Paris," said little Mildred, "Full evening dress is de rigueur."

"You see," said Mrs. Haddock. "Mildred, talk some more French for your Aunt Flora."

"I won't," said Mildred.

"Please, Mildred," said Aunt Flora, "talk some French for your Aunt Flora."

"Mildred," said Mr. Haddock, "you talk some French for your Aunt Flora, or you don't get any Toasted Fruito for dessert tonight. Papa means it."

"All right," said Mildred. "Où est l'encre?"

"You see," said Mrs. Haddock proudly.

"What does that mean, Mildred?" said Aunt Flora.

"Where is the ink?" translated Mildred obediently with a pretty toss of her curls.

"She will be a great help to you," said Aunt Flora.

"Especially if we need much ink," said Mr. Haddock.

DONALD OGDEN STEWART, *Mr. and Mrs. Haddock Abroad*

123

Fog everywhere. Fog up the river, where it flows among green aits and meadows: fog down the river, where it rolls defiled among tiers of shipping, and the waterside pollutions of a great —and dirty—city. Fog on the Essex marshes, fog on the Kentish heights. Fog creeping into the cabooses of collier brigs; fog lying out on the yards, and hovering in the rigging of great ships; fog drooping on the gunwales of barges and small boats. Fog in the eyes and throats of ancient Greenwich pensioners, wheezing by the fireside of their wards; fog in the stem and bowl of the afternoon pipe of the wrathful skipper, down in his close cabin; fog cruelly pinching the toes and fingers of his shivering little prentice boy on deck. Chance people on the bridges peeping over the parapets into a nether sky of fog, with fog all round them, as if they were up in a balloon, and hanging in the clouds.

DICKENS, *Our Mutual Friend*

124

As long as you are journeying in the interior of the Desert you
have no particular point to make for as your resting-place. The
endless sands yield nothing but small stunted shrubs; even these
fail after the first two or three days, and from that time you pass
over broad plains—you pass over newly-reared hills—you pass
through valleys dug out by the last week's storm, and the hills and
the valleys are sand, sand, sand, still sand, and only sand, and sand
and sand again. The earth is so samely that your eyes turn towards heaven,—towards heaven I mean, in sense of sky. You
look to the sun, for he is your task-master, and by him you know
the measure of the work that you have done, and the measure of
the work that remains for you to do. He comes when you strike
your tent in the early morning, and then, for the first hour of the
day, as you move forward on your camel, he stands at your near
side, and makes you know that the whole day's toil is before you;
then for a while, and a long while, you see him no more, for you
are veiled and shrouded, and dare not look upon the greatness of
his glory, but you know where he strides overhead, by the touch
of his flaming sword. No words are spoken, but your Arabs moan,
your camels sigh, your skin glows, your shoulders ache and for
sights you see the pattern and the web of the silk that veils your
eyes and the glare of the outer light. Time labours on—your skin
glows, your shoulders ache, your Arabs moan, your camels sigh,
and you see the same pattern in the silk, and the same glare of
light beyond; but conquering Time marches on, and by-and-by
the descending sun has compassed the heaven, and now softly
touches your right arm, and throws your lank shadow over the
sand right along on the way for Persia. Then again you look upon
his face, for his power is all veiled in his beauty, and the redness
of flames has become the redness of roses: the fair, wavy cloud
that fled in the morning now comes to his sight once more—
comes blushing, yet still comes on; comes burning with blushes,
yet comes and clings to his side.

Then begins your season of rest. The world about you is all
your own, and there, where you will, you pitch your solitary tent;
there is no living thing to dispute your choice. When at last the
spot had been fixed upon and we come to a halt, one of the Arabs
would touch the chest of my camel, and utter at the same time a
peculiar gurgling sound. The beast instantly understood and
obeyed the sign, and slowly sunk under me, till she brought her

body to a level with the ground, then gladly enough I alighted. The rest of the camels were unloaded and turned loose to browse upon the shrubs of the Desert, where shrubs there were, or where these failed, to wait for the small quantity of food that was allowed them out of our stores.

My servants, helped by the Arabs, busied themselves in pitching the tent and kindling the fire. Whilst this was doing I used to walk away towards the East, confiding in the print of my foot as a guide for my return. Apart from the cheering voices of my attendants, I could better know and feel the loneliness of the Desert. The influence of such scenes, however, was not of a softening kind, but filled me rather with a sort of childish exultation in the self-sufficiency which enabled me to stand thus alone in the wideness of Asia—a short-lived pride, for wherever man wanders he still remains tethered by the chain that links him to his kind; and so when the night closed round me I began to return—to return as it were to my own gate. Reaching at last some high ground, I could see, and see with delight, the fire of our small encampment, and when at last I regained the spot, it seemed a very home that had sprung up for me in the midst of these solitudes. My Arabs were busy with their bread, rattling teacups; the little kettle with her odd old-maidish looks sat humming away old songs about England, and two or three yards from the fire my tent stood prim and tight, with open portal and with welcoming look.

Sometimes in the earlier part of my journey the night-breeze blew coldly; when that happened the dry sand was heaped up outside round the skirts of the tent, and so the Wind, that everywhere else could sweep as he listed along those dreary plains, was forced to turn aside in his course, and make way, as he ought, for the Englishman. Then within my tent there were heaps of luxuries —dining-rooms, dressing-rooms, libraries, bedrooms, drawing-rooms, oratories—all crowded into the space of a hearthrug. The first night, I remember, with my books and maps about me, I wanted a light. They brought me a taper, and immediately from out of the silent Desert there rushed in a flood of life, unseen before. Monsters of moths of all shapes and hues, that never before perhaps had looked upon the shining flame, now madly thronged into my tent, and dashed through the fire of the candle till they fairly extinguished it with their burning limbs. Those who had failed in attaining this martyrdom suddenly became serious, and clung despondingly to the canvas.

By-and-by there was brought to me the fragrant tea, and big masses of scorched and scorching toast, and the butter that had come all the way to me in this Desert of Asia from out of that poor, dear, starving Ireland. I feasted like a king—like four kings —like a boy in the fourth form.

When the cold, sullen morning dawned, and my people began to load the camels, I always felt loath to give back to the waste this little spot of ground that had glowed for a while with the cheerfulness of a human dwelling. One by one the cloaks, the saddles, the baggage, the hundred things that strewed the ground and made it look so familiar—all these were taken away, and laid upon the camels. A speck in the broad tracts of Asia remained still impressed with the mark of patent portmanteaus and the heels of London boots; the embers of the fire lay black and cold upon the sand; and these were the signs we left.

My tent was spared to the last, but when all else was ready for the start then came its fall; the pegs were drawn, the canvas shivered, and in less than a minute there was nothing that remained of my genial home but only a pole and a bundle. The encroaching Englishman was off, and instant upon the fall of the canvas, like an owner, who had waited and watched, the Genius of the Desert stalked in.

A. W. KINGLAKE, Eöthen

125

THE BLESSÈD DAMOZEL

The blessèd damozel lean'd out
　　From the gold bar of Heaven:
Her eyes were deeper than the depth
　　Of waters stilled at even.
She had three lilies in her hand,
　　And the stars in her hair were seven.

Her robe, ungirt from clasp to hem,
　　No wrought flowers did adorn,
But a white rose of Mary's gift
　　For service meetly worn;
And her hair, lying down her back,
　　Was yellow like ripe corn.

Herseem'd she scarce had been a day
    One of God's choristers;
The wonder was not yet quite gone
    From that still look of hers;
Albeit, to them she left, her day
    Had counted as ten years.

(To *one* it is ten years of years:
    . . . Yet now, here in this place,
Surely she lean'd o'er me,—her hair
    Fell all about my face . . .
Nothing: the Autumn-fall of leaves
    The whole year sets apace.)

* * *

Heard hardly, some of her new friends,
    Playing at holy games,
Spake, gentle-mouth'd, among themselves,
    Their virginal chaste names;
And the souls, mounting up to God,
    Went by her like thin flames.

And still she bow'd herself and stoop'd
    Into the vast waste calm;
Till her bosom's pressure must have made
    The bar she lean'd on warm,
And the lilies lay as if asleep
    Along her bended arm.

From the fixt lull of Heaven, she saw
    Time, like a pulse, shake fierce
Through all the worlds. Her gaze still strove,
    In that steep gulf, to pierce
The swarm; and then she spoke, as when
    The stars sang in their spheres.

'I wish that he were come to me,
    For he will come,' she said.
'Have I not pray'd in solemn Heaven?
    On earth, has he not pray'd?
Are not two prayers a perfect strength?
    And shall I feel afraid?

* * *

'There will I ask of Christ the Lord
  Thus much for him and me:—
To have more blessing than on earth
  In nowise; but to be
As then we were,—being as then
  At peace. Yea, verily.

'Yea, verily; when he is come
  We will do thus and thus:
Till this my vigil seem quite strange
  And almost fabulous;
We two will live at once, one life;
  And peace shall be with us.'

She gazed, and listen'd, and then said,
  Less sad of speech than mild,—
'All this is when he comes.' She ceased:
  The light thrill'd past her, fill'd
With Angels, in strong level lapse.
  Her eyes pray'd, and she smiled.

(I saw her smile.) But soon their flight
  Was vague 'mid the poised spheres.
And then she cast her arms along
  The golden barriers,
And laid her face between her hands,
  And wept. (I heard her tears.)

               DANTE GABRIEL ROSSETTI

126

DIRGE

Never the nightingale,
  Oh, my dear,
Never again the lark
  Thou wilt hear;
Though dusk and the morning still
    Tap at thy window-sill,
Though ever love call and call
Thou wilt not hear at all,
  My dear, my dear.

               ADELAIDE CRAPSEY

127

AFTER

Take the cloak from his face, and at first
　Let the corpse do its worst.

How he lies here in the rights of a man!
　Death has done all that death can.
And, absorbed in the new life he leads,
　He recks not, he heeds
Not his wrong nor my vengeance—both strike
　On his senses alike.
And are lost in the solemn and strange
　Surprise of the change.

Ha, what avails death to erase
　His offence, my disgrace?
I would we were boys as of old
　In the field, by the fold:
His outrage, God's patience, man's scorn
　Were so easily borne.

I stand here now, he lies in his place:
　Cover the face.

ROBERT BROWNING

128

GRANDMOTHER SITS IN HER CHAIR

On the flagged walk in the sun;
She is nodding with sleep.
Her white cashmere shawl has a faint scent of camphor,
And her gown a faint scent of lavender.
Her face is soft and blank like a mask of white wool,
Her eyes are covered with a bluish film,
Like oil on water,
They pour tears when they blink in the sun,
Their shut lids are wet with tears.

'Granny, are you asleep?'
She wakes when she hears me,
Her purple lips shake in a sad, kind smile.
'Is it you, Elizabeth?'

'Yes, did you want me?
Has the time seemed very long?'
She answers, 'No.
I am quite happy.
Sitting here,
Thinking about God.'

I wonder: What does she think about him?
What goes on behind the mask of white wool,
Behind the filmed eyes?
I think she sees herself in heaven,
In a warm, comfortable place, sitting in an arm-chair,
Wrapped in a new, snow-white, heavenly shawl,
With God's arms around her,
The arms of a nice, kind man
Who knows all about Grandmother.
He is old, eternally old, the white bearded Ancient of Days,
And he loves Grandmother.
She cuddles close in his arms,
And she talks to him like a child,
She asks him to forgive her all the naughty things she has
        done,
She is so old and tired
That she falls asleep when she prays;
And sometimes she is thinking about what there will be for
        dinner,
When she ought to be thinking about him;
And sometimes she is cross with Elizabeth.
She is so tired and weak,
And she has had trouble,
God knows all about it,
How they all went away,
How they all died,
How there is nobody left but Elizabeth—
And ah well, dear God, you know what Elizabeth is.
And God tightens his arms,
And says, 'Never mind, Granny,
It's all right.
Go to sleep on my shoulder.'

I wonder whether she was really thinking about God,
Or whether she has been asleep all the time;

Sleep hangs about her still,
She is nodding with sleep.

Oh God, I, who never prayed to you,
Pray to you now:
Let me not sleep like this:
Never for me the dark calm,
The dreamless and corrupt content.
Let me die waking,
With thought a light in my brain,
And love a fire in my heart,
And afterwards
Never to rest in the folded arms of heaven,
But to go on,
Following God through the glory of the worlds for ever.
Give me, not peace,
But the bright, sharp ecstasy,
And what pang may come after.

MAY SINCLAIR, *The Dark Night*

129

ST. GOVAN

St. Govan, he built him a cell
By the side of the Pembroke sea,
And there, as the crannied sea-gulls dwell,
In a tiny, secret citadel
He sighed for eternity.

St. Govan, he built him a cell
Between the wild sky and the sea,
Where the sunsets redden the rolling swell
And brooding splendour has thrown her spell
On valley and moorland lea.

St. Govan still lies in his cell,
But his soul, long since, is free,
And one may wonder—and who can tell—
If good St. Govan likes Heaven as well
As his cell by that sounding sea?

A. G. PRYS-JONES

130

Heredity

There is a Pirate in my blood,
And a rare, great Queen:
And all that the one has understood
The other has never seen. . . .

At noon, I tread on cloth o' gold,
While the Pirate watches me—
His fingers are light in a rapier-hold
And he hungers for the sea. . . .

At night, the wind is in my hair,
And I own the wind to the sky:
But . . . the Queen's lips twist as she watches there
And she shivers as I go by. . . .

My arrogant head knows the weight of a crown,
And a Quarterdeck sired my stride;
There's a regal form in my velvet gown—
But my heart beats time to the tide!

There is a Pirate deep in me—
But his crew-command seems small;
There is a Queen—and she cannot see
Why she frets at a palace-wall.

Theta Kenyon

131

The Riveter

The street below him seemed a darkened thread,
The wild confusion and the clanging tread
Of men and beasts came to him far away,
Like distant drone of bees at break of day
    Upon the sunlit Apennines.
Above him shone a paler, northern sun;
And rifts of smoke came drifting one by one
From far beneath, and circling, circling, gently spread
A mountain-mist of gray and white above his head.

Unheedful of the vast abyss, he clung,
Steel-sinewed, to the iron beam that swung
Into the empty air. The hammer beat
Against the bolts; and, as they glowed, the heat
    Of summer days beneath the pines
Shone in his cheeks; and he was back anew
And roaming on the hills before the dew
Had left the grass. Above an alien land he hung.
Yet songs of youth and Italy were on his tongue.

Sure-poised upon the ledge, he deftly caught
The rivets as he sang. No echo sought
His words to waft their message o'er the din
Of hurrying feet that came and went within
    The shadowed depth. The far confines
Of air and vaulted sky alone have heard
The symphony of toil and song that stirred
The master builders of the rising age and brought
The strength of nature's hills to weld with living thought.

CARY F. JACOB

132

QUATRAIN

Teach me your mood, O patient stars!
    Who climb each night the ancient sky,
Leaving on space no shade, no scars,
    No trace of age, no fear to die.

EMERSON

133

A TRIOLET

I intended an Ode,
    And it turn'd to a Sonnet
It began à la mode,
I intended an Ode;
    But Rose cross'd the road
    In her latest new bonnet;
I intended an Ode
But it turn'd to a Sonnet.

AUSTIN DOBSON

134

TAVERN

I'll keep a little tavern
  Below the high hill's crest,
Where all grey-eyed people
  May set them down to rest.

There shall be plates a-plenty,
  And mugs to melt the chill
Of all the grey-eyed people
  Who happen up the hill.

There sound will sleep the traveller
  And dream his journey's end,
But I will rouse at midnight
  The falling fire to tend.

Aye, 'tis a curious fancy,—
  But all the good I know
Was taught me out of two grey eyes
  A long time ago.
             EDNA ST. VINCENT MILLAY

135

TWO CINQUAINS

November Night

Listen. . . . .
With faint dry sound
Like steps of passing ghosts,
The leaves, frost-crisped, break from the trees
And fall.

Triad

These be
Three silent things:
The falling snow . . . the hour
Before the dawn . . . the mouth of one
Just dead.
             ADELAIDE CRAPSEY

136

Four Tankas[1]

On a country road
An old woman walks;
The autumn sun casts her shadow
Long and thin.—

Milky night;
Through slender trees in drowse
A petal
Falling.—

Against the cold sky
Where the day fades swiftly
A scarecrow stands
With its torn sleeve swaying.—

The rocking horse.—
A half built block-house—
Lost laughter!

Jun Fugita

137

How do I love thee? Let me count the ways.
I love thee to the depth and breadth and height
My soul can reach, when feeling out of sight
For the ends of Being and ideal Grace.
I love thee to the level of every day's
Most quiet need, by sun and candlelight.
I love thee freely, as men strive for Right;
I love thee purely, as they turn from Praise.
I love thee with the passion put to use
In my old griefs, and with my childhood's faith.
I love thee with a love I seem to lose
With my lost saints,—I love thee with the breath,
Smiles, tears, of all my life!—and, if God choose,
I shall but love thee better after death.

Elizabeth Barrett Browning

---

[1] A tanka is a short Japanese poem expressive of one mood.

138

Spring Goeth All in White

Spring goeth all in white,
Crowned with milk-white may:
In fleecy flocks of light
O'er heaven the white clouds stray:

White butterflies in the air;
White daisies prank the ground:
The cherry and hoary pear
Scatter their snow around.

Robert Bridges

139

Without there was a pale moon up
Of winter radiance sheer and thin;
The hollow halo it was in
Was like an icy, silver cup.

Through the small room with subtle sound
Of flame, by vents the fireshine drove
And reddened. In the dim alcove
The mirror shed a clearness round.

Dante Gabriel Rossetti, "My Sister's Sleep"

140

What thou seest, when thou dost wake,
Do it for thy true love take;
Love and languish for his sake
Be it ounce, or cat or bear:
Pard, or boar with bristled hair,
In thy eye that shall appear
When thou wak'st it is thy dear.
Wake when some vile thing is near.

Shakespeare, *Midsummer Nights Dream*

141

REMEMBER

Remember me when I am gone away,
　Gone far away into the silent land;
　When you can no more hold me by the hand,
Nor I half turn to go, yet turning stay.
Remember me when no more day by day
　You tell me of our future that you plann'd:
　Only remember me; you understand
It will be late to counsel then or pray.
Yet if you should forget me for a while
　And afterwards remember, do not grieve:
　For if the darkness and corruption leave
　A vestige of the thoughts that once I had,
Better by far you should forget and smile
　Than that you should remember and be sad.

CHRISTINA ROSSETTI

142

O God of battles! steel my soldiers' hearts;
Possess them not with fear; take from them now
The sense of reckoning, if the opposed numbers
Pluck their hearts from them. Not to-day, O Lord,
O, not to-day, think not upon the fault
My father made in compassing the crown!
I Richard's body have interred new;
And on it have bestow'd more contrite tears
Than from it issued forced drops of blood:
Five hundred poor I have in yearly pay,
Who twice a-day their wither'd hands hold up
Toward heaven, to pardon blood; and I have built
Two chantries, where the sad and solemn priests
Sing still for Richard's soul. More will I do;
Though all that I can do is nothing worth,
Since that my penitence comes after all,
Imploring pardon.

SHAKESPEARE, *Henry V*

143

OZYMANDIAS

I met a traveller from an antique land
Who said: "Two vast and trunkless legs of stone
Stand in the desert. Near them on the sand,
Half sunk, a shattered visage lies, whose frown,
And wrinkled lip, and sneer of cold command,
Tell that the sculptor well those passions read
Which yet survive, stamped on these lifeless things,
The hand that mocked them, and the heart that fed;
And on the pedestal these words appear:
'My name is Ozymandias, king of kings;
Look on my works, ye Mighty, and despair!'
Nothing beside remains. Round the decay
Of that colossal wreck, boundless and bare
The lone and level sands stretch far away."

SHELLEY

144

Oh, Rome! my Country! City of the Soul!
The orphans of the heart must turn to thee,
Lone Mother of dead Empires! and control
In their shut breasts their petty misery.
What are our woes and sufferance? Come and see
The cypress—hear the owl—and plod your way
O'er steps of broken thrones and temples—Ye!
Whose agonies are evils of a day—
A world is at our feet as fragile as our clay.

BYRON, *Childe Harold's Pilgrimage*

145

For once, upon a raw and gusty day,
The troubled Tiber chafing with her shores,
Cæsar said to me, "Dar'st thou, Cassius, now
Leap in with me into this angry flood,
And swim to yonder point?" Upon the word,
Accoutred as I was, I plungèd in
And bade him follow; so indeed he did.

The torrent roar'd, and we did buffet it
With lusty sinews, throwing it aside
And stemming it with hearts of controversy;
But ere we could arrive the point propos'd,
Cæsar cried, "Help me, Cassius, or I sink!"
I, as Æneas, our great ancestor,
Did from the flames of Troy upon his shoulder
The old Anchises bear, so from the waves of Tiber
Did I the tired Cæsar. And this man
Is now become a god, and Cassius is
A wretched creature, and must bend his body
If Cæsar carelessly but nod on him.
He had a fever when he was in Spain,
And when the fit was on him, I did mark
How he did shake— 'tis true, this god did shake,
His coward lips did from their colour fly,
And that same eye whose bend doth awe the world
Did lose his lustre; I did hear him groan.
Ay, and that tongue of his that bade the Romans
Mark him and write his speeches in their books,
Alas, it cried, "Give me some drink, Titinius,"
As a sick girl. Ye gods! it doth amaze me
A man of such a feeble temper should
So get the start of the majestic world
And bear the palm alone.

SHAKESPEARE, Julius Caesar

146

Once more unto the breach, dear friends, once more,
Or close the wall up with our English dead!
In peace there's nothing so becomes a man
As modest stillness and humility;
But when the blast of war blows in our ears,
Then imitate the action of the tiger:
Stiffen the sinews, summon up the blood,
Disguise fair nature with hard-favour'd rage:
Then lend the eye a terrible aspect;
Let it pry through the portage of the head
Like the brass cannon; let the brow o'erwhelm it
As fearfully as doth a galled rock
O'erhang and jutty his confounded base,

Swill'd with the wild and wasteful ocean.
Now set the teeth and stretch the nostril wide;
Hold hard the breath, and bend up every spirit
To his full height!

SHAKESPEARE, *Henry V*

147

NATURE

As a fond mother, when the day is o'er
  Leads by the hand her little child to bed,
  Half willing, half reluctant to be led,
  And leave his broken playthings on the floor,
Still gazing at them through the open door,
  Nor wholly reassured and comforted
  By promises of others in their stead,
  Which, though more splendid, may not please him
      more;
So Nature deals with us, and takes away
  Our playthings one by one, and by the hand
  Leads us to rest so gently, that we go
Scarce knowing if we wish to go or stay,
  Being too full of sleep to understand
  How far the unknown transcends the what we know.

LONGFELLOW

148

I left no ring with her. What means this lady?
Fortune forbid my outside have not charm'd her!
She made good view of me; indeed, so much,
That sure methought her eyes had lost her tongue,
For she did speak in starts distractedly.
She loves me, sure. The cunning of her passion
Invites me in this churlish messenger.
None of my lord's ring! Why, he sent her none.
I am the man! If it be so, as 'tis,
Poor lady, she were better love a dream.
Disguise, I see thou art a wickedness
Wherein the pregnant enemy does much.
How easy is it for the proper-false

In women's waxen hearts to set their forms!
Alas, our frailty is the cause, not we!
For such as we are made of, such we be.
How will this fadge? My master loves her dearly;
And I, poor monster, fond as much of him:
And she, mistaken, seems to dote on me.
What will become of this? As I am man,
My state is desperate for my master's love;
As I am woman,—now alas the day!—
What thriftless sighs shall poor Olivia breathe!
O time! thou must untangle this, not I.
It is too hard a knot for me to untie!

SHAKESPEARE, *Twelfth Night*

149

The barge she sat in, like a burnish'd throne,
Burn'd on the water: the poop was beaten gold;
Purple the sails, and so perfumed that
The winds were love-sick with them; the oars were silver,
Which to the tune of flutes kept stroke and made
The water which they beat to follow faster,
As amorous of their strokes. For her own person,
It beggar'd all description: she did lie
In her pavillion, cloth-of-gold of tissue,
O'er-picturing that Venus where we see
The fancy outwork nature: on each side her
Stood pretty dimpled boys, like smiling Cupids,
With divers-colour'd fans, whose wind did seem
To glow the delicate cheeks which they did cool,
And what they undid did.

SHAKESPEARE, *Antony and Cleopatra*

150

Farewell, a long farewell, to all my greatness!
This is the state of man: To-day he puts forth
The tender leaves of hope, to-morrow blossoms,
And bears his blushing honors thick upon him:
The third day comes a frost, a killing frost;
And—when he thinks, good easy man, full surely
His greatness is a ripening—nips his root;

And then he falls as I do. I have ventured,—
Like little wanton boys that swim on bladders,—
This many summers, in a sea of glory,
But far beyond my depth: my high-blown pride
At length broke under me, and now has left me
Weary and old with service, to the mercy
Of a rude stream that must forever hide me.

SHAKESPEARE, *Henry VIII*

SECTION V

QUESTIONS, TOPICS FOR DISCUSSION, AND SUGGESTED READINGS

CHAPTER I

QUESTIONS AND TOPICS FOR DISCUSSION

1. Define *rhythm* according to the method given in Chapter VIII and discuss its relation to physical and mental health; to speech training.

2. Discuss the relation (*a*) between posture and poise; (*b*) between poise and social adjustment; (*c*) between social adjustment and social control; (*d*) between all these and the general subject of speech training.

3. Define *persona*

4. Discuss the relation between individual education and speech training.

5. Read the chapter on "Language" in Judd's *Psychology of Social Institutions* and discuss the author's contention that "language is the fundamental institution."

6. What practical help can the student of speech gain from the various schools of psychology?

7. Discuss the following aspects of speech training: (*a*) the scientific; (*b*) the practical; (*c*) the æsthetic; (*d*) the professional; (*e*) the social.

8. Discuss habit formation, especially in regard to speech training.

9. What connection, if any, is there between a good voice and good breeding?

10. Is it wise to attempt to develop the voice to a point beyond the general cultural development of the individual? How might such an attempt possibly be justified? What is the chief danger of such a course?

11. Suggestions for a discussion of "Education":

(a) The derivation of the word.

(b) The processes by which education can be secured.

(c) A consideration of the following aspects of education:

    (1) As a means of developing successful behavior patterns.

    (2) As a means of "learning to make transitions easily."

    (3) As a means of "securing the survival of the fittest with a minimum of suffering on the part of the unfit."

    (4) As a means of "learning to live by living."

    (5) As a means of developing a personality.

    (6) As a "release of social potentialities."

    (7) As a preparation for business efficiency.

    (8) As a preparation for social success.

    (9) As a preparation for future enjoyment.

    (10) As a preparation for leadership.

    (11) As a discipline.

(d) A comparison between:

    (1) Education and propaganda.

    (2) Education and instruction.

    (3) Education and discipline.

    (4) Education and culture.

(e) Speech training as a means and an end of education.

12. In what ways is a low state of physical or mental health usually reflected in the posture? The gait? The breathing? The voice? How is a tense, nervous condition reflected in posture, gait, breathing, voice, and manner? An aggressive nature? A cheerful disposition?

13. In what respects is an optimistic philosophy helpful? Dangerous? A pessimistic philosophy?

14. Study the posture and gait of a good many persons to see if you can formulate ideas of the correlation between posture and physical and mental states.

15. Test the James-Lange theory of emotions by standing for some time in a dejected or confident or belligerent posture and observing whether your mood gradually becomes affected by the emotional tone which the posture suggests.

16. Analyze the posture for the following types on the stage: a feeble old man; an arrogant politician; a timid, self-effacing

woman; a proud, commanding beauty; a middle-aged English butler; a trim, coquettish parlormaid; a hoydenish schoolgirl.

17. What are mannerisms and what do they signify? Should they be eliminated? If so, how?

18. Discuss the relation between fear and nerve tension. Between nerve tension and rhythm. Between rhythm and economy of effort. Between these and grace.

19. Discuss the relation between timidity and egotism.

Suggested Readings

ALLPORT, Floyd H.—*Social Psychology* (Houghton Mifflin Co.).

BLAKE, Mabelle B.—*Guidance for College Women* (D. Appleton & Co.).

BURNHAM, William H.—*The Normal Mind* (D. Appleton & Co.).

DEWEY, John.—*Human Nature and Conduct* (Henry Holt & Co.).

GRAVES, E. R.—*Personality and Social Adjustment* (Longmans, Green & Co.).

GRAY, G. W.—*"Gestalt,* Behavior and Speech," *Quarterly Journal of Speech Education,* June, 1928.

JAMES, William.—*The Principles of Psychology* (Henry Holt & Co.).

JUDD, C. H.—*Psychology of Social Institutions,* especially the chapter on "Language" (Macmillan Co.).

KOFFKA, Kurt.—*The Growth of the Mind* (Harcourt, Brace & Co.).

MILLER, A. Crichton.—*The New Psychology and the Teacher* (Jarrolds).

O'NEILL, J. M., and WEAVER, A. T.—*The Elements of Speech* (Longmans, Green & Co.).

OVERSTREET, H. A.—*About Ourselves—Psychology for Normal People* (W. W. Norton & Co.).

PARRISH, Maxfield.—"Implications of the Gestalt Psychology," *Quarterly Journal of Speech Education,* June, 1928.

ROBINSON, E. S. and F.—*Readings in General Psychology* (University of Chicago Press).

TANSLEY, A. G.—*The New Psychology and Its Relation to Life* (Houghton, Mifflin Co.).

VALENTINE, P. F.—*The Psychology of Personality* (D. Appleton & Co.).

WATSON, John B.—*Psychology from the Standpoint of a Behaviorist* (J. P. Lippincott Co.).

WELLS, F. Lyman.—*Mental Adjustments* (D. Appleton & Co.).

WOODWORTH, R. S.—*Dynamic Psychology* (Columbia University Press).

WOOLBERT, C. H.—*The Fundamentals of Speech* (Harper & Brothers).

CHAPTERS II AND III

QUESTIONS AND TOPICS FOR DISCUSSION

1. Discuss the importance of ear-training in voice and speech education.

2. Why is rhythmical control of breathing so important in voice training?

3. Discuss the advantages and disadvantages of intoning as a means of improving the voice; of the sing-and-say method; of the whispering of a passage.

4. Analyze very carefully a voice which you find particularly agreeable.

5. What difficulty do you find regarding the terms in which we describe voices?

6. Prepare a short talk for the class on the following subjects:

    (*a*) The Pleasantest Voice I Know.

    (*b*) The Most Unpleasant Voice I Know.

7. Discuss the extent to which voices indicate certain personality traits.

8. What are the results of the kind of voice training that places chief emphasis on the elimination of undesirable qualities?

9. What have you observed about voices heard over the telephone? How can you make talking over the telephone a valuable exercise in proper initiation of tone?

10. Explain phonetically the meaning of Hamlet's line, "Speak the speech, I pray you, as I pronounced it to you, trippingly on the tongue."

11. What are the advantages and disadvantages for the voice student in reading aloud (*a*) very dramatic passages, (*b*) lyrical passages, (*c*) very oratorical selections, (*d*) children's stories and poems?

12. How is the voice quality affected by each of the following: (a) happiness, (b) hate, (c) grief, (d) love, (e) contempt, (f) fear, (g) boredom, (h) interest?

13. Discuss the following subjects:
(a) A Good Voice and How to Acquire It.
(b) Is the American Voice Improving?

14. State briefly the relation between voice and (a) posture, (b) general health tone, (c) mental adjustment, (d) articulatory habits, (e) momentary moods.

15. How do you account for the fact that good singers often have poor speaking voices?

16. What does the term "elocutionary" as applied to voice usually connote? What wrong conception has brought about this feeling toward the word?

17. By what voice quality would you characterize the following personalities on the stage: (a) an intellectually critical scholar; (b) an overemotional woman; (c) an adolescent boy; (d) a spoiled child; (e) a domineering business man; (f) a dissatisfied, fault-finding person; (g) a vain, frivolous girl?

SUGGESTED READINGS

AIKIN, W. A.—*The Voice* (Longmans, Green & Co.).

BURTON-OPITZ, R.—*A Text-Book of Physiology* (W. B. Saunders Co.).

DODDS, George F.—*The Control of the Breath: an Elementary Manual for Singers and Speakers* (London, 1925).

—— and LICKLEY, J. D.—*The Control of the Breath for Speaking and Singing* (Oxford University Press).

GRAY, Henry.—*The Anatomy of the Human Body* (Lea & Febiger).

HAMILTON, Clarence Grant.—*Sound and Its Relation to Music* (C. H. Ditson & Co.).

LUCIANI, Luigi.—*Human Physiology* (Macmillan Co.).

MILLER, D. C.—*The Science of Musical Sounds* (Macmillan Co.).

MILLS, Wesley.—*Voice Production* (J. B. Lippincott Co.).

MOTT, F. W.—*The Brain and the Voice in Speech and Song* (Harper & Brothers).

MUCKEY, Floyd S.—*The Natural Method of Voice Production* (Charles Scribner's Sons).

PARISOTTI, Luigi.—*Speaking and Singing* (Boosey & Co.).

SEASHORE, C. E.—*The Psychology of Musical Talent* (Silver, Burdette & Co.).

THOMAS, Leah.—*Bodily Mechanics and Health* (Houghton Mifflin Co.).

THOMPSON, William.—*The Rhythm of Speech* (Maclehose & Jackson).

VOORHEES, Irving Wilson.—*The Hygiene of the Voice* (Macmillan Co.).

WATT, H. J.—*The Psychology of Sound* (Macmillan Co.).

ZAHN, J. A.—*Sound and Music* (A. C. McClurg & Co.).

CHAPTERS IV, V, VI, AND VII

QUESTIONS AND TOPICS FOR DISCUSSION

1. Does Henry James' arraignment of American speech strike you as unduly severe? If so, in what respects does it seem to you unjust?

2. What, briefly, is Lounsbury's attitude regarding a standard of pronunciation? To what extent do you agree with him?

3. Write out all the arguments you can think of for and against a speech standard for America, in preparation for a class discussion of the questions: (*a*) Is a speech standard desirable in America? (*b*) Is it practicable?

4. What faults of speech annoy you most? Analyze the reasons for your reaction to them.

5. If a friend asked you to help him overcome nasality, how should you proceed?

6. Can you tell by a person's speech what part of the country he comes from? If so, how?

7. Does the speech of certain parts of the country strike you as on the whole more pleasant than that of most other localities? If so, why?

8. Do you think that a speech class should try to arrive at a standard for the class? What are the chief arguments for and against this plan?

9. If such a plan were adopted, what method would you suggest for formulating the class standard? For enforcing the standard?

10. Someone has said, "The speech of many New Yorkers sounds like the flapping of an old shoe." Explain this criticism in terms of phonetics.

11. To what extent would phonetic reform in spelling affect pronunciation? (See "Reform in Nessiobia" in Grandgent's *Old and New*.)

12. Do you agree with Professor Krapp's theory that in America there are five levels of speech (literary English, formal colloquial, general colloquial, popular English, vulgar English)? If so, does this hold with reference to pronunciation as well as choice of words?

13. Discuss the extent to which our way of speaking is influenced by each of the following factors:

(*a*) The locality in which we live;
(*b*) The amount and kind of education we have received;
(*c*) The extent of our travels;
(*d*) The attention paid to our speech in our early years;
(*e*) Our temper and character;
(*f*) Our mood at the moment;
(*g*) The person or persons to whom we are speaking;
(*h*) Influence of a foreign language;
(*i*) Any other causes.

14. Define *pedantic speech*; *slovenly speech*. Give the causes of each; the best ways of overcoming each.

15. Discuss the method by which we can attain the golden mean between pedantic and slovenly speech.

16. Is there a correlation between distinctness and distinction in speech?

17. Analyze your speech habits with the help of a teacher or a friend who is both candid and sensitive to speech sounds. Which of your ineffective habits are due to physical condition? To mental attitude? To laziness? To lack of ear-training? To bad models?

18. Name as many ways as possible by which people save effort in articulation. By what criterion do you decide which of these are to be recommended?

19. What are *weak forms*? Discuss their relation to emphasis; to rhythm.

20. What is *phrasing*? What physical and mental uses does it serve?

21. What is the ideal of speech that you have set for yourself?

22. Explain all the movements of the lips, tongue, soft palate, and vocal cords in pronouncing the following words: *when, bottle, languid, area, fortune, search, dying, hidden, locked, sprinkling, tomb, shoe, she, rage, keel, ridges, sixths, writhed, chains.*

23. If you agree with Professor Krapp's classification as to the five levels of speech (see question 12 above), what seem to be the chief differences in these five levels as to (*a*) assimilation, (*b*) use of weakened forms, (*c*) clearness of articulation, (*d*) omission of sounds, (*e*) tone production?

24. Analyze the speech of the locality in which you live. Compare it with that of other parts of the country. In what respects do you consider yours better? In what respects less pleasing or effective? Can you find explanations of the special characteristics of the speech of your community? Is it changing in any noticeable way? If so, from what causes?

25. Is there an obligation on the better educated elements in a community to attempt to raise the general level of speech? If so, how can they do this without weakening the native idiom or incurring the criticism of snobbishness?

SUGGESTED READINGS

Atlantic Monthly, March, 1915.—"The Pronunciation of English in America."

BARROWS, Sarah T.—*Teacher's Book of Phonetics* (Ginn & Co.).

BORDEN, R. C., and BUSSE, A. C.—*Speech Correction* (F. S. Crofts & Co.).

BRADLEY, H.—*On the Relation between Spoken and Written Language, with Specific Reference to English* (Oxford University Press).

DE LAGUNA, G. A.—*Speech* (Yale University Press).

DE WITT, M. E.—*Euphon English and World-Standard English in America* (E. P. Dutton & Co.).

JAMES, Henry.—*The Question of Our Speech* (Houghton Mifflin Co.).

JESPERSEN, Otto.—*Growth and Structure of the English Language* (D. Appleton & Co.).

JONES, Daniel.—*An Outline of English Phonetics* (G. E. Stechert & Co.).

KENYON, J. S.—*American Pronunciation* (George Wahr).

KRAPP, George Philip.—*Modern English, Its Growth and Present Use* (Charles Scribner's Sons).

—— *The English Language in America* (Century Co.).

—— *Pronunciation of Standard English in America* (Oxford University Press).

LIDDELL, Mark H.—*The Physical Characteristics of Speech Sounds* (Purdue University, Engineering Department Bulletins 16, 23, 28).

LOUNSBURY, T. R.—*The Standard of Pronunciation in America* (Harper & Brothers).

McKNIGHT, George H.—*Modern English in the Making* (D. Appleton & Co.).

PALMER, H. E., MARTIN, J. V., and BLANDFORD, F. G.—*Dictionary of English Pronunciations with American Variants* (D. Appleton & Co.).

PEPPARD, H. M.—*Correction of Speech Defects* (Macmillan Co.).

PILLSBURY, W. B., and MEADER, C. L.—*The Psychology of Language* (D. Appleton & Co.).

RIPMAN, Walter.—*Standard and Spoken English* (E. P. Dutton & Co.).

—— *Good Speech* (E. P. Dutton & Co.).

RUSSELL, G. Oscar.—*The Vowel* (Ohio State University Press).

—— *Speech and Voice* (Macmillan Co.).

STINCHFIELD, Sarah T.—*The Psychology of Speech* (Expression Co.).

—— *The Pathology of Speech* (Expression Co.).

THOMAS, C. K.—"Recent Discussions of Standardization in American Pronunciation," *Quarterly Journal of Speech Education,* November, 1927.

WARD, I. C.—*Defects of Speech, their Nature and Cure* (E. P. Dutton & Co.).

WOOLBERT, J. M., and WEAVER, A. T.—*Better Speech* (Harcourt, Brace & Co.).

CHAPTERS VIII AND IX

QUESTIONS AND TOPICS FOR DISCUSSION

1. Discuss the difference between fact and opinion; between reasoned opinions and prejudices.

2. How do we come by our opinions? Test your methods by asking yourself with regard to some belief (for instance, your opinion as to what constitutes success, or how to use a fork, or

whether there is a life after death) what part of it you owe to each of the following:

  (a) Direct evidence of the senses;
  (b) The statements of others;
  (c) The trial and error method;
  (d) Reasoning;
  (e) Instinct or "intuition."

What of the relative value of these methods? Of the dangers of too great reliance on any one? Can you think of other methods?

3. Compare inductive with deductive reasoning, as to (a) nature, (b) the part played by each in the formation of opinion.

4. Discuss the methods of testing authority. What kinds of persons rely chiefly on authority?

5. What tests can we apply with regard to prejudice? How many persons of your acquaintance are entirely free from the following kinds of prejudice: religious, racial, political, social, professional, personal?

6. How can we avoid the extremes of credulity and scepticism?

7. How can we detect fallacies in ourselves and others?

8. Can creative thinking be taught in schools and colleges? If so, how?

9. How should one prepare to take part (a) in group discussion, (b) in a debate?

10. Discuss (a) the advantages to be gained from each of the above types of speech practice; (b) the dangers to be avoided in each.

11. Discuss all the types of introduction you know of and tell the types of speech for which each is especially adapted.

12. Explain the relation between *motivation* and *drift* in public speaking.

13. Discuss various methods of putting "authority" into a speech.

14. Explain how to organize the material of a speech. Discuss (a) the value of the logical order, that is, the arrangement of details in sequence according to time, place, cause and effect, or other types of association; (b) the value of the psychological order, that is, adaptation to the mental and emotional make-up of the audience.

15. What constitutes a good conclusion?

16. Name half a dozen different types of conclusion and discuss their relative suitability for various audiences, occasions, and kinds of subject matter. What types are always ineffective?

17. Discuss the relation between the introduction and the conclusion of a speech. Between the body and the conclusion.

18. Present in the form of a short talk the material in one of the selections in Section IV.

In order to make it an effective speech, what changes are necessary in (a) organization, (b) illustrative material, (c) style?

19. Discuss the advantages and the dangers of the use of humor in public speaking. The relation between a sense of humor and good taste.

20. Discuss imagination in public speaking, especially in connection with the following points: (a) interest and attention; (b) organization of material; (c) vocabulary; (d) delivery.

21. What do you consider the best methods of rebuttal? The best place or places for rebuttal in a speech?

22. What is *reduction to absurdity?* What arguments can you give for and against its use in rebuttal?

23. What considerations will govern your use of appeal to the emotions of your audience?

24. What are the chief differences between a purely literary style and that best suited to public speaking?

25. What is good taste in public speaking? Can it be cultivated? If so, how?

26. Suppose you were going to give a talk on the same subject to a group of college students, to children of from twelve to fourteen, and to an average mixed audience, what differences would there be in the three speeches with respect to (a) length; (b) type of illustrative material; (c) relative use of intellectual and emotional appeal; (d) vocabulary; (e) sentence structure?

27. Discuss the question of rhythm in public speaking, especially in reference to the problem of attention.

28. Make a study of the advertisements in some popular magazine to discover what instincts, or "impelling motives," are appealed to most frequently. Note also the use of various other devices to attract and hold attention. What can be learned from the study of advertisements that will be of help in public speaking?

29. Discuss the importance of transitions. Find some examples in literature of special excellence in the use of transitions. Why are clear and striking transitions even more important for the public speaker than for the writer?

30. What are the special dangers of the use of analogy in reasoning? Its special effectiveness in explanation and description?

31. Prepare a talk on the dullest subject you know, using every device you know for holding the attention of the audience.

32. Prepare a talk on a subject against which you feel that the audience has a strong prejudice. What means will be most effective in breaking down that prejudice?

33. Prepare to introduce a speaker who is known to be an authority on the subject on which he is to speak.

34. Prepare to introduce a relatively unknown substitute for a distinguished speaker.

35. Prepare to explain to an audience which has already waited a quarter of an hour for a speaker that he will arrive in ten minutes.

36. Discuss some general or disputed term like one of the following, with the idea of formulating a definition which will satisfy the whole class: *rhythm, democracy, culture, communism, socialism, propaganda, liberty, truth, concept, banality, sentiment, sentimentality, circular response, association of ideas, "emotional drive* *plexes.*

37. _the following subjects choose topics for class talks or group discussions:

Is a double standard of manners desirable? Of speech?
Personalities—born or made?
Repression or expression?
Instinctive behavior *versus* reflective behavior.
How to choose a profession.
Is America fit for democracy?
Is democracy a leveling-down or a building-up process?
Is this college democratic?
Individual responsibility in student government.
The college student's five-foot book shelf.
Seven keys to effectiveness in speaking.
Popularizing thrift; health; good speech.
If I were president of this college.
Small *versus* large colleges.

Are nationalism and internationalism reconcilable ideals?
Our latest venture in prohibition—success or failure?
Is woman suffrage justifying itself?
Militarism and pacifism—is there a *tertium quid?*
Is disarmament practicable at the present time?
What is progress?
Religion and ethics.
Morals and conventions.
Are we less moral than our ancestors?
Advantages of an international traffic system.
My "book of the year."
New light on a great man in a recent biography.
Sentiment and sentimentality.
A comparison betwen Renaissance culture and that of
    today.
Is our present American culture Anglo-Saxon?
What constitutes a good movie? A good detective story?
    A good magazine?
What is a snob? Has this college a special brand?
"Collegiate"—a term of commendation or reproach?
Some by-products of a college education.
How to tell a senior from a freshman.
Some wild bores I have known.
College wits.
College humorous publications.
Some types this college could well dispense with.
American culture contrasted with that of England or some
    other country.
Some ways of learning pantomime.

SUGGESTED READINGS

Columbia Associates.—*Introduction to Reflective Thinking*
    (Houghton Mifflin Co.).
"Coöperative Technique for Conflict" (*The Inquiry*, New York).
COVINGTON, H. C.—*The Fundamentals of Debate* (Charles Scrib-
    ner's Sons).
"Creative Discussion" (*The Inquiry*, New York).
DEWEY, John.—*How We Think* (D. C. Heath & Co.).
FOLLETT, M. P.—*Creative Experience* (Longmans, Green & Co.).
—— *The New State* (Longmans, Green & Co.).

FOSTER, W. T.—*Argumentation and Debating* (Houghton Mifflin Co.).

HALL, A. B., and STURGIS, A. F.—*Textbook on Parliamentary Law* (Macmillan Co.).

LIPPMAN, Walter.—*Public Opinion* (Harcourt, Brace & Co.).

MACPHERSON, William.—*The Psychology of Persuasion* (Methuen & Co.).

MAXCY, C. L.—*The Brief* (Houghton Mifflin Co.).

NASON, A. H.—*Efficient Composition* (New York University Press).

O'NEILL, J. M., LAYCOCK, C., and SCALES, R. L.—*Argument and Debate* (Macmillan Co.).

OVERSTREET, Harry Allen.—*Influencing Human Behavior* (W. W. Norton & Co.).

ROBERT, H. M.—*Parliamentary Law* (D. C. Heath & Co.).

ROBINSON, A. T.—*The Applications of Logic* (Longmans, Green & Co.).

ROBINSON, D. S.—*Illustrations of the Methods of Reasoning* (D. Appleton & Co.).

SHAW, Warren C.—*The Art of Debate* (Allyn & Bacon).

SHEFFIELD, A. D.—*Joining in Public Discussion* (Doubleday, Doran & Co.).

SIDGWICK, Alfred.—*The Application of Logic* (Longmans, Green & Co.).

STONE, G. P., and GARRISON, S. L.—*Essentials of Argument* (Henry Holt & Co.).

WALLAS, Graham.—*The Art of Thought* (Harcourt, Brace & Co.).

—— *The Great Society* (Harcourt, Brace & Co.).

WEST, Robert.—*Purposive Speaking* (Macmillan Co.).

WINANS, James A.—*Public Speaking* (Century Co.).

CHAPTER X

QUESTIONS AND TOPICS FOR DISCUSSION

The Intellectual Approach

1. Summarize in one clear, unified sentence the thought of each of selections 6 to 10 in Section IV.

2. Do you agree with the phrasing indicated in the phonetic transcripts of "Bredon Hill" (page 346 and selection 100) and "The Doll's House" (selections 97 and 98)?

3. Using the same system, indicate the phrasing of each of the selections 6 to 10 in Section IV.

4. Enclose in parentheses the phrases in each of these selections that are of primary importance in expressing the author's meaning.

5. Study the remaining phrases to determine which of them are used for explanation and which for intensification of the thought.

6. In the same selections underscore with a heavy straight line the words used to express the new ideas by which the thought is made progressive, and with a dotted line those used to express ideas which have already been mentioned or implied but which are structurally necessary.

7. Read these selections aloud to see that you can clearly indicate the difference between these two types of ideas.

8. In the selection from Stevenson's essay, "Child's Play" (selection 7), it will be seen that the unifying principle is that of contrast. What words must be given particular emphasis in order that this contrast may be clearly indicated?

9. In the passage from Macaulay's *Essay on Warren Hastings* (selection 8), what words must be given special emphasis in order to bring out clearly the relation of the various parts of the scene to the whole?

10. You will have observed that even these selections which are purely expository in character require something more than a merely intellectual approach. List the passages in Selections 1 to 20 that require for their adequate interpretation (*a*) a marked sense of rhythm; (*b*) a grasp of narrative technique; (*c*) imaginative response to the author's mood; (*d*) two or more of the above.

11. Note the qualities of a good public-speaking style in the passages from Meikeljohn's "The Liberal College" (selection 30); Burke's "Conciliation with America" (selection 21); Macaulay's "Speech on the Reform Bill" (selection 23); Woodrow Wilson's "The Training of the Intellect" (selection 29); and Abraham Lincoln's exposition of the "mud-sill" theory (selection 24). How can you bring out these qualities in your reading?

12. Is a purely intellectual approach an adequate preparation for the oral interpretation of any types of writing?

13. Are there any types of writing that do not need this kind of preparation for reading?

14. What connection is there between this kind of preparation and directness in oral reading?

The Rhythmical Approach

15. Read Sorley's "Song of the Ungirt Runners" (selection 51) somewhat passively until you feel the rhythm on which the poem is based. Compare the movement of the three stanzas. What differences do you note? Show how these are conditioned by changes in the thought expressed.

16. Read Millay's "The Spring and the Fall" (selection 54) in the same way until you have caught its swing. What definite changes in movement do you find in the three stanzas? Compare these changes of movement with those in Masefield's "Cargoes" and Tennyson's "Lady of Shalott." What is necessary in order to make the reading truly rhythmical instead of singsong? How much stress should be given to the word *year* in the first line? How do you read the words *in the spring of the year* the second and third times they are used? Why should the word *broke* in the first stanza be given slightly more stress than it would normally receive? Mention five or six reasons why the word *fall* in the second stanza should be given particular emphasis the first time it is used. Why is the method of emphasizing by stress used less in this poem than in Sorley's? What various means of emphasis should be used in this poem?

17. Notice the natural rhythm on which each of the following poems is based: "Against Oblivion" (selection 66), "Bredon Hill" (selection 100), "London Snow" (selection 60), "The Dead Dancer" (selection 58). To what extent does each seem to have caught the rhythm which it is supposed to represent?

18. Is your appreciation of the rhythm of "Egypt's Might Is Tumbled Down" (selection 63) increased by remembering that there is a child's song game called "London Bridge Is Falling Down"?

19. Compare the rhythmical movement of Shelley's "Night" (selection 17) with that of Byron's "There be None of Beauty's Daughters" (selection 64).

20. In getting the full swing of George Peele's "Harvesting A-Singing" (selection 72) is it helpful to remember the smooth rhythmical sweep of the arms of skilled sowers and reapers?

21. What is the special problem in reading a poem like "When I Was One and Twenty" (selection 71) in which the song quality is predominant?

22. What is the special problem in reading poetry based on a very definite metrical pattern like that of the sonnet?

23. Compare the movement of Shakespeare's sonnet "When in Disgrace with Fortune and Men's Eyes" (selection 16) with that of Keats' "On First Looking into Chapman's Homer" (selection 86). What differences do you note? Discuss the differences of technique required for a satisfactory reading of the two poems.

24. Find a poem the rhythm of which is based (a) on some kind of physical movement; (b) on a song tune; (c) on the rhythm of speech.

25. Study very carefully the rhythm of Frost's "Mending Wall" (selection 75). Note that it readily lends itself to a purely prose reading although the metre is an unusually regular form of iambic pentameter. Does this fact throw any light on the relation between metre and rhythm? (Frost himself says that his poetry is based on the rhythms of everyday speech. Does this mean that such a poem should be read as prose? If not, how should the fact that it is poetry be shown?)

26. Read the poem "On the Road to Tchi Li" (selection 87) until you feel its rhythmical pattern. Contrast this movement with that of "The Spring and the Fall" (selection 54). Which type of poem do you find harder to read?

27. Read Psalm LXV until you can make the rhythm help both to clarify and to intensify the thought.

28. Why is it often more difficult to find the rhythm of prose than of verse? Find some prose that seems to you to owe much of its power and beauty to its rhythm and prepare to read the selection as perfectly as you can.

The Narrative Approach

29. Discuss the order in which the events of "Helen of Kirconnel" (selection 101) are narrated. Can you suggest any reason for this order? What seems to you to determine the tempo or

pace of this form? Notice the subjective tone of the poem as compared with the objectivity of the earlier ballads. What difference should this make in your reading of the poem, as compared, for instance, with "Sir Patrick Spens"? What is the climax? How do you work up to it in your reading? How can you prevent the last stanza from being merely a tame repetition of the first? In general how should a refrain be treated in narrative poetry? How does your understanding of the mood and rhythm of the poem help to give unity to your reading of it?

30. What is the mood of "Proud Maisie (selection 99)? The tempo? Is she directly or indirectly described? Where is the climax? How is suspense secured? How can you make the conclusion effective?

31. What type of narration is used by Wordsworth in "Lucy" (selection 103)? Discuss the vocabulary, imagery, rhythm and mood of the poem. How can you prevent your reading of it from sounding sentimental? Insignificant? Singsong?

32. What is the mood of "When I was One and Twenty" (selection 71)? What are the chief difficulties in reading this poem?

33. In reading "Bredon Hill" (selection 100) how can the change of mood be made without destroying the unity of the poem? What part do the bells serve? What is the chief danger in the reading of the passages describing the bells? Where is the climax? What is the mood at the end? How can the intensity required by the poem be secured without making the reading seem overemotional?

34. How is the interest aroused in the selection from "The Doll's House" (selection 98)? How maintained? What is the point of view in the description of the doll's house? What indirect characterization of the children do we get?

35. What is the proper pace for "Sir Gawaine and the Green Knight" (selection 110)? What conditions determine this? How is interest aroused? Suspense increased?

36. In the quotation from Erskine's *The Private Life of Helen of Troy* (selection 107) is the interest centered primarily in the events related? If not, in what is it centered? How can the purpose of the author best be carried out? What type of humor is used? What is the difficulty in reading this kind of humorous writing?

37. In general, how does the tempo best suited to narration differ from that of description or exposition or argumentation? Why?

38. Do you classify Browning's "After" (selection 127) as a lyric, narrative, or dramatic poem? Give reasons for your classification. Try reading the poem in each of these three ways.

The Approach through Mood

39. What is the dominant mood in "Spring Goeth All in White" (selection 138)? Discuss the parts played by each of the following elements in gaining unity of impression in the poem: imagery, vocabulary, rhythm, melody secured by the use of long vowels and sonorous consonants.

40. In the two stanzas quoted from "My Sister's Sleep" (selection 139) what is the dominant mood? How is this mood intensified? How can the articulation help to carry out the author's intention in the first stanza?

41. What impression of Cleopatra does Shakespeare evidently intend to give in selection 149? Is this method chiefly that of detail or of suggestion? Note the figures of speech, the special effectiveness in choice of words. How does the rhythm help to give the effect desired? What special demands in the way of technique does a good reading of this passage make?

42. Discuss the mood of the passage from *Henry VIII* beginning "Farewell, a long farewell, to all my greatness" (selection 150). To what extent is this mood created by the use of imagery? What is necessary for the effective reading of these two figures of speech?

43. How is one's reading of the passage on tobogganing (selection 114) affected by the knowledge that Stevenson wrote it when he was in the Alps struggling against tuberculosis? Discuss the changes in pace and in tone quality necessary to give the intended impression. What special expertness is demanded by the most rapid part of the selection?

44. In the description of a fog by Dickens (selection 123), how should the words *Fog everywhere* be read? How should the constantly recurring word "fog" be read in order to secure the desired impression without the effect of monotonous repetition? What tone quality does the passage demand?

45. In the quotation from *Shadows Waiting* (selection 112), what impression is given by Persephone? Is it the usual one? Note the use of sense impressions, vocabulary, contrast, rhythm. Does the description strike you as sentimental? How can a sentimental reading be avoided?

46. By what means can the effect of a magic spell be given in the lines from Shakespeare beginning "What thou seest when thou shalt wake" (selection 140)?

47. What is the mood of the passage from *Julius Cæsar* beginning "For once, upon a raw and gusty day," (selection 145)? What was the purpose of the speaker? What means does he use to effect that purpose? Discuss in terms of pitch, volume, tone quality, articulation, the technique necessary for an adequate reading of the passage.

48. Compare the above with the passage from *Henry V* beginning "Once more unto the breech, dear friends" (selection 146). Contrast these two speeches with the passage beginning "O God of Battles" (selection 142). How can the mood of this passage be brought out? Study it particularly as to rhythm and tone quality.

49. Compare the mood of Beddoes' "Dream Pedlary" (selections 49 and 50) with that of Charlotte Mew's "The Pedlar" (selection 73). What kind of person is speaking in each? How do you get your impression?

50. Study the mood of "Ozymandias" (selection 143). By what means is unity of impression secured? Why must the word *traveler* not be too strongly accented? What is the meaning of the lines:

> "whose frown,
> And wrinkled lip, and sneer of cold command,
> Tell that the sculptor well those passions read
> Which yet survive, stamped on those lifeless things,
> The hand that mocked them, and the heart that fed."

What seems to you the highest point of intensity in the poem? In what does the effectiveness of the last lines largely consist? How should they be read in order that none of the effect be lost?

51. How many changes of mood do you find in the speech of Viola from *Twelfth Night* (selection 148)? How is it pos-

sible to make the transitions from one mood to another seem natural and convincing? In reading the speech should you rely at all on facial expression and pantomime for help in characterization or should you rely entirely on your voice? What is meant by *dramatic pause?* Where should it be used in this speech?

52. By what technical means can you express the lighter mood of such poems as "Tavern" (selection 134) and "Cupid and Campaspe" (selection 102).

53. Compare the strict metrical form of Adelaide Crapsey's "Cinquains" (selection 135) with the unmetrical structure of Jun Fugita's Japanese tankas (selection 136). Do they seem predominantly lyric or dramatic in character? What similarity of method and result do you find between these poems and stylistic Japanese paintings? Read each poem with the intensity which its concentrated emotion demands.

54. How can the interest of the hearer be sustained in a long passage like that of the description of the desert from *Eöthen* (selection 124)? What are the chief means of preventing monotony?

55. Of what practical value have you found the four approaches suggested in this chapter?

56. What do you consider the main differences between the verse of the present day and earlier poetry?

57. Read the introduction to Tassin's *The Oral Interpretation of Literature* and the chapter "The Rendering of Poetry" in Lamborn's *Expression in Reading and Writing.* Compare the two theories advocated by these writers. Formulate your own theory of reading poetry aloud.

Suggested Readings

Andrews, C. E.—*The Writing and Reading of Verse* (D. Appleton & Co.).

Auslander, Joseph, and Hill, F. E.—*The Winged Horse* (Doubleday, Doran & Co.).

Bassett, L. E.—*Handbook of Oral Reading* (Houghton Mifflin Co.).

Clark, S. H.—*The Interpretation of the Printed Page* (Row, Peterson & Co.).

Corson, Hiram.—*The Voice and Spiritual Education* (Macmillan Co.).

Curry, S. S.—*Foundations of Expression* (Expression Company, Boston).

—— *Browning and the Dramatic Monologue* (Expression Company, Boston).

Eastman, Max.—*The Enjoyment of Poetry* (Charles Scribner's Sons).

Erskine, John.—*The Kinds of Poetry* (Duffield & Co.).

—— *The Elizabethan Lyric* (Lemcke).

Fogarty, Elsie.—*The Speaking of English Verse* (E. P. Dutton & Co.).

Hubbell, J. B., and Beatty, J. O.—*An Introduction to Poetry* (Macmillan Co.).

Jacob, Cary F.—*The Foundations and Nature of Verse* (Columbia University Press).

Lamborn, E. A. G.—*Expression in Speech and Writing*, especially the chapter on "The Rendering of Poetry" (Oxford University Press).

—— *The Rudiments of Criticism* (Oxford University Press).

Lowell, Amy.—*Tendencies in Modern American Poetry* (Macmillan Co.).

Lowes, J. L.—*The Road to Xanadu* (Houghton Mifflin Co.).

Mackail, J. W.—*Oxford Lectures on Poetry* (Longmans, Green & Co.).

Monroe, Harriet.—*Poets and Their Art* (Macmillan Co.)

Morton, David.—*The Sonnet, Today and Yesterday* (G. P. Putnam Sons).

Neilson, William Allan.—*The Essentials of Poetry* (Houghton Mifflin Co.).

O'Neill, J. M., and Weaver, A. T.—*The Elements of Speech* (Longmans, Green & Co.).

Tassin, Algernon.—*The Oral Study of Literature*, especially the Introduction (A. A. Knopf).

Tomlinson, W. S.—*The Teaching of English*, especially the chapter on "Reading" (Oxford University Press).

Trevelyan, R. C.—*Thamyris, or Is There a Future in Poetry* (E. P. Dutton & Co.).

Anthologies

Davies, W. H.—*Shorter Lyrics of the Twentieth Century* (Poetry Bookshop, 35 Devonshire St., London).

De la Mare, Walter.—*Come Hither* (Constable & Co.).

GAY, Robert M.—*The College Book of Verse* (Houghton Mifflin Co.).

GORDON, Margery, and KING, M. B.—*Verse of Our Day* (D. Appleton & Co.).

MANCHESTER, F. A., and GIESE, W. F.—*Harper's Anthology, Poetry* (Harper & Brothers).

MONROE, Harriet, and HENDERSON, A. C.—*The New Poetry* (Macmillan Co.).

PALGRAVE, Francis T.—*Golden Treasury of Songs and Lyrics* (Macmillan Co.).

QUILLER-COUCH, A. T.—*Oxford Book of English Verse* (Oxford University Press).

RITTENHOUSE, Jessie B.—*The Little Book of Modern Verse*, three volumes (Houghton Mifflin Co.).

SQUIRE, J. C.—*Selections from Modern Verse*, two volumes (Martin Secker, London).

STEVENSON, Burton E.—*The Home Book of Verse* (Henry Holt and Co.).

UNTERMEYER, Louis.—*Modern American and British Poetry* (Harcourt, Brace & Co.).

WILKINSON, Marguerite.—*New Voices* (Macmillan Co.).

INDEX

503